Gay and Lesbian Rights
in the United States

Primary Documents in American History and Contemporary Issues

The Abortion Controversy
Eva R. Rubin, editor

Affirmative Action
Jo Ann Ooiman Robinson, editor

The AIDS Crisis
Douglas A. Feldman and Julia Wang Miller, editors

Capital Punishment in the United States
Bryan Vila and Cynthia Morris, editors

Constitutional Debates on Freedom of Religion
John J. Patrick and Gerald P. Long, editors

Drugs and Drug Policy in America
Steven Belenko

The Environmental Debate
Peninah Neimark and Peter Rhoades Mott, editors

Equal Protection and the African American Constitutional Experience
Robert P. Green, Jr., editor

Fair Trial Rights of the Accused
Ronald Banaszak, Sr., editor

Founding the Republic
John J. Patrick, editor

Free Expression in America
Sheila Suess Kennedy, editor

Gay and Lesbian Rights in the United States
Walter L. Williams and Yolanda Retter, editors

Genetic Engineering
Thomas A. Shannon, editor

The Gun Control Debate
Marjolijn Bijlefeld, editor

Major Crises in Contemporary American Foreign Policy
Russell D. Buhite, editor

The Right to Die Debate
Marjorie B. Zucker, editor

The Role of Police in American Society
Bryan Vila and Cynthia Morris, editors

Sexual Harassment in America
Laura W. Stein

States' Rights and American Federalism
Frederick D. Drake and Lynn R. Nelson, editors

U.S. Immigration and Naturalization Laws and Issues
Michael LeMay and Elliott Robert Barkan, editors

Women's Rights in the United States
Winston E. Langley and Vivian C. Fox, editors

This book is dedicated to the pioneering activists I have felt honored to know and to call my friends: Vern Bullough, Hal Call, Martin Duberman, Edythe Eyde, Flo Fleischman, Barbara Gittings, Harry Hay, Christopher Isherwood, Karla Jay, Frank Kameny, Jim Kepner, Morris Kight, Dorr Legg, John O'Brien, Troy Perry, Reid Rasmussen, John Rechy, and many others whose years of hard work have advanced gay and lesbian rights in the United States. Their personal example, of taking action and never giving up, helped to inspire this book.

Walter L. Williams

This book is dedicated to the butches and femmes who resisted before there was a movement, to homophile lesbians of the 1950s and 1960s, to lesbian feminists of the 1970s, and to lesbians of color of the 1980s and 1990s.

Yolanda Retter

Gay and Lesbian Rights in the United States

A Documentary History

Edited by Walter L. Williams and Yolanda Retter

Primary Documents in American History and Contemporary Issues

GREENWOOD PRESS
Westport, Connecticut • London

Library of Congress Cataloging-in-Publication Data

Gay and lesbian rights in the United States : a documentary history / edited by Walter L. Williams and Yolanda Retter.

    p. cm. — (Primary documents in American history and contemporary issues, ISSN 1069–5605)

   Includes bibliographical references and index.

   ISBN 0–313–30696–6 (alk. paper)

   1. Gay rights—United States—History—Sources. 2. Gay liberation movement—United States—History—Sources. 3. Homosexuality—United States—Public opinion. 4. Homosexuality—Law and legislation—United States. 5. Public opinion—United States. 6. United States—Politics and government. 7. United States—Social policy. I. Williams, Walter L., 1948– II. Retter, Yolanda, 1947– III. Series.
HQ76.8.U5G37   2003
305.9′0664′0973—dc21   2002035218

British Library Cataloguing in Publication Data is available.

Library of Congress Catalog Card Number: 2002035218

ISBN: 0–313–30696–6
ISSN: 1069–5605

First published in 2003

Greenwood Press, 88 Post Road West, Westport, CT 06881
An imprint of Greenwood Publishing Group, Inc.
www.greenwood.com

Printed in the United States of America

The paper used in this book complies with the Permanent Paper Standard issued by the National Information Standards Organization (Z39.48–1984).

10 9 8 7 6 5 4 3 2 1

Copyright Acknowledgments

The editors and publisher gratefully acknowledge permission for use of the following material:

Excerpts from Documents 1, 4, and 12 are taken from Walter L. Williams, *The Spirit and the Flesh: Sexual Diversity in American Indian Culture,* various pages. Boston: Beacon Press, 1986. Copyright © 1986 by Walter L. Williams. Reprinted by permission of Beacon Press.

Excerpts from Documents 34, 38, 41, 43, 44, 45, 46, 47, 48, 50, 52, 54, 55, 56, 57, 61, 70, and 157 are taken from various issues of *ONE Magazine, ONE-IGLA Bulletin,* and unpublished files in ONE Institute/International Gay and Lesbian Archives.

Excerpts from Document 39 are taken from Thomas V. Moore, "The Pathogenesis and Treatment of Homosexual Disorders: A Digest of Some Pertinent Evidence," *Journal of Personality,* vol. 14 (1945), p. 57.

Excerpts from Document 40 are taken from Zsa Zsa Gershick, "Edythe Eyde," in *Gay Old Girls.* Los Angeles: Alyson Books, 1968, pp. 47–53, 57–60.

Excerpts from Document 58 are taken from Brian Jones, "Empress I Jose," *Bay Area Reporter,* October 10, 1985, pp. 12–13.

Excerpts from Documents 59, 153, 168, 171, and 174 are taken from *Lesbian & Gay Rights and AIDS/HIV 2000: An ACLU Report.* New York: American Civil Liberties Union, 2000, various pages.

Excerpts from Document 64 are taken from Kay Tobin, "After the Ball…," *The Ladder,* February/March 1965, pp. 4–5. Reprinted with permission from Kay Tobin Lahusen.

Excerpts from Document 65 are taken from Barbara Gittings and Kay Tobin, "Interview with Ernestine Eckstein," *The Ladder,* June 1966, pp. 4–11. Original material and revisions reprinted with permission from Barbara Gittings and Kay Tobin Lahusen.

Excerpts from Documents 68 and 89 are from Mark Thompson, ed., *Long Road to Freedom: The Advocate History of the Gay and Lesbian Movement.* New York: St. Martin's Press, 1994, pp. xvii–xviii, xxiv–xxv, 1–2.

Excerpts from Document 69 are taken from Joseph S. Amster, "Reverend Troy Perry: The Cornerstone of the Gay Spiritual Movement," *The Blade,* vol. 8, no. 10 (January 2000), pp. 44–49.

Excerpts from Document 93 are taken from Randy Shilts, *The Mayor of Castro Street,* pp. 364–371. New York: St. Martin's Press, 1982. Copyright © 1982 Randy Shilts. Reprinted by permission of St. Martin's Press, LLC.

Excerpts from Document 96 are taken from Daniel C. Tsang, "Third World Lesbians and Gays Meet," *Gay Insurgent,* vol. 6 (Summer 1980), p. 11.

Excerpts from Document 98 are taken from Malcolm Boyd, "A Gay Priest Speaks Out," pp. 162 and 207, reprinted from *Long Road to Freedom: The Advocate History of the Gay and Lesbian Movement* © 1994 by Mark Thompson. All rights reserved. Used by permission from Liberation Publications Inc. [Hereafter, all Documents that appear in this work will be cited as reprinted in Thompson, *Long Road to Freedom.*]

Excerpts from Document 111 are taken from Jim Carnes, "Us and Them: 'A Rose for Charlie,'" in *The Shadow of Hate: A History of Intolerance in America* © 1995 Teaching Tolerance, Southern Poverty Law Center, Montgomery, AL. Reprinted with permission.

Excerpts from Document 113 are taken from Armistead Maupin, "Design for Living." Copyright 1985 by Armistead Maupin/Literary Bent LLC. For more on the author of this essay please visit [www.ArmisteadMaupin.com]

Excerpts from Document 114 are taken from Arnie Kantrowitz, "Friends Gone with the Wind," *The Advocate,* September 1986, pp. 42–47, 108–109. Used with permission from Arnie Kantrowitz.

Contents

Series Foreword   xvii

Acknowledgments   xix

Introduction *by Walter L. Williams*   xxi

Timeline   xxxvii

PART I: THE CLASH OF RELIGIONS   1

Document 1: Navajo Sacredness for Nadleeh   3

Document 2: Illinois Indian Transgender (1677)   5

Document 3: Miami Indian Sodomy (1702)   5

Document 4: Native American Transgendered Females   7

Document 5: Lakota Respect for Two-Spirit People (1982)   8

Document 6: The Bible: Sodom and Gomorrah   10

Document 7: The Bible: The Abominations of Leviticus   12

Document 8: The Bible: Ruth and Naomi   15

Document 9: The Bible: David and Jonathan   15

Document 10: The Bible: Jesus   17

Document 11: The Bible: Paul   19

Document 12: Spaniards' Suppression of Sodomites (1519–1540s)   22

Document 13: Virginia Sodomy Law (1610)   23

Document 14: The Execution of Richard Cornish (1624–1625)   23

Document 15: William Plaine Executed in New England
   for Teaching Masturbation (1646)   24

Document 16: African American Jan Creoli Killed and Burned
   in Dutch Colony (1646)   25

Document 17: Sara Norman and Mary Hammon Accused of
   Lewd Behavior (1649)   25

Document 18: New Haven Law Prohibits Lesbianism (1655)   26

Document 19: Puritan Sermon on The Cry of Sodom (1674)   27

Document 20: Pirates in the Caribbean (1724)   30

Document 21: Commentaries on the Laws of England (1765)   31

Document 22: Spanish Priests Condemn Transgendered
   Yuma Indians (1775)   32

Document 23: Spanish Colonial Suppression of Sodomites
   in California (1775–1777)   32

PART II: LIFE, LIBERTY, AND THE PURSUIT OF HAPPINESS: THE DEVELOPMENT OF A HOMOPHILE IDENTITY IN THE UNITED STATES, 1775–1950   35

Document 24: United States Declaration of Independence (1776)   38

Document 25: United States Constitution and Bill of Rights (1791) 40

Document 26: Bachelor Friendships of the Nineteenth Century   42

Document 27: National Women's Rights Convention (1852)   43

Document 28: Walt Whitman and the Homoerotic Poetry
   of Democracy (1860)   45

Document 29: Fourteenth Amendment to the Constitution (1868)   46

Document 30: Walt Whitman's *Democratic Vistas* (1870)   46

Document 31: Females Passing as Men (1894)   48

Document 32: Anthony Comstock Seeks to Imprison Inverts (1900)   49

Document 33: United States Navy Entraps Homosexuals (1919)   50

Document 34: Society for Human Rights (1924)   51

Document 35: *The Well of Loneliness* (1929)   55

Document 36: Sigmund Freud on Homosexuality (1935)   56

Document 37: Lesbian Challenges Georgia's Sodomy Law (1939)   58

Document 38: Lesbians in the Women's Army Corps (1945)   59

Document 39: Psychiatrists Oppose Homosexual Rights Laws (1945) 60

Document 40: *Vice Versa*, America's First Lesbian Magazine (1947)   61

Document 41: *Vice Versa* Predictions (1947)   63

Document 42: Employment of Homosexuals and
Other Sex Perverts (1950)   65

**PART III: CIVIL RIGHTS AND CIVIL LIBERTIES:
THE MAKING OF A GAY AND LESBIAN MOVEMENT IN
THE UNITED STATES, 1950–1977   67**

Document 43: Formation of the Mattachine Society (1950)   72

Document 44: Mattachine Society Meetings (1950)   73

Document 45: Mattachine Protests Police Entrapment (1952)   74

Document 46: Formation of ONE, Inc. (1952)   76

Document 47: Jim Kepner's First Mattachine Meeting (1953)   77

Document 48: Tampa Lesbian Bar Raid (1953)   78

Document 49: Daughters of Bilitis (1955)   79

Document 50: Founding of ONE Institute of
Homophile Studies (1956)   80

Document 51: Gay Bashing in Massachusetts (1956)   82

Document 52: Allen Ginsberg and the Beatniks (1956)   83

Document 53: Crittenden Report on Homosexuality
in the United States Navy (1957)   85

Document 54: Evelyn Hooker Psychological Research (1957)   86

Document 55: Supreme Court Rules ONE Is Not Obscene (1958)   89

Document 56: Mattachine National Convention (1959)   92

Document 57: A Homosexual Bill of Rights (1961)   93

Document 58: Jose Sarria Runs for San Francisco City Council (1961)   96

Document 59: ACLU Begins Gay Rights Cases (1963)   97

Document 60: Bayard Rustin, Martin Luther King,
and the March on Washington (1963)   99

Document 61: Mohave Indian Two-Spirit Person (1964)   100

Document 62: Frank Kameny Resists Job Firing (1964)   102

Document 63: Mattachine Pickets the White House (1965)   103

Document 64: San Francisco Activism (1965)   105

Document 65: Lesbian Activism and *The Ladder* (1966)   107

Document 66: Barbara Gittings and Frank Kameny Push
the Pentagon (1966)   109

Document 67: Supreme Court Excludes and Deports
Homosexual Immigrants (1967)   110

Document 68: PRIDE and *The Advocate* Magazine (1967)   111

Document 69: Rev. Troy Perry Founds the
Metropolitan Community Church (1968)   113

Document 70: Homophile Action League (1968)   115

Document 71: A Gay Manifesto (1969)   116

Document 72: Stonewall Riots in New York (1969)   118

Document 73: Gay Liberation Front and Gay Activists Alliance (1970)   120

Document 74: Gay Lib Zaps Psychologists (1970)   121

Document 75: Congress to Unite Women (1970)   122

Document 76: The Woman Identified Woman (1970)   123

Document 77: NOW Endorses Lesbian Rights (1971)   124

Document 78: Lesbian Nation (1972)   126

Document 79: Democratic Party Convention (1972)   127

Document 80: Multiple Struggles (1973)   128

Document 81: Dr. Howard Brown Comes Out (1973)   129

Document 82: National Gay Task Force Founded (1973)   130

Document 83: Lambda Legal Defense Fund (1973)   131

Document 84: Parents and Friends of Lesbians and Gays (1973)   132

Document 85: American Psychiatric Association Vote (1974)   133

Document 86: Lesbian Child Custody Rights (1974)   135

Document 87: Lesbians as the Vanguard of Feminism (1975)   136

Document 88: Gay Asians (1975)   137

Document 89: Municipal Elections Committee of
Los Angeles (1976)   138

PART IV: BACKLASH: THE REACTION TO GAY
AND LESBIAN PROGRESS IN THE UNITED STATES,
1977–1987   **139**

Document 90: Anita Bryant Defeats Miami Gay Rights
Ordinance (1977)   143

Document 91: Gay Men Harm Society (1978)   144

Document 92: Mormon Suppression of Homosexuality (1978)   145

Document 93: Harvey Milk on the San Francisco Board
of Supervisors (1978) 149

Document 94: *Gay Is Not Good* (1979) 151

Document 95: Homosexuality Is Unnatural (1979) 152

Document 96: March on Washington for Lesbian and
Gay Rights (1979) 153

Document 97: Asian American Lesbian Speaks at the
Third World Lesbian/Gay Conference (1979) 154

Document 98: A Gay Priest Speaks Out on
Fundamentalists (1980) 155

Document 99: Anita Bryant's Startling Reversal (1980) 157

Document 100: Democratic Party and Gay Rights (1980) 158

Document 101: Congressman Bauman on Opposition to
Gay Rights (1980) 159

Document 102: AIDS Strikes Gay Men (1981) 161

Document 103: Jerry Falwell Fund-Raising Letter (1981) 162

Document 104: Pope John Paul II on Controlling the Body (1981) 163

Document 105: Wisconsin Antidiscrimination Law (1981) 163

Document 106: Violence against Lesbian (1982) 164

Document 107: Merle Woo Challenges the University
of California (1982) 166

Document 108: Simultaneity of Oppression (1983) 167

Document 109: Lesbians of Color Conference (1983) 168

Document 110: Police Abuse against Gays (1983) 169

Document 111: The Death of Charlie Howard (1984) 170

Document 112: Are Gay Rights Right? (1985) 172

Document 113: Armistead Maupin's "Design for Living" (1985) 173

Document 114: AIDS and Gay Rights (1986) 175

Document 115: *Bowers v. Hardwick* Sodomy Law Case (1986) 177

Document 116: Catholic Condemnation of Homosexuality (1986) 180

Document 117: Homophobia in the Black Community (1986) 181

Document 118: Antigay Violence (1987) 182

Document 119: AIDS as God's Punishment (1987) 183

PART V: QUEER AMERICA: THE ACCEPTANCE OF SEXUAL AND GENDER DIVERSITY IN THE UNITED STATES, 1987–2000

PART V: QUEER AMERICA: THE ACCEPTANCE OF
SEXUAL AND GENDER DIVERSITY IN THE UNITED
STATES, 1987–2000   187

Document 120: ACT UP (AIDS Coalition to Unleash Power) (1987)   192

Document 121: National March on Washington for Lesbian and Gay
Rights (1987)   194

Document 122: Old Lesbians Organizing for Change (1987)   195

Document 123: Randy Burns—Gay American Indians (1988)   196

Document 124: AIDS Should Not Prevent Sexual Pleasure (1988)   197

Document 125: National Coming Out Day (1988)   198

Document 126: Congressman William Dannemeyer
Opposes Gay Rights (1989)   199

Document 127: Jewish Rabbi Acceptance of Gay and
Lesbian Rights (1989)   201

Document 128: Queer Nation (1990)   202

Document 129: Bisexuals and Gay Rights (1991)   203

Document 130: Gays in the Republican Party (1991)   204

Document 131: Democratic Party Progay Rights (1992)   205

Document 132: *Kentucky v. Wasson* (1992)   206

Document 133: Colorado Amendment 2 (1992)   207

Document 134: Oregon Measure 9 (1992)   208

Document 135: Lesbian Appointed to Federal Government (1993)   210

Document 136: Lesbians and Gay Men in the Military (1993)   213

Document 137: Military Working Group on Homosexuality (1993)   214

Document 138: Barry Goldwater on Gays in the Military (1993)   215

Document 139: Hawai'i Same-Sex Marriage Court Case (1993)   216

Document 140: March on Washington (1993)   221

Document 141: Deaf, Black, and Gay: Comparative Rights (1993)   223

Document 142: Impact of Gays on the Media (1994)   224

Document 143: PFLAG Supports Gay and Lesbian Children (1994)   226

Document 144: Catholic Condemnation of Homosexuality (1994)   227

Document 145: Ex-Gays Condemn Gay Rights (1994)   228

Document 146: Bisexual Young Woman Speaks Out (1994)   229

Document 147: Sharon Bottoms Child Custody Court Case (1994)   230

Document 148: Japanese American Citizens League Supports
Legalizing Same-Sex Marriage (1994)   232

Document 149: Lesbianas Unidas (1994) 234

Document 150: Exposing the Religious Right (1995) 235

Document 151: The Lesbian Avengers (1995) 237

Document 152: Brandon Teena Murder Trial (1996) 239

Document 153: *Romer v. Evans* (1996) 240

Document 154: Defense of Marriage Act (1996) 241

Document 155: Galluccio-Holden Adoption Lawsuit (1997) 244

Document 156: Gay and Lesbian Alliance Against Defamation (1997) 245

Document 157: Internet Publication for Gay and Lesbian Rights (1997) 247

Document 158: Intersex Society of North America (1997) 248

Document 159: Transgender Liberation (1998) 249

Document 160: Southern Baptist Convention Condemns
Homosexuality (1998) 250

Document 161: Focus on the Family (1998) 252

Document 162: Hawai'i Voters Reject Same-Sex Marriage (1998) 253

Document 163: Mrs. Shepard Speaks in Support of
Hate Crimes Laws (1998) 259

Document 164: Hate Crimes Laws Won't Stop Hate (1998) 259

Document 165: Coming Out (1998) 260

Document 166: Cyberactivism (1999) 262

Document 167: *Stan Baker v. State of Vermont* (1999) 264

Document 168: Overturning State Sodomy Laws (1999) 267

Document 169: *Dale v. Boy Scouts of America* (1999) 269

Document 170: *Boy Scouts of America v. Dale* (2000) 271

Document 171: Transgender Rights and the ACLU (2000) 276

Document 172: Laura Schlessinger Radio Show (2000) 276

Document 173: Suicide of a Gay Mormon (2000) 279

Document 174: Antigay Hate Crimes in High Schools (2000) 280

Document 175: Millennium March on Washington (2000) 282

Conclusion 285

Glossary 289

List of Gay, Lesbian, Bisexual, and Transgender Organizations 291

Selected Bibliography 295

Index 301

Series Foreword

This series is designed to meet the research needs of high school and college students by making available in one volume the key primary documents on a given historical event or contemporary issue. Documents include speeches and letters, congressional testimony, Supreme Court and lower court decisions, government reports, biographical accounts, position papers, statutes, and news stories.

The purpose of the series is twofold: (1) to provide substantive and background material on an event or issue through the texts of pivotal primary documents that shaped policy or law, raised controversy, or influenced the course of events, and (2) to trace the controversial aspects of the event or issue through documents that represent a variety of viewpoints. Documents for each volume have been selected by a recognized specialist in that subject with the advice of a board of other subject specialists, school librarians, and teachers.

To place the subject in historical perspective, the volume editor has prepared an introductory overview and a chronology of events. Documents are organized either chronologically or topically. The documents are full text or, if unusually long, have been excerpted by the volume editor. To facilitate understanding, each document is accompanied by an explanatory introduction. Suggestions for further reading follow the document or the chapter.

It is the hope of Greenwood Press that this series will enable students and other readers to use primary documents more easily in their research, to exercise critical thinking skills by examining the key documents in American history and public policy, and to critique the variety of viewpoints represented by this selection of documents.

Acknowledgments

This book would not have been possible without the resources of ONE Institute & Archives: The International Gay and Lesbian Heritage Research Center, located at the University of Southern California. If it were not for Jim Kepner, Dorr Legg, and Merritt Thompson, the forward-thinking intellectuals who founded ONE Institute in 1956, many of these documents would never have been saved. For help in finding books, periodicals, and other documents in ONE Institute's incomparable International Gay and Lesbian Archives, we are deeply grateful to the Institute's dedicated volunteer staff who have given so freely of their time for this research project: Pat Allen, Flo Fleischman, John O'Brien, Jim Schneider, Misha Schutt, Mark Thompson, Stuart Timmons, and C. Todd White.

Others who laid the basis for this book include pioneer collectors of historical documents, like Jonathan Katz, Barbara Gittings, and Martin Duberman, to more recent academic researchers like Mark Blasius and Shane Phelen. Their support and friendship have been invaluable.

We also express heartfelt gratitude to the Institute for the Study of Human Resources, for a David Cameron Legal Research Award to Walter Williams, and a Hal Call Mattachine Scholar Award to Yolanda Retter. These awards provided crucial financial support for this research. In addition, Yolanda Retter received a generous grant from University of Southern California Professor Nancy Warner, and Walter Williams received two faculty research awards from the Deans of the University of Southern California College of Letters, Arts and Sciences. These College awards paid for hiring USC History Department graduate student Thomas Cantwell, who located some important documents.

Last, thanks are due to editor Emily Birch of Greenwood Press, who was consistently supportive and extremely helpful during the publication process.

Introduction

Walter L. Williams

On this point hold firm, as with a chain of steel.
Those who deny freedom to others,
deserve it not for themselves;
and under a just god,
cannot long retain it.

> *Abraham Lincoln (Abraham Lincoln letter to Henry L. Pierce and others, April 6,*
> *1859.* Lincoln Speeches and Writings, 1859–1865 *[New York: Literary Classics*
> *of the United States, Viking Press, 1989]).*

The struggle for gay and lesbian rights in the United States is based on the idea that feelings of love and sexual attractions between persons of the same sex are natural, moral, normal, psychologically healthy, and deserving of full equality in legal, political, and all aspects of society. This movement for equality is a response to previously held ideas that homosexual behavior is unnatural, immoral, abnormal, psychologically sick, and legally, politically, and socially unacceptable. This book contains documents that explore different viewpoints about this complex issue.

THE MORALITY OF UNNATURAL BEHAVIORS

Let us begin to try to understand the controversy surrounding gay and lesbian rights by examining the idea that sexual attraction of a female for another female, or a male for another male, is "unnatural." We first have to ask: If a behavior we engage in is unnatural, does that necessarily make it wrong or immoral? If we think carefully about this, it is clear that human beings do many unnatural things every day. Think about your daily behavior and all the things you do that are not natural. Wearing clothes is not natural; we were not born wearing clothes, and these manufactured items are not part of our natural body. Most of us cut or shave the hair that grows naturally on our bodies. Some of us dye our hair a color that is not natural, or have tattoos on our bodies. Many of us undergo surgery to change the natural shape of our noses, thicken our lips, or remove natural fat deposits around our waists and hips.

Many ethical questions are raised by issues of unnaturalness. Should people be condemned because they choose to do something unnatural with their own bodies? Do people have a right to control their own bodies? If a person does not have this right, from whom must they gain permission? Who has the authority to set what is permissible and morally right for everyone else? Is it the law? If so, can voters elect new lawmakers to change the laws? Is it the scriptures of a particular religion? If so, what about people who follow a different religion? How does the law decide a religion everyone must follow, and reject the values of all other religions?

Most people in the contemporary United States believe that each person has the right to control his or her own body, even if that person chooses to do something unnatural with it. Most people also choose to accept many things that are unnatural in the areas of cultural learning and technological inventions. Right now you are doing something unnatural by reading; we do not naturally know how to read when we are born. You had to be taught how to read, and are reading this text on a manufactured piece of paper (unnaturally produced from a tree) or on a computer constructed by an unnatural robot. Most of us ride in an unnatural machine to our school or workplace, rather than walk everywhere on the legs that nature gave us. Gliding over the surface of a lake in a fiberglass motorboat is definitely not as natural as swimming. Nothing could be more unnatural than flying in an airplane. Yet, despite the plethora of unnatural behaviors we engage in, most people in modern societies take them for granted. Rather than looking down on such unnatural behaviors, we value them as evidence of human advancement and inventiveness. Part of the joy of being human lies in transcending the biological limitations that constrain us. We should not fear reading, riding, boating, flying, or any behavior just on the basis that it is unnatural. From this perspective, how can we conclude that any form of behavior should be condemned merely because it is not natural? Therefore, why should we conclude that homosexual behavior must be rejected based on the claim that it is unnatural?

HOMOSEXUAL BEHAVIOR AND NATURE

If being unnatural does not necessarily make something bad, the next question to ask is: Is homosexual behavior, in fact, unnatural? What does it mean to say that an aspect of human behavior is unnatural? Does it mean that behavior not found in nature is unnatural? If so, sexual interactions between individuals of the same sex must surely be qualified as natural, because such interactions have been documented in practically all human populations since ancient times, as well as among many species of animals in the natural world. Homosexual behavior is commonly observed in animals ranging from seagulls to elephants, and lizards to whales. Same-sex erotic behavior is particularly common among primates, humanity's closest relatives. For example, among bonobos (pygmy chimpanzees) same-sex erotic acts are notable in both females and males. Two females may form a tight bond, spending time grazing for food, resting and sleeping together, and rubbing each others' genitals for pleasure. A juvenile male may form a sexual partnership with a particular adult male, who takes the younger one under his wing and protects him and shares food. A young male learns how to become an adult partly within the context of an intimate relationship with a fully mature adult male.[1]

The overriding characteristic of nature is variation and diversity. Nature thrives with a wide variety of life forms that take advantage of numerous ecological niches, and these life forms express their behavior in innumerable ways. This includes variation in reproductive and sexual behaviors. Many species of plants reproduce through the sexual spread of the male sperm through airborne pollen. Other plants use animals, like honeybees or hummingbirds, to reproduce. When we look at a beautiful flower, we must realize that we are admiring the sexual organ of the plant. Many forms of life do not engage in sexual behavior at all, but reproduce by simply dividing in two. Others are both male and female, and reproduce by themselves. Still others are female while young, and become male later on in life.

Since a bewildering array of sexual variation is present among the many species of animals in nature, and especially among our mammalian relatives, we may conclude that it is natural for humans to exhibit sexual variation as well. Individual humans vary considerably. By observing individual people in our daily lives, we can see examples of this variation. Some people are short; some are tall. Some are lean, while others are hefty. Hair color, eyesight range, ear shape, height of the arch of the foot, and a myriad other characteristics show variation in the human body. People also have varied personalities and tastes. Some people are shy, while others are gregarious. Some people enjoy roller coaster rides, whereas others would rather sit silently by a mountain stream. Some people like to eat vanilla ice cream, while others prefer pistachio. The list of variations is endless, and is as diverse as the number of humans alive. Diversity is not a threat; it is a reality of nature.

We are all unique in some way. Do we feel pride in our uniqueness, or do we feel ashamed for being different? Do we think of our uniqueness as something perverse, or as something that is exceptional? It all depends on the values of our society, and the extent to which we internalize those social values into our personal beliefs. For example, about 10 percent of people are left-handed, making them statistically abnormal. Throughout much of European history, left-handed people were looked upon as abnormal and evil. Their left preference was believed to be a mark of the devil. Most left-handed people responded by learning to suppress their natural tendency to use their left hand, and instead learned to point, shake hands, and write with their right hand. Use of the right hand was "right," and use of the left hand was wrong. As a result, many people were closeted left-handers! It has only been within the twentieth century, after left-handedness was discovered to be genetically inherited, that prejudice against left-handed people decreased. Hand preference is no longer seen as a moral question, and teachers no longer try to force left-handed children to use their right hands. Left-handed people are different; their difference is obvious to everyone. Although left-handedness continues to be an abnormal trait in any group of people, it is no longer looked upon as something about which someone should feel ashamed. Today, many left-handed people grow up without hearing condemnation about their hand preference, and as a result most people feel neutral about their left-handedness, but some baseball players are justly proud of their leftie hardballs. One's attitude (shame, unconcern, or pride) depends to a great extent upon one's perspective.

Using labels like "abnormal" or "perverse" tends to stigmatize certain behaviors that are different. Stigma is a negative value attached by society to certain characteristics. On the other hand, other unusual traits and behaviors might be praised and valued. For example, two centuries ago Amadeus Mozart as a young boy was noted for an unusual ability to compose music. He was certainly not normal compared to other children. Instead of being looked down upon, however, his musical inclinations were lauded as exceptional and he became the most honored composer of his age. Today, in a typical high school, we might see one unusually tall person slumping over in embarrassment about this abnormality, while another might use the advantage of height to become a star basketball player. An abnormal computer nerd who is laughed at as a geek may end up becoming the wealthiest person in town because of his or her fascination with computers and technical machines.

We are all abnormal in some aspect. This is a good thing, because if everyone were the same it would be a very boring world. Variation and difference are what make the world a fascinating place. If variation exists in all aspects of human behavior, why would we expect that sexuality would be an exception? Sexual tastes, preferences, and inclinations vary among individuals, in the same way that food preferences do. Some people like coffee with cream, while others prefer tea with sugar. Some people like scrambled eggs, while others prefer their eggs fried. While this reality of variation is accepted in the case of food preferences, it is not accepted in the case of sexual variance. Few Americans would label someone as immoral because they had a preference for a certain kind of food, but we often stigmatize those who prefer certain types of sexuality. Part I of this book deals with the clash of religious views over the morality of homosexual behavior. As the documents in the following sections of the book make clear, much of the legal, political, and social attitudes related to homosexuality and bisexuality, as well as gender variance, reflect religious ideas. The battle for gay and lesbian rights in the United States goes back, in many ways, to the attitudes of religion toward sex and gender.

Considering the pervasiveness of same-sex behavior in nature, it is not surprising that the historical record also shows evidence of homoerotic desires dating back to ancient times, and in many areas of the world. One of the oldest epics of world literature is the five-thousand-year-old Mideastern Hittite story of the intimate friendship between Gilgamesh and Enkidu. Ancient Greek legends of the love between the god Zeus and the young boy Ganymede, or between the warriors Achilles and Patroclus, were made famous in Homer's *Iliad*. Homoerotic poetry, where adult men expressed their love for adolescent boys, was so common in ancient Greece that for many years "Greek" was a synonym for homosexuality. It was also referred to as "Socratic Love," after the famous teacher Socrates who was a lover of males in Athens. The term "lesbian" originated from the Greek island of Lesbos, where the famous female poet Sappho wrote poems of love to her female students.[2] This tradition of respect for same-sex love existed not only in Greece but throughout the ancient Mediterranean. Famous military leaders like Alexander the Great of Macedonia and the greatly admired Emperor Hadrian of the Roman Empire were both known to have had devoted same-sex relationships.

Traditions of same-sex love have been celebrated in other parts of the world as well. In ancient China, the Emperor Ai was famous for being so devoted to his boyfriend that when he was awakened to attend an emergency governmental meeting he cut off the sleeve of his coat rather than disturb the sleep of his partner who was resting on the coat sleeve. After that, male-male love in China was respectfully called "the love of the cut sleeve." In Japan, the great cultural hero Kobo Daishi, founder of the Shingon sect of Buddhism in the year 800, was said to have popularized male-male intimate relationships. For a thousand years after that time, homosexual behavior was highly respected in Japan, particularly among Buddhist monks, Samurai warriors ("ninja" was the name by which a warrior referred to his male lover), and kabuki theater performers.[3]

Though we know far less about female-female eroticism in other cultures, male homosexual behavior was so institutionalized among some cultures in New Guinea that they believed a boy could not mature into a man until he had engaged in many sexual encounters with adult men and absorbed their masculinizing semen.[4] Marriages between two females, or between two males, were institutionalized and socially accepted in many cultures of the world, including the Azande of East Africa, the Polynesians of Hawaii, the Aboriginal people of Australia, and the Chukchi of Siberia. Woman-woman marriage was particularly notable in Africa.[5]

Given the widespread existence of same-sex behavior in both the animal world and among many human cultures dating from ancient times to the present, the correct question is not "what causes homosexuality?" We can no more expect a straightforward answer to that question than we can to the question "what causes heterosexuality?" The basic reality is that people vary in their sexual desires, and both homosexual and heterosexual desires are expressions of a single human nature that can be expressed differently in different individuals. Some people are attracted to the other sex and some people are attracted to the same sex. Many persons through history were known to be attracted to both males and females, making bisexuality more common than perhaps any other pattern. Even though most males in cultures like ancient Greece, New Guinea, and Japan celebrated male-male love, many of those same men also married women and fathered children. Many people wanted offspring in order to have someone to take care of them in their old age.

One of the main reasons for sexual pairings and marriage, besides producing offspring, is to create long-standing intimate bonds between people. If a woman attracts the sexual interest of a man, and she marries him, ideally she gains not only the benefit of his labor and support, but also that of his relatives. This is why marriage is institutionalized in many cultures as uniting not only the two spouses, but both their families as well. A same-sex lover might also provide resources that aid in survival. Love and sexual attraction are powerful motivators for people to help one another. In short, sex and friendship are main reasons why individuals bond closely with other individuals. Whether this is done in a sexual pairing or in a nonsexual friendship, it serves the same purpose. A major purpose of intimate bonding is the development of close allies to whom one can turn in times of need. A person who bonds closely with both males and females has an evolutionary advantage.

SEX AND REPRODUCTION

The question, then, is not to try to discover what causes any particular form of sexual bonding, but to discover why a minority of the world's cultures condemns and prohibits such bonding. Much of this condemnation has to do with social attitudes toward reproduction. Obviously, much sexual behavior and sexual attraction are closely associated with reproduction of the next generation. While a woman can become impregnated by artificial insemination, without engaging in a sexual act with a man, most human pregnancies are the result of male-female intercourse. Some religious leaders have concluded that the only purpose of sex is reproduction, and that other nonprocreative expressions of sexuality are therefore morally wrong. Think about that statement, "the *only* purpose of sex is reproduction." Is this true? Or, are there many other purposes of sex, such as enjoyment, release of stress, and expression of love for another?

As mentioned above, anthropologists know that one of the most important purposes of sex for a society is the creation of close intimate bonds among nonrelated individuals. This is one reason why so many societies have incest rules, preventing people from having sex with someone in their own family. Such societies want to maximize the number of people in the family, to provide a larger support system. That is, if you marry your brother or sister, then you only have your own blood relatives to depend on. But if you marry a person who is unrelated to you, then you not only have your own blood relatives to depend on, but also your spouse and all your spouse's blood relatives. Sexual bondings to unrelated individuals are economically important. The only time such rules are not applied is when a family is already at the top level of society, and to marry an outsider would represent a lowering of the family's position because that family would then be expected to help a lower-level family. This is why the elites of hierarchical societies often favor brother-sister or cousin marriage. Examples include the pharoahs of ancient Egypt and the ali'i royalty of traditional Hawaiian culture. Many of the royal houses of Europe encouraged their members to marry foreigners who were also of royal status, rather than marry a commoner at home. Their sexual alliances and marriages often had more to do with creating political alliances than feelings of personal attraction or love.

The point is that sex has many more purposes than reproduction. A major trend that has occurred in recent decades is the idea of "sex-as-fun." This idea has been promoted especially by capitalist advertising, and by commercial publications like *Playboy*. This so-called *Playboy* ethic emerged as a major challenge to traditional Christian morality in twentieth-century American society. Commercial advertising uses sex-as-fun simply because it is so effective in selling products. Look at soda commercials, or cigarette advertisements; they do not say "it tastes good, it is good for you." Instead, the most common theme is "use our product and you will be a sexy person who will attract others as sexual partners." Because sex sells, American capitalism has a vested interest in spreading the message that sex is fun.

As a result of receiving these two contradictory messages, that "sex is only for reproduction" and "sex is fun," major tensions exist in modern society. For example, a 1990 radio commercial for the popular television prime-time soap opera *Falconcrest* advertised the program as having "all of the sin, none of the guilt." One of the reasons for the popularity of sexual scandals in newspaper tabloids and television programs is due to this combination. People can partake of their strong interest in sex, without feeling the guilt that would come from doing these things themselves. People live their sins vicariously through others.

These tensions are especially strong in someone who believes that sex is only for reproduction. To such a person homosexuality represents prohibited acts not only because it is not procreative, but also because it is done only for the enjoyment of the sexual act itself. If a person believes that sexual enjoyment is morally wrong, and should only occur within marriage for reproductive purposes, homosexual acts violate these rules. Ironically, the legal prohibition of same-sex marriage guarantees that homosexual acts can only occur outside of marriage. Legal appeals brought to the courts by same-sex couples, even if they have lived together for many years in a loving relationship and in a mutually supporting family with children, have to this point been unsuccessful.

Since every person in the United States is legally unable to marry another person of the same sex, homosexual behavior necessarily involves breaking a social rule, the one that presupposes that everyone should marry someone of the other sex. Many people want everything to be clear and in its proper place; so homosexuality seems ambiguous. It violates the notion that everything should be arranged into clear pairs of opposites: good versus evil, black versus white, savage versus civilized, man versus woman.

Homosexuality is unsettling proof that much of the world cannot be ordered into opposite categories. Those who cannot tolerate ambiguity are often those who object most loudly to the cause of gay and lesbian equality. In an ambiguous situation, intolerant people strive to reduce the ambiguity. They want to prevent the mixture of categories that, in their view, should be kept separate. An example is people who dread interracial marriages, referring to it as miscegenation.

Thus, throughout the history of the United States homosexuality has been considered as a danger, in the same way that witches were greatly feared by people in medieval Europe and in the early American colonies. Witches broke the social rules of male dominance, and homosexuals break the social rules of sexual repression. Witches were seen as being the opposite of normal people. They stayed up late at night (therefore normal people went to bed early in order to prove that they were not witches). They flew through the air on broomsticks (rather than walking as normal people did). Women were active leaders in pre-Christian Wiccan religions. This was in contrast to the male-dominated Christian churches where only males could be the top religious leaders. Witches were said to prefer dressing in black, a color associated with medieval ideas of evil. Because witches were associated with cats, Christian zealots went on rampages killing thousands of cats. This slaughter contributed to the outbreak of the bubonic plague in medieval Europe, because with fewer cats there was a sharp increase in the disease-carrying rat population.

In many ways, the antigay rhetoric of today repeats these same ideas. Like witches, homosexuals are seen as being the opposite of normal people. Something that might otherwise be seen as an advantage (being able to fly through the air, for witches, or being sexually fulfilled and unrepressed, for gays and lesbians), is converted into a stigma. Whether something is labeled a heresy or a perversion, the idea is the same: difference is a threat. As a result of the notion that there is something wrong about same-sex love, many people worry about homosexuals converting others, and recruiting children into homosexuality. This shows that they believe homosexuality is a potential for everyone. They think that any unsuspecting child can be recruited into a gay lifestyle by a single pleasurable sexual act. They see the most severe sanctions (laws against it, employment discrimination, segregation of homosexuals from schoolchildren and even from other young adults in the military) as necessary to prevent "it" from becoming rampant in society.

Those who feel that the only purpose of sex is reproduction must oppose the acceptance of homosexual behavior because it is a violation of their belief system. What this suggests is that, to gain gay and lesbian equality in the United States, a much more fundamental argument must be made against the notion that the only purpose of sex is reproduction. This is why the movement for lesbian, gay, bisexual, intersex, and transgender equality is integrally related to the movements for access to birth control, abortion, and sexual freedom in general. All of these movements argue for the acceptance of sex which is engaged in for reasons other than reproduction.

The ideology expounding sex for purposes of reproduction was taken to its illogical conclusion by Germany during the 1930s and 1940s. The Nazis strongly emphasized the need for more Aryans (Germanic peoples), in order to expand their military empire. Homosexuals, along with Jews and others the Germans considered subhuman, were put into concentration camps. Homosexuals did not reproduce and were therefore seen as useless in building the Aryan race. They were designated as a health hazard because they might infect others with their nonprocreative homosexual behavior. Nazi rhetoric against homosexuals sounds frighteningly similar to the arguments of those who oppose gay and lesbian equality.[6]

More people are beginning to question the notion that homosexuals are inferior because they do not reproduce. Today, there is almost universal agreement that overpopulation is one of the world's major problems. In the past, people who did not reproduce were considered almost as traitors, because they were not contributing to population growth. It seems ridiculous to hear someone argue that "if everybody were homosexual, the human race would become extinct." In today's world, the danger of *too much* reproduction is a greater threat to humanity's future. On this level, there is a logical connection between the gay and lesbian liberation movement and the ecology movement.

This perspective also suggests that a prime goal of the gay and lesbian liberation movement must be to legalize same-sex marriages, especially since more same-sex couples are having or adopting children. This trend toward coupling and parenthood will undercut the notion that homosexuality is antifamily. It will allow the social recognition of genuine homosexual families based on same-sex love. This is basically a struggle for the freedom to marry the person of one's choice. In United States law, the idea that no one else can legally force someone to marry against their will was introduced into the new United States as a reaction to arranged marriages in other nations. The freedom to marry was considered a personal choice outside the control of government, and an inalienable right of United States citizenship. However, in many states, the freedom to marry was originally restricted to white people. Until the Civil War, laws in Southern states prohibited anyone from marrying a black slave. Part of the progress in ending slavery was the ability of African Americans to marry legally. Still, until as late as the 1960s, some states had laws that prohibited men and women of different races from marrying. Racists predicted dire social consequences if people of different races were allowed to marry. They said they wanted to protect marriage by preventing miscegenation. Nevertheless, after many protests by civil rights activists, in 1967 the United States Supreme Court ruled that state laws prohibiting interracial marriages were unconstitutional. The right to marry the person of one's choice was deemed to be a basic freedom of United States liberty. However, at the beginning of the twenty-first century this principle—the right to marry whom we choose—still has not been applied to same-sex couples in the United States. A number of other nations, however, have legalized same-sex marriages.

PSYCHOLOGICAL REACTION FORMATION

If the right to marry a person of one's choice is so ingrained in United States law, why is there so much resistance by some citizens to the idea of same-sex marriage? The psychological theories of Sigmund Freud suggest that one reason for strong reactions against homosexuals is, ironically, because same-sex attractions are common among people. Freud said that a major reason for hatred comes from what he called "reaction formation." If a child develops a desire that she or he later finds out is severely condemned by the child's parents or significant others, then the child will internalize that condemnation by denying the existence of that desire within her- or himself. Among some people, the desire is so repressed that it may never recur, but in others unconscious thoughts may occur. In the latter case, persons strive to maintain denial, by expressing intolerance of the desire in others. Among people who still feel the desire despite learning that it is condemned, intense feelings of conflict and self-hatred arise. Freud pointed out that this repressed or latent homosexuality is quite common among people. In order to maintain their denial of this desire, people will condemn and punish others who do not repress that same desire.[7]

In this situation, anyone who is openly bisexual, gay, lesbian, or transsexual is seen as intentionally flaunting the rules, and deliberately challenging social conventions. A follower of Freudian psychology wrote: "The dread of homosexuality is the result of, and derives its tremendous force from, the wishes for homosexual expression which are present in our unconscious minds. In other words, the fear is intimately connected with the wish, and the wish is only repressed because of the dread which is conjured up by the social taboo."[8] Even if we do not want to believe Freud's claim that every person has at least some same-sex desires, it is clear that reaction formation is experienced by a large number of people. Those who recognize their own attractions to others of the same sex, especially if these attractions are held as closely guarded secrets, are often the people most likely to publicly condemn openly gay and lesbian people. By making a public statement of condemnation, they can try to convince others—and themselves—that they are not really part of the dreaded category of sexual perverts. This theory suggests that such psychological motivators for condemnation will not change until children are raised in a way that does not repress their early sexual attractions.

GENDER ISSUES

Opposition to gay and lesbian rights also relates to gender discrimination. Here we must understand the concept of heterosexism. If sexism is the belief that the male sex is superior to the female sex, then heterosexism is the belief that heterosexuality is superior to other forms of sexuality. These two forms of prejudice are closely tied. United States society has traditionally seen men as superior to women. Therefore, for a woman to dispense with a male indicates that she is not staying in her subordinate place. Likewise, for a man to become like a woman in any respect is seen as a betrayal of the superior masculine status, and as taking on the inferior feminine status.[9]

The sexist and heterosexist reaction against homosexual males is particularly strong, and is manifested in two ways. First, if a male submits to being penetrated sexually by a male, as a woman is penetrated, he is seen as being like a woman and therefore inferior. We still retain the notions that being sexually penetrated is bad, as represented by the saying "I was really screwed" meaning that something bad happened to us. Why is it considered bad? Perhaps it is because we consider women to be inferior. So when we say "Screw you" as an insult, we are really telling that person to put themselves in the subordinate status which our society has assigned to a person who takes the "insertee" role in sex. When society considers sex to be a bad thing, and women to be inferior, then this notion that sex is a means of domination will be stronger.

The second aspect of heterosexism has little to do with particular sexual behaviors, but instead focuses on personality characteristics. A female who does not act submissively or femininely is perceived as leaving the natural role for women, and rebelling against established gender values. Conversely, a male who does not conform to masculine stereotypes is seen as acting effeminate, like a woman. An effeminate male who is also homosexual violates masculine superiority in two ways. He is seen as lowering himself from the superior masculine status, and as being less than a man because women are seen as being less than men. Research has shown that the most virulent antigay bigots are those who have the most narrow and rigid ideas of what constitutes proper roles for men and women. They hold narrow views of what masculinity and femininity should be. What the research shows is that we cannot get rid of antigay prejudice without also getting rid of sexism. As long as women are considered to be inferior to men, any male who takes on a status similar to women is going to be condemned as inferior.[10]

This is why gay men should support the feminist movement. This is where gay men and feminists can be allies, because they are both opposing the privilege accorded those who are considered masculine. Lesbians are a natural bridge between the two groups, since they experience both sexist and heterosexist forms of discrimination. This perspective implies that gay men should promote lesbians as leaders in the gay rights movement, and should be supportive of feminist issues, for their own self-interest if nothing else.

THE FUNCTIONAL THEORY OF HOMOPHOBIA

The term "homophobia" has been used to describe someone's revulsion and fear of homosexuals, expressed through prejudice, discrimination, harassment, punishment, or acts of violence. Psychologist Gregory Herek sees homophobia as resulting from the psychological benefits that people derive from it. Homophobia thus has a functional role, especially for males. From the time they are small children, boys are told to "act like a man." Fear of not being a real man is an important socializing agent for boys growing up in this society. This keeps men within their traditionally defined roles in society, and forces them to counter their real desires: avoid showing fear because bravery is valued, hide pain because emotional isolation is valued, do not show love for another male because competition is valued, and do not submit to another male because dominance is valued.

It is, of course, difficult for men to attain these valued ideals, and they have to strive constantly to deal with suppressed emotions when they cannot succeed in the competitive contest. Thus, those males who are the least successful in the terms that society values (i.e., economic wealth, and domination over others), are often the ones who express the most homophobic attitudes. Homophobia becomes an easy way that they can validate their own masculinity, by seeing homosexuals as below them. Since they have failed to validate their masculinity through economic success or by commanding others, condemning homosexuals is an easy way for a man to reaffirm to others (and to himself) that he is indeed "a real man." He is not homosexual, therefore he is not like a woman. Male homophobia acts out the anger and fear that men feel at the possibility of being subjugated to another man, and of being treated the way women are treated.[11]

In his psychological research studies, Dr. Herek found that people who are strongly homophobic tend to exhibit certain attitudes:

1. They are much more authoritarian-minded than the average person, with strong feelings that it is necessary for everyone to follow the rules and not question authority.

2. They have rigid and restrictive ideas about the proper roles for men and women. They believe that women should be housewives and mothers, while men should be breadwinners and strong providers.

3. They subscribe to a conservative religious ideology that promotes the idea that homosexuality is sinful.

4. They have not been exposed to an educational setting where a diverse campus promotes a general appreciation for diversity. This applies to adolescents who have not yet attended college, or older people who never went to college.

5. They live in geographic areas where negative attitudes toward homosexuality are the norm, and their peers tend to exhibit similar attitudes.

6. They have never had close ongoing personal contact with an openly identified lesbian or gay man, as a relative, close friend, or co-worker.

If someone combines several of these characteristics, then their homophobia is even stronger. Conversely, those who are less likely to be homophobic tend to have the following characteristics:

1. They do not simply follow authority, but question things and make up their own mind about issues. They are much more independent-minded.

2. They are much more open to flexible gender roles for both women and men.

3. They believe in a religion that does not preach opposition to homosexuality, or they are not religious.

4. They are more educated (although some well-educated persons may be homophobic if they are also more authoritarian or religious, or if they have a personal problem with homosexuality due to their own repressed sexuality).

5. They live in more liberal-minded communities, and their peers are more accepting of homosexuals.

6. They have had at least one close ongoing personal contact with an openly identified lesbian or gay man, as a relative, close friend, or co-worker.[12]

Herek and other researchers emphasize the multiple origins of negative attitudes toward homosexuality. People become homophobic as a result of being told from an early age that same-sex love is unnatural, immoral, illegal, and a threat to children, to the family, to religion, and to society in general. It is because these homophobic and heterosexist views have been so dominant in society that a movement for gay, lesbian, bisexual, transsexual, and transgender rights has arisen. This movement has challenged these prejudices, and in the process has tied into the historical tradition of movements for equality and against discrimination. The essence of the argument for gay and lesbian equality is the proposition that two people who love each other should be able to do so, without social or legal interference from others. The gay rights argument says that sexual and gender identity differences need to be accepted, that sexual minorities should be treated as respectfully as any other minority. The contribution of this struggle to the modern concept of liberty is the idea that the freedom to love the person of one's choice should be considered as a basic freedom, no less important in peoples' lives than the freedom of speech, of religious expression, of assembly, and other intimate aspects of peoples' personal lives. All aspects of liberty contribute to the rich diversity that makes up the United States, and each aspect becomes a part of the fabric of democracy.

APPROACH OF THIS VOLUME

This book contains historical documents that present the story of the legal, political, religious, personal, and social struggles for the rights of lesbians, gay men, bisexuals, transsexuals, intersexuals, and transgendered persons. The book focuses on both social and government documents. Oral histories, articles in popular magazines, sermons, autobiographies, and private letters are as important as laws, court cases, congressional committee hearings, and presidential speeches. The editors have included documents that reveal different aspects of the controversy. In general, documents are arranged chronologically to show the development of the struggle over time. While space considerations necessitated the deletion of some topics, we sought to include as many representative voices and as many of the issues as would fit into one volume. The reader will find a mix of voices representing a cross section of generations, ethnicities, classes, religions, races, occupations, ideologies, and genders. The purpose of the book is to present the ideas and reasoning of the authors of the documents, and to make available multiple documents that will help clarify the controversy over gay and lesbian rights in the United States.

ENDNOTES/NOTES

1. John Kirsch and James Weinrich, "Homosexuality, Nature and Biology: Is Homosexuality Natural? Does It Matter?" *In Homosexuality: Research Implications for Public Policy,* eds. John Gonsiorek and James Weinrich (Newbury Park, CA: Sage,

1991), pp. 13–31; Bruce Bagemihl, *Biological Exuberance: Animal Homosexuality and Natural Diversity* (New York: St. Martin's Press, 1999).

2. Byrne R. S. Fone, *The Columbia Anthology of Gay Literature* (New York: Columbia University Press, 1998); K. J. Dover, *Greek Homosexuality* (Cambridge, MA: Harvard University Press, 1978).

3. Bret Hinsch, *Passions of the Cut Sleeve: The Male Homosexual Tradition in China* (Berkeley: University of California Press, 1990); Tsuneo Watanabe and Jun'ichi Iwata, *The Love of the Samurai: A Thousand Years of Japanese Homosexuality* (London: Gay Men's Press, 1989).

4. Gilbert Herdt, *Ritualized Homosexuality in Melanesia* (Berkeley: University of California Press, 1984); Gilbert Herdt, *The Sambia* (New York: Holt, Rinehart, 1987).

5. Walter L. Williams, *The Spirit and the Flesh: Sexual Diversity in American Indian Culture* (Boston: Beacon Press, 1992); David Greenberg, *The Construction of Homosexuality* (Chicago: University of Chicago Press, 1988); Stephen Murray and Will Roscoe, *Boy-Wives and Female Husbands: Studies of African Homosexualities* (New York: St. Martin's Press, 1998).

6. Richard Plant, *The Pink Triangle: The Nazi Persecution against Homosexuals* (New York: Holt, 1986).

7. "Three Contributions to the Theory of Sex." *In The Basic Writings of Sigmund Freud,* ed. A. A. Brill (New York: Modern Library, 1938); "Character and Anal Eroticism (1908)" and "Repression (1915)" In *Sigmund Freud: Collected Papers,* ed. J. Riviere (New York: Basic Books, 1959).

8. Martin Hoffman, *The Gay World: Male Homosexuality and the Social Creation of Evil* (New York: Basic Books, 1968), pp. 181–182.

9. Suzanne Pharr, *Homophobia: A Weapon of Sexism* (Little Rock, AR: Women's Project, 1988).

10. Pharr, *Homophobia*; Warren Blumenfeld, *Homophobia: How We All Pay the Price* (Boston: Beacon Press, 1992).

11. Gregory Herek, "Beyond Homophobia: A Social Psychological Perspective on Attitudes toward Lesbians and Gay Men," *Journal of Homosexuality* 10 (1984): 1–21, see p. 6; Gregory Herek, "Stigma, Prejudice, and Violence against Lesbians and Gay Men." In *Homosexuality: Research Implications for Public Policy,* eds. John Gonsiorek and James Weinrich (Newbury Park, CA: Sage, 1991), pp. 60–80.

12. Herek, "Stigma."

Timeline

1924	The Society for Human Rights in Chicago, a gay group, publishes two issues of *Friendship and Freedom*. The society is disbanded after members are arrested.
1929	*The Well of Loneliness,* a lesbian novel written by British lesbian Radclyffe Hall, is declared not obscene by a U.S. court.
1934	The Hays code becomes mandatory in Hollywood and states that "sex perversion or any inference [sic] to it is forbidden on the screen."
1939	A lesbian couple in Georgia is charged with sodomy. A judge decides that women cannot commit sodomy and dismisses the case.
1943	The Armed Forces issue regulations barring homosexuals from serving in the military.
1947–48	America's first-known lesbian publication, *Vice Versa: America's Gayest Magazine,* is typed and discreetly distributed by "Lisa Ben" in Los Angeles.
1948	The Kinsey Report notes a surprising incidence of same-sex activity among U.S. males. A similar report on women is published in 1953.
1949	D. O. Cauldwell coins the term "transsexual."
1950	President Eisenhower signs Executive Order 10450 ordering the dismissal of government workers guilty of "sexual perversion."
1950	Harry Hay, Dale Jennings, Chuck Rowland, Rudy Gernreich, and others establish the Mattachine Society in Los Angeles.
1951	Christine Jorgensen, pioneer transsexual, travels from the United States to Denmark for surgery.
1952	ONE, Inc., a publishing group, is founded in Los Angeles by Mattachine members. The group publishes *ONE Magazine,* the first nationally circulated homosexual publication.

1954   The United States Post Office confiscates *ONE Magazine* claiming that it is "obscene, lewd, lascivious and filthy." ONE, Inc. sues the Post Office and wins its case four years later.

1955   The Daughters of Bilitis, the first lesbian organization in the United States, is founded in San Francisco by eight lesbians (including two women of color). They publish *The Ladder,* the first nationally circulated lesbian periodical.

1957   The Navy creates a committee to investigate homosexuality in the military. The Crittenden Report concludes that there is no sound basis for barring homosexuals from the Armed Forces.

1961   Popular drag queen entertainer Jose Sarria is the first openly gay person to run for political office in the United States. As a candidate for San Francisco's Board of Supervisors, he receives over 6,000 votes.

1961   Illinois becomes the first state to abolish laws prohibiting homosexual acts between consenting adults.

1963   The Society for Individual Rights (SIR) in San Francisco establishes the first gay community center in the nation.

1963   African American and gay man Bayard Rustin is the organizing genius behind the March on Washington where Martin Luther King, Jr. makes his "I Have a Dream" speech. No women are invited to give a major speech that day.

1964   The first gay rights demonstration is held outside an Armed Forces recruiting station in New York City.

1964   The San Francisco police harass and arrest homosexual people at a New Year's Eve ball. Official observers include heterosexual attorneys and clergy. The case is dismissed.

1965   Members of the East Coast Homophile Organization picket the White House and other government buildings to protest antigay discrimination.

1967   The American Civil Liberties Union calls for the decriminalization of consensual sex practices, including homosexual behavior.

1967   The first Student Homophile League is organized at Columbia University. Similar groups are organized at New York University, Cornell, and Stanford.

1967   *The Advocate,* which becomes the nation's leading gay magazine, is founded.

1968   Reverend Troy Perry and friends found the Metropolitan Community Church (MCC), in Los Angeles. This is the first church founded to serve the spiritual needs of homosexuals.

1969   The American Sociology Association issues a statement in support of the rights of homosexuals and other sexual minorities.

1969   A police raid on the Stonewall Inn in New York City leads to four days of rioting by gays and lesbians, angry at police oppression. The radical Gay Liberation Front is founded soon after.

1969	*Time* magazine publishes a front-cover story on "The Homosexual: Newly Visible, Newly Understood."
1970	After being fired from his job because of suspicion of homosexuality, a United States Post Office worker in San Francisco sues and is reinstated.
1970	The first Gay Pride marches are held in New York, Los Angeles, San Francisco, and Chicago. They commemorate the anniversary of the Stonewall uprising.
1970	Due to sexism, lesbians begin to separate from cogender homosexual groups and form their own woman-only groups.
1971	Latino gay men form a support group in Los Angeles.
1971	The earliest lesbian centers open: The Gay Women's Service Center (L.A.), The Los Angeles Lesbian Center, and The Seattle Lesbian Resource Center.
1971	Frank Kameny is the first openly gay person to run for Congress.
1971	Lesbians working with allies in the National Organization for Women help pass a prolesbian resolution.
1971	*The Lesbian Tide,* the first lesbian or gay publication to have a blatant title on its masthead, is founded.
1971	Bert Chapman of Howell, Michigan, is released from prison after serving thirty-one years for having sex with another male in 1940.
1972	In the early hours of the morning, activists Jim Foster and Madeline Davis briefly speak to delegates at the Democratic National Presidential Convention.
1972	Beth Chayim Chadashim, the first gay synagogue in the United States, and perhaps the world, is founded.
1972	The Gay Community Services Center (later the Los Angeles Gay and Lesbian Center) is founded. It becomes the model for other centers around the country.
1973	The National Gay Task Force (later the National Gay and Lesbian Task Force) is founded as the first national gay and lesbian rights advocacy group.
1973	Lesbians organize a national lesbian conference which draws close to 2,000 women from twenty-six states and four countries. The conference is held at the University of California, Los Angeles.
1973	The American Psychiatric Association declares that homosexuality by itself should not be considered a psychiatric disorder.
1974	Los Angeles law student Cheryl Bratman helps file an appeal on behalf of a lesbian mother and wins one of the first custody victories for lesbians.
1974	The first federal bill banning discrimination based on sexual orientation is introduced in Congress by Bella Abzug and Edward Koch. To date it has not passed.

1974   Elaine Noble becomes the first openly gay person to be elected to a state legislature, in Boston, Massachusetts.

1974   Salsa Souls Sisters (now African Ancestral Lesbians United For Societal Change) is founded. Latina lesbian activists in Los Angeles also form a group.

1975   Leonard Matlovich, Miriam Ben-Shalom, and African American Perry Watkins are discharged from the military due to their homosexuality and they sue. The latter two are eventually reinstated and retire with benefits.

1975   Gay American Indians is founded in San Francisco by Barbara Cameron, Randy Burns, and others.

1975   The Bisexual Forum is founded in New York City.

1976   The first gay and lesbian political action committee (PAC), the Municipal Elections Committee of Los Angeles (MECLA), is founded to help elect gay- and lesbian-friendly candidates to political office. Later the Human Rights Campaign becomes the first national LGBT PAC.

1977   Leaders of national gay and lesbian rights organizations meet at the White House with Midge Costanza, President Jimmy Carter's liaison to minority communities.

1978   The Briggs Initiative, which would require gay and lesbian teachers to be fired from California public schools, is defeated by a majority of California voters.

1978   San Francisco Supervisor and gay activist Harvey Milk and Mayor George Moscone are assassinated by former Supervisor Dan White.

1979   Gay and lesbian people of color hold their first conference as part of the upcoming March on Washington.

1979   The first national March on Washington for Gay and Lesbian Rights draws over 100,000 people to the nation's capital. Similar and larger marches are held in 1987, 1993, and 2000.

1979   A national organization, of chapters of Parents and Friends of Lesbians and Gays (PFLAG), is founded.

1980   The American Jewish Congress adopts a resolution opposing antigay discrimination in employment, housing, and military service.

1980   Mel Boozer, an African American gay man, speaks on prime-time television before delegates at the Democratic National Presidential Convention.

1981   A mysterious and lethal virus is first noticed spreading within the gay male community. The virus is later named Acquired Immune Deficiency Syndrome (AIDS).

1981   Wisconsin becomes the first state to pass a comprehensive gay rights law.

1982   The National Gay and Lesbian Task Force launches a Violence Project to counter the rise of homophobic violence in the United States.

1983	Lesbians of Color in Los Angeles organize the first National Lesbians of Color Conference.
1984	U.S. Conference of Mayors passes a resolution calling for an end to antigay discrimination.
1984	In Los Angeles, Virginia Uribe founds Project 10 as a support system for gay and lesbian high school students.
1984	The City of West Hollywood is incorporated in a heavily gay area lying between Hollywood and Beverly Hills. A majority of the first city council is openly gay and the first mayor is openly lesbian.
1984	After eight years of legal battles, Los Angeles gay activist Duncan Donovan wins the right to receive the death benefit of his male lover's life insurance policy.
1985	In reaction to the invisibility and stereotypes of gays and lesbians in the media, activists in New York City found the Gay and Lesbian Alliance Against Defamation.
1986	In *Bowers v. Hardwick* the United States Supreme Court upholds the right of states to criminalize private same-sex acts. This decision is an important defeat for sexual privacy rights.
1987	ACT UP is organized in New York City to protest national inaction on the AIDS crisis.
1987	Old Lesbians Organizing for Change (OLOC) is founded to fight against ageism and for equal rights for lesbians.
1987	Prior to the second March on Washington for Gay, Lesbian, and Bisexual Rights, seventy-five people participate in the first U.S. nationwide bisexual gathering.
1987	The National Latina/o Lesbian Gay Bisexual and Transgender organization (LLEGO) is founded.
1988	First National Coming Out Day (later National Coming Out Week). The annual event affirms that coming out is a political act that helps to reduce antigay prejudice.
1988	The Black Gay Leadership Forum, later the National Gay and Lesbian Black Leadership Forum, is founded in Los Angeles.
1990	A Hate Crimes Act is passed by Congress, and signed by President George H. W. Bush. It provides for federal penalties for crimes motivated by prejudice, including those based on a victim's sexual orientation.
1990	Founding of Queer Nation, a militant direct-action challenge to heterosexism. Their slogan: "We're here, we're queer, get used to it."
1992	The Democratic Party Convention endorses gay and lesbian rights.
1993	President Bill Clinton's attempt to lift the ban on gays and lesbians serving in the military becomes the "Don't ask, don't tell" compromise.
1993	In Nebraska, transman Brandon Teena is assaulted and raped by two men. Two days later, the same men kill Teena and two friends.

1995   In Oregon, lesbian activists Roxanne Ellis and Michelle Abdill are kid-
            napped and murdered. Their killer suggests he murdered them be-
            cause they were lesbians.

1996   The United States Senate votes on a gay rights bill to ban job discrimi-
            nation on the basis of sexual orientation. The bill fails by one vote,
            50–49.

1996   The Defense of Marriage Act (DOMA) is passed by both houses of Con-
            gress. It restricts the legal definition of marriage to that between a male
            and a female.

1998   University of Wyoming gay student Matthew Sheppard is tortured
            and murdered.

2000   The Vermont legislature passes a law approving "civil unions" for
            same-sex couples, a move that grants more rights to same-sex couples
            but stops short of legalizing same-sex marriage in that state.

2000   The Supreme Court supports the Boy Scouts of America's ban on gay
            scout leaders.

Part I

The Clash of Religions

The first great cultural war in American history was between the indigenous Native Americans and the invading Europeans. Almost from the first interactions between Spanish explorers and those people they called "Los Indios," the conflict centered around the Catholic priests' attempts to convert the Indians to Christianity. Likewise, when the French and the English established their colonies in North America, they dismissed the Native American religions as savage superstitions. One of the major criticisms leveled by all Europeans against Indians was their acceptance of homoeroticism and same-sex marriages. Condemning the Native Americans for practicing sodomy, which they labeled as "diabolical and nefarious" and an "abominable sin," the colonial officials who reported back to their European overlords were amazed that the native peoples considered same-sex love to be acceptable and honorable.

What most disturbed the Europeans was the centrality of gender variance in Native American religions. While there are varieties of cultures in North America, native religions share an emphasis on the spiritual nature of all things. Instead of a creator god, native religions are animist, and focus on a multiplicity of spirits. Everything that exists—animals, plants, rocks, water, air, the moon, the sun, and the earth itself—has a spirit, and all things that exist are due equal respect because they are part of the spiritual order of the universe. The purpose of religion is not to try to condemn or to change what exists, but to accept the realities of the world and to appreciate their contributions to life. Everything that exists is created by the spirits for some special purpose. For example, sex is created by the spirits for the enjoyment of humans, and humans should be thankful for that goodness. Sex is not considered sinful or antireligious; the matters of the spirit are not opposed in any way to the matters of the flesh. Sexual desire and pleasure are sacred gifts from the spirit world.

Native American religions attach much importance to gender. According to animist religious views, the spirits give men a masculine spirit and women a feminine spirit so that their differences can complement each other. Masculine is not considered superior to feminine, but both are equally valuable. Sometimes, however, the spirits make an individual different from each of these two genders. People who are different from the usual are not stigmatized, but are seen as being more spiritual, since the spirits must have paid particular attention in making them unique. Androgynous persons are seen as having both the masculine spirit of a man and the feminine spirit of a woman. A male who has a feminine personality, or a female who has a masculine personality, are thus seen as having been blessed with *two* spirits. Because both women and men are respected for their equal but distinct qualities, a person who combines attributes of both is considered as more spiritually gifted than the average person—who has only one spirit. An androgynous Two-Spirit person, therefore, is considered a sacred person. In animist religions around the world such persons are often religious leaders. People who are different maintain an especially close connection to the spirit world. Two-Spirit persons have the talent to minister to the spiritual needs of others. Such persons are able to mediate between men and women, and between the spiritual and the temporal realms.

Rather than being looked down upon as abnormal, androgynous persons are considered exceptional, comparable to the way European cultures venerate persons with unusual musical gifts. Because women are traditionally respected in many Native American cultures, for a male to act like a woman is not shameful; it is evidence of heightened spirituality. Such persons are considered to be another distinct gender, different from both men and women. In terms of marriages, people are supposed to marry someone outside their own gender. The most appropriate marriage is between a masculine person, who is responsible for hunting or herding animals, and a feminine person, who is responsible for farming or gathering wild plants. A marriage of individuals of different genders supplies a balanced food supply of meat and plant foods. For a feminine male, then, the most appropriate partner is a masculine man; while a masculine female should marry a feminine woman. Same-sex marriages, of Two-Spirit persons with regular men or women, are therefore socially accepted in many Native American cultures. With an accepting attitude toward sexual pleasure in general, the same-sex behaviors of Two-Spirit persons are not condemned. The emphasis, however, is not on the homosexual inclinations of such persons, but on their androgynous personality which is considered sacred. Though same-sex behavior is acceptable for anyone, it is particularly associated with the androgynous Two-Spirit persons and their gender-conforming same-sex spouses.

* * *

The Navajo Indians, the largest Native American ethnic group in the United States, have a typically respectful attitude toward androgyny and same-sex marriage. In the creation story of Navajo religion, two of the most prominent characters are Turquoise Boy and White Shell Girl, who are seen as the first Nadleeh. This word means "changing one" or "one who is transformed," and is applied to androgynous persons, transvestites (those who prefer to dress in the clothing of the other sex), and intersexed hermaphrodites (persons born with ambiguous genitalia, or with both a penis and a vagina). Because of their cleverness, the Nadleeh saved the people from a flood, and invented important tools like pottery, basketry, axes, and hoes. The message of this creation story is that humans are dependent for many good things on the inventiveness of Nadleeh. Such unique individuals were present from the earliest eras of human existence, and their presence was never questioned. Since Navajos were instructed in these religious stories from childhood, a positive regard for gender variation has been passed down from generation to generation. A spiritual explanation guarantees a special place for androgynous persons, transvestites, and hermaphrodites. They are seen as part of the natural order of the universe, with a special contribution to make.

DOCUMENT 1: Navajo Sacredness for Nadleeh

In the 1930s, Willard W. Hill, an anthropologist who lived on their reservation in Arizona, said this about the Navajo people's attitudes toward Nadleeh:

The family which counted a transvestite among its members or had a hermaphrodite child born to them was considered by themselves and everyone else as very fortunate. The success and wealth of such a family was believed to be assured. Special care was taken in the raising of such children and they were afforded favoritism not shown to other children of the family. As they grew older and assumed the character of *nadle* [sic], this solicitude and respect increased....This respect verges almost on reverence in many cases....

Hill next quotes from several Navajo people to illustrate these attitudes about nadleeh:

They know everything. They can do both the work of a man and a woman. I think when all the nadle are gone, that it will be the end of the Navaho.

If there were no nadle, the country would change. They are responsible for all the wealth in the country. If there were no more left, the horses, sheep, and Navaho would all go [disappear]. They are leaders just like President Roosevelt. A nadle around the hogan will bring good luck and riches. They have charge of all the riches. It does a great deal for the country if you have nadle around.

You must respect a nadle. They are, somehow, sacred and holy.

Source: W.W. Hill, "The Status of the Hermaphrodite and Transvestite in Navaho Culture," *American Anthropologist* 37 (1935), pp. 274–278.

*   *   *

A Navajo woman interviewed by Walter L. Williams in 1982 stressed that:

Even today among traditional people, especially in the isolated rural areas, nadleeh are well respected....They are seen as very compassionate people, who care for their family a lot and help people. That's why they are healers. Nadleehs are also seen as being great with children, real Pied Pipers. Children love nadleehs, so parents are pleased if a nadleeh takes an interest in their child. One that I know is now a principal of a school on the reservation. Everyone knows that he and the man he lives with are lovers, but it is not mentioned....Nadleeh are not seen as an abstract group, like "gay people," but as a specific person, like "my relative so-and-so." People who help their family a lot are considered valuable members of the community....Missionaries and schools had a bad effect on stigmatizing homosexuality among more assimilated Indians, so it's not as open as in the past. But among traditionals nadleeh never even went underground. It has just continued; they are our relatives—part of our family.

Source: Walter L. Williams, *The Spirit and the Flesh: Sexual Diversity in American Indian Culture* (Boston: Beacon Press, 1992), pp. 18–20, 54, 63–64, 199.

*   *   *

The French explorers who first came among the Native Americans of the Great Lakes area and the upper Mississippi Valley had trouble understanding the positions of high respect that the Indians held for women, and the inclination of some males to dress like women and serve as spiritual leaders. On his first voyage of discovery down the Mississippi River from 1673 to 1677, Jesuit Father Jacques Marquette was mystified by the male Two-Spirit persons among the Illinois and other tribes. He wrote with confusion, about the Two-Spirits mixing both women's and men's roles, in his account of his explorations:

DOCUMENT 2: Illinois Indian Transgender (1677)

I know not through what superstition some Illinois, as well as some Nadouessi, while still young, assume the garb of women, and retain it throughout their lives. There is some mystery in this, for they never marry and glory in demeaning themselves to do everything that the women do. They go to war, however, but can use only clubs, and not bows and arrows, which are the weapons proper to men. They are present at all the juggleries [village events], and at the solemn dances in honor of the Calumet [spirit]; at these they sing, but must not dance. They are summoned to the [government] Councils, and nothing can be decided without their advice. Finally, through their profession of leading an Extraordinary life, they pass for Manitous—that is to say, for Spirits—or persons of Consequence.

Source: Jacques Marquette, "Of the First Voyage Made," in The Jesuit Relations, ed. Reuben Gold Thwaites (Cleveland: Burrows, 1896–1901), vol. 59, p. 129.

*   *   *

When French explorer Pierre Liette returned from living for four years in the Great Lakes area, he reported this about the Miami Indians in his memoir written in 1702:

DOCUMENT 3: Miami Indian Sodomy (1702)

Sodomy prevails more among them than in any other nation, although there are four women to one man. It is true that the women, although debauched, retain some moderation, which prevents the young men from satisfying their passions as much as they would like. There are [homosexual] men who are bred for this purpose from their childhood. When they are seen frequently picking up [women's tools…] but making no use of the bow and arrow, as all the other small boys do, they are girt with a piece of leather or cloth…a thing all the women wear. Their hair is allowed to grow and is fastened behind the head….They imitate [women's] accent, which is different from that of the men. They omit nothing that can make them like the women. There are men sufficiently embruted to have [homosexual] dealings with them.

Source: Pierre Liette, "Memoir of Pierre Liette on the Illinois Country," in *The Western Country in the 17ᵗʰ Century*, ed. Milo Quaife (New York: Citadel, 1962), pp. 112–113.

*   *   *

Most of the information gathered by Euro-American explorers about Native American social customs focused on the life of male Indians. These male explorers traded, parleyed, and interacted with men, and as a consequence knew much less about the lives of native women. Therefore, comparatively little dependable information exists in written historical documents about aboriginal women. Since sex was not often a topic of discussion between men and women, historical sources on homosexual behavior between females are practically nonexistent. Nevertheless, some comments were gathered by ethnohistorian Walter L. Williams, suggesting that female same-sex marriages were also accepted in Native American cultures. The earliest such comment was written by Pedro de Magalhaes de Gandavo, a Portuguese explorer in northeastern Brazil in 1576. While visiting the Tupinamba Indians at the mouth of a great river, he observed a remarkable group of female warriors who lived a masculine lifestyle. They joined the men's group as hunters and also went on war raids with the male warriors, using bows and arrows with great skill. According to Gandavo, these female warriors would never have sex with men. Instead, each masculine female warrior was married to a feminine woman. Gandavo was so impressed with the female warriors that he named the river that flowed through that area the River of the Amazons, after the ancient Greek legend of women warriors. This is how the Amazon River got its name.

A number of North American tribes had named categories for masculine females who married women. The feminine partner was not considered any different from other women, because she performed women's tasks and lived her life as a regular woman. The fact that she had a female husband had no bearing on her identity; she was not stigmatized as a sexual deviant in any way. Her gender identity as a woman was considered most important, and there were no categories like lesbian for these women. On the other hand, the female husband had a gender identity that was different from women and men. Such a person typically evidenced unfeminine personality characteristics from childhood. Her rough-and-tumble masculine play with boys was accepted as a message from the spirit world that she was a Two-Spirit. As she grew up, she generally became an outstanding hunter and warrior. Such females were admired for their bravery, and accepted for their uniqueness. Female Two-Spirit persons had their own separate gender identity, but were comparable to the feminine male Two-Spirits.

DOCUMENT 4: Native American Transgendered Females

With the single exception of the Navajo, those cultures that recognize alternative [gender] roles for both females and males, have distinct terminologies in their languages that are different for each sex. The Papago word translates as "Light Woman," and such women even up to the 1940s were considered simply socially tolerated variations from the norm. Among the Yumas of the Southwest, [feminine males] are called *elxa'*, while [masculine females] are called *kwe'rhame*. They are defined as women who passed for men, dressed like men and married women....She was seen as having gone through a change of spirit as a result of dreams. In growing up she was observed to hunt and play with boys, but she had no interest in heterosexual relations with them....A Yuman *kwe'rhame* married a woman and established a household with herself as husband. She was known for bravery and for skillful fighting in battle....

Mohaves also accept the fact that a [masculine female] *hwame* would marry a woman. There is even a way to incorporate children into these female relationships. If a woman becomes impregnated by a man, but later takes another lover, it is believed that the paternity of the child changes. This idea helps to prevent family friction in a society where relationships often change. So, if a pregnant woman later takes a *hwame* as a spouse, the *hwame* is considered the real father of the child....

Unlike Western culture, which tries to place all humans into strict conformist definitions of masculinity and femininity, some Native American cultures have a more flexible recognition of gender variance. They are able to incorporate such fluidity into their worldview by recognizing a special place for..."manlike women."

Source: Walter L. Williams, *The Spirit and the Flesh: Sexual Diversity in American Indian Culture* (Boston: Beacon Press, 1992), see Chapter 11 "Amazons of America: Female Gender Variance," pp. 234, 240, 242.

* * *

With centuries of oppression by Euro-Americans, much of Native American culture has been destroyed, along with the aboriginal values. In many tribes the traditional respect for Two-Spirit people has been lost, and androgynous homosexuals today are discriminated against, especially by Indians who have converted to Christianity. However, many Indian people who value their traditional Native American animist religions continue to defend Two-Spirit people. Those who respect the traditions, like Lakota medicine man Lame Deer and Russell Means, a leader of the American Indian Movement in the 1970s, have both expressed their acceptance of the special spiritual role of *winkte* the Lakota word for Two-Spirit people.

Among traditionalists of the Lakotas, *winkte* even today still have special ceremonial roles in native religions, and important economic roles in their extended families. They do the work of both women and men, and are often noted as being intelligent and artistically creative. Many of them are encouraged by their community to become adoptive parents for homeless children. They also have a reputation for generosity and hard work. By making androgyny a positive sanctified tradition, Native traditionalists successfully utilize the unique skills and insights of a class of people that Western culture has stigmatized and whose spiritual power has been wasted.

In 1982 Walter L. Williams interviewed a traditional Lakota *winkte* on the Pine Ridge Sioux reservation who was venerated as a religious leader. This fifty-two-year-old person, male in body but extremely feminine in personality, was married to a man and had raised several children whom they had adopted from alcoholic parents who were not taking good care of the children. They were respected in the Pine Ridge community for being devoted adoptive parents. Only after Walter Williams lived with this person for a month did he agree to tell his personal story. He said:

DOCUMENT 5: Lakota Respect for Two-Spirit People (1982)

I have always filled a winkte role. I was just born this way, ever since I can remember. When I was eight I saw a vision, of a person with long gray hair and with many ornaments on, standing by my bed. I asked if he was female or male, and he said "both." He said he would walk with me for the rest of my life. His spirit would always be with me. I told my grandfather, who said not to be afraid of spirits, because they have good powers. A year later, the vision appeared again, and told me he would give me great powers. He said his body was man's but his spirit was woman's. He told me the Great Spirit made people like me to be of help to other people.

I told my grandfather the name of the spirit, and Grandfather said it was a highly respected winkte who lived long ago. He explained winkte to me and said, "It won't be easy growing up, because you will be different from others. But the spirit will help you, if you pray and do the sweat [religious ceremony]." The spirit has continued to contact me throughout my life. If I practice the winkte role seriously, then people will respect me....

A few winkte marry women and have children, and still fulfill the winkte role. But most others are not permitted by the spirits to be married. It varies from one person to another....It would be unholy for me to have sex with a woman, or with another winkte. That would be wrong, and would violate the role set for me by the Sacred Pipe....

Once I asked the spirit if my living with a man and loving him was bad. The spirit answered that it was not bad because I had a right to release my feelings and express love for another, that I was good because I was generous and provided a good home for my children. I want to be remembered most for the two values that my people hold dearest: generosity and spirituality. If you say anything about me, say those two things.

Source: Pat Thunderhawk, interviews by Walter L. Williams, in Pine Ridge, South Dakota, July 1982. For further information on winkte, see Walter L. Williams, *The Spirit and the Flesh: Sexual Diversity in American Indian Culture* (Boston: Beacon Press, 1986, 1992).

*   *   *

In contrast to the accepting attitudes of Native American religions to gender and sexual diversity, the religious values brought by the Christian Europeans severely condemned homosexual behavior. The Europeans based their attitudes on certain verses in the Christian Bible. Though the Bible was written about a Hebrew culture halfway around the world from the Americas, it has probably been the single most influential book in American history. For centuries the Bible was the only book that many Americans possessed, and they learned to read by using its pages as a primer. Every verse had a huge impact on public opinion. While parts of the Bible are so obscure that their meaning is unclear, many Americans have ordered their lives around the instructions that they thought these holy scriptures gave them.

In nothing was this biblical impact more influential than issues relating to gender and sexuality. Women were exhorted to subordinate themselves to their husbands, and everyone was encouraged to avoid nakedness. Coming into intense contact with Native Americans and Africans, the English settlers sometimes felt that the Bible was the only text connecting them to civilization. The Bible's message of sexual repression was a great contrast to the more accepting sexual openness in the religions of the Indians and the Africans. Though only a few verses in the Bible deal with homosexual behavior, those verses were enough to set in motion a suppression that included murder and denial. What is clear from a reading of Biblical texts is that the most famous quotation, the story of Sodom, originally probably had nothing to do with sex at all. The most condemning words are in the Book of Leviticus, but those instructions would probably not have had much impact on Christians except for the writings of one man: the Apostle Paul. While Jesus said little about sex, Paul was focused on lust. If it were not for Paul's letters being included in the Bible, it is unlikely that Christianity would have had the antihomosexual attitudes that it did. Still, the prominence of homosexuality as a topic of twentieth-century Christian writers is surprising given the sparse textual statements of the Bible. Because these texts have had so much impact on American legal and social life, they are quoted with surrounding textual statements, to put the statements about same-sex love in context.

DOCUMENT 6: The Bible: Sodom and Gomorrah

The earliest relevant Bible text is recorded in the first book written by Moses, the Book of Genesis. One of the book's stories mentions two cities, Sodom and Gomorrah, whose "sin is very grievous" (Genesis 18: 20–21). The nature of their sin is not specified in Genesis, but Moses wrote that God sent two angels to see how they would be treated by the cities' inhabitants. Unless the angels recommended against it, God planned to destroy the two cities. The following chapter states that when the two angels came to Sodom a good man named Lot met them as they approached the gate of the city. Lot feared that the angels would not be safe if they stayed in the streets, and he pressed them to remain in his house:

[The two angels] entered into his house; and he made them a feast, and did bake unleavened bread, and they did eat.

But before they lay down, the men of the city, even the men of Sodom, compassed the house round, both old and young, all the people from every quarter. And they called unto Lot, and said unto him, Where are the men which came in to thee this night? Bring them out unto us, that we may know them.

And Lot went out at the door unto them, and shut the door after him. And said, I pray you, brethren, do not so wickedly. Behold now, I have two daughters which have not known man; let me, I pray you, bring them out unto you, and do ye to them as is good in your eyes; only unto these men do nothing; for therefore came they under the shadow of my roof.

And they said, Stand back. And they said again, This one fellow came in to sojourn, and he will needs be a judge: now will we deal worse with thee, than with them. And they pressed sore upon the man, even Lot, and came near to the door. But the [angel] men put forth their hand, and pulled Lot into the house to them, and shut to the door. And they smote the men that were at the door to the house with blindness, both small and great: so that they wearied themselves to find the door.

And the [angel] men said unto Lot, Hast thou here any besides? son in law, and thy sons, and thy daughters, and whatsoever thou hast in the city, bring them out of this place. For we will destroy this place, because the cry of them is waxen great before the face of the Lord; and the Lord hath sent us to destroy it....

[After allowing Lot and his family time to escape] Then the Lord rained upon Sodom and Gomorrah brimstone and fire from the Lord out of heaven; And he overthrew those cities, and all the plain, and all the inhabitants of the cities, and that which grew upon the ground.

Source: Genesis 19:1–13, and 24–25. (King James version of the Bible used for all Bible sources.)

*   *   *

While the text of Genesis is clear that the crowd seemed menacing, it is not clear what the men meant when they told Lot to bring out the angels "that we may *know* them." The original word in Hebrew was translated accurately by the English authors of the King James version of the Bible, and it means only *to meet*. Accordingly, there is no other moral to this story other than to show that God is displeased when travelers are treated in a threatening manner. The message that comes across in the story of Sodom is that strangers who arrive in a city should be treated hospitably, and given shelter. This view of the story of Sodom is reinforced by a reference to Sodom by Jesus in the New Testament. Since the context of Jesus' remarks has nothing to do with sexual behavior, it is clear that Jesus saw the sins of Sodom as being rudeness to travelers. When Jesus gave his disciples instructions about visiting other towns, he remarked:

whosoever shall not receive you, nor hear your words, when ye depart out of that house or city, shake off the dust from your feet. Verily I say unto you, It shall be more tolerable for the land of Sodom and Gomorrah in the day of judgment, than for that city.

Source: Matthew 10:14–15.

*   *   *

As to the nature of the unnamed "very grievous sins" committed by the inhabitants of Sodom and Gomorrah, we must examine the second book written by Moses, the Book of Exodus, to understand what Moses considered the most serious sins that were subject to God's punishment. In Exodus Moses laid down the basic moral code of the ancient Hebrews, in the form of the Ten Commandments. These commandments specified that the most serious sins involved worshiping other gods, bowing to graven images, speaking God's name in vain, working on the Sabbath, dishonoring one's father and mother, killing, stealing, lying, committing adultery, and coveting the property of others. Nowhere in these ten commandments is homosexual behavior mentioned as a sin.

Source: Exodus 20:1–17.

*   *   *

It is only in the third book of the Hebrew Bible, called Leviticus, that same-sex behavior is mentioned. It is important to understand the context of the book of Leviticus. For many pages of the book Chapters 1 through 10 offer numerous rules that priests are supposed to follow, including explicit instructions on how to slaughter animals as sacrifice to God and how to sprinkle the blood around the altar. Chapter 11 prohibits followers of the Lord from eating camels, pigs, rabbits, many types of birds, and any seafood without fins or scales (such as shrimp, crab, and lobster). Chapter 12 specifies that a woman is unclean for 41 days after giving birth to a male child and 78 days after giving birth to a female child, and she cannot come into the tabernacle until she brings an animal to a priest who will slaughter it at the altar to end her uncleanness. Several additional chapters give details of food purification techniques.

DOCUMENT 7: The Bible: The Abominations of Leviticus

Leviticus Chapter 18 pays much attention to avoiding nakedness in front of one's relatives. After all these pages of detailed instruction, prohibited sexual behaviors are dealt with only briefly in Chapter 18, and addressed only to men. It is not clear why women are not mentioned in verse 22, prohibiting them from having sex with another woman, as women are prohibited in verse 23 from having sex with an animal. What is clear in Leviticus is that the prohibition of a man having sex with another man is no more serious than having sex with his neighbor's wife, or avoiding nudity in front of his relatives, or slaughtering animals improperly, or eating pork and shrimp. All are listed as abominations. Below are the only verses dealing with sexual behavior in the whole book of Leviticus.

Thou shalt not lie carnally with thy neighbor's wife, to defile thyself with her (verse 20).

And thou shall not let any of thy seed [semen] pass through the fire to Molech, neither shalt thou profane the name of thy God: I am the Lord (verse 21).

Thou shalt not lie with mankind, as with womankind: it is abomination (verse 22).

Neither shalt thou lie with any beast to defile thyself therewith: neither shall any woman stand before a beast to lie down thereto: it is confusion (verse 23).

* * *

Chapter 19 of Leviticus follows with more rules. Verse 7 says that it is an abomination to eat leftover meat that was slaughtered over two days before. Verse 19 specifies that farmers are prohibited from planting more than one crop in a field, and people cannot wear cloth made from a mixture of linen and wool. Verse 27 prohibits men from shaving or trimming their beards. Chapter 20 of Leviticus commands the Hebrews to throw stones at a person who has violated one of the aforementioned abominations, until the person is dead:

He that giveth any of his seed unto Molech; he shall surely be put to death: the people of the land shall stone him with stones....(verse 1).

For every one that curseth his father or his mother shall surely be put to death....(verse 9).

Even he that committeh adultery with his neighbor's wife, the adulterer and the adulteress shall surely be put to death (verse 10).

And the man that lieth with his father's wife...and if a man lie with his daughter in law, both of them shall surely be put to death: they have wrought confusion; their blood shall be upon them (verses 11–12).

If a man also lie with mankind, as he lieth with a woman, both of them have committed an abomination: they shall surely be put to death; their blood shall be upon them (verse 13).

And if a man take a wife and her mother, it is wickedness: they shall be burnt with fire, both he and they; that there be no wickedness among you. And if a man lie with a beast, he shall surely be put to death: and ye shall slay the beast. And if a woman approach unto any beast, and lie down thereto, thou shalt kill the woman, and the beast: they shall surely be put to death (verses 14–16).

And if a man shall lie with a woman having her [monthly menstrual] sickness, and shall uncover her nakedness, he hath discovered her fountain, and she hath uncovered the fountain of her blood: and both of them shall be cut off from among their people (verse 18).

A man also or woman that hath a familiar spirit, or that is a wizard, shall surely be put to death: they shall stone them with stones: their blood shall be upon them (verse 27).

* * *

Chapter 21 of Leviticus follows with more rules for priests, including that a priest shall not shave his beard, or appear in public without something covering his baldness (verse 5). It is also specifies that a priest may not marry a widow or divorced woman, but only a virgin (verses 13–14). No man shall be a priest who is a dwarf, or disabled by being blind, lame, with a deformed nose, hand, foot, or back (verses 18–20). Chapters 22, 23, and 24 present still more rules, including the story of a young man who blasphemed and cursed the name of the Lord. In this story the Lord commanded Moses to gather all the people of the village to stone him to death (Chapter 24, verses 10–16). If the Hebrews followed all these rules faithfully, and killed all those who did abominations, then God promised that they would become prosperous and powerful enough to be able to enslave or slaughter the other peoples living around them.

The heathen that are round about you; of them shall ye buy bondsmen and bondmaids. Moreover of the children of the strangers that do sojourn among you, of them shall ye buy, and of their families…and they shall be your possession. And ye shall take them as an inheritance for your children after you, to inherit them for a possession; they shall be your bondmen forever….And ye shall chase your enemies, and they shall fall before you by the sword….For I will have respect unto you, and make you fruitful, and multiply you, and establish my covenant with you.

Source: Leviticus 25:44–46, and 26:7–9.

* * *

While Leviticus clearly condemned men having sex with men, it said nothing condemning female same-sex love. The Book of Ruth is a story of loving devotion of one woman for another as its central focus. While there is no mention of female-female sexuality, the story does demonstrate a tender love that can exist among women, and gives a different view than Leviticus. This story centers around Naomi, a widowed Hebrew mother and her two sons, who due to famine in their hometown of Bethlehem migrated to the land of Moab, east of the Dead Sea. There they lived for ten years, and the two sons married two women of Moab named Ruth and Orpah. When both her sons tragically died, Naomi sadly decided to return to her home in Bethlehem. The two daughters-in-law, who had grown extremely close to Naomi, wept at the thought of their mother-in-law leaving them. But Naomi insisted she had to leave, so Orpah sadly kissed her goodbye. Ruth, however, refused to separate herself from Naomi. They devoted themselves to each other, and even raised a child together. Ruth declared her love for Naomi in words that are some of the most famous of the Bible:

DOCUMENT 8: The Bible: Ruth and Naomi

And Ruth said, Intreat me not to leave thee, or to return from following after thee: for whither thou goest, I will go; and where thou lodgest, I will lodge: thy people shall be my people, and thy God my God: Where thou diest, will I die, and there will I be buried: the Lord do so to me, and more also, if ought but death part thee and me. When Naomi saw that she was steadfastly minded to go with her, then she left speaking unto her. So they two went until they were come to Bethlehem [where they lived the remainder of their lives together].

Source: Ruth 1:15–19.

*   *   *

Another view of emotional same-sex relationships is presented in the Bible story of David and Jonathan. The author wrote approvingly of the love between the two young men that was so intense it surpassed the love of a man and a woman. If such a story were written about two males today, would they be considered gay?

DOCUMENT 9: The Bible: David and Jonathan

After the young shepherd boy David became famous for killing Goliath, the leading warrior of the Hebrews' rival Philistines, he was introduced to the court of Israel's King Saul. Jonathan, the son of the king, was immediately infatuated with David. The First Book of Samuel relates this love story of one male for another.

The soul of Jonathan was knit with the soul of David, and Jonathan loved him as his own soul. And Saul took him that day, and would let him go no more to his father's house. Then Jonathan and David made a covenant, because he loved him as his own soul. And Jonathan stripped himself of the robe that was upon him, and gave it to David, and his garments, even to his sword, and to his bow, and to his girdle....

[Later, however, the unstable King Saul became so jealous of David's popularity that he decided to kill David.] But Jonathan Saul's son delighted much in David: and Jonathan told David, saying, Saul my father seeketh to kill thee: now therefore, I pray thee, take heed.... And Jonathan spake good of David unto Saul his father, and said unto him, Let not the king sin against his servant, against David; because he hath not sinned against thee, and because his works have been to thee-ward very good: For he did put his life in his hand, and slew the Philistine, and the Lord wrought a great salvation for all Israel: thou sawest it, and didst rejoice: wherefore then wilt thou sin against innocent blood, to slay David without a cause? And Saul hearkened unto the voice of Jonathan: and Saul sware, As the Lord liveth, he shall not be slain. And Jonathan called David, and Jonathan shewed him all those things. And Jonathan brought David to Saul, and he was in his presence, as in times past.

Source: First Samuel 18:1–4, and 19:1–7.

*   *   *

Later, in recurring wars with the Philistines, both Saul and Jonathan were killed in battle. When David learned of Jonathan's tragic death, the Second Book of Samuel relates his intense despair:

Then David took hold on his clothes, and rent them; and likewise all the men that were with him; And they mourned, and wept, and fasted.... And David lamented.... O Jonathan, thou wast slain in thine high places. I am distressed for thee, my brother Jonathan: very pleasant hast thou been unto me: thy love to me was wonderful, passing the love of women.

Source: Second Samuel 1:11–12, 17, 25–26.

*   *   *

While the few lines of condemnation "thou shalt not lie with mankind" in Leviticus were a part of the Hebrew Bible, Jesus never made a statement condemning homosexual behavior. He said that he had not come into the world to condemn people (John 3:17), and when presented with the example of a sexually promiscuous woman who was condemned to be stoned to death in the traditional Hebrew punishment, Jesus told those gathered that anyone who is without sin should be the first one to cast a stone at her (John 8:7). Jesus' message was that, since no one is perfect, people should be forgiving and tolerant.

Instead of condemnation of sin, Jesus spread a message in favor of love. He did not object to his disciple John being known particularly as the one "whom Jesus loved" (John 13: 23), and Jesus told his mother Mary that because of his and John's closeness that she should consider John to be her son (John 19: 27). Considering Jesus' lack of a sexual relationship with a woman, there were likely some people who concluded that Jesus and John were a loving couple.

DOCUMENT 10: The Bible: Jesus

Whatever one's opinions about Jesus' sexuality, the writings of the Disciples show that Jesus did not discriminate against diverse people. For example, one time he was approached by a Centurion soldier of the Roman army. Centurions did not marry women, and had the reputation of engaging in homosexual behavior with their male servants.[1] The soldier was distraught because his servant companion was quite ill. The Centurion told Jesus he had faith that Jesus could heal his companion. Rather than reject this man as an unworthy sinner, Jesus sympathized with the deep concern that the soldier had for his servant. Jesus complimented the Centurion, and told him:

I have not found so great faith, no, not in [all of] Israel....Go thy way; and as thou hast believed, so be it done unto thee [whereupon the servant was immediately cured].

1. John Boswell, *Christianity, Social Tolerance, and Homosexuality* (Chicago: University of Chicago Press, 1982).
Source: Matthew 8:5–8, and 10–13.

*   *   *

In another case, where Jesus was asked about the appropriateness of man-woman marriage for all people, he challenged the ancient Hebrew custom that everyone should marry. Jesus brought up the example of androgynous nonreproductive male eunuchs who were often involved in relationships with men. Rather than condemn eunuchs, Jesus spoke of them respectfully as members of the kingdom of heaven, saying:

All men cannot receive this saying, save they to whom it is given. For there are some eunuchs, which were so born from their mother's womb: and there are some eunuchs, which were made eunuchs of men: and there be eunuchs, which have made themselves eunuchs for the kingdom of heaven's sake. He that is able to receive it, let him receive.

Source: Matthew 19:11–12.

*   *   *

While Jesus never made any complaint about homosexuality, he did not shy away from attacking the things which most upset him. The things which made Jesus upset were not related to sexual behavior, but were materialist concerns like the greed of moneychangers in the temple, and the hypocrisy of the churchgoers and the wealthy. Jesus said:

It is easier for a camel to go through the eye of a needle, than for a rich man to enter into the kingdom of God.

Source: Matthew 19:24.

*   *   *

In the Sermon on the Mount, one of Jesus' most important teachings, he brought a message blessing the poor, the merciful, the peacemakers, and the persecuted; and criticizing those busybodies who are quick to judge others. Based on the actual statements that Jesus made, and the fact that he never once condemned homosexuality as a sin when it was a common occurrence in the Roman world of his time, he probably would be sympathetic toward gay men, lesbians, intersexuals, and transgendered people who are persecuted today. His words in the Sermon on the Mount speak directly to those who are persecuted in any era, and in criticism of those judgmental hypocrites who are quick to condemn others.

Blessed are the meek: for they shall inherit the earth....Blessed are ye, when men shall revile you, and persecute you, and shall say all manner of evil against you....for so persecuted they the prophets which were before you. Ye are the salt of the earth...(Matthew 5:5, 11–13).

But I say unto you. That whosoever is angry with his brother without a cause shall be in danger of the judgment: and whosoever shall say to his brother, *Raca* [an expression of contempt that implies worthlessness or effeminancy] shall be in danger of the council....Bless them that curse you, do good to them that hate you, and pray for them which despitefully use you, and persecute you....(Matthew 5:22, 44)

And when thou prayest, thou shalt not be as the hypocrites are: for they love to pray standing in the synagogues and in the corners of the streets, that they may be seen of men. Verily I say unto you, they have their reward. But thou, when thou prayest, enter into thy closet...(Matthew 6:5–6).

Judge not, that ye be not judged. For with what judgment ye judge, ye shall be judged: and with what measure ye mete, it shall be measured to you again. And why beholdest thou the mote that is in thy brother's eye, but considerest not the beam that is in thine own eye? Or how wilt thou say to thy brother, Let me pull out the mote out of thine eye; and behold, a beam is in thine own eye? Thou hypocrite, first cast out the beam out of thine own eye; and then shalt thou see clearly to cast out the mote out of thy brother's eye (Matthew 7:1–5).

*   *   *

After the death of Jesus, his disciples spread into different areas to take his message to the towns. The followers of Jesus were persecuted by many officials, including one named Saul, from Tarsus. Saul was responsible for imprisoning many of those who worshiped Jesus (Acts 8:3 and 9:1). However, Saul later claimed to have seen the spirit of Jesus, and himself became a convert. When Saul came to the original disciples with this story, they did not believe him and did not trust this new convert who had never known Jesus when he was alive (Acts 9:26). Nevertheless, despite his conflicts with the disciples, Saul changed his name to Paul and began moving from town to town preaching in the name of Jesus.

DOCUMENT 11: The Bible: Paul

After provoking riots in some places, and almost being imprisoned in others, Paul declared himself an apostle of Christ and wrote a letter to the small Christian community in Rome. In contrast to the message of love, peace, and brotherhood that Jesus emphasized, in the first chapter of the Epistle to the Romans Paul focused on lust and uncleanness:

The wrath of God is revealed from heaven against all ungodliness and unrighteousness of men....Wheretofore God also gave them up to uncleanness through the lusts of their own hearts, to dishonor their own bodies between themselves....For this cause God gave them up unto vile affections: for even their women did change the natural use into that which is against nature. And likewise also the men, leaving the natural use of the women, burned in their lust one toward another; men with men working that which is unseemly, and receiving in themselves that recompence of their error.

Source: Paul's letter to the Romans 1:18, 24, 26–27.

*   *   *

When Paul's letters were later incorporated into the New Testament along with the teachings of Jesus, Paul's new concept of homosexual behavior as unnatural was introduced into the Bible. This is also the first and only verse anywhere in the Bible that condemns same-sex affections among women. Since Jesus never said anything to condemn same-sex love, readers of the Bible are left with the conclusion that Paul's concern with lust and sin is due to his own sexual insecurities. He writes of his "carnal" desires but does not specify exactly what kind of desires he feels. He obviously feels so upset by these desires that he strives to suppress them entirely. Paul introduces a new idea into the developing Christian religion, that the concerns of the spirit are opposite the concerns of the flesh. It is only by seeing lust as against God that Paul is able to relieve himself:

I know that in me (that is, in my flesh) dwelleth no good thing: for to will is present with me; but how to perform that which is good I find not. For the good that I would I do not: but the evil which I would not, that I do....I delight in the law of God after the inward man; But I see another law in my members [body parts], warring against the law of my mind, and bringing me into captivity to the law of sin which is in my members. O wretched man that I am!...With the mind I myself serve the law of God; but with the flesh the law of sin....

The law of the Spirit of life in Christ Jesus hath made me free from the law of sin and death....For they that are after the flesh do mind the things of the flesh; but they that are after the Spirit the things of the Spirit. For to be carnally minded is death; but to be spiritually minded is life and peace. Because the carnal mind is enmity against God...they that are in the flesh cannot please God.

Source: Paul's letter to the Romans 7:18–19, 22–25, and 8:2, 5–8.

* * *

Contrast Paul's first letter to the Christian converts in Corinth, with Jesus' Sermon on the Mount. While Jesus welcomed the outcasts, Paul became the stern moralist who condemned sexuality. Paul's antisexual writings, combined with the few verses in Genesis and Leviticus, moved Christianity toward a stance of sexual repression and persecution.

The unrighteous shall not inherit the kingdom of God. Be not deceived: neither fornicators, nor idolaters, nor adulterers, nor effeminate, nor abusers of themselves with mankind, nor thieves, nor covetous, nor drunkards, nor revilers, nor extortioners, shall inherit the kingdom of God.

Source: 1 Corinthians 6:9–10.

* * *

Once Christianity became the established religion of the late Roman Empire, the tenets of Christianity spread throughout Europe. Buttressed by the teachings of Paul and subsequent leaders, the Christian Church emphasized same-sex behavior as a major form of sin. The punishment for sodomy was death, sometimes by cruel torture and other times by being burned to death. Sex between women was also punished, but female-female sex usually did not come under the definition of sodomy.

Europeans expressed a negative attitude toward same-sex love, but the Spaniards in particular seemed intent on wiping out homosexual behavior. Part of the reason for this emphasis was no doubt due to the Christian Spaniards' centuries-long struggle with the Muslim Moors for control of the Iberian peninsula. At that time Islam was relatively tolerant of homosexual behavior, and the Christians seized upon this acceptance to condemn their political enemy and take Moorish lands by conquest. King Ferdinand and Queen Isabella finally expelled the Moors and united Spain under their rule in 1492, the same year that explorer Christopher Columbus returned from his voyage across the Atlantic, announcing that he had found a new route to Asia. Subsequent explorers realized that the lands to which Columbus sailed were, in fact, not part of Asia. The Americas were a New World that the Europeans had not previously known about. Spain then entered upon a long era of imperial expansion, to conquer these new lands as they had conquered Iberia, and add them to their empire.

The native occupants of this New World, the people Columbus had incorrectly called "Los Indios" [people of the Indies], were now seen as subjects of the Spanish Empire and the Catholic Church. Priests came along with military conquistadors to convert the native peoples into willing laborers for the Crown and the church. To their horror, the Spaniards soon discovered that many of the native cultures were even more accepting of homosexual behavior than the Moors had been. Native acceptance of same-sex love was used by the Spaniards as a major justification for their conquest and subjugation of the New World. The Spanish colonial criminal code defined sodomy as a more serious crime even than murder, and punished it by death. Therefore, when the Spanish authorities even suspected a person of being a sodomite, such a person was often tortured and executed on the spot. The sorrow of the Indians at such executions is only hinted at in the surviving documents, but the great respect which Native Americans held for androgynous persons suggests that these executions were lamented greatly.

With their condemnatory attitude toward homosexual behavior, the Spaniards could easily persuade themselves that their plunder, murder, and rape of the Americas was righteous in the sight of God. The Spanish conquistadors felt that they would go to heaven by exterminating the sodomites; this was their new holy crusade.

DOCUMENT 12: Spaniards' Suppression of Sodomites (1519–1540s)

A prominent Spanish Catholic theologian, Juan Gines de Sepulveda, wrote about the American Indians:

How can we doubt that these people so uncivilized, so barbaric, so contaminated with so many sins and obscenities...have been justly conquered by such a humane nation which is excellent in every kind of virtue?"

Source: Quoted in Walter L. Williams, *The Spirit and the Flesh: Sexual Diversity in American Indian Culture* (Boston: Beacon Press, 1992), pp. 137, 138. See chapter 7 "The Abominable Sin: The Spanish Campaign against Sodomy and Its Results in Modern Latin America," pp. 131–151.

* * *

The Spaniards associated homosexual behavior with the devil. For example, after explorer Alvar Nunez Cabeza de Vaca returned from five years among the Indians of Florida, 1528 to 1533, he reported:

During the time that I was thus among these people I saw a devilish thing, and it is that I saw one man married to another, and these are impotent, effeminate men [amarionados] and they go about dressed as women, and do women's tasks, and shoot with a bow, and carry great burdens.

Source: Translated in Jonathan Ned Katz, *Gay American History* (New York: Thomas Crowell, 1976), p. 285.

* * *

Not only the Spaniards, but the English also emphasized sodomy as a major crime. Under King Henry VIII sodomy was made punishable by death. When the London Company established the first permanent English settlement at Jamestown in 1607, it took three years to establish a legal code for the colony of Virginia. Instead of using the popular English term "buggery" for nonprocreative sex, the statute writers explicitly used the religious term "sodomie." This use of terminology offers a glimpse into the close relationship between Christianity and English law.

Following is the text of the ninth provision of the 1610 Virginia legal code, dealing with sexual crimes. Note that sodomy is listed in especially condemnatory language, while adultery and rape are not. This is the first law forbidding sexual relations between persons of the same sex in British North America. Similar statutes were enacted in the other English colonies.

DOCUMENT 13: Virginia Sodomy Law (1610)

No man shall commit the horrible, detestable sins of Sodomie upon pain of death; & he or she that can be lawfully convict[ed] of Adultery shall be punished with death. No man shall ravish or force any woman, maid or Indian, or other, upon pain of death.

Source: May 24, 1610, Virginia law quoted in Peter Force, *Tracts and Other Papers, Relating Principally to the Origin, Settlement, and Progress of the Colonies in North America* (New York: Peter Smith, 1947), pp. 9–10.

* * *

The *Minutes of the Council and General Court of Colonial Virginia* of 1624 record the testimony and trial of Richard Cornish, a ship's captain who was accused of having sex with one of his crewmen. Cornish was the first of many Englishman to be put to death under a colonial sodomy law. Evidently some Virginia settlers were upset over Cornish's execution, and one of them, a man named Thomas Hatch, was even brought to trial in 1625 for criticizing the court's decision. Hatch was punished by having one of his ears cut off, and was also sold into indentured servitude for seven years for this comment. According to the court records, three witnesses testified that Thomas Hatch

DOCUMENT 14: The Execution of Richard Cornish (1624–1625)

said that in his conscience he thought the said Cornish was put to death wrongfully, whereupon this depondent [witness] said, "You were best take heed what you say, you have a precedent before your eyes the other day, and it will cost you your ears if you say such words." To which the said Thomas Hatch replied, "I care not for my ears, let them hang me if they will...."

[The Court's decision reads:] It is ordered that Thomas Hatch for his offence shall be whipped from the fort to the gallows and from thence be whipped back again; and be set upon the pillory and there to lose one of his ears, and that his [indentured] service to Sir George Yardly for seven years shall begin from the present day.

Source: H.R. McIlwaine, ed., *Minutes of the Council and General Court of Colonial Virginia, 1622–1632* (Richmond: Colonial Press, 1924), pp. 34, 42, 78, 81, 83.

* * *

Governor John Winthrop of the Massachusetts Bay Colony wrote about a man named William Plaine who was "discovered to have used some unclean practices." Plaine admitted under torture that he had committed sodomy with two men in England before he migrated to America. Winthrop reported that Plaine was executed in the New England town of Guilford because he had done

DOCUMENT 15: William Plaine Executed in New England for Teaching Masturbation (1646)

masturbations, which he had committed, and provoked others to the like above a hundred times; and to some who questioned the lawfulness of such filthy practice, he did insinuate seeds of atheism, questioning whether there was a God, etc. The magistrates and elders (so many as were at hand) did all agree that he ought to die, and gave divers reasons from the word of God. And indeed it was *horrendum facinus* [horrible crime], and he a monster in human shape, exceeding all human rules and examples that ever had been heard of, and it tended to the frustrating of the ordinance of marriage and hindering the generation [reproduction] of mankind.

Source: John Winthrop, *History of New England from 1630 to 1649*, ed. James Savage (Boston: Little, Brown, 1853), vol. 2, p. 324.

*   *   *

In the colony of New Netherland (which later was renamed New York after the English captured it), an African American slave was executed by the Dutch officials for having sodomy with a young boy in 1646. The boy, evidently also a slave, who was caught having sex with him was compelled to watch the execution of the man, and was to have faggots (kindling wood) piled around him so that he thought he was going to be burned at the stake, but then to be flogged. The boy was evidently not killed because of his young age, but the purpose of his sentence was to terrify him so much that he would not engage in same-sex behavior again. It is likely that the common public practice of burning sodomites at the stake with faggot wood, in Europe and in America, is the origin of the term "faggot" as an insult word for homosexuals. On June 25, 1646, the Dutch court proceedings record the execution of

DOCUMENT 16: African American Jan Creoli Killed and Burned in Dutch Colony (1646)

Jan Creoli, a negro, sodomy, second offense; this crime being condemned of God (Genesis c. 19; Leviticus c. 18:22, 29) as an abomination, the prisoner is sentenced to be conveyed to the place of public execution, and there choked to death, and then burnt to ashes....

Manuel Congo, a lad ten years old, on whom the above abominable crime was committed, to be carried to the place where Creoli is to be executed, tied to a stake, and faggots piled around him, for justice sake, and to be flogged. Sentence executed.

Source: E. B. O'Cakkaghan, ed., *Calendar of Historical Manuscripts in the Office of the Secretary of State, Albany, N.Y.* (Albany: Weed and Parsons, 1865), p. 103.

* * *

Records from the Plymouth Colony hold an account of the first known prosecution for illegal sexual intimacy between two women. Not covered under the sodomy laws of Plymouth, Sara Norman and Mary Hammon were not subject to the death penalty under this charge. Mary Hammon was fifteen years old in 1649, and this relative youth may have contributed to her being been "cleared with admonition" on the charge; the sodomy statute of Plymouth, for example, only held males over the age of fourteen responsible for their sexual behavior. Sara Norman, being somewhat older, however, was convicted of the charges, and was forced to publicly acknowledge her "unchaste behavior"—a far lesser punishment than a man in her position would have suffered.

Following is a portion of the court record regarding this case.

DOCUMENT 17: Sara Norman and Mary Hammon Accused of Lewd Behavior (1649)

Whereas the wife of Hugh Norman, of Yarmouth, hath stood presented [in] divers Courts for misdemeanor and lewd behavior with Mary Hammon upon a bed, with divers lascivious speeches by her also spoken, but she could not appear by reason of some hindrances unto this Court, the said Court have therefore sentenced her, the said wife of Hugh Norman, for her wild behavior in the aforesaid particulars, to make a public acknowledgment, so far as conveniently may be, of her unchaste behavior, and have also warned her to take heed of such carriages for the future, lest her former carriage come in remembrance against her to make her punishment the greater.

Source: Nathaniel Shurtleff and David Pulsifer, eds., *Records of the Colony of New Plymouth* (Boston: William White, 1855), vol. 2, pp. 137, 148, 163.

* * *

The colony at New Haven approved a body of laws in 1655; this canon was largely based on legal code of the Massachusetts Bay Colony— with a notable exception. Included in the New Haven sodomy law was a specific provision prohibiting sexual relations between women, the first of its kind in New England. The law is remarkable for its comprehensiveness—bestiality, anal sex, and masturbation as well as lesbianism are covered—and for its overt invocation of the biblical justification for judgment.
   Following is a portion of the New Haven sodomy statute.

DOCUMENT 18: New Haven Law Prohibits Lesbianism (1655)

If any man layeth with mankinde, as a man lyeth with a woman, both of them have committed abomination, they both shall surely be put to death. Levit. 20.13. And if any woman change the naturall use into that which is against nature, as Rom. I.26 she shall be liable to the same sentence, and punishment, or if any person, or persons, shall commit any other kinde of unnaturall and shamefull filthines, called in Scripture the going after strange flesh, or other flesh than God alloweth, by carnall knowledge of another vessel than God in nature have appointed to become one flesh, whether by abusing the contrary part of a grown woman, or child of either sex, or unripe vessel of a girle, wherein the natural use of the woman is left, which God hath ordained for the propagation of posterity, and Sodomitical filthinesse is committed by a kind of rape, nature being forced, through the will were inticed, every such person shall be put to death.

Source: J. Hammond Trumbull, *The True-Blue Laws of Connecticut and New-Haven* (Hartford: American Publishing Co., 1879), p. 201.

* * *

The Puritans in New England were particularly upset about sodomy. Since the Bible story of Sodom did not specifically state the nature of the sins of Sodom that led God to destroy it, the Reverend Samuel Danforth of Duxbury speculated about the ancient city's sins in a sermon to his congregation that was published in Cambridge, Massachusetts, in 1674. Danforth published his sermon to answer those people who criticized the colony's court for executing a young man for having sex with an animal. The animal was also killed because of the Puritans' belief that a man could impregnate a female animal and a monster offspring would result. Danforth justified the government's execution on the basis that if they did not kill this youth then God would destroy Massachusetts just as he had destroyed Sodom. The minister railed not only against bestiality, but also against masturbation ("self-pollution" and "the sin of Onan"), fornication (unmarried men and women having sex), adultery (a married person having sex with someone besides their spouse), and both male and female homosexual behavior. This sermon is representative of the guilt-inducing fire and brimstone style of fundamentalist Christian ministers, from the colonial era up to the present time, about all kinds of erotic bodily pleasures.

DOCUMENT 19: Puritan Sermon on The Cry of Sodom (1674)

The sins of Sodom were many and great…[but the] most grievous of all [was] abominable filthiness in all manner of Uncleanness.…[Such] wickedness cried unto Heaven for vengeance…with Fire and Brimstone.… Not only whoredom and Self-pollution, but also Adultery.…Going after strange flesh: Sodomy and Bestiality.…Filthiness with his own body alone [was the] sin of Onan [who] abhorred the lawful use of the Marriage-bed, and most impurely defiled himself.…[which was] so detestable in the sight of God.…Sodomy [is] filthiness committed between parties of the same Sex—when Males with Males, and Females with Females work wickedness. If a man lieth with mankind, as he lieth with a woman, both of them have committed an abomination: they shall surely be put to death, their blood shall be upon them, Leviticus 20:13. This sin raged amongst the Sodomites, and to their perpetual Infamy, it is called Sodomy. Against this wickedness, no indignation is sufficient.…

Some among us stand astonished…[that God would allow] a Youth…[a] Child of Religious Parents…[to be executed in a] Dreadful Example of Divine Vengeance. You pity his Youth and tender years…[but] I pray, pity the holy Law of God, which is shamefully violated…, pity the Land, which is fearfully polluted and defiled.…The execution of Justice upon such a notorious Malefactor, is the only way to turn away the wrath of God from us.…Divine Wrath…strikes a holy fear and dread…[into] Our cursed Natures.…[The] holiest man hath as vile and filthy a Nature, as the Sodomites.…[This boy's execution is God's] Instruction and Astonishment to all New England…[making people] afraid to go on impenitently in the same sins....Go to now, ye wanton and lascivious persons, go on in your Frolicks and mad Pranks....He that is a Sodomite, let him be a Sodomite still; he that is a Beast, let him be a Beast still....Justify this poor Condemned Wretch in all his Villainy....Justify Sodom in all her Abomination....

The Wrath of God [is the only thing powerful enough to] restrain the rest of our Youth, and all others....[God] hath cut off this rotten and putrid Member [to] prevent the spreading of the Infection....Detest and abominate the sin of Sodomy...[and those who] abuse themselves with mankind....[Sodomy] makes men despise the Ordinance of Marriage...[which is the] remedy [for] boiling and burning lusts....Repent...unclean Speculations, vile affections, unchaste fire...[through the] help of Christ to mortify thy lusts and crucify the flesh....Take the Sword of the Spirit, and thrust it into the bowels of thy lusts....If once thou has escaped out of Sodom, tremble to think of returning....Let the fear of God...stop thine Ears at filthy Jests, amorous Songs....Abhor all lascivious Touches, unchaste Embracings....

Let us carefully Watch over our Children, Servants, and all that are under our Care and Charge, lest they be stained and defiled....[Every man should] charge his Children and Family to beware of the wickedness. Arise, and depart out of Sodom.

Source: S. Danforth, *The Cry of Sodom Enquired Into...With a Solemn Exhortation to Tremble at God's Judgements and to Abandon Youthful Lusts* (Cambridge, MA: Marmaduke Johnson, 1674).

*   *   *

For many European males in North America, the only opportunity to escape the threat of being executed for sodomy was to go to the frontier to live with the Indians, or to become part of a group of pirates. By 1600 several European powers had made competing claims to the south Atlantic coastline and the Caribbean islands, promoting a state of confusion that was close to anarchy. In this climate, no one nation was in control. Lawlessness reigned from Carolina to Trinidad, and individual groups of seamen found that they could profit handsomely by raiding ships that were transporting huge amounts of wealth from Mexico and Central and South America. The ships sailed through the Caribbean Sea, by the Florida Keys, and across the Atlantic Ocean to Spain. Since most of this wealth was plunder that the Spanish had stolen from the American Indians, the buccaneers, as they came to be called, were in no worse moral position than the colonial authorities.

For over a century, from the late 1500s to the early 1700s, piracy turned the Caribbean and the Florida-Georgia coastline into the first of a series of Wild West areas, outside the control of any established authority. The open sea, on which ships could operate independently of national governments, offered a revolutionary opportunity for skilled seamen. From what is known of their background, most pirates came from lower class English families, and had left their parents' home (or been forced to leave) at a young age. They spent their adolescence in wandering gangs of males who camped in forests and stole from travelers. As a result of living in all-male groups that were outside the authority of church and state, and with little contact with females, most of them no doubt learned sex from the older boys. Given the slim chance for sex with a female, unless we assume that they were totally asexual, we can reasonably suggest that these boys had sex with each other.

The English sheriffs made raids on the forests to capture as many of these criminal gangs of boys as possible, and those who were captured were typically pressed into service in the Royal Navy. There they learned valuable seafaring skills, but they chafed at the brutal treatment of sailors aboard naval ships. It was these boys and young men who deserted to pirate bands at the first opportunity. If pirates captured a ship, they often offered sailors the opportunity to join their gang of buccaneers. Those who volunteered were attracted to the democratic nature of pirate society, in which practically all of the members were from lower class backgrounds like themselves. In contrast to their bitter memories of oppression in the Royal Navy, they gloried in the freedoms they enjoyed as buccaneers. They lived in an all-male community of pirates, and not being used to the company of women most of them felt nervous and uncomfortable on those rare occasions when they saw women. Since pirate lore said women were unlucky on a ship, they seldom raped women or took them as captives. For those men who remained on a pirate ship, homosexual behavior was not a variant option in their life; it was their sole sexual outlet with another person.

Colonial officials complained that pirate harbors like Port Royal, Jamaica, were "filled with sodomites," and when sailors were prosecuted for sodomy in British courts their usual defense was that they did not know that sex between two males was wrong. Long-distance sailors, where ships were at sea for several months before coming into a harbor, have long had a reputation for male-male sex. But for the buccaneers, with their very long periods at sea, and their rebellion against conventional society, it is likely that many or most of them found sex with another seaman to be preferable to celibacy. Two pirates typically paired up as mates, and they lived and fought together as a team. In accounts of pirate battles, there are numerous stories of a buccaneer dying while trying to save his mate. These were devoted, loving relationships, and many of these mates remained coupled on a permanent basis. [B. R. Burg, *Sodomy and the Perception of Evil: English Sea Rovers in the Seventeenth Century Caribbean* (New York: New York University Press, 1983).]

In a few cases, women also became pirates. The most famous were Mary Read and Anne Bonny. Mary Read was an Englishwoman who started dressing in men's clothes and passed as a man, in order to become a sailor. After pirates captured the ship she was working on, she joined them and ended up in the Bahamas. There she met a South Carolina female pirate named Anne Bonny, and they became an inseparable pair. Historian Rictor Norton has written of them:

DOCUMENT 20: Pirates in the Caribbean (1724)

[It] is more than likely, and equally significant that Anne Bonny and Mary Read were lesbian pirates. Our historical knowledge of these two women is based mainly upon the account written by Captain Charles Johnson (probably a pseudonym for Daniel Defoe) in *A General History of the Robberies and Murders of the Most Notorious Pirates*, published in 1724 shortly after Anne and Mary were brought to trial for piracy on the high seas.

We first hear of Anne Bonny, born Anne Cormac, in 1710—as a thirteen-year-old tomboy in the port of Charleston, South Carolina....Although the daughter of a wealthy lawyer and plantation owner, her red hair was cut short, her face was dirty, and her habits were rowdy. As one historian notes, Anne grew up into a strapping, boisterous girl, of a fierce and courageous temper....[After her father disinherited her] she burnt down the plantation, then fled to the British-controlled port of New Providence (on modern Nassau in the Bahamas), a haven for such pirates as Blackbeard and Captain Kidd....

[After Anne met and joined up with Mary Read, they] remained inseparable, and both alternately donned male and female clothing. In due course they took command of another ship, and Men-of-War were sent out to capture "those infamous women." They abandoned all caution and raided numerous other ships....[The] obvious enjoyment of their cross-dressing, and the fact that they acted together as a couple and obviously loved one another...suggests that they must be relevant to any history of lesbian experience.

Source: Rictor Norton, "Lesbian Pirates: Anne Bonny and Mary Read," *The Great Queens of History*, Web site [www.infopt.demon.co.uk/pirates.htm 1997], last updated January 8, 2000.

*   *   *

Sir William Blackstone, solicitor to the British Crown, codified English Common Law in his book published in 1765. It rapidly became the primary reference for judges both in England and in the American colonies. When the colonies established their independence, most of them carried over English Common Law for their criminal code, and

United States judges continued to rely on Blackstone's *Commentaries* well into the twentieth century. For example, Chief Justice Warren Burger cited Blackstone's ideas on sodomy in his United States Supreme Court decision *Bowers v. Hardwick* in 1986. Blackstone considered homosexual behavior to be so horrible that, at several places in his description, he switches to Latin language in order to spare readers from such descriptions unless they make the Latin translation. A reading of Blackstone proves the close connection between the Christian religion and Anglo-American law on matters of sex, a trend that has continued throughout the history of the United States.

DOCUMENT 21: Commentaries on the Laws of England (1765)

The crime is more detestable...of a still deeper malignity; the infamous crime against nature, committed either with man or beast. A crime, which ought to be strictly and impartially proved, and then strictly and impartially punished. But it is an offense of so dark a nature, so easily charged, and the negative so difficult to be proved, that the accusation should be clearly made out: for, if false, it deserves punishment inferior only to that of the crime itself.

I will not act so disagreeable part, to my readers as well as myself, as to dwell any longer upon a subject, the very mention of which is a disgrace to human nature. It will be more eligible to imitate in this respect the delicacy of our English law, which treats it, in it's [sic] very indictments, as a crime not fit to be named; "peccatum illud horribile, inter christianos non numinandum." [that horrible sin not to be named among Christians]....

A word concerning it's [sic] punishment. This is the voice of nature and of reason, and the express law of God, determined to be capital [i.e., punished by death]. Of which we have a signal instance, long [ago], by the destruction of two cities [the Bible story of Sodom and Gommorah] by fire from heaven; so that this is an universal, not merely a provincial, precept. And our antient law in some degree initiated this punishment, by commanding such miscreants to be burnt to death; though Fleta says they should be buried alive; either of which punishments was indifferently used for this crime among the antient Goths. But now the general punishment of all felonies is the same, namely, by hanging: and this offense...was made single felony by the statute 25 Henry VIII, c. 6.

Source: William Blackstone, *Commentaries on the Laws of England* (London, 1765), Book IV, Chapter 15, section IV.

* * *

As the Spanish imperialists expanded their empire northward from Mexico into California, they sent exploring expeditions to investigate the area and make reports. In 1775, Jesuit Father Pedro Font, who visited the Yuma Indians of the lower Colorado River valley, with the expedition of Juan Bautista de Anza, wrote in his report about some transgendered males.

DOCUMENT 22: Spanish Priests Condemn Transgendered Yuma Indians (1775)

Among the women I saw some men dressed like women, with whom they go about regularly, never joining the men. The commander called them *amaricados*, perhaps because the Yumas call effeminate men *maricas*. I asked who these men were, and they replied that they were not men like the rest, and for this reason they went around covered this way. From this I inferred they must be hermaphrodites, but from what I learned later I understood that they were sodomites, dedicated to nefarious practices. From all the foregoing I conclude that in this matter of incontinence there will be much to do when the Holy Faith and the Christian religion are established among them.

Source: Pedro Font, *Font's Complete Diary of the Second Anza Expedition*, trans. Herbert Eugene Bolton, *Anza's California Expeditions* (Berkeley: University of California Press, 1930–1931), vol. 4, p. 105.

* * *

When the Spanish Crown established a colony in California, officials found that, like most indigenous Americans, the Native Californians respected same-sex love. As they had done in other areas, the Spaniards attacked sexual and gender diversity with a ruthless suppression.

DOCUMENT 23: Spanish Colonial Suppression of Sodomites in California (1775–1777)

In 1775 the second military governor of California, Pedro Fages, wrote in his report to the Crown:

I have substantial evidence that those Indian men who both here and farther inland, are observed in the dress, clothing, and character of women—there being two or three such in each village—pass as sodomites by profession (it being confirmed that all these Indians are much addicted to this abominable vice) and permit the heathen to practice the execrable, unnatural abuse of their bodies. They are called *joyas* [jewels], and are held in great esteem.

Source: Pedro Faxes, "Supplemento Noticia del Misiones de Monterey y California por Pedro Faxes" (1775), papers of Pedro Fages, Library of the California Historical Society.

* * *

What happened when the Spanish had a chance to exert their power over the Native Californians is indicated by an incident that occurred at Saint Antonio mission near Santa Barbara in 1777. The priests reacted sharply after the arrival of a Chumash couple who came to the mission to visit another Indian who worked there as a laborer. One of the Chumash visitors, Franciscan Father Francisco Palou reported, was dressed in men's clothing,

but the other dressed like a woman and called by them a *Joya* (since that is the name they are given in their native tongue). Once the priests had been alerted, the head of the Mission went to the house with a sentry and a soldier. The couple was caught in the act of committing the nefarious sin. They were duly punished for this crime, but not with the severity it properly deserved. When they were rebuked for such an enormous crime, the man answered that the Joya was his wife! They were not seen again in the Mission or its surroundings after this reprimand. Nor did these disreputable people appear in the other missions, although many Joyas can be seen in the area of Canal de Santa Barbara; around there, almost every village has two or three. But we place our trust in God and expect that these accursed people will disappear with the growth of the missions. The abominable vice will be eliminated to the extent that the Catholic faith and all the other virtues are firmly implanted there, for the glory of God.

Source: Translated in Jonathan Ned Katz, *Gay American History* (New York: Thomas Crowell, 1976), p. 292.

Part II

Life, Liberty, and the Pursuit of Happiness: The Development of a Homophile Identity in the United States, 1775–1950

By the time of the revolt beginning in the English colonies of North America in 1775, many colonists were fed up with the cruel punishments and brutal infringements on their freedoms by British colonial officials. They reacted most to official restrictions on the intimate acts of everyday life: what one could say or write, who one could associate with, and how a person accused of a crime was to be tried. They wanted to be secure in their homes, with a right to privacy from government intrusion. They wanted to be able to assemble freely in groups, and to be able to petition the government for changes in policy, without being subjected to arrest and mistreatment. Other controversies related to the continual conflicts between different sects of Christian zealots, who each struggled to become the established religion in a colony, so that they could impose their particular brand of religion on everyone else. The official establishment of the Church of England, whose ministers were usually arrogant apologists for the British government, was also unpopular.

Crime and punishment were particular concerns of the rebel colonists. They were tired of being tried by military courts, without a jury of their peers, in trials that were sometimes kept secret. Also of concern were the number of crimes in British law that were punished by death or torture. As more colonists objected, the British Crown reacted to these rising protests by sending in His Majesty's Imperial Army to teach the upstart colonists a lesson. Direct experience with an oppressive military rule had a dramatic impact on the founding of the United States of America.

When the rebel colonists declared their independence from the British Empire in 1776, individual rights and liberties were foremost in the minds of the Founders. Firebrands like Patrick Henry declared, "Give me liberty or give me death!" saying that being able to live free from oppression was more important than life itself. This new ideology of freedom clashed with the old ideas of loyalty to the king. It also clashed with the old ideas of biblical justice. Leaders of the new government wanted not only independence from Britain, but also protection from infringements on their liberty by the newly established government of the United States. Thomas Jefferson, who wanted to free the legal system from the Bible, proposed that punishments for crimes should be reduced. Among many other reductions, he felt that those convicted of sodomy should no longer be executed.

Still, despite the new revolutionary ideology of freedom and individual rights that freed them from English control, the young United States was constrained by its Christian heritage. Most Euro-Americans continued to see themselves as Christian, and despite the sharp critique of Christianity offered by forward-thinking leaders like Thomas Jefferson, George Washington, and James Madison, the personal moral values of the general population did not much change. They continued to see women as inferior to men, and other races as inferior to those of European descent. Non-Christian American Indians were stereotyped as savages, and African American slavery was just as oppressive as before. The Bible was used to justify the inferiority of all these groups, and it would be nearly two centuries before the guarantees of freedom for citizens of the United States would be applied to them.

American popular thought particularly continued to condemn all forms of nonprocreative sex, despite the general move toward respect for individuals being able to make their own choices about how they wanted to live their lives. Why did Americans continue to condemn sexual freedom, when they moved so strongly to celebrate freedom for themselves in other regards? Perhaps an economic reason may explain why strong antisexual attitudes continued. About 90 percent of people in the new United States lived, as they had during the colonial period, on family farms. On these small farms, people survived by their own labor, and most of them never made enough money to hire other workers. However, they could reproduce additional workers by producing children. On family farms, children were put to work laboring in the fields from the time they were about six or seven years old, and they continued to work on their parents' farms until they were mature enough to inherit or purchase their own farms, or to become artisans, or to move elsewhere. Child labor was an integral part of the way the farm family survived.

Besides the need for laborers, another important economic reason for people to produce children was in order to have someone to take care of them in their old age. In contrast to the Native American extended families, where some adults who did not have children could be taken care of by their nieces and nephews, most Euro-Americans lived in simple nuclear families consisting of husband, wife, children, and perhaps an aged grandparent. In this nuclear family farm economy, it was necessary for everyone to reproduce several children in order to guarantee that at least one of these children would live long enough to support the parents in their old age. Because of a high rate of deaths for infants, women had to produce many births in order to have several children mature into adulthood. According to the first United States Census in 1790, the number of living offspring listed for the average married woman was over nine children. If we consider the large number of infant deaths that mothers experienced, which were not listed in the Census, this meant that the average American woman was almost continuously either pregnant or nursing babies during her entire reproductive cycle.

In this atmosphere, where having children was critically important for child labor on the family farm, and to insure care for the elderly, anyone without children was considered unfortunate. Someone who chose not to marry and have children was considered practically a traitor, and a potential drain on the community. Since American society was still primitive in its social organization, community institutions did not exist to take care of elderly people without children. For those unfortunate enough not to have a child to care for them in their old age, they had to depend on the kindness of their nieces and nephews, but in the nuclear family this was considered a burden because those people had their own parents to support. If someone did not have relatives, it was rare that they could live to old age. Without someone to care for them if they became ill, if they could not work to provide their own food, they would literally starve to death. Though church congregations sometimes provided gifts of charity, American society provided only limited resources to care for the poor and the infirm.

The only exception to this pattern of dependence on the rural nuclear family was in large cities. In urban areas, which held less than 10 percent of the nation's population, a small number of people were able to support themselves without children. These usually were people who had successful businesses or enough inherited wealth to hire servants to take care of them. But even these people endured much social pressure to conform to the dominant pattern of marriage. With economic, social, and religious motives all combining to pressure everyone to marry and have children, the United States became a nation of married men and women.

For women in particular, the pressure was on them to find a husband as soon as possible during their early teens to early twenties. Instead of securing her future through education or business skills, a young woman depended upon her looks and charms to attract a good husband. Those who were considered to be too ugly to attract a husband were soon labeled old maids, and were pitied. Social status for women was almost entirely dependent on being a wife and mother. If her husband were addicted to alcohol or gambling, or suffered an injury that prevented him from working the farm, a married woman would face a life of poverty. If a woman's husband died or abandoned her, she had to quickly find another husband to support her young children. While widows who were economically established on their own land could be supported by their grown children, starvation was a reality for women with small children. Orphan children were commonly taken in or adopted by another farm family, which gained value from their labor, but the mother had to locate a domestic job or starve to death. Marriage was the main economic security for American women.

*   *   *

The American colonists increasingly reacted against the harsh colonial rule of the British king, and in so doing they began constructing an Enlightenment philosophy of individual liberty and rights that would much later form the basis for the gay and lesbian rights movement. When Thomas Jefferson was asked by the rebel leaders to draw up a Declaration of Independence, he wrote revolutionary words that challenged the right of government to dictate to people. Instead, he wrote, the purpose of government is to secure "life, liberty, and the pursuit of happiness" for its people, and if a government does not do this, it is the right of people to alter or abolish it. Government, Jefferson wrote, derives its authority from the people. When the Continental Congress signed Jefferson's declaration on July 4, 1776, it committed the new independent United States of America to challenge the established idea in Europe that kings derived their authority from God, and that God's rules as written in the Bible were the basis for law.

DOCUMENT 24: United States Declaration of Independence (1776)

We hold these truths to be self-evident: That all men are created equal; that they are endowed by their Creator with certain unalienable rights; that among these are life, liberty, and the pursuit of happiness; that, to secure these rights, governments are instituted among men, deriving their just powers from the consent of the governed; that whenever any form of government becomes destructive of these ends, it is the right of the people to alter or to abolish it, and to institute new government, laying its foundations on such principles, and organizing its powers in such form, as to them shall seem most likely to effect their safety and happiness.

*   *   *

When political leaders worked to form a stronger federal government than existed under the original United States Articles of Confederation, they wrote a new Constitution in the name of "the people of the United States." The Preamble of this Constitution stated that, in addition to providing for the military defense of the nation, there were four major domestic purposes of this new government: to establish justice, tranquillity, welfare, and liberty. All of these purposes were done "to secure the blessings of liberty to ourselves and our posterity." Notwithstanding the strong statements in favor of freedom, the majority of Americans refused to agree to vote in favor of this new government until a Bill of Rights was added. They had had too much strife and controversy over religious differences during the colonial era, and wanted to make sure that a strong separation of church and state existed. This Bill of Rights marked a further move away from the establishment of the rules of the Christian Bible as a guide for government, in favor of less harsh punishments.

Many people also insisted on a firm written guarantee of the free expression of opinion, in speech, in the press, and in petitioning the government for changing the laws. They also wanted a guarantee of the freedom of people to associate with whom they want, and to assemble in groups without having their meetings being declared illegal. And they wanted to be protected from government intrusion into their private affairs, especially in the privacy of their homes. If accused of a crime, they wanted to be protected from forced testimony, to be judged by a jury of their peers, and not to be subject to cruel punishments. These issues were fresh in the minds of Americans at the time, because the British colonial government had so frequently violated those rights of intimacy, expression, and association.

The Bill of Rights was added as ten amendments to the Constitution, and adopted in 1791. By passing the Bill of Rights, the United States accepted as a mainstay of its form of government that the guarantee of people's rights to individual liberty and freedom in their personal affairs is the certain hallmark of democracy. For people who were subject to being executed as sodomites, the establishment of these legal protections was extremely important, but just as with other oppressed groups many years had to pass before these principles were actually applied. Many of these basic protections were not extended to homosexuals until the late twentieth century. The amendments which have been applied to the rights of homosexually inclined persons in recent decades are quoted here:

DOCUMENT 25: United States Constitution and Bill of Rights (1791)

Amendment 1: Congress shall make no law respecting an establishment of religion, or prohibiting the free exercise thereof; or abridging the freedom of speech, or of the press; or the right of the people peaceably to assemble, and to petition the government for a redress of grievances.

Amendment 4: The right of the people to be secure in their persons, houses, papers, and effects, against unreasonable searches and seizures, shall not be violated....

Amendment 5: No person shall be held to answer for a capital, or otherwise infamous crime, unless on a presentment or indictment of a grand jury...nor shall be compelled in any criminal case to be a witness against himself, nor be deprived of life, liberty, or property, without due process of law....

Amendment 6: In all criminal prosecutions, the accused shall enjoy the right to a speedy and public trial, by an impartial jury....

Amendment 7: In suits...the right to trial by jury shall be preserved....

Amendment 8: Excessive bail shall not be required, nor excessive fines imposed, nor cruel and unusual punishments inflicted.

Amendment 9: The enumeration in the Constitution, of certain rights, shall not be construed to deny or disparage others retained by the people.

Amendment 10: The powers not delegated to the United States by the Constitution, nor prohibited by it to the States, are reserved to the States, or to the people.

*   *   *

By the early 1800s a small network of unmarried men had emerged in Philadelphia, the largest city in the young nation, and perhaps in other large centers of population. These bachelors congregated at certain taverns to drink, eat, and socialize with other bachelors. Though these men endured pressures to marry women, and most of them did so as they got older, some of them refused to marry and became known as confirmed bachelors. The sexual alternatives for these confirmed bachelors was either to be celibate, to purchase the services of a female prostitute, or to meet their sexual needs with other males. Since homosexual behavior was still highly stigmatized as sodomy, bachelors would of course have to keep such inclinations private. But if they secretly engaged in sex with a trusted friend, the general lack of social discussion of sex served as a protection. By not discussing sex in public, they could live undisturbed as a confirmed bachelor rather than being condemned as a sodomite. Except for those who were unfortunate enough to be prosecuted under a state's sodomy law, homosexuality was not a topic of general comment, and certainly not a political issue.

A prominent example of a confirmed bachelor was James Buchanan, a political leader in the Democratic Party who was elected president in 1856. As the only unmarried president of the United States, there were backroom jokes about his close relationship with another politician named Rufus King, an effeminate man sometimes referred to as Buchanan's "Miss Nancy." Beyond this, however, the president's sexual affairs were considered his private concerns, and of no business by others. This veil of privacy also extended to Buchanan's successor Abraham Lincoln, who was elected president in 1860.

In his younger days Lincoln was a participant in the society of bachelors in Springfield, Illinois, and for several years he lived with another man named Joshua Speed. Lincoln and Speed slept in the same bed, and wrote letters to each other whenever one of them was out of town. These letters demonstrate an exceptionally close emotional bond between them. Both Lincoln and Speed felt the social pressure to marry women, though when Mary Todd pursued Lincoln, he was so nervous about being with a woman that he did not show up at his own wedding. Despite being stranded at the altar, Mary continued to pursue Lincoln until he agreed to marry her. Their marriage had many problems, and Mary resented her husband's continued closeness to Joshua Speed.

Did Abraham Lincoln and Joshua Speed, or James Buchanan and Rufus King, have sex with each other? We do not know for sure. Documentary evidence does not exist to prove that they engaged in sex with each other. They of course did not campaign for the rights of homosexuals, which at the time was totally outside the realm of political discourse. What we can say is that both these male couples lived together, were emotionally intimate, and had a long-standing commitment to each other. If they were a male and a female, they would probably be considered a loving couple. Because it was acceptable for two men to live together, even sleep in the same bed together, nineteenth-century American society's unquestioning acceptance of a bachelor category for men allowed such men to establish whatever private sexual relationship they wanted. Their sexual behavior was not brought up as a political issue.

The same acceptance was offered to unmarried women. Though generally considered unfortunate for not catching a husband during her early twenties, a woman who did not wish to marry a man could fit into the category of spinster. Many unmarried women lived with their relatives, but those who had the financial means could move in with another woman. These female-female households became so common in New England after the mid-nineteenth century that they became known as Boston marriages. As with male-male couples, the topic of sex was not discussed.

This veil of privacy over the sexual lives of people, even political leaders, existed over most of American history. As late as the 1940s and 1950s, President Franklin Roosevelt's and President Dwight Eisenhower's extramarital relationships with other women, and in the 1960s President John Kennedy's numerous sexual affairs with women, were all kept private. Though these presidents' extramarital affairs were common knowledge in Washington, they were considered the person's private business. Such matters were not reported by the press. It was only in the late twentieth century that the private sexual behavior of politicians became an acceptable public discourse and a political issue.

In the nineteenth century, the categories of bachelor and spinster could serve effectively as a cover for loving same-sex relationships. Also emphasized was the topic of same-sex friendships, which were romanticized in a very public way. Writers may not have been able to declare their right to express their homosexual desires, but they came close in their writings on friendship. In poetry especially, with its verses open to many interpretations, an argument in favor of same-sex love began to be made. A good example is contained in the works of the famous New England poet Henry David Thoreau (1817–1862). In an 1838 poem titled "Friendship" Thoreau wrote of two males he referred to as "mates" whose "roots are intertwined insep'rably." He made a reference to the prominence of male love among the ancient Greeks, by saying that among males "love cannot speak…without the help of Greek." He became even more bold in his 1839 poem "Sympathy" which suggests a bittersweet "sad remembrance" of Thoreau's intimacy with a "glorious…gentle boy" that was located deep in his emotions. After the boy moved away, Thoreau feared that he would never again find such "bliss" with another person, "nor a sympathy more rare."

Returning to this theme of male intimate relationships, in a January 1840 entry in his journal, Thoreau revealed his dream and desire to live with a male partner in a same-sex community of like-minded men in "a serene friendship land." He made reference to ancient Greek male lovers and asked:

Document 26: Bachelor Friendships of the Nineteenth Century

Why should not we put to shame those old reserved worthies by a community of such….Constantly, as it were through a remote skylight, I have glimpses of a serene friendship land [where] I would live henceforth with some gentle soul such a life as may be conceived, double for variety, single for harmony,—two, only that we might admire our oneness,—one, because indivisible.

Source: quoted in Byrne R. S. Fone, *The Columbia Anthology of Gay Literature* (New York: Columbia University Press, 1998), pp. 526–528.

*   *   *

For nineteenth-century women who wished to live in domestic partnerships with other women, the basic problem facing them was to gain economic and political independence from men. Before women could claim their right to live independently, they had to confront the idea that woman's place was solely in the home, under the control of a father or a husband. The main justification for this male-dominant view came from Christian clergy. Just as they did in condemning same-sex love, ministers quoted Bible verses telling women that God had ordained men to rule over women. Ministers ignored the teachings of Jesus and emphasized those of Paul, who was not only opposed to sexual freedom but also told wives to be submissive to their husbands. Because the Christian opposition to women's rights and to gay-lesbian rights has been so similar, arguments for women's equality and gay-lesbian equality have been closely parallel during United States history.

This similarity of an argument for individual rights can be seen in the debate held during an early National Women's Rights Convention, held at Syracuse, New York, in 1852. Various speakers favoring women's rights struggled to reinterpret the Bible toward a more favorable view of women. After listening to speakers trying to justify rights for women from biblical authority, feminist activist Ernestine Rose argued that the battle for equal rights would be won not by appealing to the Bible, but by appealing to the American Revolutionary ideals of freedom, liberty, and justice. This marked a fundamental shift in American thought, away from Judeo-Christian religion and more toward democracy. This revolutionary theme would be taken up by other independent-minded people arguing for sexual freedom in the future. Rose said:

DOCUMENT 27: National Women's Rights Convention (1852)

For my part, I see no need to appeal to any [biblical] written authority, particularly when it is so obscure and indefinite as to admit of different interpretations. When the inhabitants of Boston converted their harbor into a teapot rather than submit to unjust taxes, they did not go to the Bible for their authority; for if they had, they would have been told from the same authority to "give unto Caesar what belonged to Caesar." Had the people, when they rose in the might of their right to throw off the British yoke, appealed to the Bible for authority, it would have answered them, "Submit to the powers that be, for they are from God." No! On Human Rights and Freedom, on a subject that is as self evident as that two and two make four, there is no need of any written authority....

We ask not for our rights as a gift of charity, but as an act of justice. For it is in accordance with the principles of republicanism that, as woman has to pay taxes to maintain government, she has a right to participate in the formation and administration of it. That as she is amenable to the laws of her country, she is entitled to a voice in their enactment, and to all the protective advantages they can bestow; and as she is as liable as man to all the vicissitudes of life, she ought to enjoy the same social rights and privileges. And any difference, therefore, in political, civil, and social rights, on account of sex, is in direct violation of the principles of justice and humanity, and as such ought to be held up to the contempt and derision of every lover of human freedom.

Source: Elizabeth Cady Stanton, Susan B. Anthony, and Matilda Joslyn Gage, *History of Woman Suffrage* (New York: Fowler and Wells, 1881), vol. 1, p. 537.

*   *   *

One of the most important poets in United States history. Walt Whitman likely would not have developed his democratic ideology if it had not been for his attractions to the working-class men in his personal life. More than any previous American poet, Whitman wanted to see the breakdown of class differences, and he envisioned attractions between loving comrades as a basis for democratic equality. Whitman was inspired by Ralph Waldo Emerson's 1841 poem "Friendship," celebrating passionate male relationships, to elaborate a philosophy of male love. But Whitman went further in his celebration of same-sex love than any previous American writer. Whitman spoke of body parts in erotic ways that had never before been published in the United States.

Walt Whitman did not just look upon these male lovers as merely being connected by sexual acts. They were also, he said, united in a profound psychic and spiritual bond. He developed this theme of male comrade love most strongly in a series of poems he titled "Calamus" which was first published in the 1860 edition of his book *Leaves of Grass*. In the first Calamus poem, he calls on the reader to go with him "in paths untrodden" and to escape "from all the standards hitherto publish'd" to follow a new lifestyle of "standards not yet publish'd." After too long conforming to convention, Whitman wrote that it was at last clear to him that his soul rejoiced in the "manly attachment...of athletic love." His purpose in writing was "To tell the secret of my nights and days, To celebrate the need of comrades." In the Preface to the 1876 edition of *Leaves of Grass*, Whitman explained the political reasons why society should accept and encourage loving same-sex relationships.

DOCUMENT 28: Walt Whitman and the Homoerotic Poetry of Democracy (1860)

The special meaning of the Calamus cluster of LEAVES OF GRASS...mainly resides in its Political significance. In my opinion it is by a fervent, accepted, development of Comradeship, the beautiful and sane affection of man for man, latent in all the young fellows, North and South, East and West—it is by this, I say, and by what goes directly and indirectly along with it, that the United States of the future, (I cannot too often repeat,) are to be most effectually welded together, intercalated, anneal'd into a Living Union.

Then, for enclosing clue of all, it is imperatively and ever to be borne in mind that LEAVES OF GRASS entire is not to be construed as an intellectual or scholastic effort or Poem mainly, but more as a radical utterance out of the abysms of the Soul, the Emotions and the Physique—an utterance adjusted to, perhaps born of, Democracy and Modern Science, and in its very nature regardless of the old conventions, and, under the great Laws, following only its own impulses.

Source: Walt Whitman, *Prose Works*, ed. Floyd Stovall (New York: New York University Press, 1964), vol. 2, p. 414. See also Byrne R. S. Fone, *The Columbia Anthology of Gay Literature* (New York: Columbia University Press, 1998), pp. 528, 559, 567.

* * *

The Founding Fathers wisely recognized that problems might arise in the future that were not addressed in the Constitution of the United States, and they provided for additional amendments to be added to the Bill of Rights. In 1865 the Thirteenth Amendment was added to abolish slavery. But within the next few years it became obvious that simply ending slavery was not enough. After several white racist state governments in the South systematically violated the rights of African American freed slaves, Congress passed a Fourteenth Amendment to the Constitution, stating that state governments must guarantee equal rights for all citizens. This amendment thus extended federal protections for individual liberties not only against infringement by the national government, but also by the state governments. By greatly expanding the idea of individual rights, it has become a major legal basis for significant court decisions in the twentieth century. The Fourteenth Amendment remains an important mainstay of freedom in the United States, and along with the Bill of Rights is an important legal basis for gay and lesbian rights.

DOCUMENT 29: Fourteenth Amendment to the Constitution (1868)

All persons born or naturalized in the United States, and subject to the jurisdiction thereof, are citizens of the United States and of the state wherein they reside. No state shall make or enforce any law which shall abridge the privileges or immunities of citizens of the United States; nor shall any state deprive any person of life, liberty, or property, without due process of law; nor deny to any person within its jurisdiction the equal protection of the laws.

* * *

In 1870 Walt Whitman wrote a prose book, *Democratic Vistas*, to explain his philosophy of democracy. While he strongly favored spiritual development of individuals, Whitman felt that organized religion represented a danger to democracy. With its false certainty of intense moral right, he warned, Christianity had the tendency to lead to fanaticism and persecution. He feared a coming conflict between individual freedom and organized religion. The answer to this problem was not to get rid of religion, but to always balance it with reason, science, and appreciation for the individual will. Whitman wrote of male-female "amative love," which he associated with the material wealth and development of the nation. But same-sex "adhesive love," he said, would be the true basis of the United States' moral development in the future. He expounded a new morality based not upon the Bible, but on the ideals of freedom and democracy that he wished to encourage in the United States.

DOCUMENT 30: Walt Whitman's *Democratic Vistas* (1870)

It is to the development, identification, and general prevalence of that fervid comradeship (the [same-sex] adhesive love, at least rivaling the [heterosexual] amative love hitherto possessing imaginative literature, if not going beyond it), that I look for the counterbalance and offset of our materialistic and vulgar American democracy, and for the spiritualization thereof. Many will say it is a dream, and will not follow my inferences: but I confidently expect a time when there will be seen, running like a half-hid warp through all the myriad audible and visible worldly interests of America, threads of manly friendship, fond and loving, pure and sweet, strong and life-long, carried to degrees hitherto unknown—not only giving tone to individual character, and making it unprecedently emotional, muscular, heroic, and refined, but having the deepest relations to general politics. I say democracy infers such loving comradeship, as its most inevitable twin or counterpart, without which it will be incomplete, in vain, and incapable of perpetuating itself.

[There is a danger to democracy from organized religion, which has a false certainty] of intense moral right, and in its name and strain'd construction, the worst fanaticisms, wars, persecutions, murders, etc., have yet, in all lands, in the past, been broach'd, and have come to their devilish fruition. Much is to be said—but I may say here, and in response, that side by side with the unflagging stimulation of the elements of religion and conscience must henceforth move with equal sway, science, absolute reason, and the general proportionate development of the whole man. These scientific facts, deductions, are divine too—precious counted parts of moral civilization, and, with physical health, indispensable to it, to prevent fanaticism. For abstract religion, I perceive, is easily led astray, ever credulous, and is capable of devouring remorseless, like fire and flame....We want, for these [United] States, for the general character, a cheerful, religious fervor, endued with the ever-present modifications of the human emotions, friendship, benevolence, with a fair field for scientific inquiry, the right of individual judgment, and always the cooling influences of material Nature.

Source: Walt Whitman, *Prose Works*, ed. Floyd Stovall (New York: New York University Press, 1964), vol. 2, pp. 414–415 notes 1 and 2.

*   *   *

The way some same-sex couples gained equal rights was for one of them to leave their gender status altogether and dress in the clothes of the other gender. By passing as a person of another sex, their relationship could then be accepted by neighbors who thought they were a regular heterosexual man and woman. How many same-sex couples gained acceptance by one of them hiding their true sex is impossible to know, but it was much easier at a time when passports, drivers' licenses, and identity cards were not required. Just as some light-skinned people with African ancestry passed as white, this passing option existed for a masculine female who could convince others she was really a man, or a feminine male who could convince others he was really a woman.

We know that such arrangements were not rare because numerous nineteenth-century newspaper stories reported instances when such "passing" couples were found out. Such transgendered men were discovered to be female, or transgendered women were discovered to be male, if they had to go into a hospital, or when they died and were prepared for burial by an undertaker. One such case was revealed in Black River Falls, Wisconsin, in 1894, when the local newspaper reported that a man that everyone knew as Frank Blunt, was really a female. After Blunt was jailed for theft, the sheriff discovered the prisoner's real sex. The newspaper reported that Blunt's wife came forward to pay for an attorney and to mount a court appeal. The emotion shown by the wife suggests that they had a loving relationship.

DOCUMENT 31: Females Passing as Men (1894)

Anna Morris, alias Frank Blunt, the woman who has tried to be a man for the last fifteen years, was sentenced to the penitentiary for one year by Judge Gilson at Fond du Lac. She was arrested several months ago in Milwaukee charged with stealing $175 in Fond du Lac. It was then discovered that the prisoner was a woman, although she had worn masculine attire nearly all her life. A jury convicted her of larceny and a motion for a new trial was overruled. After the sentence had been passed Gertrude Field, a woman who claimed to have married the prisoner in Eau Claire, fell upon the neck of the prisoner and wept for half an hour. The woman has furnished all the money for Blunt's defense, and now proposes to carry the case to the Supreme Court.

Source: "Anna Morris Given One Year," *The Badger State Banner*, January 18, 1894, p. 3. See also Jonathan Ned Katz, *Gay American History* (New York: Thomas Crowell, 1976) for numerous reports of passing females being married to women, and passing males being married to men.

* * *

As founder and director of the New York Society for the Suppression of Vice, Anthony Comstock led efforts to persecute all forms of sexual behavior other than heterosexual intercourse within marriage. He opposed any form of writing that discussed sex, as well as birth control, abortion, masturbation, and same-sex love. He was largely responsible for organizing a lobbying campaign that resulted in Congress passing the 1873 Act for the Suppression of Trade in, and Circulation of, Obscene Literature and Articles of Immoral Use. This act, which became known as the Comstock Law, not only suppressed erotic illustrations and writings, but even criminalized medical information on birth control and abortion. In 1900, when writer Earl Lind wrote to Comstock and suggested that the sodomy law, with a twenty-year prison term, should be repealed, Comstock strongly disagreed. Evidently not realizing that Lind himself was homosexual, Comstock referred to homosexuals as "inverts," and said that they all should be imprisoned for life.

DOCUMENT 32: Anthony Comstock Seeks to Imprison Inverts (1900)

Inverts are not fit to live with the rest of mankind. They ought to have branded in their foreheads the word "Unclean."…Instead of the law making twenty years' imprisonment the penalty for their crime, it ought to be imprisonment for life….They are willfully bad, and glory and gloat in their perversion. Their habit is acquired and not inborn. Why propose to have the law against them now on the statute books repealed? If this happened, there would be no way of getting at them. It would be wrong to make life more tolerable for them. Their lives ought to be made so intolerable as to drive them to abandon their vices.

Source: Anthony Comstock, quoted in Earl Lind, *Autobiography of an Androgyne* (New York: Medico-legal Journal, 1918), pp. 24–25.

*   *   *

At the end of World War I many people were unsettled by the Communist Revolution in Russia. Investigations, arrests and deportations of anyone suspected of being communist, or "subversive" were begun. Subversion was seen as not only political but also as moral. In this climate of suspicion and fear, the first official federal investigation of homosexuality was published by the United States Senate, *Report of the Committee on Naval Affairs, Sixty-Seventh Congress, First Session, Relative to Alleged Immoral Conditions and Practices at the Naval Training Station, Newport, R.I.* (Washington: Government Printing Office, 1921). This investigation began in 1919 when a captain at the United States Naval Training Station in Rhode Island, heard reports of homosexual activity going on between sailors and local men at the Newport YMCA. He asked some sailors to volunteer to offer themselves sexually to these men, and after they had gathered evidence by engaging in sexual activity, to report them so the men could be arrested and tried in court. After a campaign lasting over much of 1919, several sailors and civilians were arrested plus Samuel Kent, an Episcopal chaplain at the Newport YMCA.

Reverend Kent had volunteered to be a chaplain for the armed forces in World War I, and during the influenza epidemic of 1918, he willingly risked his own life to help sailors who were dying of the disease. This record of national service meant nothing to the naval prosecutors who were trying to imprison homosexuals. In the January 1920 trial of Reverend Kent, the chief of the investigator team claimed that he could tell a man was "queer" by the effeminate way he walked and talked, and that was a basis on which his operators were assigned to investigate. While several of the undercover sailors testified that Kent engaged in sex with them to the point of orgasm, the Episcopal Church came to the aid of their preacher and defended him as an excellent minister who had done much good to help many people. He was, they said, of the highest moral character. Though he admitted inviting many of the sailors to spend the night in his room at the YMCA, Kent absolutely denied doing anything sexual with these men. After a skillful defense attorney challenged the credibility of the undercover witnesses, the jury was split and a verdict of not guilty was declared.

A number of ministers of Newport churches, including Episcopal Bishop James Perry, were so upset by the tactics of the government that on January 10, 1920, they sent a protest letter to President Woodrow Wilson. While they did not attempt to defend same-sex love, the fourteen clergymen did complain about the entrapment policies being engaged in by the Navy.

DOCUMENT 33: United States Navy Entraps Homosexuals (1919)

Those of us who have been associated in social and religious work among both army and navy call your attention to certain deleterious and vicious methods employed by the Navy Department....[Naval officials who claimed] the unusual power of detecting sexual degeneracy at sight [ordered] over a score of sailors and instructed them in the details of a nameless vice and sent them through the community to practice the same in general and in particular to entrap certain designated individuals....

It must be evident to every thoughtful mind that the use of such vile methods cannot fail to undermine the character and ruin the morals of the unfortunate youths detailed for this duty, render no citizen of the community safe from suspicion and calumny, bring the city into unwarranted reproach, and shake the faith of the people in the wisdom and integrity of the naval administration....

At the earliest moment [we call upon you to] eliminate from the navy all officials, however highly placed, who are responsible for the employment of such execrable methods....The people of the United States are entitled to the assurance that hereafter nobody who enlisted in the navy will be consigned to a career of vice....

On January 22, 1920, these ministers sent another letter to U.S. Senator Carroll Page, chairman of the Senate Naval Affairs Committee, to complain about the entrapment proceedings authorized by naval officers, which

constituted an indignity [to the] people of Newport....What are we to think of such proceedings? What recourse have we? What recourse has any innocent citizen accused by these depraved persons?

Source: Lawrence R. Murphy, *Perverts by Official Order: The Campaign Against Homo-sexuals by the United States Navy* (New York: Harrington Park Press, 1988), pp. 156–157, 161.

* * *

In 1897 Dr. Magnus Hirschfeld and other German homosexuals founded the Scientific Humanitarian Committee to challenge antihomosexual laws and attitudes in Germany. This organization, which soon became the nucleus of an international effort to organize "sexual intermediates," began sponsoring research and publication about same-sex love in different cultures throughout history. In 1906 and 1907 two directors of the Committee's Institute for Sexual Research, based in Berlin, gave several lectures in the United States, speaking before medical and scientific societies. The American free-speech lecturer Emma Goldman, who spoke out publicly in defense of homosexuals, complimented the work of this Institute.

DOCUMENT 34: Society for Human Rights (1924)

Perhaps the most striking impact of the German homosexual rights movement was due to a young American soldier named Henry Gerber. From 1920 to 1923, Gerber had served in the United States Army of Occupation in Germany. While there, he subscribed to German homosexual rights movement magazines, and visited Berlin to see the workings of Hirschfeld's Institute. When Gerber returned to the United States and took a job in the post office in Chicago, he wrote later in *ONE Magazine*:

I bitterly felt the injustice with which my own American society accused the homosexual of "immoral acts." I hated this society which allowed the majority, frequently corrupt itself, to persecute those who deviated from the established norms in sexual matters. What could be done about it, I thought. Unlike Germany, where the homosexual was partially organized and where sex legislation was uniform for the whole country, the United States was in a condition of chaos and misunderstanding concerning its sex laws, and no one was trying to unravel the tangle and bring relief to the abused....

I realized at once that homosexuals themselves needed nearly as much attention as the laws pertaining to their acts. How could one go about such a difficult task? The prospect of going to jail did not bother me. I had a vague idea that I wanted to help solve the problem. I had not yet read the opinion of Clarence Darrow that "no other offence has ever been visited with such severe penalties as seeking to help the oppressed." All my friends to whom I spoke about my plans advised against my doing anything so rash and futile. I thought to myself that if I succeeded I might become known to history as deliverer of the downtrodden, even as Lincoln. But I am not sure my thoughts were entirely upon fame. If I succeeded in freeing the homosexual, I too would benefit.

Source: Henry Gerber, "The Society for Human Rights—1925," *ONE Magazine* volume 10, n. 9 (September 1962), pp. 5–10.

*   *   *

With this purpose in mind, Gerber wrote a declaration of purpose for a "Society for Human Rights," whose name was inspired by the German homosexual rights movement. Gerber's idea became the earliest documented gay rights organization in the United States, which was chartered by the State of Illinois on December 10, 1924. Gerber persuaded six of his friends to serve on the group's board of directors, and to sign the incorporation papers of this nonprofit society. The charter of the Society for Human Rights states that its purpose is

to promote and to protect the interests of people who by reasons of mental and physical abnormalities [sic] are abused and hindered in the legal pursuit of happiness which is guaranteed them by the Declaration of Independence, and to combat the public prejudices against them.

Source: State of Illinois, Cook County, Incorporation of the Society for Human Rights, Chicago, December 10, 1924. Reprinted in Jonathan Ned Katz, *Gay American History* (New York: Thomas Crowell, 1976), pp. 386–387.

*   *   *

With no questions by the office of the Illinois Secretary of State, which approved the Society's charter, Henry Gerber's next goal was to organize a lecture series to attract as many homosexuals as possible, to get them to join the Society for Human Rights. Then he wanted to publish a magazine called *Friendship and Freedom* to educate homosexuals and keep them in touch with each other. After organizing homosexual activists, Gerber envisioned lobbying legal authorities and legislators to educate them about the reality of homosexuals' lives, and to stop the imprisonment of homosexuals. Writing in *ONE Magazine* years later, Gerber remembered the problems he had in trying to organize his initial group:

The first difficulty was in rounding up enough members and contributors so the work could go forward. The average homosexual, I found, was ignorant concerning himself. Others were fearful. Still others were frantic or depraved. Some were blasé....We wondered how we could accomplish anything with such resistance from our own people....

As secretary of the new organization I wrote to many prominent persons soliciting their support....I then set about putting out the first issue of *Friendship and Freedom* and worked hard on the second issue. It soon became apparent that my friends were illiterate and penniless. I had to both write and finance. Two issues, alas, were all we could publish. The most difficult task was to get men of good reputation to back up the Society. I needed noted medical authorities to endorse us. But they usually refused to endanger their reputations. The only support I got was from poor people....I realized this start was dead wrong, but after all, movements always start small and only by organizing first and correcting mistakes later could we expect to go on at all. The Society was bound to become a success, we felt, considering the modest but honest plan of operation. It would probably take long years to develop into anything worth while. Yet I was willing to slave and suffer and risk losing my job and savings and even my liberty for the ideal.

One of our greatest handicaps was the knowledge that homosexuals don't organize. Being thoroughly cowed, they seldom get together. Most feel that as long as some homosexual acts are against the law, they should not let their names be on any homosexual organization's mailing list any more than notorious bandits would join a thieves' union....

Unknown to Gerber, the Society's vice president Al Meininger had a wife and child. When his wife became suspicious that her husband was bisexual, she told a social worker who called the police. Al was forced to confess about his involvement in the Society for Human Rights, whereupon the other directors were all arrested. Gerber remembered that late one night a police detective and a newspaper reporter for the Chicago *Examiner* barged into his home:

He told me he had orders from his precinct captain to bring me to the police station. He took my typewriter, my notary public diploma, and all the literature of the Society and also personal diaries as well as my bookkeeping accounts. At no time did he show a warrant for my arrest. At the police station I was locked up in a cell but no charges were made against me....[The next morning I saw] a copy of the *Examiner*. There right on the front page I found this incredible story: "Strange Sex Cult Exposed." The article mentioned Al who had brought his male friends home....A raid of the flat, the report continued, had turned up...a pamphlet of this "strange sex cult" which "urged men to leave their wives and children."

What an outright untruth; what a perversion of facts....The police, I suppose, had hoped or expected to find us in bed. They could not imagine homosexuals in any other way. My property was taken without excuse. This...with the Constitution [supposed] to protect the people from unreasonable arrest and search. Shades of the Holy Inquisition....

In the Chicago Avenue Police Court, the detective triumphantly produced a powder puff which he claimed he found in my room. That was the sole evidence of my crime. It was admitted as evidence of my effeminacy. I have never in my life used rouge or powder. The young social worker, a hatchet-faced female, read from my diary, out of context: "I love Karl." The detective and the judge shuddered over such depravity. To the already prejudiced court we were obviously guilty. We were guilty just by being homosexual. This was the court's conception of our "strange cult."

The judge spoke little to us and adjourned court with the remark he thought ours was a violation of the federal law against sending obscene matter through the mails. Nothing in our first issue of *Friendship and Freedom* could be considered "obscene" of course....The following Thursday the four of us were taken before the same judge. This time two post office inspectors were also present. Before the judge appeared in court, one of the inspectors promised that he would see to it that we got heavy prison sentences for infecting God's own country.

As the trial began, our attorney demanded that we be set free since no stitch of evidence existed to hold us. The judge became angry and ordered our attorney to shut up or be cited for contempt. The post office inspectors said that the federal commissioner would take the case under advisement from the obscenity angle....[After being released on bail] I went down to the post office to report for work. But I was told that I had been suspended—more of the dirty work of the post office inspectors. Next I called upon the managing editor of the *Examiner*. I confronted him with the article in the paper. He told me he would look into the matter and make corrections, but nothing was ever done. I had no means to sue the paper, and that was the end of that....

The experience generally convinced me that we were up against a solid wall of ignorance, hypocrisy, meanness and corruption. The wall had won....After a few weeks a letter from Washington arrived advising me that I had been officially dismissed from the Post Office Department for "conduct unbecoming a postal worker." That definitely meant the end of the Society for Human Rights.

Source: Henry Gerber, "The Society for Human Rights—1925," *ONE Magazine* v. 10, n. 9 (September 1962), pp. 5–10.

*   *   *

A major controversy beginning in 1928 revolved around a well-known female novelist in England, Radclyffe Hall, who published a book that dared to depict sexual inversion. Hall, herself a mannish person who went by the nickname of "John," would today perhaps be referred to as either transgender or butch. She wrote her novel *The Well of Loneliness* to present an invert as a sympathetic main character. Many readers today would consider the book horribly apologetic and tragic, but it was a brave attempt to stand up for the rights of female-loving females. It is widely considered to be the first modern lesbian novel.

When the book was published in an American edition, it became an instant best seller. In response, the Society for the Suppression of Vice filed a complaint in the New York City Magistrate's Court, claiming that this book violated the New York State Penal Code law on indecent literature. Over eight hundred copies of *The Well of Loneliness* were seized by police, and the book's New York publisher, Donald S. Friede, was brought to trial. While Magistrate Hyman Bushel admitted that the book was a well-written work of literature that did not contain explicit descriptions of sex, he ruled on February 21, 1929, that the book should be suppressed simply because it argued in favor of the social acceptance of same-sex love. His decision is quoted below.

Donald Friede appealed Magistrate Bushel's decision, and on April 19, 1929, a three-man New York City appellate court unanimously held that *The Well of Loneliness* was not obscene. This legal battle was important as a highly publicized case that set the stage for a more public discussion of the rights of homosexuals to establish same-sex relationships.

DOCUMENT 35: *The Well of Loneliness* (1929)

The book here involved is a novel dealing with the childhood and early womanhood of a female invert....The book culminates with an extended elaboration upon her intimate relations with a normal young girl, who becomes a helpless subject of her perverted influence and passion, and pictures the struggle for this girl's affections between this invert and a man from whose normal advances she herself had previously recoiled, because of her own perverted nature....

The author has treated these incidents not without some restraint; nor is it disputed that the book has literary merit. To quote the people's brief: "It is a well written, carefully constructed piece of fiction, and contains no unclean words." Yet the narrative does not veer from its central theme....The unnatural and depraved relationships portrayed are sought to be idealized and extolled. The characters in the book who indulge in these vices are described in attractive terms, and it is maintained throughout that they be accepted on the same plane as persons normally constituted, and that their perverse and inverted love is as worthy as the affection between normal beings and should be considered just as sacred by society.

The book can have no moral value, since it seeks to justify the right of a pervert to prey upon normal members of a community, and to uphold such relationship as noble and lofty. Although it pleads for tolerance...it does not argue for repression or moderation of insidious impulses. An idea of the moral tone which the book assumes may be gained from the attitude taken by its principal character [who complains about those who] "try and make me ashamed of my love. I'm not ashamed of it; there's no shame in me."

The theme of the novel is not only antisocial and offensive to public morals and decency, but the method in which it is developed, in its highly emotional way attracting and focusing attention upon perverted ideas and unnatural vices, and seeking to justify and idealize them, is strongly calculated to corrupt and debase those members of the community who would be susceptible to its immoral influence....The courts [have] the duty of protecting the weaker members of society from corrupt, depraving, and lecherous influences, although exerted through the guise and medium of literature, drama or art. The public policy so declared was reaffirmed by the Legislature by its recent amendment to the Penal Law, making it a misdemeanor to prepare, advertise, or present any drama, play, etc., dealing with the subject of sex degeneracy or sex perversion....I am convinced that "The Well of Loneliness" tends to debauch public morals, that its subject matter is offensive to public decency, and that it is calculated to deprave and corrupt minds open to its immoral influences.

Source: People v. Friede, City Magistrate Hyman Bushel's Court of New York City, February 21, 1929. For background information on this case, see Jonathan Ned Katz, *Gay American History* (New York: Thomas Crowell, 1976), pp. 397–405.

*   *   *

A mother in America wrote to the famous Austrian psychiatrist Sigmund Freud, asking him if he could treat her son. Influenced by the German homosexual rights movement of Magnus Hirschfeld and his British ally Havelock Ellis, Freud wrote back to the woman, in English, indicating his accepting view of homosexuality and his opinion that psychoanalysis might help him live productively as a well-adjusted homosexual. He held out little hope that the son's homosexual desires would disappear, and implied that the mother should accept her son as he was.

DOCUMENT 36: Sigmund Freud on Homosexuality (1935)

I gather from your letter that your son is a homosexual....Homosexuality is assuredly no advantage but it is nothing to be ashamed of, no vice, no degradation, it cannot be classified as an illness; we consider it to be a variation of the sexual function produced by a certain arrest of sexual development. Many highly respectable individuals of ancient and modern times have been homosexuals, several of the greatest men among them (Plato, Michelangelo, Leonardo da Vinci, etc.). It is a great injustice to persecute homosexuality as a crime and a cruelty too. If you do not believe me, read the books of Havelock Ellis.

By asking me if I can help, you mean, I suppose, if I can abolish homosexuality and make normal heterosexuality take its place. The answer is, in a general way, we cannot promise to achieve it. In a certain number of cases we succeed in developing the blighted germs of heterosexual tendencies which are present in every homosexual, [but] in the majority of cases it is no more possible. It is a question of the quality and the age of the individual. The result of treatment cannot be predicted.

What [psychiatric] analysis can do for your son, runs in a different line. If he is unhappy, neurotic, torn by conflicts, inhibited in his social life, analysis may bring him harmony, peace of mind, full efficiency, whether he remains a homosexual or gets changed. If you make up your mind he should have analysis with me—I don't expect you will—he has to come over to Vienna. I have no intention of leaving here. However don't neglect to give me your answer.

Sincerely yours with kind wishes,

S. Freud

Source: Sigmund Freud, "Letter to an American Mother," *International Journal of Psychoanalysis* 32 (1951), p. 331.

* * *

The first known case of a woman challenging a sodomy law conviction occurred in Atlanta when Ella Thompson appealed her case to the Georgia Supreme Court. She had been arrested by Fulton County Sheriff J. C. Aldredge for having oral sex with another woman, and was convicted in the county superior court for violating Georgia's sodomy law. The language of sodomy laws differed widely from state to state, and the text of Georgia's sodomy law did not mention sex between two women. While she was being held in prison, Thompson's attorney appealed her conviction. On January 12, 1939, the Georgia Supreme Court issued a unanimous ruling that the crime of sodomy, as defined in the statute, could not be accomplished between two women. While this case did not challenge the constitutionality of the sodomy law, it did prevent lesbians from being prosecuted. As such, Thompson's legal appeal represents an early example of lesbian resistance to oppression. The Supreme Court ruled in her case that, even though her same-sex behavior was "loathsome," the law as it was written could not prosecute woman-to-woman sex.

DOCUMENT 37: Lesbian Challenges Georgia's Sodomy Law (1939)

This record presents the question whether the crime of sodomy, as defined by our law, can be accomplished between two women. By Code...sodomy is defined as "the carnal knowledge and connection against the order of nature, by man with man, or in the same unnatural manner with woman." Wharton, in his Criminal Law...lays down the rule that "the crime of sodomy proper can not be accomplished between two women, though the crime of bestiality may be." We have no reason to believe that our lawmakers in defining the crime of sodomy intended to give it any different meaning. Indeed the language of the Code above quoted seems to us to deliberately exclude the idea that this particular crime may be accomplished by two women, although it may be committed by two men, or a man and a woman. That the act here alleged to have been committed is just as loathsome when participated in by two women does not justify us in reading into the definition of the crime something which the lawmakers omitted.

The petitioner's conviction was a nullity and she is entitled to be discharged.

Source: Thompson v. Aldredge, 200 S.E. 799: 187 Ga. 467. *South Eastern Reporter*, vol. 200 (Jan.–March 1939) (St. Paul, MN: West, 1939), pp. 799–800.

*   *   *

World War II provided an unprecedented opportunity for young lesbians and gay men. The Japanese bombing of Hawai'i created an urgent need for troops to fight against Japan and its German and Italian allies. President Franklin Roosevelt, who did not object to his wife Eleanor's same-sex relationship with newspaperwoman Lorena Hitchcock, generally took a hands-off attitude toward homosexuality. He realized that winning the war against fascist dictatorships was more important than persecuting homosexuals. As a consequence, during the war many homosexuals were able to live in the largely single-sex environment of the armed forces without much harassment. The war also created a unique opportunity for unmarried women to work in a comparatively nondiscriminating environment. Lesbians especially flocked to the newly established Women's Army Corps (WAC). Since WAC rules specifically forbade married women from serving, and gave strong emphasis to keeping the women away from men in order to prevent pregnancies, high percentages of these women paired up in same-sex relationships. As long as they kept a low profile, most army officers did not bother them.

However, after 1945, when the armed forces no longer needed every warm body to help win the war, the army turned with a vengeance to rid itself of "sex perverts." One of the officers who tried to remove lesbians under his command was General Dwight Eisenhower. One of his assistants was Nell "Johnnie" Phelps (1922–1997), who became known as the WAC who stood up to the general. Johnnie was later an activist for lesbian and women's rights. She died in 1997 and her ashes are buried in the United States Veterans Cemetery in Los Angeles.

DOCUMENT 38: Lesbians in the Women's Army Corps (1945)

[During World War II Johnnie] enlisted in the newly created Women's Army Corps. She was sent to the South Pacific to work as a medic and lost her first [female] lover when their boat was bombed as they landed on Leyte, Philippines, in 1944. Later during that tour of duty, Johnnie was wounded and received a Purple Heart [commendation medal]. When her tour was over she reenlisted and was sent to Germany as part of the Post-WWII "Occupation" forces....

Later, Johnnie was assigned to head the motor pool for General Eisenhower's battalion. One day he asked her to prepare a list of lesbians in the units. She gave her now-famous answer: "If the general pleases, I'll be happy to do this, but you have to know that the first name on the list will be mine." At that point Eisenhower's secretary added that Sergeant Phelps's name would be second on the list and hers would be first, since she was going to type it. Johnnie estimated that 97% of the women in the units were lesbian and told the general that he would basically lose most of the battalion. She also reminded the general that the group of approximately 900 women had had no "illegal pregnancies, AWOLS or misconducts," and that every six months while under his command, they had received commendations for meritorious service. Eisenhower told them to forget the order, but later when he was President and the McCarthy witch-hunts ruined the lives of many Gays and Lesbians, Eisenhower did not intervene.

Source: Yolanda Retter, "Her/Story: Johnnie Phelps, The WAC Who Stood Up to General Eisenhower," *ONE-IGLA Bulletin* n. 5 (Summer 1998), pp. 4–5.

*   *   *

Despite the early statements of Sigmund Freud that homosexual desire is not something that psychiatry can eliminate, or that it should try to do so, many psychiatrists tried to do precisely that. Typical of many psychiatric writings is a 1945 article by Professor Thomas Moore of the Catholic University of America. Unlike most psychiatrists, Moore included his religious views in claiming that it is the duty of every person to become heterosexually married and procreate offspring. Moore explicitly opposed repeal of antihomosexual sodomy laws, on the basis that the only acceptable choices for homosexuals are either to try to become heterosexual, or to become nonsexual and cut off all personal attachments to members of the same sex.

DOCUMENT 39: Psychiatrists Oppose Homosexual Rights Laws (1945)

Various movements have been started in a number of nations to do away with penal laws against homosexuality. Before one lends support to such a movement, he should consider something more than the problem whether or not the homosexual is a sick man or a criminal. Homosexuality is to a very large extent an acquired abnormality and propagates itself as a morally contagious disease. It tends to build up a society with even a kind of language of its own, and certainly with practices foreign to those of normal society. It tends to bring about more and more unfruitful unions that withdraw men and women from normal family life, the development of homes, and the procreation of children. The growth of a homosexual society in any country is a menace, more or less serious, to the welfare of the state....Granted that some homosexuality may have a biological factor, it is still a matter of importance to control the spread of homosexuality due to psychological causes. Furthermore, it is not evident that homosexuals in whom there is perhaps a biological trend to homosexuality cannot with some effort make a normal heterosexual adjustment. Laws that would countenance the supposed biological rights of homosexuals would therefore rest on false foundations....

It would be malpractice for a psychiatrist to help the [homosexual] patient to remain in his pathological condition and feel more comfortable in its perpetuation....If we examine the matter objectively, trying to rise above the clouds of passion and desire, we will admit that a human being comes into the world to use his powers and functions in the service of God and the social order....Sex pleasure is associated with genital function in married life that children may be sought and brought into the world.

Source: Thomas V. Moore, "The Pathogenesis and Treatment of Homosexual Disorders: A Digest of Some Pertinent Evidence," *Journal of Personality* (Durham, N.C.) 14 (1945), p. 57.

* * *

Edythe Eyde is an example of how one person, working alone, can help to change society. In 1947, while she was working as a secretary for a movie production company in Burbank, California, she was inspired to produce a lesbian magazine. Because established printers would have refused to print such a publication, she was forced to type out multiple carbon copies on a manual typewriter. At the time she planned the magazine, she had not yet met any other lesbians, but she knew she was attracted only to women. In 1946 she had met other young women who lived in the same Los Angeles rooming house as she did. While chatting with them, she mentioned to her neighbors that she had no interest in dating men.

DOCUMENT 40: *Vice Versa*, America's First Lesbian Magazine (1947)

These girls looked at me and said, "Are you gay?" I said, "Well, I try to be as happy as I can under the circumstances." And they sort of snickered, and I didn't quite know what they meant—and yet I did. But I wasn't going to commit myself. So then they explained [gay], and I said, "Oh yes, I feel very much that way too, but I don't know anyone." They said, "Well, come with us next Saturday, and we'll take you to a place. And how would you like to go to a softball game with us?" I said, "OK." Actually, I hate sports, but I was interested in going and meeting a lot of [women. After the game]…they took me down to a place called the If Café.…

When we walked in, there were several girls dancing together, and I thought, Gee, how nice! And as we eased ourselves into a booth, why, somebody came out carrying a birthday cake with candles, and they sang Happy Birthday to some girl with it, and my ol' eyes just brimmed with tears, and I thought, Oh isn't this wonderful to be among girls who like girls! You know, I'd never seen anything like it. So I got up and had a few dances with them. Some of the cute things would come over to me and say, "Would you care to dance?" [Grins] And I'd say, "Mm-hmm," and I'd go and dance. So I came back there again and again and again. I thought it was a wonderful place. Actually, looking back, it was a dive.…

[I never wanted to have sex with a man,] however, I love my gay brothers. The gay boys would always say, "Well, my company is having its annual banquet at such-and-such, and we have to show up with a girlfriend; would you go with me that night?" And I'd say, "Sure," and I'd go and have a ball! I would get into a dress—well, I mean, I always wore dresses anyway—and shamble on down there with him and sit at the table, and everybody that he associated with at the office just assumed that I was his girlfriend.…

You had to really keep up an act. It wasn't like today at all. I never dreamed that I'd see the day when people would be outspoken about it at the office. I mean, in my day, if you were [discovered] they would fire you.

"No queers around here; we don't need your kind!" You had to stand for it; I mean, you just did....

The prevailing opinion of the time in different articles that appeared in the more serious things like *Reader's Digest* or some psychology magazines [was] the doctors believed that we hadn't quite matured enough to go on with a heterosexual relationship....I wasn't going to change because some book said I was a certain way. What do they know? They aren't me....

[One time when visiting a gay bar in Santa Monica, California, I saw] a bunch of policemen came in, and I thought Uh-oh. I had on slacks, but I had on my little red, sparkly earrings and some beads, I think, or a froufrou blouse to go with them and long hair, you know. And the police came over with tablets and pencils, and they said, gruffly, "What's your name?" And the music was playing so loud. So when they got to me I looked them right in the eye and said, "My name is Edythe Eyde!" And he said, "What's that?" And I said "Edythe Eyde!" Well, they couldn't tell. And he wrote something down, but I knew damn well that he didn't write anything [real] down. He couldn't tell my name or how it was spelled, and I wasn't going to spell it for him.

So then he went on to somebody else because he'd got a look at my long hair and earrings and decided I wasn't one of *those*. So then he went to a bunch of boys, and they were all sitting around a table. And there was one [feminine-looking] guy....so the police gathered around him in a circle. I had the uncomfortable feeling that they made him take his pants down to see if he was a boy or a girl. I didn't look too closely because I would have been too embarrassed, but they hid him from us anyway. And then they let him sit down again. But I thought, what a humiliating thing if that is what really happened. So then the cops stomped out. And I said, "Well, girls, I think I'll go home." And they said, "Oh, don't go yet." And I said, "Why?" And they said, "Because they lurk outside, and if anyone leaves early, then they harass them again." So I waited a full half hour or so before I left, and then I got in my car and drove home. I never went back to that place again....

[In 1947] I got the idea that there should be a gay magazine for girls. I started this magazine before I knew any [gay] girls. But I had to have sort of a fantasy life because I wasn't having much of a life that way of my own, so I devised this little magazine. At the time I was working at a place where the boss was out a lot. And he said, "I don't care what you do, as long as you look busy. If you get your work done, then you can type personal letters or anything like that, but I don't want you sitting around reading books and magazines. As long as you look busy, I don't care." So I devised this little magazine....I got the carbon paper they had in those days—they didn't have duplicating machines—and I would run it through eight copies at a time, twice. This was a heck of a lot of work. Then I would go and filch some manila folders from the supply, and I would put all these pages in there, nice and neat, staple them together. Voila! I had a magazine! I thought, well, I'll save these magazines, and then when I meet some girls, I'll distribute them. So when I met these girls [at the If Café], I distributed these maga-zines....I had no guidelines to go by; I just had to sort of make them up in my head as I went along.

Well, I would ask these girls, as I got to know them later, "Come on now, submit a story." Or, "Wouldn't you like to write a poem or movie review or something for this magazine?" "Oh, yeah, I'll think about it." They were too busy living it to care. But they always wanted the magazine. I gave it away; I never charged for it because it was a labor of my heart, and I felt that it would be almost like being a prostitute to charge. In the magazine too, somewhere in the pages, I said, "Now, when you get through with this, don't throw it away; pass it along to the next girl, keep it going, because I may not always be able to write these." And that was very prophetic because after that job ter-minated there, I wasn't [able to do it at the next office]....

I did eight or nine [issues]. I would get an occasional submission of something or other, which I was really honorbound to print, no matter how bad it was, and I used no names—there was no "poem by so-and-so, story by so-and-so": you couldn't tell who wrote what because I thought I better not use names. In those days everything had to be rather hush-hush. I did-n't even mention Los Angeles or San Francisco; you couldn't tell what city the magazine came from. But I would go down to the If Café and pass these things out until one of the girls told me, "Hey, you shouldn't bring those things here because if they catch you with them, they'll put you in jail!" I said, "Why? There's no four-letter words or dirty stories in it." She said, "It doesn't matter—if it's gay, they'll put you in jail." So that tipped me off, and I didn't do that anymore. I used to blithely mail them out through the mail. Gee, I was naïve. They had no pictures in them; the stories were not sexy at all, you know. But these girls put me wise. So then I just handed them out personally.

Source: "Edythe Eyde," in Zsa Zsa Gershick, *Gay Old Girls* (Los Angeles: Alyson Books, 1998), pp. 47–53, 57–60.

*   *   *

Edythe Eyde wrote this article and printed it in her lesbian magazine *Vice Versa* in 1947. Her predictions were amazingly accurate, and prophetic.

DOCUMENT 41: *Vice Versa* Predictions (1947)

Whether the unsympathetic majority approves or not, it looks as though the third sex is here to stay. With the advancement of psychiatry and related subjects, the world is becoming more and more aware that there are those in our midst who feel no attraction for the opposite sex....[Lesbian-themed] books such as *Diana* and *The Well of Loneliness* are available in inexpensive editions at book marts and even the corner drugstores. With such knowledge being disseminated through fact and fiction to the public in general, homosexuality is becoming less and less a taboo subject, and although still considered by the general public as contemptible or treated with derision, I venture to predict that there will be a time in the future when gay folk will be accepted as part of regular society....

Perhaps even *Vice Versa* might be the forerunner of better magazines dedicated to the third sex, which in some future time might take their rightful place on the newsstands beside other publications, to be available openly and without restriction to those who wish to read them....

In days gone by, when woman's domain was restricted to the fireside, marriage and a family was her only prospect, the home was the little world around which life revolved, and in which, unless wives were fortunate enough to have help, they had to perform innumerable household chores besides assuming the responsibility of bearing children. But in these days of frozen foods, motion picture palaces, compact apartments, modern innovations, and female independence, there is no reason why a woman should have to look to a man for food and shelter in return for raising his children and keeping his house in order unless she really wants to. Today, a woman may live independently from man if she so chooses and carve out her own career. Never before have circumstances and conditions been so suitable for those of lesbian tendencies.

Source: Edythe Eyde, "Here to Stay," *Vice Versa—America's Gayest Magazine* v. 1, n. 4 (September 1947), p. 1. Copy in ONE Institute/International Gay and Lesbian Archives.

*   *   *

In 1950 Congress was almost evenly split between Democrats and Republicans. The Republicans, who had been the minority party since 1933, used every possible argument to embarrass the Democratic administration of President Harry S. Truman and gain a majority in Congress. The Republicans, led by Senator Joseph McCarthy, claimed that the United States Department of State was infiltrated by communists. When Undersecretary of State John Peurifoy testified before a Senate committee investigating the loyalty of government workers, he admitted that ninety-one State Department employees had resigned since 1947 while under investigation for being security risks. In order to assure the senators that this had nothing to do with communism, he said that most of those who resigned were homosexuals. Instead of deflating the issue, the revelation inspired Republicans to begin a new investigation. Suddenly, in 1950, homosexuality became a major political issue.

After the head of the Washington, D.C. vice squad, police lieutenant Roy E. Blick, told the Senate that he guessed there were about 5,000 homosexual perverts in Washington, and that probably 3,750 worked for the federal government, the Senate ordered an investigation. Senator Kenneth Wherry, the Republican floor leader, chaired the Senate subcommittee. Without offering even one example of a case where this actually happened, Senator Wherry claimed that homosexuals could be blackmailed by communist spies, and thus were security risks.

Within a few months the Senate Investigations Subcommittee of the Committee on Expenditures presented its report. While the investigators interviewed numerous psychiatrists, physicians, and law enforcement officers, they evidently did not interview any open homosexuals themselves. They focused on the most effective way to fire government employees who were homosexual, rather than discussing whether such firings were advisable. The report stated with pride that between 1947 and 1950 over 1,700 applicants for federal jobs were denied employment because they had a police record of arrest for homosexuality. The committee called for the F.B.I. and police to conduct more extensive investigations into the sexual practices of employees in the future.

DOCUMENT 42: Employment of Homosexuals and Other Sex Perverts (1950)

The primary objective of the subcommittee in this inquiry was to determine the extent of the employment of homosexuals and other sex perverts in Government; to consider reasons why their employment by the Government is undesirable; and to examine into the efficacy of the methods used in dealing with the problem....Psychiatric physicians generally agree that indulgence in sexually perverted practices indicates a personality which has failed to reach sexual maturity....Homosexuals and other sex perverts are not proper persons to be employed in Government for two reasons; first, they are generally unsuitable, and second, they constitute security risks....

Persons who commit such acts are law violators. Aside from the criminality and immorality involved in sex perversion such behavior is so contrary to the normal accepted standards of social behavior that persons who engage in such activity are looked upon as outcasts by society generally. The social stigma attached to sex perversion is so great that many perverts go to great lengths to conceal their perverted tendencies. This situation is evidenced by the fact that perverts are frequently victimized by blackmailers who threaten to expose their sexual deviations....

Those who engage in overt acts of perversion lack the emotional stability of normal persons. In addition there is an abundance of evidence to sustain the conclusion that indulgence in acts of sex perversion weakens the moral fiber of an individual to a degree that he is not suitable for a position of responsibility. Most of the authorities agree and our investigation has shown that the presence of a sex pervert in a Government agency tends to have a corrosive influence upon his fellow employees. These perverts will frequently attempt to entice normal individuals to engage in perverted practices....One homosexual can pollute a Government office.

Another point to be considered in determining whether a sex pervert is suitable for Government employment is his tendency to gather other perverts about him. Eminent psychiatrists have informed the subcommittee that the homosexual is likely to seek his own kind....It is almost inevitable that he will attempt to place other homosexuals in Government jobs....The lack of emotional stability which is found in most sex perverts and the weakness of their moral fiber, makes them susceptible to the blandishments of the foreign espionage agent....Espionage organizations the world over consider sex perverts who are in possession of or have access to confidential material to be prime targets where pressure can be exerted....

There is no place in the United States Government for persons who violate the laws or the accepted standards of morality, or who otherwise bring disrepute to the Federal service by infamous or scandalous personal conduct. Such persons are not suitable for Government positions and in the case of doubt the American people are entitled to have errors of judgment...resolved on the side of caution.

Source: United States Senate Investigations Subcommittee of the Committee on Expenditures, *Employment of Homosexuals and Other Sex Perverts in the U.S. Government* (Washington: Government Printing Office, 1950).

Part III

Civil Rights and Civil Liberties: The Making of a Gay and Lesbian Movement in the United States, 1950–1977

By 1950 there existed, at least in some of the big cities of the United States, a growing population of homosexually inclined men and women with a developing sense of identity. The intellectual origins of this identity can be traced to the ideas of individual freedom contained in the Declaration of Independence, the Constitution, and the Bill of Rights. While these documents may have voiced noble sentiments of liberty, those democratic ideals were not enacted for sexual nonconformists. Persecution continued, as it had in the colonial era, based on a religious concept that same-sex behavior was a sin so horrible it should not be spoken among Christians. Just as with women, Native Americans, African Americans, and other racial minorities, for sexual minorities the promises of equal rights took another two centuries after the Revolution before substantial accomplishments could be made. The cultural war of freedom versus conformity has been the core conflict of the history of the United States, and the struggle for both women's rights and gay-lesbian rights reflect this battle.

For those who were attracted to their own sex, opportunities to meet others like themselves mainly centered in the big cities. Simply because so many people had their own jobs, to support themselves individually without the interference from meddling relatives and neighbors, life in a big city gave more people an opportunity to follow their own desires and construct their own lifestyles. Even if it only involved being able to sneak off to a public park after work, or to congregate in a tavern or restaurant, the city offered opportunities to meet others who were looking for lovers of the same sex. One could keep one's privacy from one's employer and one's landlord.

The participation of the United States in World War II would increase this trend in ways that United States military leaders never imagined. Supporting the war effort meant an unprecedented mobilization of young men and women. By uprooting so many people from their villages and hometowns, and throwing them together in large port cities where they worked at defense plants or prepared to embark for the battlefronts, the mobilization gave those with same-sex desires an opportunity to meet others who shared their attractions. At the end of the war, many of these people decided to settle in the cities where they could pursue a gay and lesbian social life. This social life, with its participation in bars and other entertainment venues, became the building blocks for a growing sense of community. And with a social network there gradually developed, at least among some individuals, a sense of identity. People who found a community of others like themselves now felt a freedom to associate. They met friends, sexual partners, and colleagues. Political organization, however, was far from the minds of most people until they were forced to start standing up for their right to be left alone.

The conflict between these individual desires for socializing and conformist pressures for social control produced raids of gay bars by police, the imprisonment of those caught in sexual acts, and a massive politicalization of homosexuality as a public issue in 1950. In response to this political attack, and the very real threat of police oppression, homosexuals began to organize to protect their rights. If the oppression had not been so real, it is doubtful that a politicized gay and lesbian movement ever would have arisen. The movement that began in Los Angeles in 1950 has not ended. Everything since that point has been an evolution of the basic idea of rights.

The 1950s marked an emergence of what became known as the homophile movement. With the founding of three main groups: Mattachine Society (1950), ONE (1952), and Daughters of Bilitis (1955), activists were able to organize and publicize an active effort to gain more rights. By resisting arrest, filing court challenges, publishing magazines and books, reaching out to academic researchers and the media, and sponsoring national conventions, the 1950s groups promoted a stronger sense of identity that formed the basis for building a community. They were still small in number, but their voices were being increasingly heard. Larger numbers of homosexuals could grow beyond thinking they were the only person in the world who felt same-sex desires.

The 1960s marked a further evolution for this beginning homophile movement, represented by two events that occurred as the decade began. First, ONE Institute held a national conference in 1961 at which the organizers called for "A Homosexual Bill of Rights." This civil liberties approach proved to be controversial in 1961, but it would soon be taken up by the American Civil Liberties Union and other groups. Second, Jose Sarria became the first openly gay person to run for public office on a platform of civil rights for homosexuals. The fact that he got 7,000 votes in his first attempt for the race for the San Francisco board of supervisors revolutionized city politics. This gave gay men and lesbians in San Francisco an inkling that it would be possible for them to band together to elect one of their own to public office. That dream was fulfilled in San Francisco with the election of Harvey Milk to the board of supervisors in 1977.

The homophile movement was transformed in the 1960s as a result of several larger trends occurring in the United States. First was the influence of the sexual revolution. Prompted by advances in medical treatments for sexually transmitted diseases, and also the invention of a birth control pill, more people felt free to engage in sex outside of marriage. With the twin dangers of pregnancy and disease reduced, there were fewer reasons for people to repress their sexuality. The right to have sex with whomever one chose became the guiding light of the sexual revolution. As heterosexuals became more open about sex for the sake of enjoyment, even outside the bonds of matrimony, this opened the door for homosexuals also to claim the right to enjoy sex with the partner of their choice. Consensual relationships, rather than heterosexual marriage, became the new moral arbiter for sex.

The second major influence was the civil rights movement. As racial issues came to the forefront of the news, homosexuals became inspired to participate in the struggle for equality for African Americans. Many white participants in the civil rights marches were gay or lesbian, perhaps because they had seen firsthand how the police and the government could cause real oppression in peoples' lives. Even those who did not participate, however, now had a new perspective on the need for people to stand up for themselves by engaging in protest demonstrations. The gay and lesbian rights movement since 1960 is in many ways a child of the African American civil rights movement.

The third trend came from the women's liberation movement. Women's rights as an issue had declined in the United States after the 1920 passage of the Nineteenth Amendment giving women the vote, but female activism reemerged in the 1960s. Due partly to the same forces that brought about the sexual revolution and the civil rights movement, women moved beyond the issue of suffrage to focus on individual liberation—"the personal is political"—and to challenge the Judeo-Christian view that women should be submissive and dependent. Women's lib calls for women to be able to have control over their own bodies resonated with those struggling for the rights of sexual minorities.

The fourth trend grew out of the protests against the war in Vietnam. By using even more confrontational tactics than the civil rights movement, the antiwar protesters brought their viewpoint to the mass media. Gay and lesbian activists saw that these tactics were effective, and actually prompted changes in government and society. The protests led to a questioning of authority, and the established way of doing things, in all areas of life including sexuality.

The fifth trend is the emergence of a counterculture in the 1960s, especially among the young generation that had been so affected by the sexual revolution, the civil rights movement, and the anti-Vietnam protests. New values of appreciation for diversity were replacing the old Christian-based conformist moral codes. For young lesbians in particular, the women's movement became the defining struggle, and their approach to the question of lesbian rights grew out of it. Lesbians began to see themselves as part of a larger women's liberation movement, and especially after 1970 gravitated away from the male-dominated gay liberation groups. Some lesbians, disgusted by the heterosexism of the women's movement, remained active in gay liberation, but others, equally disgusted by sexist attitudes of gay male activists, called for a new ideology of lesbian separatism.

The historical significance of the 1969 Stonewall uprising in New York City is clear, but has perhaps been overestimated. It certainly is NOT accurate to call Stonewall the beginning of the gay and lesbian rights movement. The modern gay and lesbian rights movement began in Los Angeles in 1950. Though the young radicals who participated in the Stonewall revolt made legitimate criticisms that the New York chapter of Mattachine was excessively cautious, this criticism does not apply so well to other places. In California especially, a gradual evolution can be seen from the homophile beginnings to gay and lesbian liberation.

Activists became increasingly militant as the 1960s progressed. New voices emerged, such as the Society for Individual Rights (San Francisco), Pride (Los Angeles), Randy Wicker (New York), Frank Kameny (Washington, D.C.), Barbara Gittings (Philadelphia), Troy Perry (Los Angeles), and the Homosexual Action League (Philadelphia). "A Gay Manifesto" was published, and *Time* magazine devoted a cover story to gay activism, all before Stonewall. Street protests and demonstrations had been held in several cities before Stonewall. Perhaps because New York City was behind the times, at least when compared to California in the late 1960s, when the explosion of outrage against oppression finally hit New York in 1969, it hit big.

The significance of Stonewall is that, rather than being a beginning, it was instead a culmination of two decades of activism. The young radicals of 1969, whether they realized it or not, stood on the shoulders of those homophile activists who had been doing steadfast work to build a community and a movement for gay and lesbian rights. While quite ready to challenge the ideas of anyone over thirty, and to dismiss the homophile activists as too cautious, gay and lesbian liberation would not have been possible without the foundations laid down by those who came before.

The real significance of Stonewall is that it captured the attention of the nation, and motivated an outpouring of lesbian and gay energy in organizing. Gay Liberation Front chapters sprang up in many locations, and Gay and Lesbian Student Unions were founded at many university campuses. The biggest legacy of Stonewall was not that it inspired more rioting, but that it inspired a massive annual outpouring of people peacefully marching in annual Gay and Lesbian Pride parades. In the mid–1960s homophile activists had joked about having a March on Washington modeled on Bayard Rustin's 1963 civil rights march, but they knew it would not be possible because most homosexuals were so deeply closeted that they would never appear in a homophile march.

Stonewall changed all that. At the first anniversary of the uprising, the Gay Liberation Front organized a huge march down Fifth Avenue. Only five years before, Frank Kameny had struggled to persuade ten to twenty volunteers to picket the White House. When he saw the thousands upon thousands of marchers in New York's 1970 Gay Pride March, he was overwhelmed at the numbers. But, while he appreciated the difference in the number of people who were coming out to be open about their lives, he also felt gratified that the militancy of the 1970 marchers was a direct outgrowth of his and others' efforts in the 1950s and 1960s.

Perhaps the biggest change between 1950 and 1977 was the number of people who had come out of the closet of hiding and shame, and emerged as gay men and lesbians who were open about their sexuality. As the 1970s progressed, and more cities started passing gay rights laws, and some states began decriminalizing same-sex behavior, it looked as if lesbian and gay liberation would soon become an accomplished fact.

* * *

In 1930, seventeen-year-old Harry Hay met a gay man in Los Angeles who told him about the arrests of the organizers of the Society for Human Rights in Chicago. Though the man told the story as a danger-ous warning that no one should try to organize homosexuals to push for equal rights, the idea sank into Hay's memory. Eighteen years later, in 1948, Hay attended a beer bust hosted by some gay male students at the University of Southern California, and they got into a wide-ranging dis-cussion about organizing homosexuals to support the presidential can-didacy of progressive Democrat Henry Wallace. Hay came up with a title and a prospectus for the group, but none of the others followed through with the idea.

Finally, after two years of intense effort, Hay convinced four other Los Angeles men to join him in founding an organization that was to be "devoted to the protection and improvement of society's Androgynous Minority." Its 1950 prospectus, written by Hay under a pseudonym, proclaimed:

DOCUMENT 43: Formation of the Mattachine Society (1950)

In order to earn for ourselves any place in the sun, we must…[work] for the full class citizenship participation of Minorities everywhere, in-cluding ourselves. We, the androgynes of the world, have formed this re-sponsible corporate body to demonstrate by our efforts that our physiological and psychological handicaps need be no deterrent in inte-grating 10% of the world's population towards the constructive social progress of mankind.

Source: Eann MacDonald [pseudonym for Harry Hay], "Preliminary Concepts, In-ternational Bachelors Fraternal Orders for Peace and Social Dignity," (Los Angeles: privately printed, July 7, 1950). In the files of ONE Institute International Gay and Lesbian Archives, Los Angeles.

* * *

In a 1998 interview, Harry Hay recalled the fear of police arrest that was common among members of the Mattachine Society. To preserve everyone's security, Hay drew upon his past experience in the Communist Party and set up a secretive organization where only the five founders knew all the details of the various subgroups of Mattachine.

DOCUMENT 44: Mattachine Society Meetings (1950)

These were the days of intense police raids on both Gay bars and house parties. Entrapment, blackmail, job firings, financial ruin, wrecked families, violence, vindictive court trials and incarceration in prisons and mental institutions were all too common. Our founding five set up Mattachine along the classic lines of revolutionaries with separate cells, or guilds, whose attending members would remain unknown to each other. We allowed no photographs to be taken, and insisted nothing be put down in writing—no notes, no phone lists, or anything that could be used for blackmail or turned over to the F.B.I.

We decided to call ourselves Mattachine after...medieval peasant monks who wore masks....We too were forced to wear masks on the job and elsewhere. Paranoia was such at our early meetings that we had to promise total secrecy. Some newcomers were blindfolded and driven around in circles before taken to a meeting. Others came accompanied by members of the opposite sex as a cover for their safety....We had five such guilds in the Los Angeles area, each operating independent of the others. Those people attending one guild's discussion group were unaware of the activities of another group....In each guild, however, there were one or two members who reported back regularly to the founding group of five. The guild gatherings might have up to 50 people in attendance, crowded into a private residence....

Mattachine was important because it got us to stop thinking of ourselves in negative terms. For years we had been told that we were sick and criminal, perverts and degenerates. Any cop could tell you what a homosexual was. We weren't a separate people, a natural phenomenon, according to them. No, we were heterosexual persons who performed depraved homosexual acts and had been led astray by a choir-master or a scout-master....

It was important, therefore, to establish another word for ourselves, one that would combat the negative images. At Mattachine we decided to call ourselves Homophiles [after the Greek word "homo" (the same) and "philos" (love of)], emphasizing the love aspect of our relationships and de-emphasizing the sexual. Gay was still a coded word used only by those in the scene....By using homophile in our literature, in the courts and elsewhere, we effectively confused and defused our enemies....

We believed that as a special people we had made significant contributions for thousands of years, and we were determined that we continue contributing as openly Gay people in present-day society and for all time....[We] used to talk about the snake pit of despair we all were in before the emergence of Mattachine, how far we've come, and how much further we have yet to travel.

Source: Ernie Potvin, "Harry Hay Remembers Jim Kepner," *ONE-IGLA Bulletin* n. 5 (Summer 1998), pp. 14–16.

* * *

In 1952 one of the original cofounders of the Mattachine Society, Dale Jennings, was arrested in Los Angeles by a vice squad detective on the charge of soliciting to commit a homosexual act. Most people arrested on such charges pled no contest in order to keep their names out of the newspapers, and were released after paying a steep fine. The numbers of men arrested on such charges provided a large sum of money each year for the Los Angeles Police Department. Resentful of such extortion, the Mattachine Society decided to use Dale Jennings's arrest as a test case to challenge the pervasive mistreatment of homosexuals by police. Mattachine leaders organized a Citizens' Committee to Outlaw Entrapment and raised money to hire a lawyer. At his arraignment, to the great surprise of the judge, Jennings called for a trial by jury. In *Los Angeles v. William Dale Jennings*, May 19, 1952, Jennings freely admitted during his trial that he was a homosexual. However, he said that he was not guilty of solicitation, but that the plainclothes policeman had entrapped him because he was a single man in an area where homosexuals congregated. He explained to the jury that this kind of police harassment was commonly done to homosexuals, and that he was standing up for his equal right to walk on the sidewalks just like other people. As a result of publicity about Jennings's unprecedented stand, the Mattachine Society grew rapidly in Los Angeles. Jennings described his trial in the first issue of the organization's *ONE Magazine*:

DOCUMENT 45: Mattachine Protests Police Entrapment (1952)

The trial was a surprise. The attorney [George Shibley], engaged by the Mattachine Foundation, made a brilliant opening statement to the jury....[saying] the only true pervert in the court room was the arresting officer....The jury deliberated for forty hours and asked to be dismissed when one of their number said he'd hold out for guilty till hell froze over. The rest voted for straight acquittal. Later the city moved for dismissal of the case and it was granted....

Yes, I gave my name and publicly declared myself to be a homosexual, but the moment I was arrested my name was no longer "good" and this incident will stand on record for all to see for the rest of my life. In a situation where to be accused is to be guilty, a person's good name is worthless and meaningless. Further, without the interest of the Citizens' Committee to Outlaw Entrapment and their support which gathered funds from all over the country, I would have been forced to resort to the mild enthusiasm of the Public Defender. Chances are I'd have been found guilty and now be either still gathering funds to pay the fine or writing this in jail.

Yet I am not abjectly grateful. All of the hundreds who helped push this case to a successful conclusion, were not interested in me personally. They were being intelligently practical and helping establish a precedent that will perhaps help themselves if the time comes. In this sense, a bond of brotherhood is not mere blind generosity. It is unification for self-protection. Were all homosexuals and bisexuals to unite militantly, unjust laws and corruption would crumble in short order and we, as a nation, could go on to meet the really important problems which face us. Were heterosexuals to realize that these violations of our rights threaten theirs equally, a vast reform might even come within our lifetime. This is no more a dream than trying to win a case after admitting homosexuality.

Source: Dale Jennings, "To Be Accused, Is To Be Guilty," *ONE Magazine* v. 1, n. 1 (January 1953), p. 10.

*   *   *

In late 1952 in Los Angeles, a group of Mattachine members, plus others who were involved in the Knights of the Clock, a social club of gay and lesbian interracial couples, decided to publish a magazine called *ONE*. Because it was still illegal for homosexuals to congregate, they had to be vague about their purpose, but they had a clear mission of creating the first number-one gay magazine in America. On February 7, 1953, ONE filed for incorporation as a California nonprofit corporation. Besides Mattachine confounder Dale Jennings, other founders of ONE were a diverse mix of people, including an African American man named Merton Bird and his white lover W. Dorr Legg, Mexican American Antonio Reyes and his white lover Don Slater, and Jewish activist Martin Block.

Under the leadership of W. Dorr Legg, Don Slater, and Irma "Corky" Wolf, ONE, Inc. began publishing *ONE Magazine* in 1953, the first national publication to advocate equal rights for homosexuals. The group rented an office in downtown Los Angeles, where a lecture series was begun. They also established a peer counseling center, and a lawyer referral service for those persons who were entrapped by police vice squads. ONE became a virtual community center for Los Angeles gays and lesbians.

The articles of incorporation for ONE, Inc. boldly state that the organization's primary purpose is to promote research "on homosexuality from the scientific, historical and critical point of view, and to aid in the social integration and rehabilitation of the sexual variant." Its three main goals are listed as follows:

DOCUMENT 46: Formation of ONE, Inc. (1952)

1. To publish and disseminate magazines, brochures, leaflets, books and papers concerned with medical, social, pathological, psychological and therapeutic research of every kind and description pertaining to socio-sexual behavior.

2. To sponsor, supervise and conduct educational programs, lectures and concerts for the aid and benefit of all social and emotional variants and to promote among the general public an interest, knowledge and understanding of the problems of such persons.

3. To stimulate, sponsor, aid, supervise and conduct research of every kind and description pertaining to socio-sexual behavior.

Source: Files of ONE Institute/International Gay and Lesbian Archives. See also W. Dorr Legg, David Cameron, and Walter Williams, *Homophile Studies in Theory and Practice* (San Francisco: GLB and ONE Institute Press, 1994), pp. 442–445; and "40 Year Dedicated Activist Dorr Legg Dies at 89," *ONE-IGLA Bulletin* n. 1 (Spring 1995), p. 4.

* * *

Jim Kepner had tried to organize homosexuals in San Francisco in the 1940s, but without success. After fruitlessly searching public libraries for books and articles about same-sex love in 1942, Kepner had dedicated his life to gathering and preserving as much constructive information about sexual variance as possible. By diligently searching bookstores, using every spare dollar he had to buy rare books, and clipping every article he could find in periodicals, Kepner laboriously built what became known as the International Gay and Lesbian Archives. The Jim Kepner Library, part of ONE Institute that is now housed at the University of Southern California, is the largest collection of its kind in the world. When Kepner moved to Los Angeles in 1952 he was amazed to hear of the new Mattachine Society. He got involved with the group just in time to witness its factionalization. After 1953 the headquarters of Mattachine shifted to San Francisco, and many of the radical members in Los Angeles, like Jim Kepner, shifted their attention to join ONE, Inc. Still, Mattachine and its philosophical founder Harry Hay had a tremendous impact on Kepner. After his lesbian friend Betty Perdue took him to his first meeting in 1953, Kepner was inspired to write down his feelings.

DOCUMENT 47: Jim Kepner's First Mattachine Meeting (1953)

Can you fall in love with a roomful of men? I did. Trying for ten years to find another gay to join in fighting for our rights, here was a roomful. Already committed, already organized, talking of building community, a really handsome intelligent lot....I burst with love and zeal, grateful to be invited into membership. We'd hid in the dark 2,000 years, ignorant of ourselves, afraid, persecuted. No more hiding! No more damned hiding! We were on the move, and I was part of it. I loved that roomful of men.

Source: Jim Kepner, "A Roomful of Men: Los Angeles, January 1953," *ONE-IGLA Bulletin* n. 5 (Summer 1998), p. 14.

* * *

The late 1940s and early 1950s were years of intense political persecution for Florida's lesbian and gay communities. Flo Fleischman was a student at the University of Tampa, and was a writer for the university's student newspaper, but in 1950 she was prevented from becoming editor because of rumors about her lesbianism. Discouraged, Fleischman dropped out of school and became active in the city's underground gay scene.

The few gay bars were usually owned by the Mafia, who made money payoffs to the police to keep them away. If a bar owner did not make a payment on time, the police would make a raid, arrest the customers, and haul them off to jail. Fleischman was caught up in some of these raids and subjected to police harassment. After years of discrimination, in 1956 she and a friend left for Southern California where she hoped life would be better. She was not an activist again until 1963, when she organized a group of professional lesbians in the Los Angeles South Bay area. Many of them were so afraid of losing their jobs that they would not reveal their real name at meetings. When Fleischman affiliated the group as a chapter of the lesbian group Daughters of Bilitis, in 1965, many of the women dropped out and refused to associate with her.

Undeterred, in 1965 Fleischman went on to help establish the Council on Religion and the Homophile, and joined the gay Metropolitan Community Church (MCC) in 1971. Eventually she graduated from MCC's Samaritan Theological Seminary and became a pastor in the church. In 1995 she joined the board of directors of ONE Institute and became its president two years later. Looking back on her life of activism, she recalled:

DOCUMENT 48: Tampa Lesbian Bar Raid (1953)

Coming out publicly in "my day" was unheard of—coming out privately was dangerous enough. "My day" was the 1940s, and as a young lesbian in Florida I was acutely aware of the threats, insults, prejudice and beatings hurled at my kind. Most of all it was the constant hammering in our heads that we were somehow "unworthy to walk this earth."...The message was being delivered loudly from virtually every pulpit by strident ministers and priests who ranted and raved on the sins of homosexuality. Addressing any such person who might be in their congregation, they'd tell us we were "going to burn in hell" if we didn't turn to heterosexuality. It was a recurring theme.

Their message, thank God, was one I would never accept. It did however bring considerable stress at times into my life. Times like when my church newsletter declared "homosexuals are an abomination of God."...Staying hidden in "my day" was an absolute necessity.

At school the greatest stress from being different was the inability to find other people like myself. Organized lesbian and gay groups were unheard of. No matter what social group one joined in "my day," you were obliged to attend their events accompanied by the opposite sex. I rebelled by becoming an introvert with plummeting grades and a lost will to exist....[In 1949, when] I entered the University of Tampa, it was the day I came out, not publicly but privately, to myself and a few intimate friends. Coming out publicly would mean being ostracized with attacks from many directions. It happened anyway. I had been feature editor of the university newspaper and nominated for editor when I was reported to the Dean's office [in 1950]. This resulted in loss of my position and removal from the paper's staff. By the end of the semester I was forced to leave college entirely for being "too overt a homosexual." The greatest blow came the next day from my girlfriend who left me a "Dear Flo" letter telling me we were through. She couldn't withstand the stigma of being known as a "woman lover."

In "my day" Tampa had mostly mixed lesbian/gay bars, all sleazy. One called Charlie's was for women only and a real dump. One afternoon [in 1953] I strolled in looking for a buddy....I had put my hand on the barmaid's shoulder and asked if she had seen my friend when, from out of nowhere, I was whirled around and heard [from an undercover vice policewoman] "let's go, you lesbian, you're under arrest for lewd and lascivious conduct." All of us were hauled off to jail.

Unwarranted random bar raids were just another part of the times during "my day." And this day, like many others, the cops were showing pocket-size porno books to all the lesbians, promising to let them off if they would have sex with them. No one took up their offer and instead spent the rest of the night in jail. I faced up to them threatening to sue and they let me off....

In years to follow, I witnessed other degrading incidents in which vice squads jostled innocent lesbians and gays out of bars and violated their human rights in a number of different ways. Later, as a pastor for several Metropolitan Community Churches, these experiences were to help me in ministering to others. Although "my day" for coming out may have occurred in Florida during the '40s, the '90s are "my day" to serve with pride on the board of ONE Institute where my story and countless numbers of others are being preserved for generations to come.

Source: Rev. Flo Fleischman, "Lesbian Reflections on the Frightening Forties," *ONE-IGLA Bulletin* n. 2 (Spring/Summer 1996), p. 10.

*   *   *

Daughters of Bilitis (DOB) was the first known lesbian organization in the United States. Before this group formed, lesbians created networks of friendship and support by meeting at bars, on beaches, at house parties, and softball games. In 1955, Marie, a Pilipina, suggested forming a social club for lesbians as an alternative to the bars. Eight women met in September of that year. Two were women of color (besides Marie, there was one Chicana), and the group was a mix of blue- and white-collar workers. A woman named Nancy suggested the name Bilitis, after a woman by the same name who may have lived on the island of Lesbos and known the poet Sappho. A year later, the organization began publishing *The Ladder*. Later, two of the founding members wrote about DOB's statement of purpose.

DOCUMENT 49: Daughters of Bilitis (1955)

The purpose of Daughters of Bilitis, a women's organization to aid the Lesbian in discovering her potential and her place in society, was spelled out. The organization was to encourage and support the Lesbian in her search for personal, interpersonal, social, economic and vocational identity. The DOB social functions would enable the Lesbian to find and communicate with others like herself, thereby expanding her social world outside the bars. She could find in the discussion groups opportunity for the interchange of ideas, a chance to talk openly about the problems she faced as a Lesbian in her everyday life. Also available to her would be DOB's library on themes of homosexuality and women in general. In educating the public to accept the Lesbian as an individual and eliminate the prejudice which places oppressive limitations on her life style, the group proposed an outreach program: to sponsor public forums, to provide speakers for other interested civic groups, and to publish and disseminate educational and rational literature on the Lesbian. DOB also announced its willingness to participate in responsible research projects, and its interest in promoting changes in the legal system to insure the rights of all homosexuals.

Source: Del Martin and Phyllis Lyon, *Lesbian/Woman* (New York: Bantam, 1972), p. 243.

*   *   *

Along with ONE, Inc. cofounder W. Dorr Legg and Professor Merritt Thompson of the University of Southern California, Jim Kepner saw the need for an educational research center for the homophile movement. In 1956 they founded ONE Institute and began holding seminars, sponsoring lectures, and supporting research. Jim Kepner became editor of *ONE Institute Quarterly of Homophile Studies*, the first academic journal in what would later come to be called Gay and Lesbian Studies. Kepner's philosophy of homophile equality is represented in a letter he wrote to United States Senator Thomas Hennings and to Dr. Robert Hutchins of the Ford Foundation. Kepner's words, based on civil liberties guarantees in the Bill of Rights, had a huge impact in inspiring more activists to come out in support of gay and lesbian rights.

DOCUMENT 50: Founding of ONE Institute of Homophile Studies (1956)

Dear Sirs: The commendable and forthright work of each of you in spotlighting the erosion of civil liberties, at a time much threatened by conformity and a distorted concept of national security, leads us to hope you may be willing to turn attention to the wrongs suffered by a group shunned like lepers by most defenders of liberty and justice.

More maligned than even Communists, and lacking bold allies or a developed sense of community, each homosexual seems to stand alone as an outcast—a secret sinner dreading exposure that may come at any time. Those assuming such a minority to be a small band of willfully perverted criminals can perhaps approve such social ostracism. However, [Indiana University Professor Alfred] Kinsey revealed what other researchers had indicated: that this is far too large a group to be repressed without severe consequences to society....Kinsey's figures [in his 1948 book, *Sexual Behavior in the Human Male* and his 1953 book *Sexual Behavior in the Human Fe-*

male] indicate some 18 million men (and smaller numbers of women), who, having completed at least one such overt act, might be considered homosexual by the law....

In general, one need not argue a point of justice on the basis of the number of persons involved. Yet so great is antihomosexual prejudice that an appeal founded solely on justice, right, or scientific evidence finds but few listeners....Laws that place a burden of criminal guilt on a third of the populace and make one in ten an "abominable" outlaw are serious laws indeed....

Homosexuals are subjected to constant fear and insecurity, slander and vilification, discrimination in employment, and sudden waves of persecution during which basic legal rights may be totally ignored. In their rights to peaceably assemble, and to be secure against unreasonable search and seizure, homosexuals have been particularly wronged. We cite the unfair handling of homosexuals in the armed services and in government security cases, and the effects of inept sex offender registration laws, new criminal psychopath laws with vague definitions and indeterminate sentences not based on specific proven acts, and the loose interpretation of "catchall" statutes such as vagrancy laws.

The homosexual is doggedly frustrated in exercise of what the Declaration of Independence calls the inalienable right to life, liberty, and the pursuit of happiness....Finding himself different from most men, he nonetheless cannot change his impulses at will. He hears the glib talk of cure, and often tries to get cured, but months or years of "treatment" do not alter his basic drives. His problem becomes one of satisfying or denying his desires, donning a social mask so neighbors and business associates won't recognize what he is, and hoping he can keep safe from police and blackmailers....

In the public mind, homosexuality is identified with all manner of perversions and sex crimes, such as rape and child molesting. But statistics show that corruption of minors and crimes of violence are about equally distributed among heterosexuals and homosexuals, and in either group, represent a minority....

Search of homes of suspected homosexuals without warrant and seizure of address books and correspondence have been common police practice. "Vice" officers regularly entice citizens into compromising positions to make an arrest. Nor is it rare to hear of vice officers suggesting to their victim that charges can be dropped for a cash payment....The thoroughgoing discrimination against the homosexual is unnecessary to the preservation of social order—it threatens order, in encouraging excesses of police power, in making a large class of potentially useful citizens antisocial, in creating festering spots of fear and hatred, in thwarting the lives and natural development for millions who have no alternative, and in magnifying dangerous guilt feelings in other segments of the population.

Public hysteria and attacks on homosexuals have increased as the subject comes more into the light. [Sociologist] David Riesman has suggested that as the Negro progressively escapes his role as public scapegoat, and as the Communist hunt grows stale, the bigoted are likely to turn to homosexuals for attack.

What would be the consequences of relaxing some parts of the restrictions? Would the walls of morality come tumbling down? Would men desert heterosexual monogamy? Would the birthrate fall disastrously? Only if heterosexuality was assumed to be unnatural and enforced only by restrictive law. Most men, basically heterosexual, will remain so without legal force. And the homosexual minority will remain generally as it is despite prejudice, laws, or mores. In no society, past or present, no matter how restrictive, has homosexuality been absent. In no society, no matter how permissive, has the natural impulse of the majority been impaired by granting freedom to inverts....

The American ideal holds that the country is large enough for people with different concepts of right and wrong to live together in harmony. The nations we decry are those where conformity has done its worst, where all thought and action must fit what is officially acceptable. In our own country there have been shortcomings in our practical application of this ideal, but we always have faith that we can overcome them. The homosexual feels that it is his turn to receive fairness and tolerance.

Source: Lyn Pedersen [pseud. for Jim Kepner], "An Open Letter: Do Constitutional Guarantees Cover Homosexuals?" *ONE Magazine* (January 1956). [Reprinted in Jim Kepner, *Rough News—Daring Views: 1950s Pioneer Gay Press Journalism* (New York: Haworth Press, 1998), pp. 217–220, 264–269.]

* * *

In the 1950s, anyone accused of being homosexual was subject to attack by violent bullies, who knew the police would seldom make an arrest for violence against a sexual pervert. The range of violence extended even into the schools, where any boy who was not masculine was subject to continual torment. Gay novelist Paul Monette wrote in his memoirs about an incident he observed in 1956 when he was in the sixth grade at Central School in Andover, Massachusetts. Monette saw the class bully, Vinnie O'Connor, harassing a meek boy in the school hallway.

DOCUMENT 51: Gay Bashing in Massachusetts (1956)

Vinnie and a group of three or four others had somebody pinned in a corner. Vinnie was snarling and shoving. "Yeah, you're a homo, ain't ya? Little fairy homo. Ain't that right?" Then he shot out a fist and slammed his victim's head against the wall. A bustle of students streamed past to their lockers, eyes front and pretending not to see...."Homo, homo, homo," Vinnie kept repeating, accompanying each taunt with a savage rabbit punch. The victim pleaded, terrified but trying not to cry. It was Austin Singer, a meek, nervous kid....He vigorously denied the homo charge, choking it out between punches, which only made Vinnie angrier. He growled at two of his henchboys, who pinned poor Austin's face to the wall.

Vinnie made a hawking sound and spit a glob of phlegm on the brick beside Austin's face. "Come on, homo—lick that off." Austin whimpered and tried to pull back. Vinnie brought up his knee into Austin's kidney, making him cry out...."Lick it, homo," Vinnie hissed. One of the brute lieutenants pushed Austin's face along the brick, scraping it raw. And now Austin, broken, surrendered whatever dignity was left. His tongue lolled out, and he licked up the phlegm while the bullies cheered. "Swallow it!" Vinnie commanded. From where I stood, by my locker, I saw in a daze of horror, the self-disgust in Austin's face as he got it down without retching.

Vinnie and his boys sprang away, shrieking with laughter. Instantly I busied myself with my lunchbox, terrified they would notice me. As they swaggered away, neither I nor anyone else made a move toward Austin—slumped in the corner as if it would have been easier to die than survive this thing. We all went hurrying away.

Source: Paul Monette, *Becoming a Man: Half a Life Story* (New York: Harcourt Brace Jovanovich, 1992), pp. 34–35.

*   *   *

A reaction to the conformist 1950s began when poets in San Francisco and Los Angeles challenged the dominant mainstream morality. Part of this challenge was focused on sexual values, and this was especially due to the influence of openly gay writers Allen Ginsberg and William Burroughs. The 1950s group they helped popularize as the Beatniks was the forerunner of the 1960s counterculture movement and the sexual revolution. Throughout his life Ginsberg stayed on the forefront of gay liberation, giving a radical speech at the 1979 March on Washington for Gay and Lesbian Rights, and he also defended the North American Man-Boy Love Association's efforts to abolish age of consent laws. In 1997, longtime activist Jim Kepner wrote of the historical impact that the Beat writers had on the movement for gay and lesbian rights.

DOCUMENT 52: Allen Ginsberg and the Beatniks (1956)

When poet Allen Ginsberg and novelist William Burroughs died within a few months of each other [in 1997] the general press praised their role in initiating a break from conformity during the 1950s, but made little mention of their influence on Gay life and culture....[Ginsberg was] a virtual one-man Gay Liberation movement—[when] most Gays were then as much into suit-and-tie conformity as the rest of the U.S....The stark homosexual passages in William Burroughs' staccato 1959 book *Naked Lunch* created a national sensation. Homosexuality was not a main Beatnik theme, but almost no other English language writers had dealt with it so often, so explicitly and without apology. Most homosexuals then, even those who were sexually active, tended to be guilt-ridden and to believe what the authorities said: that homosexuality was sinful or sick. Where *ONE Magazine* had been censored for addressing the subject positively but very discretely, Ginsberg, Burroughs and Corso in that otherwise super conservative period described their sex activity affirmatively and earthily—and were cheered, even among many young heteros who were ready to break out of 1950s conformity....

Ginsberg remained an icon of that much wider [1960s counterculture] movement, leading "Aums" at gigantic peace marches, at the 1968 Yippie confrontation outside the Democratic Convention in Chicago, delivering a ringing manifesto at the Chicago Conspiracy trial, and leading the 1967 anti-war "levitation" of the Pentagon. The hippies, like the Beats before, provided an alternate identity to many homosexuals who were not yet ready to identify publicly as Gay—and license to break out of "straight" costumes....

[When I heard Ginsberg speak] his performance was electrifying, with the frankest homosexual poetry I had ever heard delivered to any audience, and this audience was primarily heterosexual....He appeared on stage in the lotus position alongside Mark, a soft youth who gloried in sharing the limelight. After leading the audience in a long "Aum," Ginsberg gave Mark a long kiss, and every closet queen in the audience shuddered in fear....When he recited "Please Master!"—the most erotic S&M [sadist & masochist] poem I'd ever heard read in public, the auditorium was electric. Many Gays were visibly embarrassed, but the young heteros cheered loudly....[He had] a voice of power, of deep sincerity, not polished, but cutting to essential issues.

The Beats helped move American culture from intolerable conformity, and Gays from overwhelming fear and shame, to a new sense of freedom and assertiveness. Few young Gays today realize how much the life they take for granted is partly owed to Ginsberg.

Source: Jim Kepner, "When the Beat Died," *ONE-IGLA Bulletin* n. 4 (Winter 1997–98), pp. 14–16.

* * *

In late 1956 the secretary of the Navy appointed a panel, chaired by naval captain S. H. Crittenden, Jr., to review the Navy's policies regarding homosexuality and to recommend any revisions of these policies that they deemed necessary. After hearing testimony from a number of people, including psychiatrists, personnel officers, and the director of Naval Intelligence—the department in charge of ferreting out homosexuals and discharging them from the Navy—the Crittenden Board issued its report on March 15, 1957. Buried by the Pentagon for decades, the Crittenden Report was finally released, in truncated form, after extraordinary efforts by scholars and multiple appeals under the Freedom of Information Act. The Crittenden Report concluded that homosexual behavior in and of itself did not render one incapable of performing his or her duties adequately. Rather, the report stated that naval policy was shaped by social attitudes toward homosexuality, and recommended that—while not getting ahead of society's notions about tolerance—the Navy continue to monitor the situation and make changes accordingly. Following are the most pertinent parts of the Report.

DOCUMENT 53: The Crittenden Report on Homosexuality in the United States Navy (1957)

The Board noted that in the area of sexual perversion, only homosexuality is covered by specific directives, although other categories are equally violative of moral codes, laws, and accepted standards of conduct....The homosexuals disclosed represent only a very small proportion of homosexuals in the Navy, and that homosexual behavior by persons who are not exclusively homosexual is even more common....A concept which persists without sound basis in fact is the idea that homosexuals necessarily pose a security risk. It is difficult to determine just how this idea developed, but it seems that it first appeared in governmental directives in 1950, in the report of the Hoey Committee. This Committee, however, based its recommendation on "the *opinions* of those best qualified to know, namely, the intelligence agencies of the Government."However, no intelligence agency, as far as can be learned, adduced any factual data before that Committee with which to support these opinions...Some intelligence officers consider a senior officer having illicit heterosexual relations with the wife of a junior officer or enlisted man much more of a security risk than the ordinary homosexual. The matter of indiscretion would appear to be of more importance than the question of the nature of any sexual activity. There is some information to indicate that at least some homosexuals are quite good security risks....Many exclusively homosexual persons have served honorably in all branches of the military service without detection....Based on testimony of record, the practice of the other services and its own experience, the Board has little difficulty in reaching the conclusion that mandatory discharge of all one-time, non-habitual offenders is not in the best interest of the naval services....The ineffectiveness as a deterrent of the policy of court-martial and *confinement* for *all* homosexual offenders has...been illustrated....The other than honorable discharge should not be *mandatory* for any class of offender....To exhibit, profess or admit homosexual *tendencies* is not an offense, any more than tendencies toward alcoholism for example, and where such tendencies are controlled during naval service, the individual should not be placed in a position of being separated with an undesirable discharge because of such tendencies....The exclusion from service of all persons who, on the basis of their personality structure, could conceivably engage in homosexual acts is totally unfeasible in view of the large proportion of the young adult male population which falls in this category....*Recommendations*: a. Maintain in great part the present service approach to the problem of homosexual behavior. b. Be alert to keep abreast of any widely accepted changes in the attitude of society at large toward the overall problem. c. The service should not move ahead of civilian society nor attempt to set substantially different standards in attitude toward or action with respect to homosexual offenders.

Source: S. H. Crittenden, "Report on Homosexuality in the United States Navy," Papers of the Secretary of the Navy, March 15, 1957, pp. 2, 4, 5, 6, 7, 11, 15, 22, 24, 25, 38, 56.

* * *

When she first took a job as a professor of psychology at the University of California at Los Angeles, Dr. Evelyn Hooker knew very little about homosexuality. Unlike psychiatrists who came into clinical contact only with homosexuals who wanted to try to suppress their same-sex feelings, Hooker and her husband had met several openly gay men on a social level as neighbors. These gay men, many of whom were active in the Mattachine Society and ONE, had no interest in repressing their homosexuality. Having no vested interests in making money by claiming to cure homosexuality, Hooker began to do the first psychological research on homosexuals who were *not* in therapy. In 1997 an obituary for Hooker summed up the influence of this heterosexual woman in establishing the intellectual basis for gay and lesbian rights.

DOCUMENT 54: Evelyn Hooker Psychological Research (1957)

Few Gays today know that 30 years ago we were virtual wards of the psychiatric profession. They had power to explain us to the world, to pronounce us sick, and to subject those of us who fell into their hands to any treatments then fashionable: "therapy," imprisonment, castration, shock treatment, etc. While many of them sincerely wished to help, and a few of them did, they mostly labeled us as neurotic or psychotic, unstable and fixated at an infantile level of sexuality—and raged at us when we rejected their judgment.

Two persons did the most to revolutionize that: Dr. Alfred C. Kinsey…and Dr. Evelyn Gentry Hooker….While teaching psychology at UCLA and living in gay Santa Monica Canyon, it hadn't occurred to her that the derogatory textbook paragraphs about homosexuals would apply to friends and neighbors [like]…philosopher Gerald Heard and novelist Christopher Isherwood. Her pioneering research was urged on her by a particularly bright student, Sam From, who, impressed by her tremendous energy and humanity, challenged her to get acquainted with his Gay friends and their lives, to study them and put to the test what psychiatrists were saying about them….

She applied for and received a National Institute of Mental Health grant (the man in charge flew out to make sure she was not Lesbian, then recommended funding her study). She set up a controlled experiment to test the accepted view that Gays were by definition neurotic, unstable, infantile, and identifiable. "Projective tests" in wide use were assumed to be able to identify homosexual leanings, even in persons who didn't know they had them, and to prove that homosexuals were neurotic. Thousands had lost government and private jobs for seeing the "wrong" thing in the eight Rorschach inkblots…or for giving "wrong" responses to the Thematic Apperception Test (TAT)….Certain answers were interpreted as showing the testee was homosexual and mentally disturbed.

In 1953, the pioneer homophile groups Mattachine and ONE helped her recruit 74 exclusively Gay men who'd never been in therapy or in trouble with the law….She gave the matched pairs the Rorschach, TAT and other tests, and took the results blind to top experts who were sure they could identify homosexuals from the test results alone. Asked to evaluate the responses, they could not tell which were by homosexuals. They "knew" that all homosexuals were maladjusted, but rated more than half of the Gays as better adjusted than the heteros! This astonished even Hooker. The tests showed no difference between the Gay and non-Gay groups. Her study disproved many homophobic assumptions made universally by psychologists at the time and proved that these tests, taken alone, could not identify homosexuals….

She published her then highly controversial results in two careful articles, "The Adjustment of the Male Overt Homosexual," in the *Journal of Projective Techniques*, 1957 and 1958, and kept in touch for years with those she'd interviewed, becoming intimate with Gay life, combining scientific objectivity with warmth, commitment and humor. She spoke widely, infuriating professional homophobes….[and] became convinced that the subject would better be approached from a sociological viewpoint. In the *Journal of Psychology* 1956, her "Preliminary Analysis of Group Behavior of

Homosexuals" looked at how the Gay community gives support for those who didn't find it in their early background....

Dr. Stanley Yolles, Director of the U.S. Public Health Service's National Institute of Mental Health, appointed her in September 1967 to head a Task Force on Homosexuality....[In] 1969 the Task Force recommended, with minor dissents, additional research and education, intensive research on possible prevention and treatment factors, repeal of legal penalties on private adult consensual homosexual acts, and the ending of employment discrimination. The Nixon Administration buried the report and fired Dr. Yolles....

In 1992 David Haughland made the moving documentary [film] "Changing Minds: The Story of Dr. Evelyn Hooker" [which] was nominated for an Academy Award....She denied being a hero, as many called her, saying that curiosity and empathy rather than courage had impelled her research, but she added that even as a child, she knew she would do something to better the lot of mankind. She'd demolished the prevailing dogma that homosexuals were inherently abnormal and helped legitimize homosexuality.

Source: Jim Kepner, "A Memory of Dr. Evelyn Hooker," *ONE-IGLA Bulletin* n. 3 (1997), pp. 10–11.

*   *   *

ONE Magazine, which began publication in 1953, quickly became the leading voice of the homophile movement. An attorney read each article to make sure it was not sexually explicit, thereby putting the editors at risk for arrest. In addition, the writers used aliases. For example, William Dorr Legg wrote as "Bill Lambert" and "Hollister Barnes," Irma Corky Wolf as "Ann Carll Reid," and art director Joan Corbin signed her work "Eve Elloree."

Their fears were well founded. Within a year of the magazine's first publication, Los Angeles postmaster Otto Oleson refused to allow the October 1954 issue of *ONE Magazine* to be sent to subscribers through the mail, on the basis that it was obscene. If Oleson's charge was upheld, ONE officers could be subject to fines or imprisonment. Instead of cowering, ONE's leaders approached the issue as few homosexuals did at the time, seeing themselves as a persecuted minority deserving equal rights and freedom of the press. ONE sued the United States Post Office, becoming the first homophile organization to initiate a court case for equal constitutional protections. In 1956 they lost, when a federal judge ruled in *One, Inc. v. Oleson*, that the magazine was obscene. ONE's attorney Eric Julber then appealed to the Ninth Circuit Court of Appeals, claiming that homosexuals should be recognized as a legitimate segment of the American populace. They lost again, when the Appeals

Court ruled (241, F. 2d. 771) that *ONE* was "lewd, obscene, lascivious and filthy." Not giving up, the intrepid band of ONE activists appealed the case all the way to the United States Supreme Court.

By the time the appeal reached the Supreme Court in January 1958, the court had already made a ruling on obscenity. A few months earlier, in *Roth v. U.S.* (354 U.S. 476), the justices stated that to be declared legally obscene, a published work as a whole must appeal to the average person's "prurient interest." The Court said that a nonprurient discussion of sex behavior and problems is an important topic of human interest, and entitled to constitutional protections of freedom of speech and of the press. Therefore, a general discussion of sexual issues and controversies could not be censored by government officials. Without hearing oral arguments, the Supreme Court made a unanimous decision that the guidelines of the Roth decision also applied to discussions of homosexuality, and that *ONE Magazine* was not obscene. The justices overturned the Court of Appeals decision, and ordered the postmaster to allow *ONE Magazine* to be sent through the mail. This decision was an important victory in the struggle for gay and lesbian rights; all future gay, lesbian, bisexual, and transgendered newspapers, in a sense, owed a debt to the legal challenge initiated by ONE.

The strength of purpose that the leaders of ONE felt is represented in an article written by ONE cofounder Dorr Legg in 1958. Its provocative title was placed on the cover of the magazine: "I Am Glad I Am a Homosexual." This article and others like it published in *ONE Magazine* refute the notion that all homophile activists in the 1950s were conservative, cautious, and apologetic.

DOCUMENT 55: Supreme Court Rules ONE Is Not Obscene (1958)

"I am proud of being a homosexual." This powerfully affirmative statement, made by a speaker at the Constitutional Convention of the Mattachine Society, in April 1953, acted as an electrifying catalyst. Some few applauded its forthrightness. Others, whether consciously or not, [agreed] with popular opinion—that homosexuality is wrong: that it is sinful; that it is shameful....

The admitted homosexuals are a smaller group, comprised mainly of those claiming to be more intellectually sophisticated, and of the flaming queens. This group, in whatever terms, expresses pride in its homosexuality, finding nothing either sinful or shameful in it. They feel that homosexual men and women should be in every way as free to practice their sexual preferences as are other segments of the population; that they should enjoy the same legal and social privileges as others, no more, but also, no less. They feel themselves under no obligations whatever to conform to the particular social standards of any particular community; that instead of their adjusting to popular mores, the mores should be adjusted to their own wishes....

This rugged individualism has an almost anarchistic quality that is yet as American as the "hot dog." It is in the spirit of that old Colonial flag, emblazoned with a rattlesnake and the motto, "Don't tread on me." This is the individualism of the queen, flaunting makeup and a bracelet or two in the face of an amused or embarrassed public, and of the intellectual....[challenging] the unhealthy manifestations of a society so sick, a culture so unsure of itself that it shrinks in horror from some of the greatest and basically elemental forces of man and nature, while striving feverishly at an impossible repression. Is it proposed that the honest man, the upright woman, shall lend themselves to the furtherance of such sickness, such unhealthiness, such weakness? Should they not rather strive to lead their blind fellows out of this nasty-minded neuroticism?...

Some of the most shining stars in the human firmament have been homosexual. Without these great men and women the world in which we live today would indeed be a sad, drab place—less moral. Who doubts this knows neither religion, history, nor art.

Like other homosexuals who have self-respect and a natural pride, I am proud of being a human being, quite as capable as any of my fellows of doing good work, to the extent of my individual abilities. In addition, I feel sure that my particular way of life has given me certain insights into human problems and character that most heterosexuals apparently lack....[Due to having experienced discrimination first hand] the homosexual discovers in himself a sympathy for the poor and oppressed of all kinds denied to all but the saints. Being utterly untouched by their interests and concerns he has an unerring eye for the follies and foibles of his heterosexual brothers and sisters, so unerring in fact that he often finds himself cast in the role of sympathetic adviser and confidant....

Do these concepts seem shocking, or startling? If so, the reader should prepare himself to continue being shocked, for ideas such as these are present today in the minds of many homosexuals. They will be expressing them more and more vigorously as time goes on. Their day is on the march. They are actively, resiliently proud of their homosexuality, glad for it. Society is going to have to accustom itself to many new pressures, new demands from the homosexual. A large and vigorous group of citizens, millions of them, are refusing to put up any longer with outworn shibboleths, contumely and social degradation.

Like the rest of my brothers and sisters I am glad to be a homosexual, proud of it. Let no one think we don't mean business, or intend to enforce our rights.

Source: Hollister Barnes [pseudonym for Dorr Legg], "I Am Glad I Am a Homosexual," *ONE Magazine* August 1958, pp. 6–9.

*   *   *

In 1953, several hundred people who were involved in Mattachine Society gatherings held a general membership meeting at the First Unitarian Universalist Church in Los Angeles. It was a contentious meeting and as a result, Harry Hay and the other original founders of the Mattachine Society resigned from the board of directors. A new group of officers, led by Harold Call of San Francisco, shifted the organization to Northern California. Call, a masculine anticommunist journalist and businessman, was very different from the left-wing androgynous labor organizer Harry Hay. Whereas Hay emphasized that androgynes were fundamentally different from heterosexuals in their essential being, and had organized Mattachine to build self-respect among homosexuals themselves, Call wanted to shift focus toward gaining tolerance for homosexuals by changing heterosexuals' prejudicial attitudes. He criticized Hay's introspective approach as ineffective, and felt that gay people would be able to feel better about themselves when general societal prejudice was reduced. In the meantime, he encouraged homophiles to start businesses to increase their economic power in society, and to become professionally educated in order to gain more influence over the public presentation of homosexuality in established institutions and the mass media.

Harold Call wanted to make Mattachine a more democratic and open organization, moving it from being a secretive marginalized leftist group into the mainstream of American society. He wanted to promote a general sexual freedom in society, with same-sex behavior accepted as a part of a larger movement for social and sexual liberation in general. In order to accomplish this, Call invited newspaper editors, psychiatrists, theologians, and other recognized authorities—even when they did not agree with Mattachine's viewpoint—to speak to the group. A brilliant and tireless publicist, Call gave interviews to newspapers, talked with television reporters, spoke to numerous mainstream community groups in San Francisco, and lobbied local religious leaders and politicians. He even made the first documentary films about homosexuals, and showed them at every opportunity. He stressed that, except for their sexual preferences, most homosexuals were similar to other Americans. He wanted to minimize the differences between homosexuals and heterosexuals by saying that "we're the same as you, except for what we do in bed." Most of Call's work focused on San Francisco, but he founded and edited *The Mattachine Review* to spread his approach nationally.

Gradually the Mattachine Society spread from California to other states, and members started holding annual conventions. The most successful was held at a major hotel in Denver, Colorado, over Labor Day weekend in 1959, with delegates from California, New York, Illinois, Massachusetts, Georgia, Michigan, Louisiana, New Jersey, Hawaii, Kansas, and Wyoming, as well as Colorado. This convention generated unprecedented favorable press coverage. The four-day meeting included speeches by prominent homophile leaders like Del Martin and Jim Kepner, a speech on legal problems facing homosexuals by the director of the Colorado chapter of the American Civil Liberties Union, and speeches by sympathetic heterosexual psychiatrists, psychologists, and anthropologists. A prominent Colorado politician also spoke about the need to repeal state sodomy laws. The September 5 issue of the *Denver Post* quoted Harold Call on the convention theme of "New Frontiers in Acceptance of the Homophile." Call explained the purpose of the convention for the mainstream readers of the newspaper:

DOCUMENT 56: Mattachine National Convention (1959)

The idea is to talk frankly about what homosexuality really is, and the intelligent attitude to take in facing the problems it poses for society.... Among those you love most deeply there is likely to be at least one homosexual: a son or daughter, brother or sister. Most homosexuals are NOT insane, stupid, willfully perverted, unnatural or socially incompetent as is often believed....Most can and do lead useful and productive lives....But homosexuals as such have only limited social and civil rights....This is why a group of responsible, socially conscious citizens, including many who are not themselves homosexual, has formed the Mattachine Society...to encourage medical and social research pertaining to socio-sexual behavior and to publish the results of such research. It sponsors educational programs to aid social and emotional variants and seeks to promote among the general public an understanding of the problems of such persons.

Source: Quoted in "Tangents," *ONE Magazine* v. 7, n. 10 (October 1959), pp. 14–15.

*   *   *

Since 1955 ONE Institute had been sponsoring a Midwinter Institute in Los Angeles, as a gathering of homophile activists from across the nation. For the seventh Midwinter Institute, in January 1961, the announced theme was "A Homosexual Bill of Rights." ONE's director W. Dorr Legg asked activists to choose which drafting committee they wanted to participate in, and to come up with wording for equal rights for lesbians and gay men in specific areas. Inspired by the Bill of Rights in the United States Constitution, the goal of the organizers was to plan a blueprint for gay and lesbian rights for the upcoming decade. Lesbian leaders of the Daughters of Bilitis considered this agenda to be too radical, and they led a movement of women out of ONE. They were joined by assimilationist men, who believed that homosexuals should strive to blend in with the general society, and not agitate for special rights as homosexuals. This split weakened ONE, and the radical organizers of the Institute were not able to come up with a final document. However, the suggested topics for consideration in the program mark the beginnings of a list of demands for equality that would culminate in the later Marches on Washington for Gay and Lesbian Rights. ONE's suggested topics for drafting committees, which were clearly ahead of its time, included:

DOCUMENT 57: A Homosexual Bill of Rights (1961)

Drafting Committee I: Preamble

1. The right to non-conformity; the right of choice (free will); the line between individual and group rights.

2. Do homosexuals have the right to demand the status of a minority group? Must the wishes of the majority be accepted? The right to civil disobedience.

3. Can democratic voting procedures determine moral and ethical questions? Does the State have authority to prescribe sex behavior? Do homosexuals have the right to set up their own standards of sex behavior—as individuals, as a group?

Drafting Committee II: Social Rights

1. Work rights. The right to employment without discrimination in either private or public capacity; the right to military service without prejudice or penalty.

2. Fiscal rights. The right to equal insurance privileges; to own and bequeath real or personal property on an equal footing with other portions of society; the right to inheritance; equal tax rights; to own and conduct businesses on equal footing with others.

3. Social rights. To choose one's mode of dress; to determine suitable public and private behavior; to participate freely in community affairs and public life; to social facilities and privileges (dancing, sports, etc.).

4. Family rights. The right to parental respect and understanding; the right to social equality with heterosexual brothers and sisters; the right to have children, if desired.

5. Personality rights. The right to be free from social discrimination; the right to be free from social contempt; freedom from slander.

Drafting Committee III: Religious Rights

1. Doctrinal rights. The right to be theologically evaluated as are other members of society; the right to be as free from religious denunciation as anyone; the right to have homosexual love accorded no lower rank than heterosexual love.

2. Institutional rights. The right to take active part in church work; to hold church offices without prejudice; to equal treatment as a church member.

3. Rights of equity. The right to be free of religiously-imposed mask-wearing (hypocritical behavior); the right to equal treatment by both clergy and organizations, i.e., to official attitudes and conformity with actual practices.

4. The right to church-approved homosexual marriage for those who wish it.

5. The right to freedom from religious interference (for the non-religious).

Drafting Committee IV: Scientific Questions and Overpopulation

1. The right to have scientific study of homosexuality freed of value judgments; the right to have scholars study human behavior without censoring out homosexual factors; the right to free, frank, scientific reporting.

2. The right to have homosexuality studied objectively, i.e., without an ever-present heterosexual frame of reference; the right to have homosexuality presented as simply a mode of behavior, not a deviation, a variation, perversion, inversion, etc.

3. The right to serious, scientific treatment of the role of the homosexual concerning overpopulation; eugenics, artificial insemination.

4. The right to impartial sex education of young people concerning homosexuality; the right to require scientists to fearlessly seek out and present factual information on the topic to adolescents; the right to demand objectivity from social scientists and case workers concerning the topic.

5. The right to defense from faulty court testimony by psychologists, psychiatrists, etc.

Source: Files of ONE Institute/International Gay and Lesbian Archives.

*   *   *

By the 1940s, alarmed at the growing number of bars in San Francisco that catered to homosexuals, the California state department of Alcoholic Beverage Control (ABC) started a campaign to close down such bars as "disorderly houses." The ABC would send a spy into a bar, and if he saw effeminate men or masculine women he would telephone the police to arrest the customers and levy a large fine to the owner of the bar. When the ABC raided the Black Cat bar in 1948, instead of paying the fine the owner hired a lawyer who sued the ABC for violating his civil rights. Eventually the case worked its way up to the California State Supreme Court, which ruled in the bar owner's favor.

Meanwhile, in the 1950s San Francisco police were arresting three hundred to four hundred gay people per week on charges like solicitation and lewd behavior. The typical result is that the person would have to hire a lawyer for about $250, who would negotiate with the judge for a no contest plea, pay a fine averaging $50, and be given six months' probation. Such costs were considered the price for being homosexual, and the money that went to pay lawyers, police, and the courts essentially constituted a tax on the emerging gay community. An employee of the Black Cat, a Latino drag queen named Jose Sarria, finally stood up to this extortion, and began advising every arrested gay person to plead not guilty and demand a trial by jury. Eventually, when enough people started doing this, it so clogged the city courts that a judge ordered the police to back off.

Jose Sarria would entertain the Black Cat audience with clever drag spoofs on opera. His ever-more-elaborate opera shows, in which he sang both male and female roles, were so funny that they attracted packed crowds to the bar. Jose mixed serious comments, telling people to "be proud of who you are" and "don't worry about what people think," along with his humor. Sometimes after his show he would lead the entire audience down the block to the city jail, where he would lead the crowd singing "God save us nellie queens" to the arrested homosexuals inside waiting arraignment. This was his way of building a sense of solidarity among gay people, to give them strength to demand a jury trial.

By the early 1960s Jose Sarria was the most notable gay person in San Francisco. He would become even more famous after being crowned as the first Empress of the Imperial Court, an organization of drag queens that sponsored shows and supported various gay and nongay charities and political candidates.

In 1960, after listening to homophobic politicians rant and rave against the "threat of sexual perversion," Jose decided to do what no openly gay person had ever done in the United States—to run for public office on a platform of freedom for homosexuals. While having no thought that he would actually win a seat on the San Francisco Board of Supervisors, Sarria wanted to use the 1961 election as an opportunity to let the city establishment know that gay people constituted a significant percentage of the electorate, and that they were not going to take any more abuse by the police. A reporter for the *Bay Area Reporter* later interviewed Sarria to summarize what happened.

DOCUMENT 58: Jose Sarria Runs for San Francisco City Council (1961)

In 1960—to the delight of some and the dismay of many in the emerging gay community—the Sunday afternoon opera queen decided to run for San Francisco Supervisor. "I said in 1960 that we have 10,000 votes in this town and we could win an election," Jose said. "They told me I was full of shit."

The one thing you never tell Jose is that he can't accomplish something. With the determination of the spurned, Jose set about to prove his point. "I needed $25 and 35 signatures [to file as a candidate]. The $25 was easy. But I couldn't get the signatures. Many told me they were behind me, but that they just could not sign. Nobody wanted to endorse a known homosexual...."

[After finally collecting the signatures, Jose filed with the city clerk as a candidate.] To say that the political establishment was horrified by the prospect of a queen in City Hall would be an understatement. Both Republicans and the Democrats refused to list Jose—a tactic to keep him off the ballot. "I went in to the Democrats and told them I had been a Democrat all my life and you cannot deny me the right to run. And if you do I will sue your ass and take you all the way to the Supreme Court," Jose said. Since the Black Cat case was by this time headed for the Supreme Court, it was not an idle threat.

The Democrats listed Jose—but city leaders packed the ballot....Jose didn't win—"If I would have won, I would have died!" he said—but his 7,000 votes shocked the city. In an era when most Americans still would not utter the word "homosexual," a barmaid opera queen whose best Sunday suit was a red dress had won 7,000 votes for public office. San Francisco would never be the same....

[After losing the election] Jose took the next natural step: declared himself ruling monarch of the gay community....Many in the emerging gay community saw Jose's camp as a potential embarrassment to them—even though Jose had by now written the book on gay lib in San Francisco. The biggest gay meetings ever were held—all to argue over whether a drag queen should be allowed to represent the gay community...."Here is the problem," the Empress Jose told the audience. "You don't want a man dressed up as a woman running around town representing you. So let me tell you...if you don't agree, I'll do it anyway...." Few can doubt that the Empress I Jose reigns still. He is the Queen Mother of the gay community.

Source: Brian Jones, "Empress I Jose," *Bay Area Reporter* October 10, 1985, pp. 12–13.

* * *

The American Civil Liberties Union (ACLU) has been the major institution in the twentieth century to challenge infringements of individual rights in the United States. It sends lawyers, most of whom volunteer to take precedent-setting cases *pro bono* [without charging a fee], to argue for civil rights legal suits in court. Many of the nation's modern advances in civil rights have been made by ACLU attorneys.

However, during the 1950s, the ACLU refused to take cases relating to the federal government's policy of firing gay men and lesbians as security risks, or challenging laws that criminalized homosexual behavior. Activists in Los Angeles, San Francisco, New York, and Washington, D.C. convinced their local ACLU chapters to appeal to the Union's national board of directors. In 1963 the national ACLU agreed to accept gay and lesbian rights as an important aspect of the battle for civil liberties in the United States. According to a history of the ACLU Lesbian and Gay Rights Project, by project director Matt Coles, 1963 was an important turning point, as the organization jumped into the struggle for gay and lesbian rights.

DOCUMENT 59: ACLU Begins Gay Rights Cases (1963)

In that year it brought its first important challenge to federal civil service rules which allowed lesbians and gay men to be fired on the basis of sexual orientation [*Scott v. Macy*]. It took twelve years, but the U.S. Civil Service Commission eventually changed those rules in response to another ACLU sponsored case. Also in 1963, the ACLU brought its first challenge to a state sodomy law [*Enslin v. Walford*, followed by *Delany v. Florida* in 1967]....

The ACLU dockets of the '60s read like primers on just how bad things were only thirty years ago....Police didn't just raid gay bars. They shuttered them, particularly if they allowed people to dance or, god forbid, hold hands. They also sat outside bars and took down license plate numbers to intimidate people into staying away....[vice squads conducted] "sting" operations designed to entrap gay men into making passes at police officers. It would be years before those operations would cease in some parts of the U.S. [though police in many locales continue to do such stings today]. Throughout the '60s the ACLU fought government attempts to deport lesbians and gay men. Those efforts culminated in the [ACLU's] first U.S. Supreme Court case on gay rights, *Boutillier v. The Immigration and Naturalization Service*. We lost....

By the early 1970s, the issues were changing. Employment discrimination cases became more common. The ACLU brought its first challenge to an anti-gay military policy in 1970 [*Schlegel v. U.S.*, which also lost]. Even more interesting, issues that are still hotly contested today started appearing on ACLU dockets in the '70s. In 1972, well ahead of its time, the ACLU brought the first challenge to a ban on same-sex marriage...[*Baker v. Nelson* and *McConnell v. University of Minnesota* where the ACLU defended a] librarian fired because he attempted to marry his partner....In 1973 the ACLU took on the defense of a much honored teacher in Washington who lost his job for being gay. Although we lost the [*Gaylord v. Tacoma*] case, we forced a university in Mississippi in 1977 to recognize a lesbian and gay student group [*Mississippi Gay Alliance v. Mississippi State University*]....In 1976 *Voeller v. Voeller* [the ACLU mounted a] defense of a gay father denied visitation with his children....

In 1980 Wisconsin passed the first statewide law against employment discrimination based on sexual orientation. In the '70s and early '80s, twenty-one states got rid of sodomy laws, and in a 1980 ACLU case [*People v. Onofre*], New York's highest court struck down its sodomy law as a violation of the right to privacy....[Other prominent ACLU cases included] a 1982 case in which the ACLU brought a suit [*Brinkin v. Southern Pacific*] for funeral leave for a gay man whose lover died....[In 1984 *National Gay and Lesbian Task Force v. Oklahoma* was a great victory when the United States] Supreme Court strikes down a law targeting teachers who support gay rights.

Source: Matt Coles, "Looking Back: Lesbian and Gay Rights, AIDS, and the ACLU," *Lesbian & Gay Rights, AIDS/HIV, 2000: An ACLU Report* (New York: American Civil Liberties Union, 2000), pp. 5–7.

*   *   *

Bayard Rustin (1910–1987) was an African American pacifist who had been imprisoned during World War II for resisting the draft, and later for challenging segregation laws in the South. As a prominent officer in the pacifist Fellowship of Reconciliation, he went to India at the invitation of Gandhi's Congress Party, and served as an advisor to Ghana's President Kwame Nkrumah. In 1953 Rustin was arrested again, this time by a policeman in Pasadena, California, who accused Rustin of engaging in sex with two young men in the backseat of a car. He served sixty days in jail on a morals charge, and was forced to resign his position in the Fellowship of Reconciliation.

Having been abandoned by the pacifist movement, Rustin gravitated to the black civil rights movement. By 1956 he was integral to the campaign to challenge segregation on buses in Montgomery, Alabama, and he became one of the most trusted advisors of the boycott's leader Dr. Martin Luther King, Jr. Rustin influenced King, especially by bringing his direct experience with the philosophy of nonviolence as practiced by Gandhi. King knew of Rustin's homosexuality and was supportive of him.

In 1963, when civil rights leaders decided to organize a massive March on Washington for equality, veteran African American leader A. Philip Randolph proposed Rustin as the person most capable of organizing the march. Some were nervous that Rustin's homosexuality would subject them to criticism, so they prevailed upon Randolph to serve as the formal leader of the march, with Rustin doing the actual work as his deputy. Despite this plan, South Carolina's segregationist leader Senator Strom Thurmond made a speech in the Senate denouncing Rustin for sexual perversion, and inserted a copy of Rustin's police booking slip from the 1953 morals arrest into the *Congressional Record*.

Rustin's quiet dignity, in not denying his gayness and not retreating when his homosexuality was publicized, became an example for many gay and lesbian activists. He was not deterred, but continued to work feverishly in organizing the march. He put together the most influential march in the history of the United States, helping to bring about the Civil Rights Act of 1964 and the Voting Rights Act of 1965. Rustin became an almost legendary figure in the civil rights movement.

The high point of the march was the "I Have a Dream" speech given by Martin Luther King, Jr. This became King's most famous speech, and an inspiration for all people around the world who were struggling against discrimination and prejudice of any kind. King's words inspired many gay and lesbian activists, who shared with him the dream that one day the United States would live up to the true meaning of its ideology, and be transformed into an oasis of freedom, justice, and equality.

Years later, King's widow Coretta Scott King came out in support of the gay Human Rights Campaign, and said that she was convinced that if her husband had lived longer he would have become a major voice in favor of gay and lesbian rights. She knew from King's close personal relationship with Bayard Rustin that he did not discriminate against gay people, and that he favored equality for everyone.

Bayard Rustin's prominence in civil rights organizing inspired many other gay, lesbian, bisexual, and transgendered persons of all races to become activists. According to Jervis Anderson, Rustin's biographer, after Thurmond's attacks on his homosexuality,

DOCUMENT 60: Bayard Rustin, Martin Luther King, and the March on Washington (1963)

Randolph's faith in his handpicked organizer remained unshaken. "Mr. Rustin," he said in a statement prepared for the press, "has more than satisfactorily conducted himself in the position with which he has been entrusted; and we have not the slightest intention of permitting his separation from that position. [We will not allow]…corrupt, undemocratic elements to deprive our movement of so capable a leader.…"

[After the march was an astounding success, congratulations poured in for Bayard Rustin.] History, Roy Wilkins wrote some years later, "has attached the name of the Reverend King to the march, but I suspect it would be more accurate to call it Randolph's march, and Rustin's."…

"Dr. King will go down in history as Lincoln did after the Gettysburg Address," Charles Bloomstein said. "But if there had been violence that day the media would have seized upon it, and King's great speech would have been drowned out. Bayard's masterful planning of the march made King's speech both possible and meaningful."

[The work that Rustin did] reflected not only his fine sense of political timing but also his eye for spontaneous moments in history that can seldom be successfully reorchestrated. "The march," he said in retrospect, "made Americans feel for the first time that we were capable of being truly a nation, that we were capable of moving beyond division and bigotry. I think it will be quite some time before there will be another such spiritual uprising in the hearts of the people. The human spirit is like a flame. It flashes up and is gone. And you never know when that flame will come again."

Source: Jervis Anderson, *Bayard Rustin: Troubles I've Seen* (New York: HarperCollins, 1997), pp. 251, 264.

*   *   *

By the 1960s Americans were beginning to take a more respectful attitude toward Native American values, and this included more accepting Indian attitudes toward sex. In 1964 ONE Institute sent a reporter to interview Elmer Gage, a thirty-five-year-old Mohave Indian at his home on the Colorado River Reservation. On the reservation Elmer was universally known as homosexual, and though some Mohaves sometimes made fun of him about it, he was generally accepted. He was respected as the best Mohave craftsman and beadworker of his generation, and he was a traditional Bird Dancer. He lived with his elderly grandmother and took care of her. More than a few Mohave men had sexual relations with him. Elmer Gage evidenced a psychological self-acceptance that was rare among white homosexuals of the time. *ONE Magazine* published this interview in 1965 to inspire others to take a more self-accepting attitude and to be true to their own self. Asked by the interviewer if he considered being gay a disadvantage, Elmer replied:

DOCUMENT 61: Mohave Indian Two-Spirit Person (1964)

*   *   *

E: I can't say if it's a disadvantage being gay because I've been this way so long. Who knows? It's a disadvantage being a lot of things. It's a disadvantage not having money, a lot of things….Do I like being made fun of? I don't like it much. When they start to talk about me I just go along with it. I'm not crazy about it. But, for the most part, we all get along. They don't mean any harm by it.

Q: How did you learn about sex?

E: From other boys my age. Of course, it took me awhile to get it all straight in my mind. But we played around a lot and I enjoyed it. Now most of those kids are married and have children of their own….But some of the boys run around with me. We have a good time. Oh, I don't mean like sex all the time. I mean we have a good time like friends—singing Mohave songs and dancing….

Being gay has its disadvantages. But I don't think I would like to change. I guess I'm on my own personal little warpath—not against whites but against heterosexuals who think everyone should be like them. I'm not always happy, but I am always me. And they can like it or lump it. Life's too short to spend your time being something you don't want to be. Like the old saying, "To thine own self be true." I'm true to myself and my own nature. I think that's all anyone has a right to ask of me.

Source: Bob Waltrip, "Elmer Gage: American Indian," *ONE Magazine* 13 (March 1965), pp. 6–10.

* * *

The gay rights movement took a militant turn in the 1960s partly due to the determination of Frank Kameny. He grew up in New York City's immigrant Jewish community, entered college at age fifteen, and after serving in the army during World War II, went on to get his Ph.D. in astronomy from Harvard University. He was hired by the United States Map Service to make sky surveys. After teaching astronomy at Georgetown University, and gaining "superior" ratings from his United States civil service superiors, his promising scientific career suddenly came to a halt in 1957 when a government investigator found evidence that Kameny was a homosexual.

Dr. Kameny did not deny the charge but fought his dismissal through all levels of the Civil Service administrative appeals process. He wrote letters to congressmen and to President Eisenhower, but got no response. He then hired a lawyer to challenge his firing in court, but his suit to regain his job was defeated at every level. After running out of money, the lawyer gave up, but Frank Kameny did not. He wrote his own brief, and submitted an appeal to the United States Supreme Court. In 1961 he learned that the Supreme Court had declined to review his appeal.

Dr. Kameny had lost his government security clearance when he was fired, and as a result he could not find another job for nearly two years. The brilliant astronomer was reduced to poverty, and had to get food from the Salvation Army. Most people would have retreated into depression, but Frank Kameny got angry at the injustices and economic discrimination he had faced. In 1961 he spearheaded the formation of the Mattachine Society of Washington (MSW). Though he took the name of the California-based Mattachines, his group was completely independent. He shaped MSW into a group that put civil liberties and law reform as its top priority. Influenced by the increasing militancy of the African American civil rights movement, Kameny championed a bold, strong, uncompromising, and militant stance that called for absolute equality for homosexuals. At a homophile conference in 1964, Kameny spoke of the need to use a vigorous, social-protest model for the movement, just as black people were doing. He rejected the idea that homosexuals would win acceptance by depending upon sympathetic heterosexual experts to make their case. Homosexuals themselves, he argued, were the true experts on homosexuality, and they should not be cowed by ignorant psychiatrists parading as authorities. He formed an alliance with the Washington, D.C. chapter of the American Civil Liberties Union, convincing them to condemn government investigations of peoples' private sexual behavior.

With an amazing energy level, Kameny brought court suits, served as counsel to government employees who were being investigated for homosexuality, wrote letters to congressmen, sent out press releases, testified before official hearings, and traveled widely to spread his message that homosexuals should be proud of who they are. Adapting the civil rights statement "Black Is Beautiful," Kameny coined the slogan, "Gay Is Good." He wanted homosexuals to stop internalizing society's view that their sexual feelings were sick, and instead to realize that the real sickness was society's prejudice. He explained his civil libertarian approach in numerous speeches and the following interview.

DOCUMENT 62: Frank Kameny Resists Job Firing (1964)

We place our government on notice that we are unwilling any longer to be selected out. Everything heterosexuals have, we're going to have. We've been shoved around for three thousand years and we're tired of it and we're starting to shove back. And we're going to keep shoving back until we are guaranteed our rights. We are organizing stepped-up resistance by the homosexual minority the country over—against the implementation of the federal government's antihomosexual policies—resistance by individuals and by groups, by formal legal process and by demonstration and other methods. There are more of us than there are Justice Department lawyers to cope with our cases, and we will swamp them and the courts with a tide of litigation!....

It is time to open the closet door and let in the fresh air and the sunshine; it is time to doff and to discard the secrecy, the disguise, and the camouflage; it is time to hold up your heads and to look the world squarely in the eye as the homosexuals that you are, confident of your equality, confident in the knowledge that as objects of prejudice and victims of discrimination you are right and they are wrong, and confident of the rightness of what you are and of the goodness of what you do; it is time to live your homosexuality fully, joyously, openly, and proudly, assured that morally, socially, physically, psychologically, emotionally, and in every other way; Gay is good. It is.

Source: Kay Tobin and Randy Wicker, *The Gay Crusaders* (New York: Paperback Library, 1972), pp. 89, 133–134.

* * *

Convinced by his own experience that attempting to convince authorities was not very effective, Frank Kameny led the Mattachine Society of Washington to begin a dramatic confrontation against the federal government. He saw government, psychiatry, and churches as the three top archenemies of gay and lesbian rights. It was ironic, he wrote, that in World War II he fought Germans to establish freedom for stigmatized minorities in Europe, and now had to fight the United States government to establish freedom for stigmatized homosexuals in America. In 1965 thirteen Mattachine members arrived with signs to picket in front of the White House. To show their patriotism, the picketers carried signs protesting Fidel Castro's government discrimination against homosexuals in Cuba, but other signs protested similar mistreatment by the United States government. Television coverage guaranteed publicity for this first-ever protest by homosexuals in front of the presidential mansion.

With the success of this picket, Mattachine members went to Philadelphia on July 4, to do a similar picket at Independence Hall and the Liberty Bell. In front of the building where Thomas Jefferson first read the Declaration of Independence to the Continental Congress, Kameny pointed out the contradiction between the promise of "life, liberty, and the pursuit of happiness" for all Americans, with the fact that in the 1960s homosexuals had none of these guarantees. In *The Ladder*, Kameny spelled out his strategy to gain gay and lesbian rights.

DOCUMENT 63: Mattachine Pickets the White House (1965)

There was, and is, a feeling that given any fair chance to undertake dialogue with our opponents, we would be able to impress them with the basic rightness of our position. Unfortunately, by this approach alone we will not prevail because most people operate not rationally, but emotionally, on questions of sex in general, and homosexuality in particular.

It is thus necessary for us to adopt a strongly positive approach, a militant one. It is for us to take the initiative—the offensive, not the defensive—in matters affecting us. It is time that we begin to move from endless talk (directed in the last analysis by us to ourselves) to firm, vigorous action.

We are right; those who oppose us are both factually and morally wrong. We are the true authorities on homosexuality, whether we are accepted as such or not. We must demand our rights, boldly, not beg cringingly for mere privileges, and not be satisfied with crumbs tossed to us.

The question of homosexuality as a sickness is probably the most important single issue facing our movement today. There are some who say that we will not be accepted as authorities, regardless of what evidence we present, and therefore we must take no positions on this matter but must wait for the accepted authorities to come around to our position—if they do. This makes us a mere passive battlefield across which conflicting "authorities" fight their intellectual battles. I, for one, am not prepared to let others dispose of me as they see fit. I intend to play an active role in the determination of my own fate.

Source: Frank Kameny, in *The Ladder* v. 9, n. 8 (May 1965), pp. 14–20.

*   *   *

The Mattachine Society and the Daughters of Bilitis (DOB), both headquartered in San Francisco, considered the local bar scene to be less than respectable and hopelessly apolitical. They also considered bars damaging because of the alcoholism that resulted from gay peoples' regular attendance at these drinking establishments. But though some customers had drinking problems, other people went to the bars as social centers more than just to drink. Police harassment had finally prompted the bar owners, and their customers, to respond politically. After Jose Sarria's astounding 1961 campaign for the San Francisco Board of Supervisors, his supporters organized the League for Civil Education and began publishing a newspaper, *LCE News*. The emphasis was to encourage gay men and lesbians to register to vote, and to begin a bloc vote for local candidates for public office who would be favorable to gay rights. The newspaper's editor, Guy Strait, knew that to get significant numbers of followers he would have to distribute the newspaper in the city's gay bars. In order to attract readers he detailed examples of police mistreatment of gays. Within a couple of years he started receiving paid advertisements from political candidates who realized they could attract gay votes by campaigning for police department reform.

The bar owners themselves, who were fed up with continued raids by the police, organized a Tavern Guild in 1962. Two years later this

Guild supported the formation of the Society for Individual Rights (SIR), to be their political mouthpiece. The main leader to emerge in SIR was Jim Foster, who had been expelled from the United States Army in 1959 because of his homosexuality. His dishonorable discharge prompted him to become activist, and he moved to San Francisco because of its growing reputation as a "gay mecca." Foster combined popular social events with militant political action to raise gay people's awareness in his adopted city. SIR began to publish a monthly magazine, opened a gay community center, sponsored voter registration drives, held meetings for candidates to speak, brought legal suits against the police, and organized demonstrations. As he became more political, Foster became a force within the San Francisco Democratic Party. Heterosexual candidates for local political office lobbied for his support in exchange for their promise to support gay and lesbian rights. Foster became convinced that involvement in the Democratic Party was the most effective strategy for gay people to attract heterosexual supporters, and he eventually established the first gay and lesbian Democratic Club.

The other group of heterosexuals to whom San Francisco activists reached out were local Christian ministers. One of the most influential was Reverend Cecil Williams, an African American minister who recognized the similarities between antiblack and antigay discrimination. Williams and other liberal heterosexual ministers agreed with gay activists to open a dialogue between the churches and the gay and lesbian community. Along with representatives from the Society for Individual Rights, the Mattachine Society, the Daughters of Bilitis, and the Tavern Guild, these ministers formed The Council on Religion and the Homosexual in 1964. In order to raise funds for the new group, and to demonstrate their support for the gay community, the ministers decided to host a costume ball on New Year's Eve. What happened at this dance was a turning point, reported in early 1965 by *The Ladder*, which energized gays and lesbians by the activism of sympathetic heterosexuals in the struggle against police oppression.

DOCUMENT 64: San Francisco Activism (1965)

Dozens of police swarmed in and around California Hall in San Francisco on New Year's Day, invading a benefit costume ball organized by the Council on Religion and the Homosexual. A line-up of police cars, one paddy wagon, plainclothes and uniformed officers, and police photographers greeted over 600 patrons at this supposedly gala event. Attending the ball were prominent ministers in the San Francisco area, as well as many members of their congregations....

Arrested were three attorneys and a housewife who challenged inspectors from the sex-crimes detail by insisting the police needed either a warrant, or information that a crime was being committed, in order to enter the hall. The four were charged with obstructing police officers. A clergyman was threatened with arrest....

"Angry Ministers Rip Police" said one newspaper headline over a report of a press conference held by the ministers on January 2. The clergymen accused the police of "intimidation, broken promises, and obvious hostility...." San Francisco newspapers carried a stream of letters and articles about the ball. Wire service reports were picked up by newspapers around the country. Radio and TV (including BBC) discussed the repercussions from the ball and also took up the subject of homosexuality in general....

Del Martin, DOB treasurer and a member of the Council, commented that "this is the type of police activity that homosexuals know well, but heretofore the police had never played their hand before Mr. Average Citizen....It was always the testimony of the police officer versus the homosexual, and the homosexual, fearing publicity and knowing the odds were against him, succumbed. But in this instance the police overplayed their part....Police action in this affair will be contested in court to establish the right of homosexuals and all adults to assemble lawfully without invasion of privacy."

The homosexual-dance cause celebre (see "After the Ball" in the February/March LADDER) closed on a technicality in court.

On New Year's Day in San Francisco, police had harassed a benefit costume ball organized by the Council on Religion and the Homosexual to raise funds for its work. Three attorneys and a woman ticket-taker had been arrested. The Council hoped that the trial might pave the way to a substantive decision concerning homosexuals' rights of legal assembly and privacy. But the court hearing was cut short when the judge ordered a not-guilty verdict because of confusion in the State's formal complaint that the lawyers and the woman had interferred with police entry to the ball.

Before the premature close of the trial, however, the court heard some colorful explanations from the testifying chief of the police department's sex-crimes detail. When asked why police photographers had snapped pictures of guests arriving at the hall where the dance was held, Inspector Nieto replied that police "wanted pictures of these people because some of them might be connected to national security." Nieto was also asked why he took along to the ball more than a dozen officers and a policewoman plus the two photographers. He side-stepped with the assertion, "We went just to inspect the premises."

Source: Kay Tobin, "After the Ball...," *The Ladder* February–March 1965, pp. 4–5, and June 1965, p. 16.

*   *   *

As a college student in 1950, Barbara Gittings felt so isolated as a lesbian that she began diligently searching in books for every mention of homosexuality she could find. Eventually she learned about ONE Inc. in California. For her vacation in 1956 Gittings flew from Philadelphia to the West Coast and made contact with leaders of ONE and the Mattachine Society, who put her in touch with the recently organized Daughters of Bilitis (DOB). Gittings attended her first DOB meeting where she met organizers Del Martin and Phyllis Lyon. Two years later in 1958 they tapped her to start a New York chapter of DOB, and Gittings was elected its first president. In 1963, assisted by her photographer lover Kay Tobin Lahusen, Gittings became editor of DOB's publication *The Ladder*, the first national lesbian magazine.

Soon Gittings met Frank Kameny. His militant civil rights approach inspired her to become more confrontational and activist. The gay rights movement in the 1960s was strongly influenced by tactics of the African American civil rights movement. Gittings and Tobin participated in gay pickets at the White House and the Pentagon in Washington in 1965, and at Independence Hall in Philadelphia every July Fourth from 1965 through 1969. In *The Ladder* they highlighted these direct-action protests. While DOB's board of directors favored a more cautious approach such as influencing sympathetic heterosexual authorities, Gittings via *The Ladder* emphasized pickets for civil rights and challenges to the sickness label which hampered the drive for equality for homosexuals.

To boost distribution of *The Ladder*, she persuaded a handful of progressive bookstores in Philadelphia and New York to sell the magazine on their shelves; no gay/lesbian bookstores existed at that time. She added the out-of-the-closet subtitle "A Lesbian Review" to attract attention, and began featuring Kay Tobin's photographs of actual lesbians on the magazine's covers, with interviews inside encouraging more readers to come out as open lesbians. For example, in the June 1966 issue Gittings published an interview with an African American woman who was then vice-president of the New York chapter of Daughters of Bilitis, with her photo on the cover. The back cover had another photo of the same lesbian, showing her picketing in front of the White House with a sign that said "Denial of Equality of Opportunity Is Immoral." This interview subject was much more militant than most members of Daughters of Bilitis, yet she shared many other gay people's prejudices about gender-nonconformist masculine females and feminine males.

DOCUMENT 65: Lesbian Activism and *The Ladder* (1966)

Picketing I regard as almost a conservative activity now. The homosexual has to call attention to the fact that he's been unjustly acted upon. This is what the Negro did....I do regard picketing as a form of education! But one thing that disturbs me a lot is that there seems to be some sort of premium placed on psychologists and therapists by the homophile movement. I personally don't understand why that should be. So far as I'm concerned, homosexuality per se is not a sickness. When our groups seek out the therapists and psychologists, to me this is admitting we are ill by the very nature of our preference. And this disturbs me very much....

Homosexuals are invisible, except for the stereotypes, and I feel homosexuals have to become visible and to assert themselves politically. Once homosexuals do this, society will start to give more and more....Any movement needs a certain number of courageous people, there's no getting around it. They have to come out on behalf of the cause and accept whatever consequences come....

I don't find in the homophile movement enough stress on courtroom action. I would like to see more test cases in courts, so that our grievances can be brought out into the open. That's one of the ways for a movement to gain exposure, a way that's completely acceptable to everybody....We should concentrate on the discrimination by the government in employment and military service, the laws used against homosexuals, the rejection by the churches....

Also, I think we ought to have for officers of our organizations people who are ordinary-looking men and women. I feel very strongly that a woman who's very masculine, or a man who's very effeminate, should not be an officer in the homophile movement. This is my personal opinion. Our officers shouldn't be the stereotypes, for God's sake! We're trying to counteract the notion that homosexuals are like that....We need more "intellectual" and "professional"-level people in the movement....

Some homophile groups are [too conservative], with the same sort of predisposition to take things easy, not to push too fast, not stick their necks out too far. For instance, demonstrations, as far as I'm concerned, are one of the very first steps toward changing society....In the homophile movement, some segments will have to be so vocal and so progressive, until they eventually push the ultra-conservative segments into a more progressive line of thinking and action....

Source: Barbara Gittings and Kay Tobin, "Interview with Ernestine Eckstein," *The Ladder* June 1966, pp. 4–11.

* * *

In 1966 the leaders of the Daughters of Bilitis pressured Barbara Gittings to resign as editor of *The Ladder* because she was too radical for them. Instead of feeling defeated, however, Gittings simply redirected her efforts. Freed from her time-consuming work in DOB, Gittings plunged into a strong alliance with Frank Kameny to work on reducing discrimination against homosexuals. The two of them soon became an effective team, being interviewed on radio and television shows, assisting lawyers in court suits, sending press releases, speaking at colleges, and organizing demonstrations. Both Gittings and Kameny lived frugally and held minor jobs that were easy for them to leave, giving up their own personal financial security in favor of activism. Their selfless devotion to helping others inspired them to attend numerous security clearance hearings as co-counsels for government employees being accused of homosexuality. When they went to hearings, often held in the Pentagon, they always made sure to dress very conservatively. Gittings talked about the tactics they used in 1966:

DOCUMENT 66: Barbara Gittings and Frank Kameny Push the Pentagon (1966)

I wore a dress, and heels and hose, and Frank always had on a suit, white shirt, and tie. We looked great, but there was one jarring note we employed to unsettle the hearing examiners. We wore one or two slogan buttons with blatant messages that were completely out of step with the rest of our conventional attire. The little buttons made statements like "Cheers for Queers," "Gay is Good," and one of the most deliberate eyepoppers of all time, "Pray for Sodomy!"

Publicity was the objective. So we held press conferences for the benefit of sharp-eyed reporters. And, when we first went into a hearing room, we made certain to shake hands with all adversary participants so those persons could not avoid reading our buttons. Throughout the rest of the day they had to either look at us or consciously ignore us, but they wouldn't be able to forget what our buttons said.

As I grew older, I found that I cared less about what people thought. When the first invitations came to go [be interviewed] on radio, I was scared, but I accepted. As it turned out, I enjoyed it. I was always ready to do something different, and I haven't had any regrets. Good times were part of the early years, even though you never knew what was going to happen....Every time I had to make a decision to put myself forward or stay back, to use my real name or not, to go on television or decline, to get out on some of the earliest picket lines or remain behind, I usually took the public position because there weren't many of us yet that could afford the risk.

Source: Troy D. Perry and Thomas L. P. Swicegood, *Profiles in Gay and Lesbian Courage* (New York: St. Martin's Press, 1991), pp. 168–169.

*   *   *

The United States Immigration and Naturalization Service (INS) regularly excluded or deported any immigrant who was discovered to be homosexual. Under Sections 1182 and 1251 of Title 8 of the United States Code, those "afflicted with psychopathic personality, or sexual deviation, or mental defect" could be excluded from the United States. With the help of the American Civil Liberties Union, a gay immigrant challenged this exclusion in *Boutilier v. INS*, but in 1967 the United States Supreme Court ruled against the immigrant and ordered him deported. For over a decade after that, the INS used this decision to justify deporting homosexuals. Even after the president of the American Psychiatric Association wrote a letter to the INS commissioner pointing out that homosexuality was no longer classified as an illness, the INS refused to change its policy. The executive director of the American Civil Liberties Union also requested the INS to halt its deportations of homosexuals, but in vain. On August 8, 1974, INS Acting General Counsel Sam Bernsen replied to these requests:

DOCUMENT 67: Supreme Court Excludes and Deports Homosexual Immigrants (1967)

The United States Supreme Court in *Boutilier v. INS*, 387 U.S. 118 (1967) stated its conclusion that the Congress used the phrase "psychopathic personality" not in the clinical sense but to effectuate its purpose to exclude from entry all homosexuals and other sexual perverts. The Supreme Court upheld the Service position that an alien is deportable if he was excludable under Section 212(a)(4) of the Immigration and Nationality Act on the ground that he was a homosexual at the time of entry....Naturalization, as you undoubtedly know, is a judicial function. However, the Service position is that a petitioner for naturalization who is or has been a homosexual during the relevant statutory period is precluded from establishing the good moral character required for admission to citizenship. See Petition of Olga Schmidt, 289 N.Y. Supp. 2d 89 (1968). Although some courts have admitted homosexuals to citizenship, *In re Labady*, 326 F. Supp. 924 (1971), this Service will continue to recommend to the courts that homosexuals be denied citizenship on the ground that they do not possess the good moral character required for citizenship.

Source: Howard Brown, *Familiar Faces, Hidden Lives: The Story of Homosexual Men in America Today* (New York: Harcourt Brace Jovanovich, 1976), p. 232.

*   *   *

Gay activism in Los Angeles was debilitated in 1965 by internal squabbling within ONE Institute, which under Dorr Legg's leadership was focusing on education, and Don Slater's faction, which saw the publishing of *ONE Magazine* as more important. Rather than compromising, or allowing different individuals to develop both education and publishing, Legg and Slater each tried to take over the organization. This led to a tragic court suit which factionalized ONE, and both sides were weakened. Discouraged by the in-fighting, the following year ONE Institute cofounder Jim Kepner joined a new generation of gay rights activists to form a new group called Personal Rights in Defense and Education (PRIDE). While a number of homophile activists of the 1950s believed in equality for homosexuals, they could never marshal large numbers of people to turn out for public protests. What changed by the 1960s was the fact that more people were starting to come out publicly as gay and lesbian, and the example of massive public protests offered by the civil rights movement and the anti-war movement. Kepner served as a bridge between the old homophile movement and the new mass protest approach.

DOCUMENT 68: PRIDE and *The Advocate* Magazine (1967)

As with previous homophile groups, a top priority of PRIDE was concern over police harassment, but it could draw on the rebellious mindset of the '60s generation to prompt large-scale demonstrations and protests against the Los Angeles Police Department.

[For] Los Angeles homosexuals, as in most urban centers, fear and loathing ruled the day; anxiety over the capricious nature of law enforcement agencies when it came to homosexuality—bar raids, illegal entrapment, and a widespread application of "lewd conduct" laws—made just about anybody open for arrest at any time....It was the particularly brutal Los Angeles Police Department raid on the Black Cat bar in the first hour of 1967 that put the players in motion. Police swept into the Black Cat shortly into the New Year, severely beating an employee and arresting others there and at another nearby Silver Lake gay bar. A few weeks later, PRIDE organized its largest public protest ever in response to the attack, two and a half years before another police raid on the Stonewall Inn in New York City would similarly ignite gay men and lesbians on the East Coast. The Los Angeles gay community was galvanized, and PRIDE swelled with new members.

Source: Mark Thompson, ed., *Long Road to Freedom: The Advocate History of the Gay and Lesbian Movement* (New York: St. Martin's Press, 1994), pp. xvii–xviii. [Hereafter referred to as Thompson, *Long Road to Freedom*.]

* * *

Central to gay activism was the need for communication of gay community concerns, yet by the mid 1960s both *ONE Magazine* and *The Mattachine Review*, as well as *The Ladder*, were all in decline. Seeing this void, in 1967 three Los Angeles activists involved in PRIDE—Dick Michaels, Bill Rand, and Sam Winston—took the initiative to expand PRIDE's newsletter into a national gay magazine. They wanted to build a publication with widespread circulation, to get the word out about what was happening. The almost nonexistent coverage of gay news by mainstream newspapers made the need for a gay newspaper all the more urgent.

Though PRIDE disbanded in 1967 due to internal squabbling, it left an important legacy with the emergence of its newspaper *The Advocate*. Within a year it had become the largest gay periodical in the nation. It not only let activists around the United States know what was happening, and helped to publicize gay rights arguments, but it also marked the first time that businesses began to do significant advertising in a gay publication. Many gay organizations got started by first announcing their meetings in *The Advocate*. The banner headline in the first issue, in September 1967, blazed, "Gay Power," and the editorial stated:

We feel *The Advocate* can perform a very important service as the newspaper of the homophile community—a service that should be delayed no longer. Homosexuals, more than ever before, are out to win their legal rights, to end the injustices against them, to experience their share of happiness in their own way. If *The Advocate* can help in achieving these goals, all the time, sweat, and money that goes into it will be well spent.

The editorial of the second issue stated:

[Our] day will come. We do not ask for our rights on bended knee. We demand them, standing tall, as dignified human beings. We will not go away.

Source: The Advocate, September 1967, and October 1967. Quoted in Thompson, *Long Road to Freedom*, pp. 1–2.

* * *

Troy Perry was an ordained minister in a strict fundamentalist Christian Church. When he discussed his feelings of attraction for other males with another minister, the pastor told him to marry a woman and that would cause his same-sex desires to go away. After following that advice, Perry was dismayed to find that his feelings did not go away. Eventually he discussed the issue with his wife and they agreed to end their marriage. Although Perry came out as a gay man, he still did not want to abandon Christianity. After a number of churches rejected him, in 1968 he established the Metropolitan Community Church (MCC). In his role as the MCC minister, Rev. Perry became a leading gay rights activist, modeling his social justice work on the work of Martin Luther King, Jr. and other preachers who had become leaders in the civil rights movement. In an interview by editor Joseph Amster of *The Blade* magazine Perry recalled his history of activism in MCC.

DOCUMENT 69: Rev. Troy Perry Founds the Metropolitan Community Church (1968)

My church had excommunicated me...and told me that God couldn't possibly love me. That started a journey where I found that God really did love me. I say to people, 31 years after the founding of the Metropolitan Community Churches, that "God didn't create you so God could have something to sit around and hate." In early 1968 I'd gone through a suicide attempt. I'd taken the attitude that...[if] God couldn't love me and my family couldn't love me, then life wasn't worth living. I crawled into a bathtub, cut both my wrists, hoped I would die. Thank God I didn't....

[The next morning while praying I spoke to God and said] "You can't love me. The church has told me that over and over again...." Then God spoke to me in that still, small voice in the mind's ear and said, "Troy, don't tell Me what I can and can't do. I love you; you're my son. I don't have stepsons and -daughters." With that, I knew without a shadow of a doubt that I could be gay and Christian....

[After talking with other homosexuals who felt that God had abandoned them, later that year I prayed to God and asked] "If you want to see a church started as an outreach to the gay and lesbian community, but with its doors open to all, You just let me know when." And that still, small voice in my mind's ear let me know, "Now." With that, I took out an ad in *The Advocate*...and invited people to come and worship with me. On October 6, 1968, twelve people showed up in the living room of my home. Nine friends, three strangers, one person of color, one Jew, one female, one heterosexual couple....The rest is history....

Within two years of the founding of the church, we owned our original piece of property here in Los Angeles. It was the first piece of property ever owned by a gay organization in America....[After that church building was burned by arsonists, instead of giving up I decided] to start other Metropolitan Community Churches and to start the denomination and to give full time to that. We've seen incredible growth. We have 310 churches now, 48,000 members. About a quarter of a million people a year attend our churches....Our clergy are very involved in the local justice issues.... Where we find oppression, we have to help bring deliverance. "You've got to do more than just pray about things," I tell people. "You got to put legs on your prayers." And it means, get out and do something. So we've been at the forefront [of the struggle for gay and lesbian rights]....

We have had 21 of our churches arsoned and burned down to the ground in our 31 year history. But we've never, ever, left a city where we've faced persecution. We've had four of our clergy murdered....I was slapped in the face, called names, threatened with death. [Yet,] in the last year and a half, I've been invited to the White House three times...to be honored for my work in American society. We sat down at breakfast for two hours and 20 minutes with the President of the United States. So, things change....

I will not back away from who I am. I thank God for it. I believe my homosexuality is a gift from God. Because I know it is, I know I don't have apologies to give to anyone....

[In the 1960s and 1970s, in dealing with opposition like police brutality,] we didn't back away if the police did something. If they raided a bar, we came down hard. We held demonstrations, we surrounded the police station. I fasted and prayed for 16 days in downtown Los Angeles. After the first Gay Pride parade, I was arrested. I said I would fast and pray until somebody in city government talked to me. Sixteen days later, City Councilmember Bob Stephenson and his wife Peggy—who, later after he died, became a city councilmember from the Hollywood area—came and started a conversation with me about making a difference here in L.A. Later, in 1973, I was appointed to the Los Angeles County Human Relations Commission. I was the first gay individual in American history to be appointed to a human relations commission....

[The perception that gay rights began in 1969 with New York's Stonewall riots is] not true. The gay rights was already...getting ready to crest. We look to that as a time when gay people stood up in one city, but we were already standing up out here, too. MCC was founded nine months before Stonewall took place....I'm eternally grateful to God for people like Harry Hay, who, in 1950 started the Mattachine Society. Those folks started paving the way....

[As a result of the progress in gay and lesbian rights] it's a wonderful world out here. In the long run, once you stand up for yourself, it can make all the difference in the world....To the young people I say, "Don't be afraid; there's all kinds of resources. Get on the Internet and find them."

Source: Joseph S. Amster, "Reverend Troy Perry: The Cornerstone of the Gay Spiritual Movement," *The Blade* (Laguna Beach, California) v. 8, n. 10 (January 2000), pp. 44–49.

* * *

Organizations like SIR (Society for Individual Rights) in San Francisco and HAL (Homophile Action League) in Philadelphia were liminal (bridge) groups standing politically between the homophile organizations of the

1950s and early 1960s, and the gay liberation groups of the 1970s. HAL was founded in 1968 by former members of Philadelphia Daughters of Bilitis. This group announced that its purpose was political and thus social action rather than "fitting in" was going to be their approach to fighting for lesbian and gay rights. During its years of existence, HAL members challenged commonly held negative views about homosexuality, hosted and attended movement conferences, fought against discrimination, opposed police raids and entrapment, fought legal battles to improve their legal standing, and pressured the mainstream media to provide more visibility and fewer stereotypes. In short, they helped move the struggle for homosexual rights toward gay pride and activism.

The Organization's first newsletter carried this editorial:

DOCUMENT 70: Homophile Action League (1968)

This newly formed group, open to both men and women, has adopted the name "Homophile Action League," and has as its main purpose "to strive to change society's legal, social and scientific attitudes toward the homosexual in order to achieve justified recognition of the homosexual as a first class citizen and a first class human being."

This far reaching goal will be sought through a variety of means. A major emphasis will be placed on informing and enlightening the public, through the utilization of the mass media and diverse publications. Another focus will be on assisting homosexuals in the battle to secure their constitutional rights and to deal effectively with all manner of publicly-sanctioned discrimination against them. Still another vehicle for implementing our purpose will be the initiation of and participation in social action projects, such as organizing a boycott of business firms whose personal policies discriminate against homosexuals.

We wish to emphasize that word "ACTION" in our name. There is much work to be done and it is our intention to do it. We are *not* a social group. We do *not* intend to concentrate energies on "uplifting" the homosexual community, for such efforts would be badly misplaced. It is our firm conviction that it is the heterosexual community which is sadly in need of uplifting and it is in that direction that our action will be focussed [sic].

Source: *Homophile Action League Newsletter* (1968); p. 1. Copy in ONE Institute and Archives.

* * *

Carl Wittman was active in the 1960s radical New Left group Students for a Democratic Society (SDS) in Philadelphia, before moving to San

Francisco to work in the labor union movement. Wittman came out in San Francisco, and drew inspiration from the Black Power movement, the sexual revolution, feminism, and the hip counterculture movement, applying their principles on behalf of gay men's freedom. In early 1969 he wrote A Gay Manifesto which offered new ideas of gay liberation and respect for effeminate queens. Wittman's Manifesto was widely printed in underground leftist newspapers, where radicals who were gay and lesbian encountered it. Wittman, who later went on to found a rural gay commune in Wolf Creek, Oregon, captured the mood of 1969:

DOCUMENT 71: A Gay Manifesto (1969)

Where once there was frustration, alienation, and cynicism, there are new characteristics among us. We are full of love for each other and are showing it; we are full of anger at what has been done to us. And as we recall all the self-censorship and repression for so many years, a reservoir of tears pours out of our eyes. And we are euphoric, high, with the initial flourish of a movement....

Our first job is to free ourselves; that means clearing our heads of the garbage that's been poured into them...[such as] male chauvinism: All men are infected with male chauvinism—we were brought up that way....Male chauvinism, however, is not central to us. We can junk it much more easily than straight men can. For we understand oppression. We have largely opted out of a system which oppresses women daily—our egos are not built on putting women down and having them build us up. Also, living in a mostly male world we have become used to playing different roles....

To pretend to be straight sexually, or to pretend to be straight socially, is probably the most harmful pattern of behavior....If we are liberated, we are open with our sexuality. Closet queenery must end....Being open is the foundation of freedom....

Conclusion: An Outline of Imperatives for Gay Liberation:

1. Free ourselves: come out everywhere; initiate self-defense and political activity; initiate counter community institutions.

2. Turn other gay people on; talk all the time; understand, forgive, accept.

3. Free the homosexual in everyone: we'll be getting a good bit of shit from threatened latent [homosexuals]: be gentle, and keep talking and acting free.

4. We've been playing an act for a long time, so we're consummate actors. Now we can begin to be, and it'll be a good show!

Source: International Gay and Lesbian Archives. [Reprinted in Karla Jay and Allen Young, eds., *Out of the Closets* (New York: Douglas, 1972), pp. 330–340, and in Neil Miller, *Out of the Past* (New York: Vintage Books, 1995), pp. 385–387.]

*   *   *

The large gay community in New York City made less progress in gay
and lesbian rights than California did, partly because the New York Mattachine Society was so cautious. A younger generation of students and
working-class youth reacted against this cautious approach. Many of
them had already engaged in demonstrations in favor of revolutionary
movements, and in protests against the Vietnam War. As a mood of revolutionary resistance gripped New York City, these countercultural
young gays and lesbians were reaching the point of explosion. June 27,
1969, was the fateful date. That was the day of the funeral of a gay icon,
the famous movie star and singer Judy Garland. Many of those people
who gathered that evening at places like the Stonewall, a bar in the
heart of the gay section of Greenwich Village, were in no mood to be
pushed around by the police.

The night a contingent of police entered the Stonewall arresting
drag queens, and forcing everyone else to leave the bar while the police collected their payoff from the bar's Mafia owners. The smoldering anger suddenly exploded into attacks on the policemen. A lesbian
resisted arrest, while a drag queen who confronted a policeman was
beaten to a bloody pulp. A large crowd gathered outside the bar began
to throw rocks and break the windows of the bar. Someone threw a
burning trashcan toward the door, blocking the exit. As the police
called for reinforcements, a larger crowd arrived. For three nights,
protesters ran through the streets of Greenwich Village, evading police attacks while breaking windows and shouting "Gay Power!"
While plenty of protests had been pioneered in Los Angeles and San
Francisco, no outright riot by gays and lesbians had ever occurred in
American history. Allen Ginsberg noted that, for the first time, gays
had lost "that wounded look."

One of the participants in the uprising was an eighteen-year-old
Latino named Rey Rivera, who had gone to the Stonewall that
evening to have a drink. Profoundly effeminate, Rivera usually
dressed in women's clothes, and went by the drag name of Sylvia Lee.
From earliest memories, Rivera had always been feminine and preferred doing girls' things, and as a result was subjected to extreme
cruelty by neighborhood kids while growing up. As a teenager, Sylvia
had dropped out of school and escaped to downtown to hang out
with the drag queens on New York's Forty-Second Street. Rivera had
finally found some kindred spirits, but they were often harassed and
arrested by the police. Rivera explained that personal background of
involvement in the antiwar and black liberation protest movements
of the late 1960s, had helped to lead the way into gay and transgender activism.

DOCUMENT 72: Stonewall Riots in New York (1969)

[In 1968] I got involved with a lot of different [protest] things because I had so much anger about the world, the way it was, the way they were treating people. When the Stonewall happened, it was fabulous....I was drinking at the bar, and the police came in to get their payoff as usual...[with their] inhumane, senseless bullshit. They called us animals; we were the lowest scum of the earth....

I don't know if it was the customers or if it was the police, but that night everything just clicked. Everybody was like, "Why the fuck are we doing all this for? Why should we be chastised? Why do we have to pay the Mafia all this kind of money to drink in a lousy fuckin' bar? And still be harassed by the police?" It didn't make any sense. The people at the bars, especially at the Stonewall, were involved in other [protest] movements. And everybody was like..."Why do we have to keep on putting up with this?" Suddenly, the nickels, dimes, pennies, and quarters started flying. I threw quarters and pennies and whatnot. "You already got the payoff, and here's some more!"

To be there was so beautiful. It was so exciting. I said, "Well, great, now it's my time. I'm out there being a revolutionary for everybody else, and now it's time to do my thing for my own people." It was like, "Wow, we're doing it!...[Police oppression] is what we [had] learned to live with at that time. Until that day.

So we're throwing the pennies, and everything is going off really fab. The cops locked themselves in the bar. It was getting vicious. Then someone set fire to the Stonewall. The cops, they just panicked. They had no backup. They didn't expect any of this retaliation. But they should have. People were very angry for so long.

Source: Rey "Sylvia Lee" Rivera, quoted in Eric Marcus, *Making History: The Struggle for Gay and Lesbian Equal Rights, 1945–1990* (New York: HarperCollins, 1992), pp. 190–192.

*   *   *

The year after the Stonewall riots was an important one for gay rights in New York City. Within a few weeks of the riots, radicalized young gays formed the Gay Liberation Front (GLF). They organized a rally of about four hundred lesbians and gay men, singing "We Shall Overcome" and chanting "Gay Power!" Many of the GLF members had come from a radicalized culture of protest, and were dismissive of mainstream values and politics-as-usual. They did not beg for understanding, as the homophiles had, but demanded equality. They were not concerned about creating a favorable public image for homosexuals, but tried to "blow people's minds." They wanted liberation in all aspects of life.

Challenging New York laws prohibiting same-sex dancing in public, GLF organized a series of dances. After New York University denied a request by students to hold a gay and lesbian dance on campus, and sent police to attack GLF protestors, more than 2,000 people rioted. GLF conducted a week-long sit-in to protest the University's antigay policies. GLF thinking quickly spread to major university campuses around the nation, and also energized gay protests in other cities. GLF Los Angeles organizers like Morris Kight were soon being widely quoted in the local media, far outdistancing the publicity that had been generated by previous homophile groups.

GLF meetings were chaotic and unfocused. Revolutionary rhetoric flourished, and since all revolutionary struggles were seen as one movement, GLF paid as much attention to issues of racism, capitalism, and exploitation of the poor and labor classes as to gay rights. However, after antiwar and Black Power leaders criticized gay participation in their demonstrations, a majority of GLF members decided to withdraw from leftist groups and restrict themselves to activism solely for gay and lesbian rights. They broke away to form the Gay Activists Alliance (GAA), and picketed, did sit-ins, and perfected the fine art of the "zap."

A zap was done not only to embarrass the target homophobe, but also to gain media attention by doing creative photogenic protests. For example, when GAA learned that a New York credit bureau included reports of homosexuality in its credit reports supplied to banks, the president of the company defended his agency's assumptions that someone is a homosexual by saying "If one looks like a duck, walks like a duck, associates only with ducks, and quacks like a duck, he is probably a duck." In response, twelve GAA protesters dressed up in duck costumes and picketed the company's offices while quacking loudly. To get the protesters to leave, the company promised to stop including information on sexual behavior in its credit reports.

Another example of GAA direct action occurred after *Harper's* magazine printed an article in its October 1970 issue condemning homosexuality as the worst tragedy parents could imagine for any of their children. Members of GAA barged unannounced into the New York offices of *Harper's*, and when the publisher refused to print GAA's rebuttal article from a parent who accepted a gay child, GAA staged an all-day sit-in. During the ensuing long discussion, however, the editors did promise to think carefully before publishing such prejudiced comments in the future. GAA decided to confront heterosexism whenever possible, whether generated by the media, business, or politicians.

Whereas Mattachine had politely sent questionnaires to politicians, who usually ignored them, GAA members confronted campaigning politicians in public and demanded to know their stand on gay rights. If the politician avoided them, a group of GAA members would follow them in a crowd, chanting "Crime of silence, crime of silence!" and "answer homosexuals!" GAA confrontations with local political candidates forced the latter to speak out on the question of gay and lesbian rights, and attracted new candidates who welcomed the chance to speak at GAA meetings. In New York City politics, gays and lesbians were beginning to be seen as a voting bloc.

Gay men and lesbians in other cities, including those who had previously been at the forefront of the struggle in Los Angeles, San Francisco, and Washington, D.C., now took their cues from the new radicalism that exploded in New York. The 1970s saw the spread of confrontational gay and lesbian liberation throughout the nation.

Gay and lesbian liberationists organized marches on June 28, 1970, to commemorate the first anniversary of the Stonewall riots. Gay Liberation Front Los Angeles sponsored a brash parade with 1,200 people marching down Hollywood Boulevard, while Chicago had several hundred marchers. Stonewall became the event used to mark an annual celebration of Gay Pride. It was in New York City, however, that the biggest Gay Pride march took place. An estimate of 10,000 to 20,000 people marched from the gay area of Greenwich Village to the center of the city. *The New York Times*, which had only briefly mentioned the Stonewall riots a year before, gave the Gay Pride March front-page coverage. The *Village Voice* captured the excitement of the march:

DOCUMENT 73: Gay Liberation Front and the Gay Activists Alliance (1970)

Thousands and thousands and thousands, chanting, waving, screaming—the outrageous and the outraged, splendid in their flaming colors, splendid in their delirious up-front birthday celebration of liberation.... They swept up Sixth Avenue, from Sheridan Square to Central Park, astonishing everything in their way. No one could quite believe it, eyes rolled back in heads, Sunday tourists traded incredulous looks, wondrous faces poked out of air-conditioned cars. My God, are those really homosexuals? Marching? Up Sixth Avenue?

Source: Jonathan Black, "A Happy Birthday for Gay Liberation," *Village Voice* July 2, 1970, p. 1.

*   *   *

Gay activists realized that they could not gain respect for gay rights as long as homosexuality was conceived as an illness. Society's response to an illness is to try to cure it rather than to accept it as a valid option for people. When the Los Angeles Gay Liberation Front found out that a meeting of the Behavioral Modification Conference would be showing a film about shock therapy for homosexuals, about forty GLF members decided to attend the meeting at the Los Angeles Biltmore Hotel. When the film showed ways that psychologists could use electric shocks to decrease a man's same-sex attraction while showing him photographs of naked men, GLF members raised shouts of "Barbarism!" "Medieval torture!" and "This is disgusting!"

A group of GLF members that included Don Kilhefner, Morris Kight, and Del Whan turned on the lights and took over the microphone from the psychologist who was narrating the film. Morris Kight told the audience that even if a person came to the therapist and claimed to want to undergo the electric shocks, it was still a barbaric practice. The very existence of such techniques, he concluded, was prejudicial. Kight told the psychologists that each of them in the room was a participant in what amounted to torture, and they must assume responsibility to stop such barbaric practices.

Kilhefner, who would later receive his Ph.D. in psychology and become a gay-affirmative therapist, refused to give up the microphone despite numerous objections from psychologists in the audience. About twenty psychologists left the auditorium, but the rest remained and eventually agreed to form a dozen small discussion groups. In the discussions, which went on for more than an hour, GLF members attempted to get across the idea of a valid gay lifestyle to many conference participants who had never before thought of their shock therapy as oppressive. Here is what Kilhefner had to say to the psychologists to get them to pay attention, which typified the confrontational approach of GLF:

DOCUMENT 74: Gay Lib Zaps Psychologists (1970)

I'm a firm believer in free speech. But what you people out there call free speech in fact has been a monologue for over a half century. And we would like to start a dialogue. Right now the GLF is suggesting that this morning be reconstituted. If a dialogue is to begin, let it begin now. You have been our oppressor for too long, and we will take this no longer. We are going to reconstitute this session into small groups, with equal numbers of GLF members and members of your profession. We're going to be talking about what you as psychologists are going to do to clear up your own fucked minds....This is what we're going to be doing. Anybody who can't dig it, we ask you to leave.

Source: Originally appeared in *The Advocate* in 1970. Reprinted in Thompson, *Long Road to Freedom*, pp. 38–39.

*   *   *

After the 1966 founding of the National Organization for Women (NOW), heterosexists regularly tried to discredit it by claiming NOW was a front for lesbianism. Stung by this criticism, NOW founder Betty Friedan publicly denounced what she saw as a lesbian plot to infiltrate NOW. She referred to lesbians as a "lavender menace." Numerous lesbians who had been inspired to get involved in NOW on behalf of women's rights, reacted with dismay. Many, like Ivy Bottini and Rita Mae Brown, who had worked hard to build the New York chapter of NOW, felt betrayed by heterosexual NOW members. In November 1969 NOW organized a Congress to Unite Women, but deleted the name of the lesbian organization Daughters of Bilitis from the press release listing the endorsers of the Congress. Lesbians decided to fight back.

In New York City in May 1970, on the opening night of the second annual Congress to Unite Women, seventeen women wearing T-shirts labeled "Lavender Menace" interrupted the proceedings and took control of the stage. For the rest of the evening, they forced the Congress to confront the lesbian issue, by talking about their lives as lesbians and the reasons lesbians in particular are drawn to feminism. They announced the formation of consciousness-raising groups for women who were interested in discussing the relationship between lesbianism and feminism. As a result of this confrontation, and after much discussion, the Congress voted to adopt a set of resolutions put forth by the Lavender Menace. These resolutions confronted the issue head-on, by defending lesbian rights. The resolutions stated:

DOCUMENT 75: Congress to Unite Women (1970)

1. Be it resolved that Women's Liberation is a Lesbian plot.

2. Resolved that whenever the label "Lesbian" is used against the movement collectively, or against women individually, it is to be affirmed, not denied.

3. In all discussions on birth control, homosexuality must be included as a legitimate method of contraception.

4. All sex education curricula must include Lesbianism as a valid, legitimate form of sexual expression of love.

Source: Sidney Abbott and Barbara Love, *Sappho Was a Right On Woman* (New York: Stein and Day, 1972), p. 115. [Quote reprinted in Neil Miller, *Out of the Past* (New York: Vintage Books, 1995), pp. 375–376.]

* * *

In 1970 a collective publishing under the name Radicalesbians printed a pamphlet calling on the women's movement to stop avoiding the lesbian issue, and to define lesbians as women who give primary attention to relationships with other women. This definition shifted emphasis away from sexual behavior, and toward relationships and activism, thus helping to support the concept of political lesbians. They felt that lesbians—by being totally oriented toward women's interests— were a major asset for the women's movement, and that feminist groups should stop treating them as a menace and an embarrassment. They argued that those women who are in relationships with other women should be valued and respected. This woman-centered approach also meant a move away from gay men's organizations, as lesbians concentrated on building their movement in alliance with other women. Those who were uncomfortable dealing with the sexism of gay men, and the heterosexism of heterosexual women, decided that the solution was to develop lesbian separatist projects where they could work and live solely with other lesbians.

DOCUMENT 76: The Woman Identified Woman (1970)

Lesbian is a label invented by the Man to throw at any woman who dares to be his equal....Affixing the label lesbian not only to a woman who aspires to be a person, but also to any situation of real love, real solidarity, real primacy among women, is a primary form of divisiveness among women: it is the condition which keeps women within the confines of the feminine role, and it is the debunking/scare term that keeps women from forming any primary attachments, groups, or associations among ourselves.

Women in the [feminist] movement have in most cases gone to great lengths to avoid discussion and confrontation with the issue of lesbianism....But it is no side issue. It is absolutely essential to the success and fulfillment of the women's liberation movement that this issue be dealt with. As long as the label "dyke" can be used to frighten women into a less militant stand, keep her separate from her sisters, keep her from giving primacy to anything other than men and family—then to that extent she is controlled by the male culture. Until women see in each other the possibility of a primal commitment which includes sexual love, they will be denying themselves the love and value they readily accord to men, thus affirming their second-class status. As long as male acceptability is primary—both to individual women and to the movement as a whole—the term lesbian will be used effectively against women....

Our energies must flow toward our sisters, not backward toward our oppressors. As long as woman's liberation tries to free women without facing the basic heterosexual structure that binds us in one-to-one relationship with our oppressors, tremendous energies will continue to flow into trying to make the "new man" out of him.

Source: Radicalesbians, "The Woman Identified Woman" (Pittsburgh: Know, Inc., 1970). Reprinted at [http://scriptorium.lib.duke.edu/wlm/womid/] in the On-line Archival Collection of the Women's Liberation Movement, Special Collections Library, Duke University.

*   *   *

After the 1970 Congress to Unite Women passed a prolesbian resolution, more lesbians began to join the National Organization for Women, and more feminist activists began to come out of the closet. Particularly significant was the 1970 coming out as bisexual of Kate Millett, author of the influential feminist book *Sexual Politics*. When *Time* magazine published an article saying that her disclosure would discredit the feminist movement, heterosexual NOW leaders like Gloria Steinem, Susan Brownmiller, and Flo Kennedy spoke out in defense of lesbian rights. Some feminists who did not have sex with other women began to publicly refer to themselves as "political lesbians," as a statement of political solidarity with lesbians. Only by making a public statement, they argued, could they undercut the notion that lesbianism was an accusation to be feared.

DOCUMENT 77: NOW Endorses Lesbian Rights (1971)

Meanwhile, members of the Los Angeles chapter of NOW worked with members of Lesbian Feminists to pass a prolesbian resolution in 1971. The Los Angeles NOW Newsletter printed a position paper that offered a justification for this new openness.

[Lesbians] found a natural outlet in the women's liberation movement that seemed to view women in a new way and promised a new pride and sisterhood for every woman, in search of equality and independence. Lesbians became active in NOW and in other groups, fighting for all the feminist goals, including child care centers and abortion repeal.... But instead of finding support from their sisters, lesbians discovered that NOW and other liberation groups reflected some of the same prejudices and policies of the sexist society they were striving to change.... Asking women to disguise their identities so they will not "embarrass" the group is an intolerable form of oppression, like asking black women to join us in white face....

Some members of NOW object that the lesbian question is too controversial to confront right now, that we will weaken the movement by alienating potential and current members who are comfortable with NOW's "respectable" image. The same argument, that women would be frightened away, was raised a few years ago when NOW took a bold stand on the controversial abortion issue. The argument did not prove prophetic then, and we do not believe it is valid now. We are, after all, a reform movement, with revolutionary goals. The D.A.R. can be "respectable"; but as Susan B. Anthony pointed out: "Cautious, careful people always casting about to preserve their reputation or social standards, can never bring about a reform."

It's encouraging to note that feminists are not so easily frightened. Since the Resolution supporting lesbians was passed in Los Angeles two months ago, the chapter has increased, not decreased, in membership. If a few cautious, careful people scurried away, the loss was imperceptible. And we are stronger now because many women feel more relaxed and are freer to work with us towards NOW goals.

Source: "Position Paper: Justification for L.A. NOW Resolution Supporting Our Lesbian Sisters," *Los Angeles NOW Newsletter* August 1971, p. 7.

* * *

At the national convention of the National Organization for Women in September 1971, the delegates repudiated Betty Friedan's condemnation of lesbians as a "lavender menace." The convention passed a resolution which stated:

Be it resolved that NOW recognizes the double oppression of lesbians;
Be it resolved that a woman's right to her own person includes the right to define and express her own sexuality and to choose her own life-style; and
Be it resolved that NOW acknowledges the oppression of lesbians as a legitimate concern of feminism.

Source: Sidney Abbott and Barbara Love, *Sappho Was a Right On Woman* (New York: Stein and Day, 1972), p. 134. [Quote reprinted in Neil Miller, *Out of the Past* (New York: Vintage Books, 1995), p. 378.]

* * *

In 1973, Jill Johnston, a writer for the *Village Voice*, published a series of essays, under the title "Lesbian Nation." She was one of the first lesbians working in the media, to come out, and her book struck a chord in many lesbians. For a time, the phrase "Lesbian Nation" was used as a metaphor for an ideal place where lesbians lived and worked together in autonomous harmony and abundance on behalf of a better world. It was understood that such a place did not really exist, but the concept served as a point of inspiration.

DOCUMENT 78: Lesbian Nation (1972)

Within just two years the meaning of the word lesbian has changed from private subversive activity to political revolutionary identity....The purpose of feminist analysis is to provide women with an awareness of their servitude as a class so that they can unite and rise up against it....The lesbian is the woman who obviously unites the personal and the political struggle to free ourselves from the oppressive institution. The lesbian argument is first and foremost...the (re) development of the moral, physical, intellectual, strengths of women whatever the social consequences of that may be.

It is the banding together of fugitives which constitutes the phenomenon of revolutionary opposition....It is this commitment by choice, full-time, of one woman to others of her class that is called lesbianism....[Ti-Grace] Atkinson correctly placed the lesbian as that tiny minority within the Oppressed [groups] who refused to play out its proper political function in society....Lesbians are...challenging by [their] very existence if not by overt action, the exclusive political dominion of the heterosexual institution by which women are maintained as the subservient caste. By this definition lesbians are in the vanguard of the resistance....Historically lesbians have had two choices: being criminal [being a lesbian] or going straight....The totally woman-committed woman, or lesbian...is the political nucleus of a woman's or lesbian state—a state that women cannot achieve by demand from the male bastion but only from within exclusive woman strength building its own institutions of self support and identity....[Lesbian] is now a generic term signifying activism and resistance and the envisioned goal of a woman committed state.

Source: Jill Johnston, *Lesbian Nation: The Feminist Solution* (New York: Touchstone, Simon and Schuster, 1973), pp. 275–279.

*   *   *

As "gay ghettoes" in Los Angeles, San Francisco, and New York became known, gay men and lesbians from smaller towns and cities yearned to join these vibrant communities. While homosexuals had been migrating to the largest cities for decades, the migration reached a groundswell in the early 1970s. Even though Los Angeles had been the birthplace of the movement for gay and lesbian rights, and even though New York was the site of the Stonewall rebellion, by the 1970s no city personified gay liberation more than San Francisco.

The city had a proud bohemian heritage and nonconformist tolerance, but part of the reason for San Francisco's popularity as a migration site was economic opportunity. In the 1960s San Francisco had been transformed from a blue-collar manufacturing center to the headquarters of a number of national corporations. Entertainment sectors also blossomed as the city became the nation's leading tourist resort. Within these areas of growth, jobs were available for mobile young office workers and service industry employees. Middle-class educated gay men, often willing to work for lower wages than heterosexuals with children to support, filled the need perfectly. Corporations cared more about their profit margins than about the off-hours sexual behavior of their employees, and they were happy to accept whatever qualified employees they could find in the booming economy. As San Francisco became famous as a gay mecca, migrants poured into the city. Many were fleeing severe persecution in the American heartland, and once they got to the dreamland of California a mood of celebratory relief entered the gay community. Discos proliferated, as gay men enjoyed dancing the night away.

The Society for Individual Rights (SIR), which had been so effective in San Francisco in the 1960s, became transformed into the Alice B. Toklas Memorial Democratic Club under the leadership of Jim Foster in 1971. When liberal United States Senator George McGovern of South Dakota ran for the Democratic nomination for president in 1972, he came out in favor of gay rights. In a well-organized campaign, Foster's gay Democratic club quickly gathered one-third of all the signatures that McGovern needed to get on the ballot in the California Democratic primary. Foster became a major Democratic operator in the Bay Area.

When the Democratic National Convention met in Miami and awarded the party nomination to McGovern, the grateful candidate gave Jim Foster and lesbian activist Madeline Davis the opportunity to give nationally televised addresses on gay rights at the convention. This was the first time that openly gay people had given speeches on gay and lesbian rights to a national television audience. Foster began with a note of pride:

DOCUMENT 79: Democratic Party Convention (1972)

We do not come to you pleading your understanding or begging your tolerance. We come to you affirming our pride in our lifestyle, affirming the validity to seek and maintain meaningful emotional relationships and affirming our right to participate in the life of this country on an equal basis with every citizen.

Source: Quoted in Neil Miller, *Out of the Past* (New York: Vintage Books, 1995), pp. 396–397.

*   *   *

Like most white-dominated social movements, the lesbian and gay movement has had trouble dealing with its own racism. Lesbians of color have had to struggle against both racism in the larger society and racism within the lesbian and gay movement. Lesbians of color consider the struggle against racism in the lesbian community to be as important as their struggle for lesbian rights. Over several decades efforts have been made to build bridges across ethnicity and race. Community dialogues and antiracism forums and workshops sometimes created change. But more often, the differences were not bridged. Below is a statement by a group of lesbians of color who attended the historic West Coast Lesbian Conference in Los Angeles in 1973. It is one of the earliest public statements made by lesbians of color about racism in the lesbian movement.

DOCUMENT 80: Multiple Struggles (1973)

The workshop on racism began by trying to define racism and by giving examples from our lives, as to how racism functions. Because of the magnitude of the problem we got bogged down. So we dealt with each other instead....We decided to make proposals to make the next conference better with regard to the problem of racism....Racism is here. We don't like it and we don't want to see it any more [sic], particularly from our lesbian sisters....Del Martin [a white activist] pointed out that in her travels across the country she has not seen one lesbian organization that has successfully dealt with the issue of racism. Racism is an issue that we have yet to come to terms with. We must, for there is no greater oppression than that which comes from a sister.

Source: "Report From the Racism Workshop," *The Lesbian Tide* June 1973, p. 19.

*   *   *

On October 3, 1973, Dr. Howard Brown, former chief health officer of the city of New York, made a speech at a conference of physicians in support of gay rights. He became the first nationally prominent physician to come out as openly gay, and his openness generated much publicity in the mass media. He later became a director of the National Gay Task Force, and wrote his autobiography, *Familiar Faces, Hidden Lives*. When *The Advocate* asked him to write an article explaining his decision to come out, he wrote:

DOCUMENT 81: Dr. Howard Brown Comes Out (1973)

The people who basically led me to my decision were the brave men and women of the Gay Activists Alliance who have fought so magnificently for gay rights in New York City. Though I had helped them behind the scenes, really I was like the other successful homosexuals I know. I stayed hidden and let these gallant boys and girls work hours and days and even be beaten up in a fight that really I should have joined. Whenever I hear criticism of these magnificent fighters for human rights from pompous, closeted, successful gays, I get so enraged I can hardly continue my friendship with them....The gay heroes of New York will rank in history with leaders in the fights against economic and racial oppression. These gay leaders moved me, just as leaders of other [civil rights] fights had earlier.

It is one measure of how society has really oppressed me, that though I had been active in the fight for the poor and for civil rights, it never occurred to me that I could fight for the rights of homosexuals. The gay freedom fighters redefined my previous feelings of shame at being a homosexual into a sense of rage that society could do this to me and so many of the people I loved.

Now it seemed that I could help the cause by saying, "Here I am. I'm gay, a queer, a fairy, a faggot, and there are so many like me that you can't shame or hurt us any longer."...[Society] must not deprive any of us homosexuals of our basic human dignity. This right to dignity has noting to do with success or an acceptable image.

Am I glad I made the announcement? You bet I am.

Source: Howard Brown, reprinted in Thompson, *Long Road to Freedom*, p. 88.

*   *   *

In 1973 infighting developed within the Gay Activists Alliance. In response, GAA president Bruce Voeller left the organization and, with veteran homophile activists Barbara Gittings and Dr. Frank Kameny, founded the National Gay Task Force (NGTF). Dr. Voeller, a professor of biology at Rockefeller University, also recruited other respected professionals to be on the NGTF board, like Dr. Howard Brown and Dr. Martin Duberman, a prize-winning author and history professor at the City University of New York. Duberman was also a founder of the Gay Academic Union.

Voeller wanted NGTF to bring more professionalism to the issue of gay and lesbian rights. He wanted to synthesize the homophile and the liberationist approaches into a new hybrid that would be more effective. The goal of the group was to become a gay version of civil rights organizations like the NAACP. While NGTF began with a focus on changing the mass media, especially television news studios, its national political focus eventually led it to move its headquarters to Washington, D.C. NGTF later changed its name to the National Gay and Lesbian Task Force, to affirm its inclusion of lesbians. In his autobiography, Duberman reported his memories about the 1973 founding of NGTF.

DOCUMENT 82: National Gay Task Force Founded (1973)

We held a sparsely attended press conference to announce the official launching of the new organization, with Howard speaking succinctly and eloquently of the need to mobilize national resources on behalf of the gay struggle for civil rights. Though pleased to lend my name and energy to NGTF—and its board of directors did turn out to be very much a working board—I had serious doubts about the new organization from the beginning. The same night of the press conference, I set down my conflicted feelings in my diary: "NGTF clearly wants to pattern itself on the ACLU or NAACP—which means it can make a valuable contribution, but in the liberal, reformist mode: 'let us in' rather than 'let us show you new possibilities.' Structurally, too, I can sympathize with wanting to do away with the marathon GAA membership discussions on whether to buy one or two typewriters, but decisions from the top down may carry limitations as severe (if different from) those of participatory democracy—especially since it's not clear in whose name we're speaking...."

The gay movement in general was heading into the same set of interlocking dilemmas that have characterized protest movements throughout our history. How to prevent a radical impulse from degenerating into reformist tinkering? How to mobilize a constituency for substantive change when most of the members of that constituency prefer to focus energies on winning certain limited concessions, like civil rights legislation, and show little interest in joining with other dispossessed groups to press for systemic social restructuring? How to appeal to a country on behalf of an oppressed minority when the country...smugly assumed its prejudices and values were somehow divinely ordained?

Source: Martin Duberman, *Cures: A Gay Man's Odyssey* (New York: Dutton, 1991), pp. 291, 297–298.

*   *   *

Gays and lesbians in the United States have historically fought homophobia through any means possible, including the courts. With the help of sympathetic lawyers, judges, and lawmakers, they were, at times, able to win cases that increased their civil and human rights. Eventually, the gay and lesbian community formed its own legal arm. The Lambda Legal Defense Fund's first case was fighting on its own behalf to gain nonprofit status. Since the 1970s, it has been a strong voice on behalf of the struggle for gay and lesbian rights.

DOCUMENT 83: Lambda Legal Defense Fund (1973)

Lambda was the first organization in the country (and probably the world) to establish itself principally to fight for lesbians and gay men in the courts and within the legal profession. However, in 1972, a New York court denied Lambda's application to become a non-profit legal organization on the grounds that Lambda's "stated purposes are on their face neither benevolent nor charitable, nor, in any event, is there a demonstrated need for this corporation." According to the court, "[i]t does not appear that discrimination against homosexuals, which undoubtedly exists, operates to deprive them of legal representation."

Fortunately for all of us, New York's highest court overturned this ruling in 1973. Yet, this first case both underscored the community's need for legal representation by and for lesbians and gay men, and has also served as an example of the last twenty-five years of lesbian and gay legal activism— where underdogs fight hard and occasionally triumph, winning the right to exist, to speak, to be free from discrimination, and to change the hearts and minds of those who act on misconceptions of who we are.

Lambda has spent the last twenty-four years challenging our courts and our constitutional system to open up the promises of liberty and equal treatment to lesbians, gay men, and people with HIV/AIDS. In the process, we have won significant victories both in and out of the courtroom. By widely publicizing our cases, we break the silence that has traditionally surrounded our lives and tell the real stories about ourselves. We work under the belief that legal change comes not in the vacuum of a courtroom or because of the exceptional skills of lesbian and gay lawyers, but because the citizens of this country have come to believe that certain ideas, actions, and prejudices must not be reinforced by our courts.

Source: Lambda Legal Defense Fund Web page: [http://www.lambdalegal .org/cgi-bin/pages/about/history]

*   *   *

One of the most difficult challenges facing lesbian, gay, bisexual, and transgendered (LGBT) youth is rejection by their families. Since 1973, a group called Parents and Friends of Lesbians and Gays (PFLAG) has helped parents and other family members understand their LGBT and

gender-nonconformist children. From its New York and Los Angeles beginnings, PFLAG has established support groups in many smaller, more
conservative cities. It has now grown to over four hundred chapters
worldwide, with more than 70,000 members and a staffed headquarters
in Washington, D.C. According to PFLAG's Web site:

DOCUMENT 84: Parents and Friends of Lesbians and Gays (1973)

It started simply, almost accidentally. In 1972 the *New York Post* published
a letter from Jeanne Manford, whose gay son had been beaten badly at a
protest, while police stood by....Two months later, Manford and her son
Marty marched in New York's gay pride parade together. Manford carried
a sign which read, "Parents of Gays: Unite in Support for Our Children."
The crowd screamed, yelled and cried as Manford approached....In March
1973, New York City Parents of Gays held its first meeting. Nearly 20 people gathered in a Methodist church in Greenwich Village to share their stories and support each other....[In 1976, Adele and Larry Starr] launched the
Los Angeles group, the first parent's group to apply for non-profit, tax exempt status....[In 1981] 30 people met at the Starr's home in Los Angeles to
write bylaws for a national organization....

[Today] we've taken our place at the national table....Ten years ago we
were an afterthought. Now people call us to testify before Congress. We all
did what we did because of the love [for] our children.

Source: Carolyn Wagner, "PFLAG's Rich Past Provides Solid Foundation for Future" in PFLAG Web site [http://www.pflag.org/about/history.html]

*   *   *

For several years gay and lesbian activists like Frank Kameny, Barbara
Gittings, Ron Gold, and Bruce Voeller lobbied members of the American Psychiatric Association (APA) to stop labeling homosexuality as a
mental disorder. The activists combined noisy militant protests, quiet
one-on-one dialogue with prominent psychiatrists, and participation in
APA panels. They also had the strong support of nongay allies like Dr.
Judd Marmor, professor of psychiatry at the University of Southern California, who had published his research showing that same-sex attractions are not a sickness. By exerting pressure from outside the APA,
along with personal influence from the inside, they were able to persuade the APA board of trustees to make a unanimous vote on December 15, 1973, to remove homosexuality from its official list of
psychiatric disorders. With homosexuality no longer labeled as a men-

tal illness by the nation's leading psychiatric association, a major justification for the denial of gay and lesbian rights was now removed.

In response to this vote, psychiatrist Charles Socarides demanded a vote of the full membership of the APA. Socarides had built his career on "curing" homosexuals, by techniques like electric shock treatments, and he was not about to relinquish his authority on the subject. He saw homosexuality as a danger to society, and advocated detention camps for homosexuals. Interestingly, Socarides could not prevent his own son from becoming homosexual. Eventually his son became a gay activist and in 1994 was appointed by President Bill Clinton as White House liaison for gay and lesbian issues.

After a four-month campaign to the membership of the APA in early 1974, the members' secret ballots on the Socarides referendum were mailed in. Bruce Voeller went to the APA headquarters on the morning that the election and referendum results were to be announced. He reported to *The Advocate* his private thoughts on that fateful day:

DOCUMENT 85: American Psychiatric Association Vote (1974)

It's nine-thirty in the morning, April 9, and Frank Kameny and I are again sitting in the board room at the headquarters of the APA in Washington, D.C....We learn that our item, the Socarides referendum, will be the last item reported from a long ballot....Frank and I sit waiting, repeatedly photographed by cameras searching for hints of our feelings, observing us like some sort of parlor-broken zoo animals brought in to hear our fate. I turn to Frank and tell him I'm nervous for the first time in over a year, and he smiles and says he's not....

What to say to the press if we lose, what to say if we win. I fussed for four hours over rhetoric and wordings, only to decide finally that if we win, I will simply say that the way has now been cleared to get on with the real issue, from which our attention and energies have been so irritatingly pulled. All gay women and men call on their fellow citizens and the APA to address the real issue—injustice to one's fellow human beings. These are the abuses the century-old categorization of homosexuality as a mental disorder served to bulwark....

[The APA official teller announces results on] the election to the 1975 presidency of the APA: Judd Marmor, professor of psychiatry at the University of Southern California, has won! Marmor and his two opponents strongly supported gay rights and opposed the Socarides referendum. All three signed a letter the National Gay Task Force had sent (at a cost of some three thousand dollars) to eighteen thousand members of the APA, urging defeat of the Socarides referendum. But Marmor was particularly known for his opposition to the sickness model. Frank and I sit, anxiously hopeful that the Marmor victory augurs success on our issue. The tension in the room grows....The teller finally comes to our lives. A stereotypical hush falls on the room. The teller reads the referendum, in which a yes vote is a vote for us. Frank and I lean forward to hear as cameras click away. "Yes, 4,854 votes, or 58 percent." We've done it! "No, 3,810 (37.8 percent), abstaining, 367 (3.6 percent)." We've won!...

Our costly letter has perhaps made the difference. Throw away the defeat speech and tell the world to cut the sickness crap and start helping us get our rights—start teaching that the real struggle is for recognition that gays love and care for each other; that to be gay is to have a life-permeating affection for one's fellow beings. If you can't stand or understand affection and caring, you're a homophobe.

I must make it my first job to send the news and my thanks to the many people who helped get out the letter to APA members. Gay people come through when much is at risk and a photo finish looks imminent. People who'd never contributed before sent in fives and tens. Several nongay psychiatrists contributed....

Whatever else, all gays, not just those few of us lucky enough to be in the movement, can now view themselves with pride—pride they should have had all along, but that's easy for us to say. We're a day nearer the time when young gays will look at us with incomprehension and some embarrassment when we reminisce about such things as being in the closet and being told we're sick.

Source: Bruce Voeller, "Suspenseful Wait for Vindication," *The Advocate* n. 187 (May 8, 1974), pp. 1 & 24, quoted in Thompson, *Long Road to Freedom*, pp. 105–106.

*   *   *

Because so many lesbians came out only after having been heterosexually married, and having children, many of those who divorced their husbands were faced with bitter child custody battles in the courts. While gay men hardly ever gained custody, lesbians were at least able to take advantage of the common courtroom presumption that a child should stay with its mother. However, even this advantage was often lost if a mother's lesbianism became known by the court. A few victories in the courts, however, were occurring in this crucial right facing lesbians who wanted to stay with their children. In 1974 Cheryl Bratman, then a law student, filed an appeal on behalf of a lesbian mother in Los Angeles. The court granted custody to her, making it one of the nation's first legal victories for lesbian mothers. Based on an interview with Bratman, *Lesbian Tide* publisher Jeanne Cordova wrote an article advising lesbians how to win custody of their children.

DOCUMENT 86: Lesbian Child Custody Rights (1974)

In order to win custody of her child in court, a lesbian mother needs a special lawyer, the right judge, social workers, psychiatrists, an alcoholic or absent husband, in-laws who don't contest, money, great commitment and energy, an impeccable background, community and political support and a state which has passed laws favorable to gay rights....In child custody cases the burden of proof (that the child should be taken) rests with the state, in-laws, or relatives, not with the biological parent....[But] the moment the word lesbian is mentioned in a court room, the burden of proof shifts....

It is not enough for the defending mother to call upon her opposition (husband, in-laws, state) to "prove it." Ignorance and prejudice are so rampant in the minds of most judges that "inference" alone is often more than enough to swing the decision....The question of whether or not the mother's sexual orientation negatively affects her children is sometimes not even considered....[A successful case needs declarations from the children] saying they wanted to remain with their mother, and statements from psychiatrists, child psychologists, social workers, etc., showing that it would be detrimental to take the young women from their mother....The lesbian parent's battle is never really over. Opposing parties can contend for the child until she/he reaches the age of 18....

[Often] the husband is so upset that his wife left him for another woman that he will use the custody as a battle of revenge. The lesbian mother must, therefore, assess the time, money and vengeance her ex-husband is prepared to invest in the struggle. Similarly, she must evaluate her own resources of money, energy and stamina. In making this decision, the gay parent must also realize publicity and/or subpoena might also cost her her job, her career, her friends and alienation from family.

Source: Jeanne Cordova, "How to Win a Lesbian Custody Case," *Lesbian Tide* July–August 1974, pp. 20–21.

*   *   *

In the 1970s, lesbian feminists developed a philosophy that lesbianism is a practice that grows out of feminist theory. This view assumes that many women have the flexibility to develop same-sex feelings and can feel more fulfilled in an egalitarian relationship with another woman than in a dominant-submissive marriage with a man. Rita Mae Brown, who went on to write the humorous best-selling lesbian novel *Rubyfruit Jungle*, articulates in this essay the concept of lesbianism as women's liberation. It was written while she was a member of the "Furies," a collective of white lesbians living together in Washington, D.C. Their name suggested women's outrage at how they are treated.

DOCUMENT 87: Lesbians as the Vanguard of Feminism (1975)

Lesbianism, politically organized, is the greatest threat that exists to male supremacy. How can men remain supreme, how can they oppress women if women reject them and fight the entire world men have built to contain us? The beginning rejection is to put women first....Committing yourself to women is the first concrete step toward ending that common oppression. If you cannot find it in yourself to love another woman, and that includes physical love, then how can you truly say you care about women's liberation?...Relationships between men and women involve power, dominance, role play, and oppression. A man has the entire system of male privilege to back him up. Another woman has nothing but her own self. Which relationship is better for you? It's obvious.

If women still give primary commitment and energy to the oppressors how can we build a strong movement to free ourselves? Did the Chinese love and support the capitalists? Do the Viet Cong cook supper for the Yankees? Are Blacks supposed to disperse their communities and each live in a white home? The answer, again, is obvious. Only if women give their time to women, to a women's movement, will they be free. You do not free yourself by polishing your chains....

[Lesbianism] offers you potential equal relationships with your sisters. It offers escape from the silly, stupid, harmful games that men and women play, having the nerve to call them "relationships." It offers change....As you change yourself, you will begin to change your society also. A free, strong self cannot live in the muck that men have made....You will discover the thousand subtle ways that heterosexuality destroyed your true power; you will discover how male supremacy destroys all women....You will find love and that you are beautiful [and] strong.

Source: Rita Mae Brown, "The Shape of Things to Come," in Nancy Myron and Charlotte Bunch, eds., *Lesbianism and the Women's Movement* (Baltimore: Diana Press, 1975), pp. 70–73.

*   *   *

In his book on Gay Asians in pre-AIDS Los Angeles, Editor Eric Wat quotes from a 1972 letter sent by Hung Nung to the leftist Asian journal *Bridge*:

DOCUMENT 88: Gay Asians (1975)

"I am Asian, a male and gay. For the past year I've gotten involved with the Asian Movement, or at least tried—I have been scorned, ridiculed and rejected by many so-called sincere Asian Movement people, especially males. I won't pretend that I'm not gay, just as I'm proud to be Asian. And the two are not mutually exclusive."

Source: Eric Wat, *The Making of a Gay Asian Community: An Oral History of Pre-AIDS Los Angeles*. Lanham, MD: Rowman & Littlefield, 2002.

* * *

Nung's struggles were not unique. Below is the testimony of another gay Asian man, who felt that coming out would compromise his political activities on behalf of his ethnic community.

In the early 1970s, Gil Mangaoang was an activist working against the sociopolitical oppression of Filipinos and he was gradually becoming aware of his gay orientation. Below is a portion of an essay he wrote examining his experiences managing his multiple identities as a gay Filipino American activist.

While I was discovering my Filipino-American identity and was immersed in the political struggle of social justice for Filipinos both in the U.S. and the Philippines, I was struggling with my sexual identity. I wanted to understand not only what it meant to be gay, but also to participate as an openly gay male in society. Initially I felt that these two identities—Filipino and gay—were contradictory and irreconcilable. To come out in the Filipino community would be double jeopardy, being openly gay would further jeopardize the serious consideration my political viewpoints would be given in the Filipino community. To come out in mainstream society would force me to confront the homophobic attitudes of society at large in addition to the racial discrimination that I was already subjected to as an ethnic minority. Gradually I began to understand that the discrimination and homophobia I perceived were two sides of the same coin, and that in fact, there were similarities of oppression (later I would recognize that racism as a social dynamic also permeates the gay subculture). I had to take responsibility for defining what my life was to be as a gay Filipino American man and I have found that the process of liberation is a continuous one.

Source: Gil Mangaoang, "From the 1970s to the 1990s: Perspective of a Gay Filipino American Activist," *Amerasia Journal* v. 20, n. 1 (1994), pp. 33–44.

* * *

Inspired by the feminist idea that "the personal is political," some gay people began to recognize the need to address personal psychological issues before people could be motivated to contribute money and time in support of gay and lesbian rights. *The Advocate*'s editor Mark Thompson wrote about innovative projects first developed in Los Angeles to help gay men and lesbians get over their sense of inferiority and shame about being homosexual, and to inspire them to become activists. As a result of these programs, Thompson saw Los Angeles as "the ATM machine of gay activism," which supplied much of the money contributed for gay and lesbian rights.

DOCUMENT 89: Municipal Elections Committee of Los Angeles (1976)

Rob Eichberg, a psychologist with a long history of grassroots activism…started a consciousness-raising group for gay men in Los Angeles, out of which sprang the idea for a political action committee. "We needed a project and decided to change the face of gay rights in Los Angeles by passing a municipal gay-rights resolution," remembers Eichberg. David Mixner, a political consultant then handling Tom Bradley's mayoral campaign, and businessman Tom Scott were among those recruited in the formation of the Municipal Elections Committee of Los Angeles (MECLA), which by 1976 was holding hundred-dollar black-tie dinners and other upscale fundraising events. "We raised more money in a shorter time than any other gay group," explains Eichberg, and by the following year MECLA was able to effectively lobby the City Council into passing a gay-rights resolution.

MECLA's dramatic coup [led] Eichberg to come north and inspire gay men in the [San Francisco] Bay Area to similar achievement. The psychologist created a training seminar…[which] was well received, and [*The Advocate*'s editor David] Goodstein immediately asked Eichberg to consider taking the workshop "on the road." He proposed forming an organization—to be known as "The Advocate Experience"—which would help gay people overcome low self-esteem, addictive behavior, and other problems brought about by society's intolerance. Backed with Goodstein's money and Eichberg's know-how, The Advocate Experience was launched in 1978.…Soon the Consciousness-raising experience was attracting hundreds of gay men and lesbians.…Graduates of The Advocate Experience went on to establish some of the gay community's leading organizations—[including] the Human Rights Campaign Fund, the Stop AIDS Project, the Public Awareness Project, and National Coming Out Day.

Source: Thompson, *Long Road to Freedom*, pp. xxiv–xxv.

Part IV

Backlash: The Reaction to Gay and Lesbian Progress in the United States, 1977–1987

The gay and lesbian rights movement had only begun in the United States in 1950, but by 1977 it had made amazing progress. Most astounding was the change in the self-image of homosexuals. While many remained closeted, most had begun to reconceptualize themselves as persons deserving equal rights. One of the main goals of the early homophile movement was to challenge the medical model that looked at homosexuality as a mental illness. In 1974, after the American Psychiatric Association voted to remove homosexuality from the official list of mental disorders, this goal was largely accomplished. By 1977 many homosexually inclined people had developed a strong, proud gay or lesbian identity.

The second main area of accomplishment for gay and lesbian rights was in the field of law. With the efforts of the pioneering homophile organizations and their successors, and the help of supportive allies in influential national organizations like the American Civil Liberties Union and the National Organization for Women, court suits and legislative changes were won. Liberal politicians in the big cities were beginning to respond to gay voting blocs. Police sometimes still harassed gay men and lesbians, but militant gay rights activists had challenged the most odious forms of police oppression.

Instead of seeing homosexuals as immoral criminal elements, a new generation of more progressive police officials began to take a cooperative approach to the gay community. A major reason for change in law enforcement attitudes was due to the gradual decriminalization of consensual sex. By 1977 eighteen states had repealed their sodomy laws, and over forty cities had passed ordinances to protect people from discrimination on the basis of sexual orientation.

The rise of a strong sense of gay or lesbian identity allowed the development of a sense of community. The idea of like-minded people struggling for their rights fulfilled the vision of homophile pioneers. As a result of their vision, and their work, strong gay and lesbian communities were able to flower in several large cities. The situation had progressed from 1952, when Dale Jennings was a lone person defending his rights in a public forum, to 1977 when many thousands marched openly in gay pride parades. Community strength was reflected in the political influence of organizations like the Municipal Elections Commission of Los Angeles, the Alice B. Toklas Democratic Club in San Francisco, and the National Gay Task Force in New York. All these trends were highlighted by the election of openly gay politician Harvey Milk to the San Francisco Board of Supervisors in 1977.

On the national level, a congressional bill amending the 1964 Civil Rights Act, to protect people from being discriminated against on the basis of sexual orientation, had thirty-nine cosponsors in the House of Representatives by 1977. President Jimmy Carter pledged to sign this bill once it passed Congress. In the same year, Carter's assistant Midge Costanza welcomed representatives of gay and lesbian organizations for a formal meeting at the White House. This was the first time such an invitation had been offered to lesbian and gay activists by the federal government. All in all, 1977 began as a very good year for gay and lesbian rights in the area of the law.

While significant improvements had been accomplished in the psychiatric and legal arenas, the one institution which had not changed was the Judeo-Christian religious tradition. In 1977 a fundamentalist movement emerged, which united conservative Protestants, Catholics, and Orthodox Jews in common cause against gay and lesbian rights. This backlash was predicted by classic sociological theory, which suggests that whenever a new social movement is established and makes notable gains, a countervailing reaction typically follows.

Gay and lesbian activists, concentrating on building strong communities and gaining influence in mainstream society, did not pay much attention to what was going on in the 1970s among conservative Protestants, Catholics, and Orthodox Jews. These other minorities were feeling increasingly uneasy about the massive social changes of the 1960s. America had gone through unprecedented changes, including

African American challenges to the segregationist order in the South, popular uprisings against the war in Vietnam, and student revolts on the campuses. Conservatives felt left out and alienated from the secular directions in which the United States was moving.

Two revolutions that occurred in the 1960s and 1970s which especially worried social conservatives were women's liberation and sexual liberation. Both challenged fundamentalist Christian and Orthodox Jewish values, which emphasized women's subordination to men and the sinfulness of sex outside of marriage. By the 1970s, many of the social changes advocated by the '60s radicals were becoming widely accepted in American society. It was no longer only hippie revolutionary males who sported long hair, but many young men. Middle-class young women were moving into the job market as never before, they were more likely to file for divorce rather than to remain in an unhappy marriage, and many were having sex outside of marriage. The pervasiveness of the sexual revolution convinced many fundamentalists that America was in moral decline.

To prevent sin, fundamentalists felt they had to reassert biblical values among the young. They started calling for Bible readings and prayer in public schools, in order to protect children from the looser sexual mores of the general society. While an earlier generation of social conservatives in the late nineteenth and early twentieth centuries had tried to prevent nonprocreative sexual acts like masturbation and birth control, by the 1970s such acts were so accepted that it was hopeless to try to suppress them. Instead, fundamentalists seized upon two issues that were less accepted, and where they felt they could influence moral standards. These issues were abortion and homosexuality.

Fundamentalist preachers—who depended upon contributions for their income—realized that opposition to abortion and gay rights was an effective way to attract church members and contributions. Abortion and homosexuality were seen as prime indicators of society's sinfulness, since both marked sex for purposes other than reproduction.

For people who felt guilty about their own imperfections, it was comforting to be able to condemn others who were seen as even more sinful. With an attitude that sexual liberation in general was against God's rules, fundamentalists got very upset with people who not only violated the rules of the Bible, but who claimed that there was nothing wrong with such free sexual behavior.

Fundamentalists stress that "the only purpose of sex is procreation" and that it should be done only within the confines of marriage. With this viewpoint, homosexual behavior is inherently sinful because it cannot be procreative and it is outside marriage. Sexual liberationists claimed that the enjoyment of the sexual act itself should be acceptable, and that it is good for two people to express their love for and attraction to each other.

This view went against the basic values of sexual repression found among fundamentalists. Fearing the rapid changes in society regarding sexual practices, many Americans were attracted to the antigay backlash.

Sensing the popularity of the reaction building against gay liberation, conservative Republicans welcomed fundamentalists into a new Republican coalition. Rev. Jerry Falwell founded a new national fundamentalist group called the Moral Majority, and gave his blessing to Ronald Reagan in the upcoming 1980 presidential campaign. Reagan added the antigay and antiabortion views of the rising fundamentalist voting bloc to his own conservative economic and military vision. The election of 1980 was primarily decided over issues of foreign policy and the economy, but gay and lesbian rights suffered after the election of Reagan and his conservative followers. Ideas that had previously been limited to hardcore conservatives now moved into the mainstream of American public opinion.

The fundamentalist message that "the wages of sin is death" seemed to be coming true in 1981, when a strange new disease started killing gay men. Eventually named Acquired Immune Deficiency Syndrome (AIDS), it devastated the gay male community. Fundamentalists lost no time in asserting that AIDS was God's punishment for homosexuality. The problem with this analysis is that it eventually became clear that lesbians had the lowest rate of AIDS of any sexual group in the world. More heterosexuals were getting AIDS than lesbians. If AIDS were to be seen as God's curse, a number of lesbian activists pointed out, then lesbians must be God's Chosen People. Some lesbian activists pointed out the reality that a woman who had sex solely with other women and avoided sex with a man greatly reduced her chances of contracting AIDS.

Despite the lack of threat to the health of their own community, many lesbians threw themselves wholeheartedly into a campaign to help those who were sick. The Reagan administration, in contrast, could not bring itself to mention the disease, even as AIDS was rapidly reaching epidemic proportions. At that point, a bitter debate surfaced within the gay community. Activists who defended the sexual liberationist gains of the 1970s were confronted by activists who felt the need for a drastic reordering of gay male sexual behavior. Meanwhile, many gays felt that they were being looked upon as lepers, to be abandoned to their sad and tragic fate.

In contrast to the 1970s, when the situation for gay and lesbian rights seemed to be increasingly positive, by the 1980s the political dominance of conservative Republicans foreshadowed a reactionary period of opposition to gay and lesbian rights.

Sources: John Boswell, *Christianity, Social Tolerance and Homosexuality* (Chicago: University of Chicago Press, 1980); S. M. Maret, "Attitudes of Fundamentalists towards

Homosexuality," *Psychological Reports* 55 (1) (1984), pp. 205–206; J. S. Maynor, "Fundamentalist Ministers vs. Gay Rights Groups," *TV Guide* 28 (46) (1980), pp. 16–20; H. Rice, "Homophobia: The Overlooked Sin," *Church and Society* 73 (2) (1982), pp. 5–13.

* * *

Responding to the lobbying of Miami's large gay community, in 1977 the Dade County Commission voted to pass an ordinance protecting people from job discrimination on the basis of sexual orientation. Christian pop singer Anita Bryant, a resident of Miami, was inspired by her fundamentalist minister to start a campaign to overturn this ordinance. Suggesting that the inclusion of gay people in the country's antidiscrimination law violated the rights of Christians, she organized Save Our Children, Inc. Claiming that the gay community was recruiting children into the homosexual lifestyle, she saw a need to discriminate against homosexuals by keeping them away from children. This meant that any teachers or other persons working with children should be fired if it became known they were homosexual.

With this emotional appeal to Save Our Children Bryant's followers collected 65,000 signatures on a petition to force a referendum on the ordinance. Although Bryant spoke about a "well-organized, highly financed, and politically militant group of homosexual activists," her own well-organized, highly financed, and politically militant group of fundamentalist Christians overwhelmed the weak gay activist alliance in Miami. When the vote was held on June 7, 1977, Dade County voters overwhelmingly repealed the gay rights law. Fresh after this victory, Bryant took her campaign national, to turn the tide against gay and lesbian rights. She even consented to be interviewed in *Playboy* magazine, where she justified her antigay activism.

DOCUMENT 90: Anita Bryant Defeats Miami Gay Rights Ordinance (1977)

[Homosexuals] were asking for special privileges that violated the state [sodomy] law of Florida, not to mention God's law....Why do you think homosexuals are called fruits? It's because they eat the forbidden fruit of the tree of life....I was standing up for my rights as a mother to protect my children after I realized what the threat the homosexuals were posing meant....[The antidiscrimination ordinance] would have made it mandatory that flaunting homosexuals be hired in both the public and parochial schools....If they're a legitimate minority group, then so are nail biters, dieters, fat people, short people and murderers....I have no respect for homosexuals who insist that their deviant lifestyle is normal. We pray for them, we try to lead them out of it....I love the sinner but I hate the sin.

Source: "Playboy Interview: Anita Bryant," *Playboy* (May 1978), pp. 73–96, 232–250.

* * *

Building upon the success of Anita Bryant's antigay campaign in Florida, in 1978 California State Senator John Briggs sponsored an initiative to remove gay employees from public schools. Briggs warned that if his initiative were not passed, soon homosexual teachers would take over entire schools. Briggs's leaflets featured lurid warnings that gay male teachers would seduce young boys in their classes. After a bitter campaign, California voters rejected this initiative. Still, the presence of gay male teachers was seen as a threat in the classroom. The issue of lesbian teachers was practically ignored, as attention focused on the evils of male homosexuality. A good example of this emphasis is contained in the following document by leading conservative journalist Michael Novak, who argued that homosexuality is a danger to society because everyone should reproduce children. Without strong heterosexual marriages to reproduce children, he warned, the future of society "looks bleak indeed." He did not mention whether he condemned nonreproducing heterosexuals as well. Novak thought that women were less important in society, that the battle between men and women needed to continue, that homosexuals had opted out of this battle, and that the modern decline in masculinity "suffocates the male principle." Therefore, he saw male homosexuality as a greater danger.

DOCUMENT 91: Gay Men Harm Society (1978)

In past ages, homosexuality was sometimes construed as a danger to the human race because it meant (a) a decline in population, or (b) a decline in those masculine qualities essential for survival. What happened in the socialization of the young male was perceived to be of greater significance, and of greater risk, to the race than what happened to the female....Lesbianism may suggest infantile pleasure and regression, but it does not threaten the public, at least not to the same extent that male homosexuality does....Female homosexuality seems somehow more natural, perhaps harmless. Male homosexuality seems to represent a breakdown of an important form of socialization....

Homosexuals absent themselves from the most central struggles of the individual, the struggle to enter into communion with a person of the opposite sex. That is the battle most at the heart of life. Excluded from this struggle, whether by choice or by psychic endowment, the homosexual is deprived of its fruits. Those fruits are a distinctive honesty, realism and wisdom taught by each sex to the other: that complementarity in which your humanity is rejoined and fulfilled. Apart from this civilizing struggle there is a lack....Half the human mystery is evaded. The second [problem] is the instability of homosexual relationships, an instability that arises from the lack of the full dimension of raising a family. Apart from having and raising children, a couple can hardly help a degree of self-preoccupation....

Thirdly, the homosexual faces a particular sort of solipsism, which is difficult to escape simply through companionship. Homosexual love is somehow apart from the fundamental mystery of bringing life into the world, and sharing in the birth and death of the generations. It is self-centered....Society has a strong interest, in private and in public, in encouraging heterosexuality and in discouraging homosexuality.

Source: Michael Novak, "Men Without Women," *The American Spectator* October 1978. [Reprinted in Lisa Orr, ed., *Sexual Values: Opposing Viewpoints* (San Diego: Greenhaven Press, 1989), pp. 79–82.]

* * *

In the 1970s the Church of Jesus Christ of Latter-Day Saints, or Mormons, became a leading voice in opposition to gay and lesbian rights. While the Mormons themselves had been subjected to extreme prejudice and discrimination in the nineteenth century, once they gained acceptance they enthusiastically discriminated against other groups like homosexuals and African Americans. While most psychiatrists stopped using electric shocks to try to destroy homosexual desires, the psychology department at the Mormons' Brigham Young University (BYU) in Utah became a leading exponent of this treatment. In 1978 a closeted gay psychology student at BYU wrote a blistering critique of his church. His article was published in *The Advocate* and generated letters in subsequent issues from other gay Mormons, who supported the accuracy of his critique. He wrote:

DOCUMENT 92: Mormon Suppression of Homosexuality (1978)

The Church generally takes two approaches toward "curing" the homosexual. The first is a sort of positive-thinking approach wherein supportive counsel is given to encourage the young man to think manly thoughts, do masculine things, date, even in some cases "mess around" a little with women, and to put all notions of homosexuality out of his mind. He is urged to be prayerful, repent any past transgressions, be faithful, get married, and settle down.

This method is encouraging to the naive but quickly runs into difficulty. If the young man goes along with the persistent urging of almost everyone around him to get married, his predicament becomes much more complicated. If he candidly reveals to the authorities that he remains homosexual in spite of all efforts to change, he is made to feel guilty and his intentions are doubted. Most quietly and simply withdraw from this kind of destructive counseling. Many are embittered permanently against the Church, while still homosexual.

The other therapy encouraged by the Church is, ironically, regarded as more professional. This is the behavioral therapist's approach. Curiously enough, BYU is coming to be preeminent in applying conditioning therapy for the treatment of homosexuality. Let me tell you briefly of a young man who recently "successfully" completed his treatment...[at] the BYU counseling service. He was given a battery of tests and interviews, then was assigned to a conditioning therapy program coupled with hypnosis and supportive counseling. He came out of these sessions nauseated, shaking, and with mild burns on his arms. For nearly two years this therapy lasted, during which time he felt confident he was changing and that homosexuality was behind him.

Shortly after this, he met a friend, whom I shall call Bob. Bob was talented, intelligent, and handsome. Immediately upon his introduction to Bob, he knew that nothing really had changed. They were soon great friends, and he knew that all of what had happened in therapy, painful as it had been, had not even scratched the surface of who he always was.

This young man's experience, like many others', including my own, discredits the proposition of reconditioning the homosexual. This story is duplicated over and over. Right now, young men are going into the BYU Smith Family Living Center to be strapped with electrodes and shocked out of homosexuality. Has it not occurred to you that in shocking the young man, you are chipping away at his ability ever to love another human being? From what set of values do you say that a man is "improved" when, following shock therapy, he can love neither a man nor a woman? Will Mormons now join the long, shameful tradition of religious fervor working its inhumanity upon mankind, epitomized in the now famous slogan "Kill a queer for Jesus"? The prospects are not encouraging.

Source: Quoted in Thompson, *Long Road to Freedom*, p. 170.

*   *   *

When Harvey Milk quit his job in New York and moved to San Francisco in 1972, he used his savings to open a camera shop on Castro Street. At that time, the Castro area was a run-down, Irish, working-class neighborhood, but gay men were starting to move into the inexpensive dilapidated old Victorian houses and fix them up. Milk saw an opportunity for political activism, but rather than join the city's organized gay political clubs he impulsively decided to run for the city's governing Board of Supervisors only a year after his arrival.

The city's leading gay activist, Jim Foster, believed that gay rights could most effectively be accomplished by creating gay voting blocs to support sympathetic heterosexual politicians. Though he was a liberationist, Foster believed that San Francisco was not yet ready for an openly gay politician. He preferred to continue building his solid base of alliances within the Democratic Party. When Milk came to Foster asking for his support, the veteran activist dismissed the recent arrival as an impulsive upstart. Milk did not let this opposition from the city's gay establishment dissuade him. Rejecting Foster's gradual approach, Harvey Milk felt that gays would never gain equality until they were present in all levels of government. To everyone's surprise, Milk ran a strong campaign, coming in tenth in a field of thirty-two candidates.

With this initial strong showing, Milk spent the next two years forging a political alliance with San Francisco's labor unions, and developing the Castro neighborhood as the center of the gay community. By 1975 Milk was well known, and on his second electoral campaign was almost elected to the Board of Supervisors. Liberal Mayor George Moscone appointed Milk to a city permits board, as well as naming lesbian activists Jo Daley and Phyllis Lyon to the city's Human Rights Commission and Del Martin to the Commission on the Status of Women. Moscone, recognizing that gays were becoming part of the city's economic establishment as well as a political voting bloc, decided to make gay rights one of his major political planks.

In 1977 Harvey Milk made a third run for the city Board of Supervisors in San Francisco. This time, he won. He quickly formed an effective alliance with Mayor Moscone, and by virtue of his position became the new leader of the gay community in San Francisco. Milk realized that his position allowed him to exert influence on a national scale, and he made speeches directed to a national audience. He issued an invitation for gays to leave the persecution and prejudice of their hometowns and migrate to San Francisco, or at least visit as tourists. Gay tourism helped to make San Francisco the nation's most visited city.

By 1978, however, Supervisor Milk's mood had dampened. Prompted by the success of Anita Bryant's Save Our Children campaign in Florida, and with California State Senator John Briggs's initiative on the ballot to prohibit gays from being teachers, Milk debated Briggs before numerous voter forums. Senator Briggs not only played on fears of gay men as child molesters, but also felt that a teacher who was openly gay or lesbian— even if nothing sexual ever happened with students—was not appropriate as a role model for youth. Harvey Milk demolished Briggs's arguments, and helped turn the tide to defeat the Briggs Initiative.

Meanwhile, Milk spearheaded progressive and gay rights measures on the San Francisco Board of Supervisors, and he received numerous death threats from conservatives. When he sponsored a gay rights city ordinance the only vote in opposition was cast by Dan White, a Catholic former policeman who had been the only conservative elected to the Board of Supervisors. Realizing he was outnumbered on a number of issues, White decided to resign in the fall of 1978. Mayor Moscone accepted his resignation, but ten days later after the San Francisco Police Officers' Association lobbied him to return to the board, White changed his mind and asked for his seat back. Moscone had already chosen someone else to fill the empty seat, and with Harvey Milk's support Moscone refused White's request. On November 27, 1978, Dan White brought his police pistol to City Hall and shot and killed both the mayor and Harvey Milk. The entire city, especially the gay community, was in shock.

Six months later, Dan White was put on trial for murder. The jury consisted solely of white heterosexual Catholics. When the jury returned a verdict of voluntary manslaughter, rather than murder, many gay people took this as a sign that a gay person could be killed with impunity. Without a conviction for murder, Dan White would be free in five years. The night after the verdict was announced, an angry crowd marched on City Hall and burned a dozen police cars. The police counterattacked, bursting into a gay bar in the Castro and bludgeoning everyone in sight.

While this "White Night Riot" tragically resulted in one hundred gay people and sixty-one police being hospitalized, it was a crisis that represented a turning point. The city's new mayor Diane Feinstein and the rest of the supervisors sympathized with the gay community's anger over the murders and the injustice of the lenient verdict given to Dan White. A new police commissioner was appointed, and he worked to reduce anti-gay prejudice among the police. Many bigoted police resigned from the force, and new trainees were recruited from the nonwhite, gay male, and lesbian communities. At last the long-simmering battle between the San Francisco police and the gay community was over, and the San Francisco Police Department became one of the most progressive law enforcement agencies in the nation. The city government also responded, providing grants to gay community projects and hiring more lesbian and gay citizens in city government. San Francisco became more of a progay oasis as a more conservative mood spread over the nation.

Much of this progress in San Francisco was directly due to the hard work, creativity, and martyrdom of Harvey Milk. His vivid speeches against the right-wing zealots who were attacking gays, and the liberals who remained silent on the issue, helped to inspire many San Franciscans to support equality. An example of his powerful gay rights rhetoric is his keynote speech at the rally in front of City Hall, following the Gay Freedom Day Parade on June 25, 1978. Over a quarter million people marched for gay and lesbian rights, making it the largest gay rights march in the nation up to that time.

DOCUMENT 93: Harvey Milk on the San Francisco Board of Supervisors (1978)

My name is Harvey Milk—and I want to recruit you. I want to recruit you for the fight to preserve your democracy from the John Briggs and the Anita Bryants who are trying to constitutionalize bigotry. We are not going to allow that to happen. We are not going to sit back in silence as 300,000 of our gay brothers and sisters did in Nazi Germany. We are not going to allow our rights to be taken away and then march with bowed heads into the gas chambers. On this anniversary of Stonewall I ask my gay sisters and brothers to make the commitment to fight. For themselves, for their freedom, for their country....

Blacks did not win their rights by sitting quietly in the back of the bus. They got off!...We are coming out to fight the lies, the myths, the distortions! We are coming out to tell the truth about gays!

For I'm tired of the conspiracy of silence. I'm tired of listening to the Anita Bryants twist the language and the meaning of the Bible to fit their own distorted outlook. But I'm even more tired of the silence from the religious leaders of the nation who know that she is playing fast and loose with the true meaning of the Bible. I'm tired of their silence more than of her biblical gymnastics!

And I'm tired of John Briggs talking about false role models. He's lying in his teeth and he knows it. But I'm even more tired of the silence from educators and psychologists who know that Briggs is lying and yet say nothing....I'm tired of the silence, so I'm going to talk about it. And I want you to talk about it.

Gay people, we are painted as child molesters. I want to talk about that. I want to talk about the *myth* of child molestations by gays. I want to talk about the *fact* that in this state some 95 percent of child molestations are heterosexual....I want to talk about the *fact* that some 98 percent of the six million rapes committed annually are heterosexual. I want to talk about the *fact* that one out of every three women who will be murdered in this state this year will be murdered by their husbands. I want to talk about the *fact* that some 30 percent of all marriages contain domestic violence....Today I'm talking about the *facts* of heterosexual violence and what the hell are you going to do about that??? Clean up your own house before you start telling lies about gays....

I'm tired of our so-called friends who tell us we must set standards. What standards?

The standards of the rapists? The wife beaters? The child abusers? The people who ordered the bomb to be built?...The people who built the concentration camps—right here in California, and then herded all the Japanese-Americans into them during World War II....What standards do *you* want *us* to set? Clean up your act, clean up your violence before you criticize lesbians and gay men because of their sexuality....It is madness to glorify killing and violence on one hand and be ashamed of the sexual act, the act that conceived you, on the other....

There is a difference between morality and murder. The *fact* is that more people have been slaughtered in the name of religion than for any other single reason. That, that, my friends, that is the true perversion!...

What are you going to do about it? You must come out...to your relatives. I know that that is hard and will upset them but think of how they will upset you in the voting booth. Come out to your friends, if indeed they are your friends. Come out to your neighbors, to your fellow workers, to the people who work where you eat and shop....Once and for all, break down the myths, destroy the lies and distortions. For your sake. For their sake. For the sake of the youngsters who are becoming scared by the votes from Dade to Eugene.

If Briggs wins he will not stop. They never do. Like all mad people, they are forced to go on, to prove they were right! There will be no safe "closet" for any gay person. So break out of yours today—tear the damn thing down once and for all!...

I call upon lesbians and gay men from all over the nation, your nation, to gather in Washington one year from now....And we will tell you about America and what it really stands for....Let me remind you what America is. Listen carefully.

On the Statue of Liberty it says: "Give me your tired, your poor, your huddled masses yearning to breathe free." In the Declaration of Independence it is written: "All men are created equal and they are endowed with certain inalienable rights." And in our National Anthem it says: "Oh, say does that star-spangled banner yet wave o'er the land of the free."

For Mr. Briggs and Mrs. Bryant...and *all* the bigots out there: That's what America is. No matter how hard you try, you cannot erase those words from the Declaration of Independence. No matter how hard you try, you cannot chip those words from off the base of the Statue of Liberty. And no matter how hard you try you cannot sing the "Star Spangled Banner" without those words.

That's what America is. Love it or leave it.

Source: Harvey Milk, "That's What America Is" June 25, 1978, speech, quoted in Randy Shilts, *The Mayor of Castro Street* (New York: St. Martin's Press, 1982), pp. 364–371.

* * *

Despite the progay votes of the American Psychiatric Association, conservative writers who opposed lesbian and gay rights continued to use the older outdated psychiatric literature to assert that homosexuals brought on their own problems, and that homosexuality should be treated as a mental disease. Writers like Frank du Mas used the old psychiatric disease model as justification for overturning gay rights laws.

DOCUMENT 94: *Gay Is Not Good* (1979)

The homosexual, already deviant in one aspect of his life, may assert his strong conscious or unconscious antisocial tendencies by deliberate confrontations with social taboos and the forces of law and order. It seems reasonable to conclude, therefore, that in the very great majority of instances, the homosexual himself is deliberately, though often unconsciously, responsible for difficulties with the police....When they go into the streets they are deliberately asking for confrontation with the police and other authorities. They interfere with the civil liberties of heterosexual citizens, just as they claim they themselves have been abused....

It is often part of a homosexual's character to place himself in a situation where he will be humiliated, rejected, harassed, and degraded. One world-famous authority [psychiatrist Edmund Bergler, author of *Homosexuality: Disease or Way of Life?* (New York: Hill and Wang, 1957)] on homosexuality believes that "injustice collecting" is a major character trait of most if not all homosexuals....

What can heterosexuals do to combat the political influence of homosexuals?...Heterosexuals will now have the difficult time of undoing much of the damage already done and of stemming the homosexual tide that no longer threatens but has actually engulfed much of our society....

Perversions have no special rights. I believe homosexuals do have a special class of rights that many other citizens do not. They have the rights of all sick people. They have "patient rights" or "client rights," but that is all. They have the same rights as schizophrenics, necrophiliacs, and all others who need our understanding, our compassion, our help....

Homosexuality has played a significant role in the moral poverty and derangement of our society. Heterosexuals are just beginning to insist on their "rights." We have reason to hope that in the future more and more people will understand that gay is not good.

Source: Frank M. du Mas, *Gay Is Not Good* (Nashville: Thomas Nelson, 1979), pp. 131, 133, 135, 248, 257.

* * *

Conservative magazines have continued to publish articles about the unnaturalness of homosexuality. Though this author does not define what is "appropriate to the nature of man," he suggests that, in order to live a complete life, a person must produce children. He does not address the issue of overpopulation, or the morality of encouraging every person to reproduce. He seems to feel that having children is the only way that a person can make a contribution to "the dialogue of the generations," but he ignores adoption as a means for homosexuals to do this. Given the overwhelming need for humanity to restrict further increases in world population, a reader might wonder why people should be condemned for not reproducing.

DOCUMENT 95: Homosexuality Is Unnatural (1979)

Homosexuality is, in a certain sense, unnatural....I use the term "natural" here to mean "appropriate to the nature of man," for I am at a loss to know what other term to use in dealing with the obvious fact that human bodies seem more obviously designed for heterosexual intercourse than for homosexual, both as to technique and to purpose....And it seems to me that one cannot honestly ignore the relation of sex to reproduction....The fact is that homosexuality generally entails a renunciation of responsibility for the continuance of the human race and of a voice in the dialogue of the generations....It is harder to live a complete life than a partial one, and easier to live in fantasy than in reality.

Source: Samuel McCracken, *Commentary* January 1979, pp. 19–29. [Reprinted in Lisa Orr, ed., *Sexual Values: Opposing Viewpoints* (San Diego: Greenhaven Press, 1989), p. 81.]

* * *

In answer to the increasingly powerful backlash against gay and lesbian rights, and also to celebrate the tenth-year anniversary of the Stonewall uprising in New York, activists planned to follow Harvey Milk's suggestion for a national March on Washington for Lesbian and Gay Rights. Inspired by the 1963 March on Washington for civil rights, which helped to mobilize public opinion in favor of equality for African Americans, the idea of a national march for lesbians and gays generated opposition from leaders of some gay groups. Despite this, over a hundred thousand lesbians, gay men, bisexuals, and transgendered people—as well as their families and friends—gathered from throughout the United States and on October 14, 1979, rallied at the Washington Monument.

The march had an intense personal impact on those who came to participate in it. For some, it represented their personal coming out, as they informed their families, friends, and co-workers of their participation. Most had never been in a gay rights march before, and indeed for many this event was their first experience in gay activism. Significant numbers of participants stayed to lobby their senators and representatives, and went home inspired to work for lesbian and gay rights on a local or professional level.

Especially notable in the march was the presence of people of color. Over five hundred African Americans, Asian Americans, Latin Americans, and Native Americans were in Washington to participate in the first national Third World Lesbian/Gay Conference, held near Howard University on October 12–15. They marched together from the conference site to join the full march in downtown Washington. The excitement and inspiration of this conference and march on those who attended is reflected in a news report written by Daniel Tsang, a Chinese gay activist from Southern California.

DOCUMENT 96: March on Washington for Lesbian and Gay Rights (1979)

The early morning march through the Black neighborhood and through Chinatown was the first time Black and Asian lesbians and gay men had paraded through our own neighborhoods. The mood of the marchers was jubilant, and the reaction from onlookers more surprise than hostility. The dozen or so Asian lesbians and gay men chanted "We're Asian, Gay and Proud!" as the street signs turned Chinese at the edge of Chinatown. Many of the Asian marchers faced deportation for so visibly coming out as lesbian or gay, under a reactionary McCarthy period law which bars gay people from abroad from entering this country.

At noon the marchers joined with others forming the main March on Washington and marched as the Third World contingent, right behind the lesbians and handicapped gays who led off. The Third World marchers expressed pride in their gayness and solidarity with national liberation struggles abroad....Heading the Third World contingent was a small group of Native Americans, holding a sign proclaiming "The First Gay Americans."

The march culminated a weekend of intense discussion among Third World lesbians and gay men who attempted to reconcile being both people of color and lesbian or gay in a racist and homophobic society. Participants heard a moving address by keynote speaker Audre Lorde, Black feminist lesbian, and discussed racism and sexism in various workshops. Conferees late Saturday also heard solidarity statements from socialist compañeros from Mexico, who had somehow managed to avoid detection and enter the country....

The high level of political awareness and militancy among the majority of conference participants suggests that the largely white-dominated gay movement, ten years after the uprising at the Stonewall Inn in New York, now faces a threshold in its history. The next decade may see an autonomous Third World lesbian and gay movement developing.

Source: Daniel C. Tsang, "Third World Lesbians and Gays Meet," *Gay Insurgent* 6 (Summer 1980), p. 11.

*   *   *

On October 13, 1979, the day before the national March on Washington for Lesbian and Gay Rights, Asian American lesbian activist Tana Loy gave an address before the Third World Lesbian/Gay Conference. The excitement she felt was shared by many at this groundbreaking conference. Loy's speech is an example of the political importance of personal identification with a specific lesbian and gay community as an important basis on which to build an activist movement. Even something as simple as a gathering of like-minded people in a room can be a major inspiration for those who work for lesbian and gay rights. The feminist slogan "the personal is political" is demonstrated in Loy's speech.

DOCUMENT 97: Asian American Lesbian Speaks at the Third World Lesbian/Gay Conference (1979)

The strength that comes from being here and being out with you is...what happened to us at the Asian American caucus, what happened to us personally and politically. Somehow we felt—immediately and immensely in tune with each other....In the context of this history making conference, we Asians, gay Asians...have for the first time, for many of us, with open hearts and minds, run toward each other. (Applause)

And we all know that for a Third World lesbian and gay man, to do something that personal is highly political. It is very much as though we had been in a wasteland....But today we are going toward each other, and we are sharing our strength with each other, and with all our brothers and sisters here today....[We acknowledge] the fears and frustrations that keep our own people in the closet as Asians and as lesbians and gay men. Many of us cannot even come out for fear of deportation; and yet I know there are many Asians who are going to be out on that street tomorrow, knowing that's a reality in their lives.

In our short time together, a support system has evolved from which we have drawn our strength, from each other and from all of you here. And out of this strength we have collectively decided to march together as Asians. (Applause) We come to you to share our strength, as we have come out strong with each other. We express our strength and power with all of you; with all of us. Because when we are out tomorrow it will be the Third World lesbian and gay people, side by side, as one voice, to say no to racism, no to sexism, and no to anti-gay bigotry.

Source: Tana Loy, "Who's the Barbarian?" *Gay Insurgent* 6 (Summer 1980), p. 15.

*   *   *

Episcopal Priest Malcolm Boyd was well known as the author of a number of books that presented a progressive view of Christianity. His outspokenness in the civil rights movement of the 1960s, and his later public coming out as a gay man in the 1970s, helped lead the Episcopal Church to take a strong stand for equality. As a prominent clergyman, he was in a prime position to challenge antigay fundamentalist viewpoints and to show that all Christians do not support discrimination. He recalled his feelings about gay and lesbian rights in the late 1970s, and the close connection between gay rights and religion:

DOCUMENT 98: A Gay Priest Speaks Out on Fundamentalists (1980)

My past involvement in civil rights and the anti-Vietnam war movement made the subject of gay rights a thrilling and demanding one for me. I had been jailed numerous times during the sixties for civil protest, marched with Martin Luther King, Jr., and had been arrested twice for leading peace Masses inside the Pentagon. So, the challenge of civil rights for gays became an intensely felt struggle. I experienced the full joy of being a proud and open gay man. My gay memoir, *Take Off the Masks* [Garden City, NY: Doubleday, 1978] was published, I fell in love, and I appeared on national TV as a guy who was gay and happy about it. Thousands of letters poured in from gay people who responded positively to my message.

Soon, however, I would be more sober about the whole experience. Queer-haters responded to my coming out with negativism and hate. And, as a spiritual leader, I would come to grips with the savage gulf that exists between my gay brothers and lesbian sisters, on the one hand, and much of organized religion, on the other....

As gays, we must not beg anymore. We claim freedom that is our authentic right. No one can "give" it to us. The establishment churches, as part of the power structure, respect power. We must show them ours....

Never forget: The religious question is central to gay politics. The antigay position is predicated on the fundamentalist religious proposition that, in effect, "The majority of American Christians, which is the majority of Americans, are not and never will be prepared to approve or accept the open practice of homosexuality." What the Bible is construed to say about homosexuality is the bottom line of the gay political struggles.

It is necessary for gays to deal with the religious question creatively and take the initiative rather than be put on the defensive about it. If gays let the religious question go by default, a major communications disaster will occur. Gays need to approach the religious question in a very positive way. Untapped political strength will be the result. God is not antigay, nor is the Bible. Only churchianity is....

Jesus speaks of love. He acts out of love. If many of his so-called followers openly deny love and show hate, they're not the "good people" at all.

Source: Malcolm Boyd, "A Gay Priest Speaks Out," quoted in Thompson, *Long Road to Freedom*, pp. 162, 207.

*   *   *

After Anita Bryant led the successful effort to overturn Miami's gay rights ordinance in 1977, she established two foundations—Anita Bryant Ministries and Protect America's Children—to oppose gay and lesbian rights on the national level. By 1979, over 400,000 people from across the nation had donated more than $2 million to these foundations. With this money, plus her own considerable wealth from her records, concerts, and Florida Orange Juice Commission sponsorships, she financed a huge antigay rights campaign.

In 1980 Anita Bryant made an astounding admission. In an interview with the *Ladies' Home Journal*, she admitted that her campaign against homosexuals was tied up with her own inner insecurities. When she was growing up in the middle of the Oklahoma Bible Belt, she said, she was traumatized by her parents' divorce. A family breakup is traumatic enough for any child, but especially for a child being raised in a fundamentalist church. As a divorcee, her mother became an outcast. Soon after Anita married Bob Green, she realized she had made a big mistake. The money from her successful music recording career supported him and their children, yet she felt that he tried to act dominant over her and mistreat her. While they smiled for the cameras as a model happy couple, privately their lives were falling apart. Bryant finally admitted the hypocrisy of her life in 1980, and she filed for divorce. She was immediately thrown out of her church. The betrayal of her fundamentalist colleagues led her to make this public statement about the sexism of the Christian Church.

Both Anita Bryant and her husband ended up as broken people, grieving and depressed. She had become so politically controversial that she could not get new recording contracts and concerts. Meanwhile, national gay and lesbian organizations led a boycott of Florida orange juice, which was so effective that the Florida Orange Juice Commission did not renew her advertising contract. Deprived of this income, her foundations fell apart and she had to sell her house to pay her debts. Anita and her three youngest children moved back to her mother's house in Oklahoma, where she became even more of an outcast to her fundamentalist neighbors than her mother had been. With her entertainment career destroyed her life was miserable. The hatreds and prejudices she had helped to arouse toward gay people had turned back on her. Learning the hard way what it meant to be an outcast, she reflected:

DOCUMENT 99: Anita Bryant's Startling Reversal (1980)

Divorce was what I feared most....When I was growing up in the Bible Belt, the kind of sermon I always heard was—wife submit to your husband, even if he's wrong....[When I married Bob] I had such doubts about getting married and I was depressed all through the honeymoon. Our problems never ended after that. It was obvious to anyone around us by the way we cut each other verbally and embarrassed each other....He saw me as a meal ticket....I felt like a caged animal, smothered, stymied, and I saw that he was miserable too....Bob had a hate, a contempt for me. Who can withstand constant rejection—no respect, no trust, no affection, no love life, no recognition as a worthwhile human being? Something's got to give....I hit bottom enough I wanted to [commit suicide]....The home atmosphere was devastating....

[In early 1980, when Anita filed for divorce, her church threatened] that if I did not submit to my husband they would have me excommunicated.... I've about given up on the fundamentalists, who have become so legalistic and letter-bound to the Bible....Fundamentalists have their head in the sand. The church is sick right now and I have to say I'm even part of that sickness. I have had to stay in pastors' homes and their wives talk to me. Some pastors are so hard-nosed about submission and insensitive to their wives' needs that they don't recognize the frustration—even hatred— within their own households....There are some valid reasons why militant feminists are doing what they're doing. Having experienced a form of male chauvinism among Christians that was devastating, I can see how women are controlled in a very ungodly un-Christian way....

[I can also see how fundamentalists have] a personal vendetta about gays. They harbored hatreds....I guess I can better understand the gays' and the feminists' anger and frustration. As for the gays, the church needs to be more loving, unconditionally, and willing to see these people as human beings, to minister to them and try to understand....[Nowadays] I'm more inclined to say live and let live....I know now there are no easy answers. I'm learning every day, growing and changing....The answers don't seem quite so simple now.

Source: Cliff Jahr, "Anita Bryant's Startling Reversal," Ladies' Home Journal v. 97, n. 12 (December 1980), pp. 60–68.

*   *   *

Though the Democrats were defeated in the election of 1980, lesbians and gay men continued to build gay strength within the Democratic Party bureaucracy. An unprecedented seventy-seven elected delegates to the 1980 Democratic National Convention were openly gay and lesbian. Gay and lesbian rights gradually became more accepted by the national Democratic establishment as an integral plank in the party platform and an integral part of the coalition that made up a liberal voting bloc. A dramatic high point of the convention occurred when over four hundred delegates signed a petition to place the name of Mel Boozer, an African American gay man, in nomination as the Democratic candidate for vice president of the United States. While Boozer withdrew his name from consideration, his electrifying speech compared the black civil rights movement and the movement for gay and lesbian rights.

DOCUMENT 100: Democratic Party and Gay Rights (1980)

I rise in anguished recognition of more than twenty million Americans who love this country, and who long to serve this country in the freedom that others take for granted. Twenty million Lesbian and Gay Americans whose lives are blighted by a veil of ignorance and misunderstanding....Now more than ever, fairness, equal justice, and compassion are under attack by the forces of the extreme right. But we also believe that the ideals embedded in our Constitution by the founders of the Republic are alive and well in the Democratic Party....We are pleased that the platform of our party calls for an end to this kind of discrimination....Is this not the same party which has championed the causes of every minority which has come before us?...Is this not the same party that has sought to include women on an equal basis? Is this not the same party which has led the battle for civil rights in Black America?

Would you ask me how I dare to compare the civil rights struggle with the struggle for Lesbian and Gay rights? I can compare them and I do compare them, because I know what it means to be called a nigger and I know what it means to be called a faggot, and I understand the difference, in the marrow of my bones. And I can sum up that difference in one word: NONE. Bigotry is bigotry.

Source: "Text of Mel Boozer's Speech," *Washington Blade* August 21, 1980, p. 6.

* * *

One of the most conservative leaders of the Republican Party in the 1970s, Congressman Robert E. Bauman of Maryland, opposed gay rights. He was a founder and national chairman of Young Americans for Freedom and of the American Conservative Union. A strict Catholic, Bauman was married and had children. But despite his conservative political views he had been sexually active with other boys and young men since he was eight years old. Even after marriage his same-sex feelings were so strong that he sometimes sought out young men for sexual purposes. His beliefs that these urges were sinful, and his efforts to deny to himself that he was queer, led him to drink heavily and become an alcoholic. Despite turmoil in his marriage, Bauman managed to keep his homosexuality secret until 1980.

However, on September 3, 1980, just two months before his reelection to Congress, F.B.I. agents informed him that they had been investigating his visits to gay bars, and had extracted confessions from bar employees that he had paid them for sex. Congressman Bauman was charged with solicitation for having sex with a twenty-six-year-old man. Newspapers published the stories, and the conservative leader suddenly found himself in the middle of a huge public scandal. Later, in his autobiography, Bauman wrote that his strong conservative stance in politics was at least partly a result of his own self-hatred.

DOCUMENT 101: Congressman Bauman on Opposition to Gay Rights (1980)

This was my way of fighting the dread threat of homosexuality even as I was fighting within myself....That my ignorance hurt others I did not even consider....Fearful of my own sexuality, still trying to maintain the inner sham...I twice voted against homosexuals receiving equality of treatment under the law that all American citizens deserve....How wrong I was in taking these stands was to be forcefully driven home to me in a few years as I myself felt the sting of economic discrimination because of my own belatedly accepted sexuality. I was wrong in my votes....I acted in public consistent with my religious and moral beliefs, even if my private life was totally inconsistent....I have learned the bitter lessons of discrimination....It is small wonder ultimately others would see much of my life as hypocrisy....In a desperate effort to create my illusion of self-esteem I adopted conservative politics with a fervor amounting to neurotic escape. It would be my refuge from the unacceptable inner reality....[pp. 194–199, 234–235].

[After being defeated for reelection to Congress in 1980 due to his sex scandal, Bauman tried to get an appointive position, but his many Republican friends refused to hire him. His wife divorced him and took their children away, and she was awarded a prominent position in the Reagan administration. Left without a job, Bauman gained a heightened awareness of the discrimination facing gay people. He gradually accepted himself as gay and realized the need to challenge prejudice. In 1983 he spoke in favor of gay rights at the annual meeting of the American Bar Association, and attempted to organize other gay conservatives to come out in favor of gay equality. But, he wrote, gay conservatives] did not wish to come out of the closet in spite of their obviously gay private lives. They did not want their names on even a "secret" mailing list or even to write contribution checks....The closets of Washington are full of gay Republicans...in high Reagan administration posts, some in the White House. They serve in the Congress and populate the circles of power that exist in law firms, public relations firms, lobbying groups, political action committees, even conservative organizations and the Republican party structure as well. Their names appear on the White House guest list and feature articles on them can be seen in the *Washington Post*....It can be argued their lives are the essence of hypocrisy....[pp. 261–262].

Source: Robert E. Bauman, *The Gentleman from Maryland: The Conscience of a Gay Conservative* (New York: Arbor House, 1986) pp. 194–199, 234–235, 261–262.

*   *   *

In 1981 the United States Centers for Disease Control (CDC) reported an outbreak of a rare form of skin cancer among gay men. The CDC named the underlying condition Acquired Immune Deficiency Syndrome (AIDS), and concluded that AIDS results from a virus called Human Immunodeficiency Virus (HIV). The first AIDS article to appear in the gay press occurred when novelist Larry Kramer wrote in the *New York Native* on August 24, 1981, calling for gay men to avoid promiscuous sexual behavior. Those who did not want to give up sexual liberation pointed out that promiscuous lesbians were not getting AIDS, and even promiscuous gay men who avoided anal intercourse were rarely infected. Many feared, though, that sexual freedom would be swept away in the reaction against AIDS.

Kramer helped form the Gay Men's Health Crisis (GMHC) to educate gay men to keep them from getting infected, to take care of the sick, and to raise money for medical research on AIDS. Those who agreed with Kramer worked to restructure their sexual lives, and also agitated to close down gay bathhouses where promiscuous unsafe sex was occurring. Sexually transmitted diseases put a brake on the freewheeling sexual lifestyle of the 1970s, as many gay men settled into monogamous relationships, became celibate, or carefully followed safer sex guidelines. The federal government's tepid response to the AIDS epidemic prompted a new generation of gay men and lesbians, who were experiencing anti-AIDS discrimination while going through the personal sorrow of having friends sicken and die, to a new wave of activism. Kramer remembered:

DOCUMENT 102: AIDS Strikes Gay Men (1981)

There was only one thing that made me an activist, and that was AIDS....[Before AIDS] you just didn't want to get involved. It was not chic; it was not something you could brag about with your friends....When there was a news story on television about the gay pride parade, people would sit in front of the TV set and make fun of it....[Even now, in the United States] there are 24 million gay people out there, and the biggest gay organization has no more than 15,000 to 25,000 gay people on a mailing list. We have surprisingly few rights and surprisingly little power for the numbers that we represent....The reality is that most people—in this city, anyway—just want to be successful and do their work and live their lives and have a modicum of enjoyment. That's all most people want to do. They don't want to get involved; they don't want to make waves....

I think we are a very special people and capable of so much more....I think being a gay man—even today with AIDS—is a wonderful thing. I love being gay...[but] having to face AIDS is almost like a bum rap. Nevertheless, I think we are very lucky. We have...a responsibility to put more into the world, to be upstanding in a dignified way for what you represent. Maybe I shouldn't expect so much, but I expect a lot from everyone. I'm also disappointed in straight people [who have] done exceedingly little to help us in this fight. We have certainly helped them in many fights.

Source: Eric Marcus, *Making History: The Struggle for Gay and Lesbian Equal Rights, 1945–1990* (New York: HarperCollins, 1992), pp. 422, 425, 427–429.

* * *

One of the most powerful leaders of the New Right coalition that helped elect Ronald Reagan to the presidency was Jerry Falwell. A fundamentalist Christian preacher who pioneered the drive to get evangelicals involved in politics, Reverend Falwell spoke often about the sinfulness of homosexuality in his "Old-Time Gospel Hour" sermons which were televised from his Baptist Church in Lynchburg, Virginia. Because homosexuality proved to be a sure-fire way to get Falwell's followers to send in money, he often resorted to this topic as a fund-raiser. An example is a 1981 fund-raising letter that he sent out which included his position on gay and lesbian rights. After AIDS became known Falwell added references to AIDS as God's punishment for sin, but his opposition to lesbian and gay rights was set long before AIDS arrived.

DOCUMENT 103: Jerry Falwell Fund-Raising Letter (1981)

With God as my witness, I pledge that I will continue to expose the sin of homosexuality to the people of this nation. I believe that the massive homosexual revolution is always a symptom of a nation coming under the judgement of God.

Romans 1:24–28, Paul clearly condemns the sin of homosexuality. In verse 28, when a nation refuses to listen to God's standard of morality, the Bible declares, "God gave them over to a reprobate mind."

Recently, 250,000 homosexuals marched in the streets of San Francisco. Several weeks ago, 75,000 more were marching in the streets of Los Angeles. The homosexuals are on the march in this country.

Please remember, homosexuals do not reproduce! They recruit! And, many of them are out after my children and your children....

Let me repeat, a massive homosexual revolution can bring the judgement of God upon this nation. Our children must not be recruited into a profane lifestyle.

Source: Fund-raising letter from the "Old-Time Gospel Hour" (1981), reprinted in Perry Deane Young, *God's Bullies: Native Reflections on Preachers and Politics* (New York: Holt, Rinehart and Winston, 1982), p. 307.

* * *

When Pope John Paul II toured the United States, he reiterated that homosexual acts are sinful. The pope's reasoning seems to be related to the need for people to repress the desires of their body, and not to give in to lust. By controlling the body, he claims, a person can experience holiness. He is following St. Paul's view of the spirit and the flesh as opposites. In a commentary on Paul's letter to the Corinthians, in the Bible, the pope explained:

DOCUMENT 104: Pope John Paul II on Controlling the Body (1981)

The parts of the body that seem to be weaker are indispensable and those parts of the body we think less honorable we invest with the greatest honor. St. Paul's remarks about the less honorable or less presentable parts of the body reflect the sense of shame felt by mankind since the loss of original innocence and the subjection to concupisence, particularly to the lust of the flesh.

The parts in question are not objectively less honorable or respectable in themselves. They are such only on account of that sense of shame that urges us to surround our body with honor—to control in holiness and honor. It is precisely by controlling the body in holiness and honor that we overcome the present discord within us. We restore harmony by purity of heart.

Source: Pope John Paul II, quoted in Thompson, *Long Road to Freedom*, p. 222.

*   *   *

Despite losses on the federal level, in certain liberal areas of the nation gay and lesbian rights continued to make progress. In 1981 Wisconsin became the first state to adopt a nondiscrimination law that included protection against discrimination on the basis of sexual orientation. Other states used the Wisconsin list of protected categories to draft legislation in this area.

DOCUMENT 105: Wisconsin Antidiscrimination Law (1981)

Section 12: It is the declared policy of this state that all persons shall have an equal opportunity for housing regardless of sex, race, color, sexual orientation, handicap, religion, national origin, sex or marital status of the person maintaining the household, lawful source of income, age or ancestry....This section shall be deemed an exercise of the police powers of the state for the protection of the welfare, health, peace, dignity, and human rights of the people of this state.

Section 13: The equal rights council shall...educate the people of the state to a greater understanding, appreciation and practice of human rights for

all people, of whatever race, creed, color, sexual orientation, national origin, to the end that this state will be a better place in which to live.

   Section 14: The practice of denying employment and other opportunities
to, and discriminating against, properly qualified persons by reasons of
their age, race, creed, color, handicap, sex, national origin, ancestry, sexual
orientation, arrest record or conviction record, is likely to foment domestic
strife and unrest, and substantially and adversely affect the general welfare
of a state by depriving it of the fullest utilization of its capacities for production. The denial by some employers, licensing agencies and labor
unions of employment opportunities to such persons solely because of
their age, race, creed, color, handicap, sex, national origin, ancestry, sexual
orientation, arrest record or conviction record, and discrimination against
them in employment tends to deprive the victims of the earnings which are
necessary to maintain a just and decent standard of living, thereby committing grave injury to them....

   Except where permitted by law, a person shall not: Deny an individual
the full and equal enjoyment of the goods, services, facilities, privileges,
advantages, or accommodations of a place of public accommodation or
public service because of religion, race, color, national origin, age, height,
weight, handicap, marital status, sexual orientation, student status, or because of the use by an individual of adaptive devices.

Source: Wisconsin State Laws of 1981, Chapter 12, sections 12–14, and (3)(b)(i).

*   *   *

   In 1982 at a press conference in Indianapolis, Kathleen Sarris spoke
   on behalf of Justice, Inc., a lesbian and gay rights group. Her speech,
   along with antigay comments from Christian ministers, was widely covered by local television stations. She later testified before a congressional investigating committee about the repercussions.

DOCUMENT 106: Violence against Lesbian (1982)

   Within 24 hours of the press conference, I began receiving threatening
telephone calls and letters. The phone calls and letters were religious in nature; they spoke of acting in the name of God or Jesus and exacting retribu-
tion. They also spoke of my leading people to become sodomites, and that
this person would put an end to my work. My initial response was that it
was an annoying hoax, and it would die down and go away. Instead, the
letters and telephone calls continued with systematic regularity. I decided
to move out of my home....Within days, the letters and phone calls resumed. It was very apparent that I was being tracked....[I] went to talk

with the Indianapolis police. Their response was there was nothing they could do, and if I couldn't stand the heat, I should get out of the kitchen! After a couple of weeks the letters and phone calls stopped. I assumed the person got tired of playing the game.

Then, approximately two weeks after the letters stopped, I was leaving my office and as I turned to lock the door, I felt the barrel of a gun in the back of my head. He pushed me back into the reception area. For the next three hours, he beat me with his fists, his gun, and his belt. I was sexually molested and, ultimately, I was raped. Throughout the assault, he talked about how he was acting for God; that what he was doing to me was God's revenge on me because I was a "queer" and getting rid of me would save children and put an end to the [gay] movement in Indiana.

At the end of his torture, he had me stand up; I was facing the desk in the reception area, and he again put his gun to the back of my head. I heard him draw back the hammer, and the chamber clicked into position. It was at that point it occurred to me that I had nothing to lose, I picked up an object from the desk and swung around and hit him in the head. While he was stunned, I kicked him and he lost the gun. We struggled for about ten minutes until he finally knocked me unconscious. When I regained consciousness, about an hour later, he was gone....

[After calling a hospital ambulance] I was in the Emergency room for eight hours; I suffered a concussion, hair line fracture of my right cheek bone, dislocation of my jaw, and damage to my left knee. While I was in the Emergency room, the detectives were able to piece together the whole scenario of the past few months. It was then that I learned the Indianapolis Police department could have attempted to get fingerprints and conducted a paper and ink analysis on the letters; also, they could have ordered a tracer on my telephone. The Indianapolis police chose not to give me any help....

It has been four years since the assault, and the pain is still very real....I live with constant fear that it will happen again. I also live with the knowledge that because of my orientation, because I chose to exercise what I believe are my constitutional rights, my life has no value to certain people.

Source: Kathleen Sarris testimony, Hearing before the Subcommittee on Criminal Justice of the Committee on the Judiciary, House of Representatives, 99th Congress, Second Session on Anti-Gay Violence; October 9, 1986, pp. 164–165). Washington; Government Printing Office, Serial No. 132. [Reprinted in Gregory M. Herek and Kevin T. Berrill, eds., *Hate Crimes: Confronting Violence Against Lesbians and Gay Men* (Newbury Park, CA: Sage Publications, 1992), pp. 201–203.]

*   *   *

In 1982 Merle Woo's teaching contract in Asian American Studies at UC Berkeley was not renewed. Woo, a popular teacher and activist, argued that her termination was due to her politics and identification as a lesbian feminist, unionist, student rights advocate, and her leadership role in the Freedom Socialist Party and Radical Women. Her cause was taken up by a number of progressive organizations and a legal battle ensued. In 1983, Woo spoke about her case:

DOCUMENT 107: Merle Woo Challenges the University of California (1982)

They fired me because I was visible. I took my protected free speech rights seriously, spoke out against the imminent death of Ethnic Studies, spoke out about who I am, totally and fully and with dignity. The four year rule [under which she was not rehired] was simply a pretext used to try to silence my criticism and outspoken politics.

In 1984, a jubilant Woo announced that she had been rehired in the Education Department with back pay:

After nearly two years of waging a free speech battle, we have merged victorious. I am returning to teach at UC Berkeley. Personally I am overjoyed to be teaching again. I have taught for 13 years focusing on people of color and women's issues. My victory comes in a wave of workers organizing against UC's union-busting tactics. The freedom to speak your mind is not a luxury, but a constitutional right, and if we don't use it, we'll lose it.

Two years later Woo's contract was not renewed and she sued. In 1990, as the case made its way through the legal maze, Woo learned that she had cancer. Prefering to not use up her energy in the arduous litigation process, she dropped her case.

Sources: Merle Woo Defense Committee, "News Release #6," March 29, 1983, p. 2; Merle Woo, "Press Statement on Merle Woo's Free Speech Victory," February 17, 1984, pp. 1–4.

*   *   *

In 1983, African American activist Barbara Smith edited a book called *Home Girls: A Black Feminist Anthology*, in which she wrote that women of color, especially lesbians, understood that major systems of oppression are multifaceted and interlocking. Smith's thinking was influenced by her membership in the Combahee River Collective, an African American feminist organization founded in Boston in 1974. Their manifesto became a feminist classic, in which they concluded that, as black women, they saw black feminism as the logical political movement to combat the simultaneous oppressions faced by them.

DOCUMENT 108: Simultaneity of Oppression (1983)

The concept of the simultaneity of oppression is still the crux of a Black feminist understanding of political reality and, I believe, one of the most significant ideological contributions of Black feminist thought....This multi-issued approach to politics has probably been most often used by other women of color who face very similar dynamics, at least as far as institutionalized oppression is concerned. It has also altered the women's movement as a whole....Approaching politics with a comprehension of the simultaneity of oppressions has helped to create a political atmosphere particularly conducive to coalition building....Some of the issues we have worked on are reproductive rights, equal access to abortion, sterilization abuse, health care, child care, the rights of the disabled, violence against women, rape, battering, sexual harassment, welfare rights, lesbian and gay rights, educational reform, housing, legal reform, women in prison, [against] aging, police brutality, [for] labor organizing, anti-imperialist struggles, anti-racist organizing, nuclear disarmament and preserving the environment....We have done much. We have much to do....I believe that everything is possible. But there are challenges we face as Black feminists that we can neither bury nor ignore.

Source: Barbara Smith, ed., *Home Girls: A Black Feminist Anthology* (New York: Kitchen Table: Women of Color Press, 1983) pp. xxxi–xxxv.

*   *   *

Activists have often been divided between those who favored mass political mobilization and those who favored personal change as a way to change society. At conferences politicos were often at odds with personal-change activists. Particularly as conservatives under the leadership of President Ronald Reagan dominated 1980s national politics, many activists retreated from politics and focused instead on building stronger groups within the lesbian and gay community. An example of this dynamic took place in 1983 at the first national Lesbians of Color Conference held at a rural retreat in Malibu, California. Over two hundred women attended and there were many difficult discussions over race and politics. Nancy Reiko Kato, a progressive socialist, later wrote about the lack of political focus at the conference. She wanted to see a multiracial alliance of women of various sexualities uniting together to accomplish equality for everyone, and abandoning separations of sexuality and skin color.

DOCUMENT 109: Lesbians of Color Conference (1983)

Los Angeles Lesbians of Color organized the conference so that "we may begin to know each other, reach out, touch and trust, to form lasting alliances and friendship." Unfortunately, what they had in mind were primarily personal and social, rather than political, alliances.

There is nothing at all wrong with getting to know each other. But at a time when lesbians of color desperately need to mount national strategies to fight against everything from anti-abortion attacks to gaybashing to social service cuts to repressive immigration legislation to union busting, getting to know each other is not enough.

This conference had great potential as a starting point for strategizing and organizing against rightwing reaction. But it shortchanged those women who came for serious political discussion and active proposals for fighting back that they could take home to their communities. Most of the workshops were aimed...to retreat from political commitment.

But there is no real retreat from politics, or from the racism, sexism, and class oppression that permeate capitalist society, including the movements for social change. The anti-political atmosphere at the conference actually gave rise to two very definite brands of political ideology, lesbian separatism and cultural nationalism, both of which express capitulation to racist and sexist divisiveness and thrive in an atmosphere of political retreat.

Separatism and cultural nationalism are exclusionary by nature. Separatists see men—and straight women—as the enemy. Cultural nationalists see culture and color as the only bases for interaction and alliance. Both attack all those who do not look, think, or act like they do....Some lesbians of color are looking for a safe space, thinking safety is where we are all the same. But in reality, safety is where we can unite with others to defeat the right wing, capitalism, and the patriarchy.

Source: Nancy Reiko Kato, "Lesbians of Color Conference: The Politics of 'Sisterhood,'" in *Voices of Color*, ed. Yolanda Alaniz and Nellie Wong (Seattle: Red Letter Press, 1999), pp. 30–34.

*   *   *

Police brutality and discrimination against gays and lesbians has been an ongoing problem, but it was only in late 1983 that activists from the National Gay Task Force were able to get Congress to pay attention to the problem. In early 1984, *The Advocate*'s Washington, D.C., staff reporter Larry Bush included in his "Capitol Report" column a summary of this testimony.

DOCUMENT 110: Police Abuse against Gays (1983)

For the first time, a Congressional panel heard testimony on police harassment of gays during a New York City hearing last November. James Creedle of Black and White Men Together and Kevin Berrill, director of the National Gay Task Force's Violence Project, told the House Subcommittee on Criminal Justice that gays and lesbians face abuse from police because of their sexual orientation, and called on Congress to take steps to correct the problem. "If we are serious about the eradication of [police] brutality from [the black] community," testified Creedle, "then we must acknowledge the widespread abuses which occur daily against lesbians and gay males. The point is that as a black gay man, I often ask, 'From whom do I need protection?' And more often than not, the answer is, 'I need to be protected from the police!'"

Creedle recounted his visit to Blues (a Manhattan bar frequented by black gays) the day after a police raid that received substantial press attention and is now being investigated by the office of New York Mayor Edward Koch. Creedle likened the destruction to what he had seen during his tour of duty [as a soldier] in Vietnam. "Broken bottles, glasses, and mirrors were strewn about the floor. Blood was everywhere splattered on the floor, on the walls, on equipment—a total wasteland."

"To be a victim of a crime, especially a violent crime, is a terrible ordeal," Berrill said. "But when that crime against you is committed by those who are responsible for protecting you, the pain and rage are even greater."

Source: Larry Bush, "Capitol Report: Police Abuse Against Gays," quoted in Thompson, *Long Road to Freedom*, p. 269.

*   *   *

Jim Carnes, of the Teaching Tolerance project of the Southern Poverty Law Center, wrote the following article based on the trial transcripts of the case of Charlie Howard. He included this story as an example of the types of discrimination faced by minorities in American history, from the Quakers in colonial New England, to nonwhites in the nineteenth and twentieth centuries. He included Charlie Howard as an example of discrimination against gender nonconformity. Charlie was a slight, effeminate, young gay man from Portsmouth, New Hampshire.

From childhood he was laughed at as a sissy, and in high school he was bullied, physically abused, and derided as a fag. Upon graduating he left Portsmouth so as not to be an embarrassment to his family, and to get away from the unending torment. After drifting a few years he ended up in Bangor, Maine, where his luck seemed to change.

DOCUMENT 111: The Death of Charlie Howard (1984)

He found a warm community of friends at the Unitarian Church, which had a number of openly gay members. The church also sponsored Interweave, a gay and lesbian support group....The acceptance he felt among the Unitarians was a new experience. Here he found a place to express his own openness and sense of humor, his love for life. He started attending services regularly and soon decided to undertake the preparation required for membership.

The Unitarian Church and Interweave were the only two organizations in Bangor that welcomed homosexuals. Many of the other churches, in fact, were openly hostile. Fundamentalist preachers used their pulpits to blame gays and lesbians for many of society's ills. There were no gay bars in town, and local clubs routinely kicked out couples of the same sex who tried to dance together. Most of Charlie's friends had experienced verbal harassment, and several had been physically attacked....One day in the grocery store a middle-aged woman suddenly started shouting at him, "You pervert! You queer!" Everyone stared. Charlie dropped his basket and walked slowly toward the door, terrified. Just before exiting, he choked back his fear, turned, and blew a kiss at the cluster of hateful faces.

This confrontation seemed to mark a turning point for Charlie. The stares of strangers began to spook him a little more after that. Sometimes he was afraid to leave his apartment. He stepped outside one morning and found his pet kitten lying dead on the doorstep. It had been strangled. Charlie's friends wished they could shield him from such cruelties, but they knew he would have to come to his own terms with a perilous world. He wasn't the only one for whom church and Interweave meetings sometimes felt like shelters in a storm.

Interweave sponsored a potluck supper on the night of Saturday, July 7, 1984. When the party broke up around 10 o'clock, Charlie talked his friend Roy Ogden into walking downtown with him to check his post office box. They headed up State Street. Midway across the bridge spanning Kenduskeag Stream, in the heart of Bangor, Charlie noticed a car slowing down just behind them. He thought it was one belonging to some high school boys who had harassed him a few days earlier. When they stopped the car and got out, he knew that he was right.

The three young men [Shawn Mabry, Daniel Ness, and Jim Baines] had just left a party to look for more beer when they spotted Charlie....."Hey, fag!" one boy yelled. Then the three started running. Roy and Charlie took off, but Charlie tripped on the curb and fell hard onto the walkway....Charlie scrambled to stand, but the boys grabbed him. They threw him back down and laid into him with kicks and punches.

"Over the bridge!" shouted Jim Baines. Daniel grabbed Charlie under the arms and lifted. Jim got him by the legs. Charlie was gasping now. He snatched enough air to yell, "I can't swim!" From the far end of the bridge, Roy heard his plea.

Jim and Daniel heaved Charlie up onto the guardrail. They had to pry his hands loose. Shawn gave the shove that sent him over. They looked down at the black water 20 feet below and congratulated themselves....

The boys spotted Roy Ogden watching from the end of the bridge and promised him he'd be sorry if he ever told anyone. When they got back to the car, they were laughing. Roy waited for the car to disappear. He could still hear the boys whooping and hollering. Then he ran along State Street till he found a fire alarm....

Shawn, Daniel, Jim went back to their party. Everyone could see they had a story to tell. "We jumped a fag," they said, "and threw him in the stream." The other kids laughed and pumped them for details, then resumed dancing and drinking. Around 1 A.M., rescue divers pulled the body of Charlie Howard, 23, out of the Kenduskeag, a few hundred feet downstream from the bridge.

Daniel Ness turned himself in the next morning, as soon as he heard the news. He couldn't believe Charlie was dead. They never intended to kill anybody—they just meant to "show" him. Shawn Mabry and Jim Baines decided to hop a freight train out of town but...all three were [arrested for murder,] convicted and sentenced to detention at the Maine Youth Center.

On the Monday night after Charlie Howard's murder, more than two hundred people crowded into a memorial service at the Unitarian Church. Afterward, a candlelight procession crossed the bridge. Charlie's mother had requested that someone drop a white rose into the water. The marchers moved on to the main police station, where they stood silently in the street. Hecklers from the crowd of onlookers shouted obscene names. A week later, at the spot on the bridge where Charlie Howard was tossed over, someone spray-painted three words: "Faggots Jump Here."

Source: Jim Carnes, "Us and Them: 'A Rose for Charlie,'" in *The Shadow of Hate: A History of Intolerance in America* (Montgomery, AL: Teaching Tolerance Project of the Southern Poverty Law Center, 1995), pp. 113–119.

* * *

Roger Magnuson published a book in 1985 that questioned the legal basis for gay rights laws. In particular he argued against applying to sexual minorities the antidiscrimination laws that applied to racial and religious minorities. In his argument he ignored the fact that followers of a religion have a choice about their behavior to participate in religious events, and that their religious practice was not an "unchangeable status."

DOCUMENT 112: Are Gay Rights Right? (1985)

Proponents of "gay rights" laws rely heavily on an analogy to other human rights legislation. If human rights laws have provided protection to other minorities, why not add one more group to those protected from discrimination? Hitching their wagon to the broadly based support Americans have traditionally given civil rights laws, "gay rights" advocates have made surprising progress in the past decade.

The human rights analogy cannot withstand careful analysis. Adding homosexual behavior to a list of classes that includes racial and religious minorities makes no sense. It expands the reach of such laws from their initial limits—protecting a particular unchangeable, and morally neutral, status like race—to include an entire galaxy of perverted behavior.... At least five common characteristics typify protected classes:

1. A demonstrable pattern of discrimination...

2. Causing substantial injury...

3. To a class of people with an unchangeable status...

4. Which has no element of moral fault...

5. Based on criteria that are arbitrary and irrational...

In short, "gay rights" laws meet none of the traditional requirements for human rights protection. Homosexuals have never been able to demonstrate a convincing pattern of discrimination that causes them substantial socioeconomic injury. They are a class of people linked together through behavior, not unchangeable status. Their actions are not morally neutral. Reasonable people—for reasons of deep-seated moral conviction, of health, of psychological stability, or of common sense—may wish to take a person's homosexual lifestyle into account in their decision-making, all without the slightest tinge of bigotry or irrationality.

Source: Roger J. Magnuson, statement in *Gay and Lesbian Rights*, ed. D. Newton (Santa Barbara, CA: ABC-CLIO, 1994), pp. 106–107.

*   *   *

North Carolina native Armistead Maupin moved to San Francisco and came out as a gay writer. He became phenomenally successful as the author of the best-selling *Tales of the City* novels about life in 1970s San Francisco. He also became an outspoken advocate for gay and lesbian rights. When asked for his suggestions for how to have a fulfilled life, Maupin emphasized above all the need to be open and honest about oneself. Gay rights can never be accomplished, he emphasized, without lesbians, bisexuals, gay men, and transgendered people doing these things:

DOCUMENT 113: Armistead Maupin's "Design for Living" (1985)

*** Stop begging for acceptance. Homosexuality is still anathema to most people in this country—even to many homosexuals. If you camp out on the doorstep of society waiting for "the climate" to change, you'll be there until Joan Rivers registers Democratic. Your job is to accept yourself—joyfully and with no apologies—and get on with the adventure of your life.

*** Don't run away from straight people. They need variety in their lives just as much as you do, and you'll forfeit the heady experience of feeling exotic if you limit yourself to the company of your own kind. Furthermore, you have plenty to teach your straight friends about tolerance and humor and the comfortable enjoyment of their own sexuality....

*** Refuse to cooperate in the lie. It is not your responsibility to "be discreet" for the sake of people who are still ashamed of their own natures. And don't tell me about "job security." Nobody's job will ever be safe until the general public is permitted to recognize the full scope of our homosexual population.

Does that include teachers? You bet it does. Have you forgotten already how much it hurt to be fourteen and gay and scared to death of it? Doesn't it gall you just a little that your "discreet" lesbian social-studies teacher went home every day to her lover and her cats and her [lesbian] Ann Bannon novels without once giving you even a clue that there was hope for your own future? What earthly good is your discretion, when teenagers are still being murdered for the crime of effeminacy? I know, I know—you have a right to keep your private life private. Well, you do that, my friend—but don't expect the world not to notice what you're really saying about yourself. And about the rest of us....

When I began my book tour, a publicist in New York implored me to leave his name out of it, because "my family doesn't know about my, uh, lifestyle." Maybe not, but they must be the dumbest bunch this side of Westchester County; I could tell he was gay *over the telephone*. When my own father learned of my homosexuality (he read about it in *Newsweek*), he told me he'd suspected as much since I'd been a teenager. I could've made life a lot easier for both of us if I'd had the guts to say what was on my mind.

*** Learn to feel mortal. If AIDS hasn't reminded you that your days are numbered—and always have been—then stop for a moment and remind yourself. Your days are numbered, babycakes. Are you living them for yourself and the people you love, or are you living them for the people you fear? I can't help thinking of a neighbor of mine, a dutiful government employee who kept up appearances for years and years, kept them up until the day he died, in fact—of a heart attack....Appearances don't count for squat when they stick you in the ground (all right, or scatter you to the winds), so why should you waste a single moment of your life seeming to be something you don't want to be?

Lord, that's so simple. If you hate your job, quit it. If your friends are tedious, go out and find new ones. You are queer, you lucky fool, and that makes you one of life's buccaneers, free from the clutter of two thousand years of Judaeo-Christian sermonizing. Stop feeling sorry for yourself and start hoisting your sails. You haven't a moment to lose.

Source: Armistead Maupin, "Design for Living," quoted in Thompson, *Long Road to Freedom*, pp. 283–285.

*   *   *

A changed attitude toward AIDS sufferers occurred in 1985, when famed actor Rock Hudson was hospitalized with HIV disease. Practically every American had seen the handsome masculine man in numerous movies and television programs, but most people were not aware that he was gay. More than any other case, Hudson's illness and death put a human face on AIDS. Hudson was a personal friend of Ronald Reagan, and his death finally prompted the president to make his first address on AIDS—five years into the epidemic. After Hudson's other close friend actor Elizabeth Taylor joined the board of the American Foundation for AIDS Research, support for AIDS funding became chic. As America saw the gay and lesbian community's dedicated efforts supporting people who were ill, and the touching sentiments of the panels of the AIDS Quilt sponsored by The Names Project, a different image of gay people emerged in the public mind. Rather than shadowy figures lurking in an alien and threatening sexual underworld, lesbians and gay men now seemed much more human and whole personalities to mainstream Americans.

Faced with the lack of funding by the government, more gay men and lesbians joined AIDS service organizations. Many who had never been inspired to commit time or resources to the struggle for gay and lesbian rights now saw the need to stand up for themselves as a matter of life or death. Lesbians rallied to support their gay brothers. Wealthy gay men who had never given to a gay rights group opened their checkbooks when their friends became ill. Organizations like the Human

Rights Campaign, which gives money to politicians who support gay and lesbian rights and AIDS issues, grew larger. While AIDS was a tragic setback for the gay male community, it ironically helped to strengthen gay and lesbian rights just because so many more people were now actively involved.

This changed attitude could be seen in New York City where, after years of defeats, in 1986 activists managed to persuade a majority of New York's City Council to approve a gay rights law. In the midst of the horrible losses of many friends and loved ones to AIDS, activist Arnie Kantrowitz reported in *The Advocate* his bittersweet feelings that came with the final passage of this law:

DOCUMENT 114: AIDS and Gay Rights (1986)

So many of our people have proven to be heroic throughout this [AIDS] tribulation....These are not stereotypical, flighty, sex-addicted faggots. These are humanity at its finest. Do our critics know how often we are society's servants, its comforters and nurturers? While they excoriate us for being frivolous fun-seekers, we work as nurses and therapists and teachers beyond our proportions in the populace. There is more to the gay lifestyle than Sunday brunch. It takes nobility and perseverance and dignity and courage to be gay and proud in the face of condemnation and injustice, violence and death. I have never been so proud of our people as I am today....

The AIDS crisis has brought homophobes of every stripe out of the woodwork, and their fulminations against us have inadvertently helped to make some decent people aware of the real threats faced by the gay community and of the need for legislation to protect us. When New York City's gay-rights bill, Intro 2, surfaced once again in the City Council, our enemies called us abominations and sinners, negative role models and child molesters, trying to impose their primitive values on our lives. While Pope John Paul II counsels his priests to refrain from involvement in secular affairs, Cardinal O'Connor shamelessly lobbies with legislators and politicizes his pulpit....

Before I left the closet in 1970, I was so intimidated by ignorance and hatred that I tried to kill myself twice, but I survived to see the best years of my life. Once again the ignorance and hatred surround me, but Intro 2 gives me some hope that if I can endure through this dark time, something better may follow. Who knows? If we work at it, we might win still more: perhaps even the right to marry and the legal, social, and economic advantages that come with it. Whatever we achieve, we must not let the next generation become complacent and take these treasures for granted, or they will be lost to us again.

As I stood with Vito and my lover, Larry Mass, amidst the throng in Sheridan Square, surrounded by friends celebrating the passage of the law we had all fought so long and hard for, I felt a quiet pride. (I did some leaping and whooping too.) We have made it the hard way, and we will have to fight to preserve what little we have gained. Some of us will not survive to see the future, but those of us who do must learn the infinite value of human life. Our enemies today foolishly turn their backs on us and fail to appreciate how much we have to give, but their rejection only makes us stronger and more self-reliant.

Source: Arnie Kantrowitz, "Friends Gone With the Wind," *The Advocate* September 1986, pp. 42–47, 108–109, quoted in Thompson, *Long Road to Freedom*, pp. 300–302.

* * *

Both those favoring and opposing gay and lesbian rights recognize the crucial importance of sodomy laws. Many people have been imprisoned over the years, some for long terms, but even though criminal prosecution has declined in recent decades, the existence of these statutes in the lawbooks places an onus of criminality on anyone who engages in same-sex acts. Sodomy laws have been used by judges as justification to prevent lesbians and gay men from gaining legal protections in everything from basic civil rights to child custody. With sodomy laws on the books, judges have concluded, why should governments confer equality on a class of people categorized as criminal?

The case that finally resulted in a court challenge began almost by accident. Early in the morning of July 5, 1982, in Atlanta, Michael Hardwick was given a ticket by a policeman. Hardwick dutifully mailed in his fine, but the paperwork did not go through and in three weeks the policeman arrived at Hardwick's apartment with a warrant. The officer saw the door slightly ajar, and when he pushed it open he observed Hardwick having oral sex with his boyfriend. He arrested them and took them to the Atlanta City Jail.

Michael Hardwick was so upset at being arrested and taken to jail for engaging in an intimate act in the privacy of his own home, that with the help of the American Civil Liberties Union he sued Georgia's attorney general Michael Bowers in federal court. The basis of his suit was that the Georgia sodomy law placed him and other homosexuals in imminent danger of arrest, and that this law was beyond the reach of state regulation because it violated the Ninth and Fourteenth Amendments to the United States Constitution.

After hearing the case, the Supreme Court justices were evenly split. Four justices, led by Byron White, found the Georgia sodomy law to be constitutional, while another four justices, led by Harry Blackmun, defended Michael Hardwick's right to privacy in his own home. Justice

Lewis Powell was ambivalent, but in the end he voted against Hard-wick. This five-to-four decision became the basis on which sodomy laws were declared to be constitutional.

Later, after he retired, Justice Powell was asked about this decision; he replied that his deciding vote in *Bowers v. Hardwick* was a mistake. [John C. Jeffries, Jr., *Justice Lewis F. Powell, Jr.* (New York: Scribner, 1994)]. If this one judge had changed his mind, state sodomy laws would have been declared an unconstitutional infringement on the fun-damental freedom of Americans. Without sodomy laws, other bases for discrimination against homosexuals would have much more chance of being overturned. This decision was one of the biggest legal defeats for gay and lesbian rights in the twentieth century.

DOCUMENT 115: *Bowers v. Hardwick* Sodomy Law Case (1986)

Justice White delivered the opinion of the Court.

The issue presented is whether the Federal Constitution confers a funda-mental right upon homosexuals to engage in sodomy and hence invali-dates the laws of the many states that still make such conduct illegal and have done so for a very long time....Respondent would have us announce, as the Court of Appeals did, a fundamental right to engage in homosexual sodomy. This we are quite unwilling to do. It is true that despite the lan-guage of the Due Process Clauses of the Fifth and Fourteenth Amend-ments, which appears to focus only on the processes by which life, liberty, or property is taken, the cases are legion in which those Clauses have been interpreted to have substantive content, subsuming rights that to a great extent are immune from federal or state regulation or proscription. Among such cases are those recognizing rights that have little or no textual support in the constitutional language....

This category includes those fundamental liberties that are "implicit in the concept of ordered liberty," such that "neither liberty nor justice would exist if [they] were sacrificed"...[or] are "deeply rooted in this Nation's his-tory and tradition." It is obvious to us that neither of these formulations would extend a fundamental right to homosexuals to engage in acts of con-sensual sodomy. Proscriptions against that conduct have ancient roots. Sodomy was a criminal offense at [English] common law and was forbidden by the laws of the original states....In fact, until 1961, all fifty states out-lawed sodomy, and today, twenty-four states and the District of Columbia continue to provide criminal penalties for sodomy performed in private and between consenting adults. Against this background, to claim that a right to engage in such conduct is "deeply rooted in this nation's history and tradi-tion" or "implicit in the concept of ordered liberty" is, at best, facetious.

Nor are we inclined to take a more expansive view of our authority to discover new fundamental rights imbedded in the Due Process Clause....Respondent asserts that there must be a rational basis for the law and that there is none in this case other than...that homosexual sodomy is immoral and unacceptable. This is said to be an inadequate rationale to support the law. The law, however, is constantly based on notions of morality, and if all laws representing essentially moral choices are to be invalidated under the Due Process Clause, the courts will be very busy indeed. Even respondent makes no such claim, but insists that majority sentiments about the morality of homosexuality should be declared inadequate. We do not agree.

Justice Blackmun, with whom Justice Brennan, Justice Marshall, and Justice Stevens join, dissenting:

This case is no more about "a fundamental right to engage in homosexual sodomy," as the Court purports to declare, than *Stanley v. Georgia* was about a fundamental right to watch obscene movies....Rather, this case is about the most comprehensive of rights and the right most valued by civilized men, namely, "the right to be let alone." The statute at issue denies individuals the right to decide for themselves whether to engage in particular forms of private, consensual sexual activity....Like Justice Holmes, I believe that "it is revolting to have no better reason for a rule of law than that it was laid down in the time of Henry IV. It is still more revolting if the grounds upon which it was laid down have vanished long since, and the rule simply persists from blind imitation of the past." I believe we must analyze Hardwick's claim in the light of the values that underlie the constitutional right to privacy....

The Constitution embodies a promise that a certain private sphere of individual liberty will be kept largely beyond the reach of government.... Only the most willful blindness could obscure the fact that sexual intimacy is a sensitive, key relationship of human existence, central to family life, community welfare, and the development of human personality. The fact that individuals define themselves in a significant way through their intimate sexual relationships with others suggests, in a Nation as diverse as ours, that there may be many "right" ways of conducting those relationships, and that much of the richness of a relationship will come from the freedom an individual has to choose the form and nature of these intensely personal bonds.

In a variety of circumstances we have recognized that a necessary corollary of giving individuals freedom to choose how to conduct their lives is acceptance of the fact that different individuals will make different choices....The Court claims that its decision today merely refuses to recognize a fundamental right to engage in homosexual sodomy; what the Court really has refused to recognize is the fundamental interest all individuals have in controlling the nature of their intimate associations with others.

The behavior for which Hardwick faces prosecution occurred in his own home, a place to which the Fourth Amendment attaches special significance....The right of an individual to conduct intimate relationships in the intimacy of his or her own home seems to me to be the heart of the Constitution's right to privacy.

Source: Michael Bowers, Attorney General of Georgia v. Michael Hardwick. United States Supreme Court 478 U.S. 186 (Decided June 30, 1986).

*   *   *

Except for the antigay fundamentalist and conservative evangelical churches, mainstream American religious denominations were sharply divided on the issue of support for gay and lesbian rights in the 1980s. The United Church of Christ, the Unitarian Universalist Association, the Quakers, the Episcopal Church, and the Reform Jewish Congregations all spoke out strongly against discrimination. They also began offering ceremonies of union for same-sex couples, and ordaining openly gay and lesbian clergy. Some denominations, like the Methodists, the Presbyterians, and the Lutherans, underwent much controversy over the issue, with some congregations blessing same-sex couples, while other congregations opposed it. These Protestant churches became more split over this issue than any issue since opposition to slavery and the ordination of women clergy.

A fierce debate on homosexuality also raged within the Roman Catholic Church, especially following the 1979 publication of *The Church and the Homosexual* by John J. McNeill [Kansas City, MO: Sheed Andrews and McMeel, 1976]. Reverend McNeill, a Jesuit priest, argued that the Bible verses used to condemn homosexuals are more accurately translated as a condemnation of lustful sex devoid of devotion and commitment. He said that monogamous same-sex relationships are essentially marriages, and should be considered morally good. Some bishops in the United States spoke out in favor of a new theology of sexuality which sees both heterosexual and homosexual love as God's creation

For a time a group of moderates within the Catholic hierarchy suggested a compromise, whereby homosexual acts were conceived as a sin but homosexual inclinations were "morally neutral." With this view that everyone is a sinner, they allowed the gay and lesbian Catholic group Dignity to hold group meetings in Catholic churches. Some church leaders spoke out in favor of gay and lesbian rights laws, and deplored homophobic violence. Other clerics felt that it was unfair to expect all homosexuals to remain celibate, and quietly accepted congregants who were in same-sex relationships.

However, in 1986 Pope John Paul II decided to crack down on Catholics in the United States who preached a more accepting view of same-sex love. The pope held strict views concerning the prohibition of birth control, abortion, and homosexuality. He took moves to castigate dissenters, and to silence progay opinions by papal order. Rev. McNeill and other progressive Catholic clerics were forbidden from writing or speaking about same-sex love, and Dignity was prohibited from celebrating mass on church property. In response, thousands of lesbian, gay, bisexual, and transgendered Catholics left the church in the United States, and continued holding independent masses under Dignity's direction.

On October 30, 1986, a document on homosexuality was issued by the Vatican's office in charge of the orthodoxy of Catholic belief, the Congregation for the Doctrine of the Faith. This document, published under the name of the pope and Joseph Cardinal Ratizinger, called even an inclination toward homosexuality "an objective disorder."

DOCUMENT 116: Catholic Condemnation of Homosexuality (1986)

The issues of homosexuality and the moral evaluation of homosexual acts have become a matter of public debate. Since this debate often advances arguments and makes assertions inconsistent with the teaching of the Catholic Church…special concern and pastoral attention should be directed toward those who have this condition, lest they be led to believe that living out this orientation in homosexual activity is a morally acceptable option. It is not….Ministers must ensure that homosexuals will not be misled by this point of view so profoundly opposed to the teaching of the Church….

Ministers will reject theological opinions which dissent from Church teaching….[Many dissenters] are bringing enormous pressure to bear on the Church to accept the homosexual condition as though it were not disordered and to condone homosexual activity. One tactic used is to protest that any and all criticism of, or reservations about, homosexuals, their activity and lifestyle, are simply diverse forms of unjust discrimination.

Christians who are homosexual are called, as all of us are, to a chaste life. As they dedicate their lives to understanding the nature of God's personal call to them, they will be able to receive the Lord's grace so freely offered in order to convert their lives more fully to His way….It is only in the [heterosexual] marital relationship that the use of the sexual faculty can be morally good. A person engaging in homosexual acts therefore acts immorally…. Homosexuality may seriously threaten the lives and well-being of a large number of people.

Source: Pope John Paul II and Joseph Cardinal Ratizinger, "Statement on Homosex-uality," submitted by Catholic Oregonians for Truth, and quoted in *Voters' Pamphlet*, State of Oregon General Election, November 3, 1992, p. 94.

*   *   *

People of color who are gay and lesbian face difficult struggles when their ethnic communities reject them. They often feel that they are being made to choose between their personal feelings and their community's norms. Since they already face the racism of the larger society, being re-jected by their own community is very difficult. Cheryl Clarke, an African American lesbian activist, wrote a notable essay titled "Failure to Transform: Homophobia in the Black Community" that was pub-lished in Barbara Smith's book *Home Girls: A Black Feminist Anthology* (New York: Kitchen Table, 1983). In it Clarke wrote of the pain felt by black lesbians and gay men in facing public denunciation from other black people, when they should be appreciated for their manifold con-tributions to the African American community.

Unfortunately, in too many cases, communities of color do not sup-port their lesbian and gay kinfolk. For example, in 1990, as part of Gay Pride Month, the Gay and Lesbian Librarians in Los Angeles included Langston Hughes in their list of notable gays and lesbians. They were met by a severe backlash from a number of African American librarians. With the approval of the Latina who was then the Los Angeles City Li-brarian, thousands of taxpayer-funded flyers were destroyed and new ones without Hughes's name were printed. The librarian, who is other-wise known as a progressive person, had bowed to the pressure.

Below is an excerpt from an essay in an anthology of writings by African American gay men. In it, the author writes about the difficulties facing him in his "home" community.

DOCUMENT 117: Homophobia in the Black Community (1986)

Two of the most difficult aspects of being black and gay are the lack of ac-ceptance and affirmation, shown me by my community, and its failure to utilize the talents of black gays. The black community could benefit a great deal from channeling the energy of its gay brothers and lesbian sisters....Separating the black homosexual from the black heterosexual serves only to widen the existing gaps in our community....If we ever hope to empower ourselves in this country, we must accept each other as we are with our myriad differences; we have no other choice....I'm nineteen years old and working toward a...degree in journalism. It pains me to realize that

I may not be allowed to serve my community with my education....In order to serve my community, I must give up all pride in myself, and my way of living and loving....How can we, after escaping so many years of oppression, turn around and oppress others?...

I don't want to be labeled faggot anymore than I want to be called nigger. I have been forced by society to pay a price for being black. I don't want to pay yet another price when I come home....By dismissing black gays, the black community denies a considerable portion of its identity. Does the sexual orientation of James Baldwin or Langston Hughes invalidate their insightful writings? It's ironic: so often, the rights that people want for themselves, the rights for which they would die, are precisely the rights they would deny others. We have fought for years for equal opportunity and equal treatment. I want the same when I come home.

Source: Stephan Lee Dais, "Don't Turn Your Back on Me," in *In the Life: A Black Gay Anthology*, ed. Joseph Beam (Boston: Alyson, 1986), pp. 60–62.

*   *   *

By the mid-1980s antigay violence was becoming endemic in the United States. Darrell Yates Rist of New York City gave personal testimony in *The Advocate* in 1987 about the most recent of many instances of violence to which he had been subjected. In this instance, a neighbor kicked his dog and swung a briefcase at him, calling him faggot.

DOCUMENT 118: Antigay Violence (1987)

I'd been fag-bashed in the lobby of my building just two years before—by five drugged teenaged boys with a sharpened pole, which they smashed across my face, shattering my glasses and driving tiny, brittle shards into my eyes. This time—as fast as the visions people see an instant before they think they're about to die—a lifetime of insults and assaults, of violence of one kind or another just because I'm gay, flashed across my mind. I screamed, "Take *this* from a fag!" and slammed my fist into the man's contorted face. With the fiery arc of my arm, its drive propelled by years of smoldering anger, I burned away just one more pattern of apologizing for who I am.

It is 1987, and I'm an outlaw in America—cut out of the Constitution by last summer's Supreme Court ruling, which defined the way I love as criminal. In twenty-four states and Washington, D.C., I can be punished by as little as a two-hundred-dollar fine or as much as a twenty-year prison term.

Statistics portray a virtual reign of antigay terror in the eighties. Reported assaults against gay people soared 80 percent in the first six months of 1986, while the number of men in New York City murdered just because they're gay doubled. Twenty gay men have been stabbed to death in New

York City's Chelsea district alone in this past year—many of them mutilated beyond recognition. Police found all the bodies castrated. The ritual of cutting off the victim's cock and balls, according to police, is common in the murders of gay men.

My lover and I have been assaulted several times—sometimes with fists, sometimes with bottles and rocks, sometimes with sticks or bats, once with the barrel of a gun. Every attack was accompanied by shouts of "queer" or "faggot"—terrifying slurs because they resonate with the threat of violence. They are epithets we all know well, of course—and not just from our assailants. We were raised from childhood—in our homes, at school, with friends—on their vicious sound and the hatred they convey. For, unlike "nigger" and "kike," the words "queer," "faggot," "lezzie," and "dyke" still pass in this society as acceptable comment or harmless jest. On the street, at the gym, at cocktail parties, at the office, even from some of our friends and family, we still hear the epithets and feel their hateful weight.

Source: Darrell Yates Rist, "Drawing Blood," quoted in Thompson, *Long Road to Freedom*, p. 313.

*   *   *

Conservative Christians often emphasize sex outside of marriage as a major sin, and in the 1980s used the AIDS epidemic as proof that God was punishing homosexuals. They never mentioned the extremely low rate of AIDS infections among lesbians, or the fact that women might be much less likely to get AIDS by having sex with another woman rather than with a heterosexual man. They also seldom acknowledged that the most common sexual behavior by which HIV is transmitted worldwide is by heterosexual intercourse. That statistic is not explained as God's judgment on heterosexuals in general.

An editorial in *Christianity Today* speculates about the cause of AIDS and suggests:

DOCUMENT 119: AIDS as God's Punishment (1987)

Especially among Christians, in fact, the urge to speculate has been almost irresistible. Why? The main way to get AIDS is to commit a certain kind of sin. In the U.S., about 73 percent of the people diagnosed with AIDS are homosexual and bisexual males. Hence, the speculation: Is the deadly disease God's judgment on homosexuals? Already, a number of articles have appeared in conservative Christian publications suggesting AIDS is God's punishment for homosexual behavior. We may cringe at this notion, but we cannot dispute it. The Bible condemns homosexual acts as sin, and the wages of sin is always death. God's holy anger is set against all sin. He will not be trifled with and he will not be mocked. What we sow we will reap—if not now, certainly in eternity.

God may indeed be using AIDS to confront homosexuals with their sin. And since the disease is spreading to the heterosexual population, God may also be confronting all forms of promiscuity. There is literally no such thing anymore as "safe sex" outside the boundaries of marriage as God intended it. AIDS could be one dramatic method God is using to wake up a sinful society to the realities of sin and judgment.

Source: "The Judgment Mentality," *Christianity Today* March 20, 1987. [Reprinted in Lisa Orr, ed., *Sexual Values: Opposing Viewpoints* (San Diego: Greenhaven Press, 1989), pp. 68–69.]

*   *   *

Rev. Billy James Hargis, a prominent fundamentalist Christian minister in the 1980s, often wrote about sexual sins. Writing in the magazine of the Christian Crusade in 1987, he claimed that God causes diseases like AIDS to spread even to children, in order to teach people not to have sex outside of heterosexual marriage. He also ignored the lack of AIDS in the lesbian community, and did not address the reality that many male homosexuals avoid getting infected with HIV disease by engaging in safer same-sex behaviors.

AIDS, as well as herpes, is a result of the judgment of God on a nation which has despised His stern commandments regarding sex....This AIDS plague is a shout from heaven, saying "You've gone too far." As the Lord speaks in judgment, the guilty must suffer, and many innocent along with the guilty. AIDS is undoubtedly one of the last plagues. The end of our age is near....Authorities want $2 billion a year to fight AIDS. What is needed, beyond everything else, is to repent and get right with God....

Some disagree with this conclusion that herpes and AIDS is [sic] the judgment of God upon unrepentant sinners, by saying that many non-homosexuals have also contracted AIDS although they are not guilty of any wrongdoing....The sins of a few compared to the whole [population] can cause an epidemic among the masses who become their innocent victims. This is not the fault of God. Instead it is the fault of those who sinned, and who inflicted their fellow human beings with this awful plague....

Don't blame God because a little child somewhere is dying of AIDS that he got from a needle during treatment or surgery in a hospital. If anyone is to blame, it is the person who spread the disease....These innocent children are not guilty. Then someone says, "What about the woman whose husband has infected her with AIDS?" The sin is of the man who infected her.

The sin is not hers. But, it rains on the just and the unjust. All of this debate about an unmerciful God is not going to change that....If we cannot check our ungodly sexual lusts, then not only should we expect the consequences, but others will also suffer, and perhaps die, because of our sin.

Source: Billy James Hargis, "AIDS: Sign of the Times!" *Christian Crusade* v. 34, n. 5 (1987). [Reprinted in Lisa Orr, ed., *Sexual Values: Opposing Viewpoints* (San Diego: Greenhaven Press, 1989), pp. 65–68.]

*   *   *

An article in a publication of the Worldwide Church of God included homosexuality as one of the results of the sexual revolution that must be suppressed.

Nothing in recent decades has jarred free-swinging sexual attitudes and lifestyles—and will continue to do so—more than incurable sexually transmissible diseases....The sexual revolution of the '60s has set us up for...sexually transmitted viruses [which] are the fruits of that sexual revolution....Human nature is such that many individuals who do not strongly adhere to high sexual standards of mutually faithful, monogamous marital sexual relations often willingly blind their mind to dangers of these diseases and other serious consequences. Long ago, the Creator revealed to man that sexual relations are to be confined to marriage to protect the family unit and bless all society. Premarital, homosexual and other extramarital sex acts are forbidden in numerous instructions of Scripture. Millions, however, have rejected the Creator's revealed instructions....

Millions are bereft of any purpose in life but that of fulfilling their own desires and pleasures. Many respect no authority or values but their own. The Bible describes such "perilous times." "If it feels good, do it," was commonly preached...[but] such thinking could kill you. Will you be among the millions who will not face up to the staggering dangers of AIDS and more than 20 other serious sexually transmissible diseases until it is too late? You must if you care about your future and loved ones. The moral message of STDs and AIDS is SCREAMING at us!

Medical science has, belatedly, been forced to agree with what sexual morality has taught for thousands of years. The best defense against contracting AIDS and most serious sexually transmissible diseases is sexual abstinence before marriage and sexual faithfulness within marriage—for *both* partners. Many scoff at such morality. But it's no longer a scoffing matter if you want to protect your own life and that of your mate.

Source: Donald D. Schroeder, "The Moral Message Behind STDs," *The Plain Truth* February 1988. [Reprinted in Lisa Orr, ed., *Sexual Values: Opposing Viewpoints* (San Diego: Greenhaven Press, 1989) pp. 38–42.]

Part V

Queer America: The Acceptance of Sexual and Gender Diversity in the United States, 1987–2000

As conservative Republican dominance continued in the 1980s, the agenda of the Christian fundamentalist movement was receiving much more serious attention than were campaigns for gay and lesbian rights. Especially with conservative Christian rhetoric that God causes AIDS, the Reagan administration opposed massive public health expenditures to fight the disease. Therefore, comparatively little was done on the federal level to conquer the AIDS epidemic. Efforts to distribute safer-sex information in colleges and high schools met with extreme resistance by the Catholic Church, which objected to the mention of condoms. Though the Catholic hierarchy's objection had more to do with the church's historic resistance to birth control, activists were furious that denying information to young people was threatening their lives. The federally sponsored safer-sex literature that was finally distributed to teenagers was worded so vaguely that they could not tell what specific behaviors (like mutual masturbation, body rubbing, interfemoral sex, and even oral sex, which is much safer than intercourse) would help them remain uninfected. Under the influence of the conservative Christians, the main message that went out to young people was to abstain from sex entirely, outside of heterosexual marriage.

The outrage that arose about government inaction, especially by people who were dying of AIDS, became strong enough in 1987 that a new militancy arose. It became obvious to gay men that the tepid government response to AIDS was determined by the fact that the disease was hitting a population considered by the fundamentalists as expendable. AIDS activists contrasted the lightening government response to an outbreak of mysterious deaths of attendees at an American Legion convention, with a hesitancy on the disease that was decimating gay men.

The building outrage against AIDS was combined with a reaction to the Supreme Court's 1986 *Bowers v. Hardwick* decision. The fight for gay and lesbian rights would be required to pressure for sodomy law repeal in each state, rather than depending on the federal government to decriminalize same-sex behavior in the entire nation.

The response to these setbacks resulted in a new era of militancy. The formation of ACT UP in New York City marked a move from lobbying to street action, from begging to demanding. The militancy of activists like Larry Kramer was typical of this new style. Activists also planned a second March on Washington for Lesbian and Gay Rights, to bring more political pressure on Congress. A major purpose of the march was to inspire people to take their outrage back into their local communities, where they could more effectively pressure for reforms on the local and state levels. The National Gay and Lesbian Task Force started a "Fight the Right" campaign to challenge religious right-wing dominance in local and state governments. A National Coming Out Day campaign encouraged more gays and lesbians to be open in their daily life, and to discuss gay and lesbian rights with their friends, relatives, and co-workers. The Gay and Lesbian Alliance Against Defamation took on the responsibility for influencing the mass media, especially the Hollywood film and television industry, to present more accurate and positive representations of gay and lesbian characters in movies and TV.

Another response of gay and lesbian activists was to continue to build their influence within the Democratic Party. By this time the years of dedicated work of many lesbians and gay men for the party had resulted in a firming of support for lesbian and gay rights within the party platform. Activists looked for a candidate for president who was firmly committed to their goals. The candidate who emerged with the strongest progay position in the presidential campaign of 1988 was Jesse Jackson. Though Jackson was not able to gain the party's nomination, his idea of a Rainbow Coalition caught on. Lesbians and gay men were considered an integral part of this coalition, no longer marginalized to the fringes.

The Democrats were defeated by Republican Vice President George Bush, who won the presidential election of 1988, but Arkansas Governor Bill Clinton prepared to run against Bush in 1992. Clinton was a younger leader, part of the 1960s generation who had come of age during the sexual revolution and the era of gay and lesbian liberation. Clinton had close friends and staff members who were openly gay, and he felt an acceptance and comfortableness around gay people that previous presidents did not have. During the 1992 campaign Clinton reached out to gay and lesbian voters, and touched their hearts. He told them that his vision for the future of the United States included the lesbian and gay community as an integral part of the nation. In response, gay and lesbian volunteers worked for his campaign, and gay money poured into the Clinton campaign war chest.

When Bill Clinton was elected president in 1992, gays and lesbians were jubilant. They were an important part of the Democratic Party coalition that had elected him, and the new president promised to include them in his government. Where Clinton came through most strongly was to appoint openly gay and lesbian people to high office in the executive branch of the government. His attorney general, Janet Reno, also threw the weight of the Justice Department into the fight for lesbian and gay rights. For the first time, gay men, lesbians, bisexuals, and transgendered people from other nations could apply for political asylum to be admitted to the United States. If they could prove that they were subject to persecution on the basis of their sexual orientation in their home country, the United States would grant them asylum just as it does for other people who are persecuted by oppressive governments. This has resulted in a number of gay activists being granted political asylum by the courts of the United States Immigration and Naturalization Service.

At the same time, the Clinton administration had trouble accomplishing changes in other areas. The same Immigration and Naturalization Service that now grants asylum for gay activists does not recognize the right of residency for same-sex partners of United States citizens. If a United States citizen goes abroad and falls in love with a person of the other sex, they can get married and the Immigration and Naturalization Service quickly approves admission of that foreigner to the United States. Not only does this spouse receive legal residence status, but they also get a work permit and can easily qualify for the benefits provided to citizens. On the other hand, if a United States citizen goes abroad and falls in love with a person of the same sex, none of these benefits are available. In fact, being open about their relationship may make it even more difficult for the same-sex partner to gain legal admission to the country. Gay activists have argued that this provision, based solely on the basis of the sex of the partner, constitutes discrimination on the basis of sex and is a special right reserved solely for heterosexuals. While several other nations have moved to admit same-sex partners as they do other-sex partners of their citizens, the United States government made no move to change the immigration regulations on this issue. The ironic result is that it is easier for a gay person from a persecuting nation to gain admission to the United States than it is for a person from a nation that does not discriminate against gay people, but who has a loving relationship with a United States citizen.

The biggest disappointment for gay rights involved Clinton's back-tracking on his promise to lift the ban against lesbians, gay men, and bi-sexuals serving in the armed forces. Although Clinton tried to make such a change right after he was sworn into office, a strong challenge emerged in the Joint Chiefs of Staff and in Congress. Instead of standing up to the Pentagon, and establishing his reputation as a strong com-mander-in-chief, the new president retreated. The gays-in-the-military fiasco showed clearly that the national gay and lesbian rights organiza-tions were unable to match their foes in terms of political strategies, or-ganizational efficiency, and financial resources. Unlike President Harry Truman, who stood up to segregationists when he ordered the racial de-segregation of the armed forces in 1947 by executive order, Clinton showed weakness under pressure. As a result of his rapid retreat in the face of the generals' opposition, it took him a long time to overcome this image that he was a weak president.

Clinton likewise demonstrated weakness during the 1996 presiden-tial campaign, when Republican strategists in Congress cleverly passed the Defense of Marriage Act (DOMA). This act defined marriage as being solely between a man and a woman. This was another heterosexual priv-ilege, another special right reserved solely for heterosexuals. The Repub-licans wanted to enact DOMA into law to prevent legal recognition of same-sex marriages that might be recognized due to a ruling of the Hawai'i state supreme court. Though the president recognized that the Constitution gives states the right to regulate marriages, and this repre-sented an unprecedented intrusion of the federal government into states' rights to define marriage as they see fit, he knew that if he vetoed the bill he would suffer in the upcoming election. He chose to take the safe way out, to guarantee his own reelection, by signing the most explicitly anti-gay law ever passed by the United States government.

Clinton also disappointed his gay and lesbian supporters by not hav-ing the Justice Department take a supporting role in a case before the United States Supreme Court, regarding the constitutionality of Col-orado's Amendment 2. This amendment would prevent local govern-ments from passing laws to prevent discrimination on the basis of sexual orientation. In 1996 the United States Supreme Court ruled in *Romer v. Evans* that the State of Colorado could not infringe on the rights of local governments like this. This was the biggest Supreme Court victory for gay and lesbian rights in the twentieth century, and after this decision ef-forts to repeal local gay rights laws fizzled.

Those Americans who were in opposition to Clinton's progay poli-cies helped to elect more antigay Republicans to Congress in the midterm 1994 elections. A pattern of two steps forward, one step back, and then forward and back again, characterized the 1990s. Even though the issue of gay and lesbian rights was still a major point of disagreement among Americans, at least the subject was being debated as a central issue in the nation's politics and mass media. The issue was no longer invisible, it was no longer an embarrassing topic to be mentioned only in gutter language or as a joke. It was now an object of serious political discussion. Despite his partial support and backtracking, Clinton had done for gay and lesbian rights what President John F. Kennedy had done for African American civil rights. For the first time in American history, a president spoke out firmly and repeatedly against discrimination on the basis of sexual orientation. However much he faltered, Bill Clinton's historical contribution was to put the power of the presidency behind the struggle for equality for lesbians and gay men.

The most amazing, and surprising, advance for gay and lesbian rights in the 1990s was in the economic arena. As more people came out of the closet and refused to hide their same-sex relationships, they demanded protection from discrimination at work. With a prosperous economy and a tight job market, more and more employers and corporations recognized that they could not afford to lose good workers. They also recognized that they could not afford to alienate a significant market sector of customers. Surveys showed that gay people established strong brand loyalty to products of companies that treated them respectfully and supported gay rights. Boycotts against antigay companies, like Coors Beer and Cracker Barrel Restaurants, were also effective. Not because of some suddenly discovered great moral concern, but simply to advance their own profits, companies started advertising in gay magazines and sponsoring booths at Gay Pride festivals. In terms of personnel policies, many companies realized they needed to attract and retain the best-skilled employees, no matter what their inclinations in their personal lives. More private employers started including sexual orientation in their company nondiscrimination policies. Homophobic supervisors and personnel directors either changed their approach or lost their jobs to others who appreciated the advantages offered by a diverse workforce.

Increased exposure of gay issues in the mass media also, over time, made the issue less shocking to people in the mainstream. Gay rights was no longer a new and alien idea, but a simple reality of life in the modern United States. That which is seen all around oneself is usually accepted by many people in a pragmatic way. In contrast to the shocking gay liberationist rioting in 1969, the gender-conforming gay or lesbian couple down the street who attended PTA meetings and helped out in neighborhood beautification projects seemed much less threatening. Economic realities and media exposure accomplished what political tactics had largely failed to do. In an ironic turn of events, a radical call for a "Queer Nation" had been accomplished in a much more mundane acceptance of the reality of diversity. Gay men, lesbians, bisexuals, transgenders, and transsexuals, and even a newly recognized group of intersexed people, were now seen simply as part of the larger mosaic that made up the population of the United States. In contrast to earlier decades, in the 1990s corporate America and the mass media proved to be strong supporters of gay and lesbian rights. These fundamental changes were, to a great extent, due to the simple decision of massive numbers of lesbians, gay men, bisexuals, intersexed, and transgendered persons to stop hiding and to live their lives openly. The strategy of coming out of the closet to one's friends, relatives, co-workers, and associates was, ultimately, the most important factor in reducing discrimination.

* * *

ACT UP was formed in 1987 in response to the unwillingness of the government to take action against the AIDS crisis. Brash, rude, and impolitic, ACT UP's motto was "United in anger and committed to direct action to end the AIDS crisis." ACT UP's first demonstration was a sit-down strike of 250 people on Wall Street, the heart of the nation's financial district. Their purpose was to call attention to pharmaceutical companies' profits from the AIDS crisis by charging prohibitive prices for many AIDS drugs. ACT UP chapters soon formed across the United States. Many ACT UP members were youth of a new generation and they were joined by veteran activists, both gay and lesbian. ACT UP's methods were reminiscent of those of Gay Liberation in the 1970s. On one occasion they entered St. Patrick's Cathedral in New York City and chanted "Stop the Inquisition!" These actions were meant to shock opponents of lesbian and gay rights and call attention to the plight of people with AIDS.

Many lesbians also joined the battle. Theirs was a significant act of altruism since lesbians have the lowest rate of HIV infection of any group in the United States. Some lesbians questioned whether this focus on a gay male disease was going to deflect energy and resources away from the lesbian movement. Others felt that their gay brothers needed help and that homophobes did not distinguish between gays and lesbians. One of these was Maxine Wolfe a longtime lesbian activist in New York City. In an interview with Laraine Sommella in 1995, she recounted her involvement with ACT UP.

DOCUMENT 120: ACT UP (AIDS Coalition to Unleash Power) (1987)

The people who came to the first meeting of ACT UP included individuals from GMHC (Gay Men's Health Crisis) who had become totally disaffected by [GMHC's] unwillingness to do any political stuff. There were people from the PWA [People With AIDs] Coalition who wanted to get out on the streets....There was also the SILENCE = DEATH Project, which...[placed posters] on the streets, to get the message out to people: "Why aren't you doing something?" So they created the SILENCE = DEATH logo well before ACT UP ever existed, and the posters at the bottom said...."Turn anger, fear, grief into action."...

When Larry Kramer came to speak, in March 1987...there was a very particular audience in that room....He had been screaming for years and nobody had done anything. From my point of view, there was a whole group of people there ready to do something....At some point [Larry] yelled, "What are you gonna do?"...Soon after, [ACT UP] did their first Wall Street action. They did not have a lot of people come to their meetings until after [New York City's] Gay Pride that June....I had marched behind them at the Gay Pride March and saw this incredible "thing," which was a [representation of] a concentration camp with wire all around and people inside. There were people outside the wire dressed in masks and military gear and handing out flyers....

If you can imagine, there is always this tension in the Gay Pride March in New York because the majority come to it for a celebration and they do not want it to be anything political at all....ACT UP took that leadership role in that Gay Pride march and marched in the middle of a "space" that is apolitical and often commercial....The New York ACT UP style was wonderful...writing leaflets that you could read and I think more importantly, not relying only on the written word but also [on] visual media....We focused on what would stand out, what would show up....We would [also] pretend to be almost anything if we could get in somewhere....ACT UP was about organizing the unorganized...it was about mobilizing a community that had not been organized to do this kind of direct action in the last twelve or fourteen years. Secondly, ACT UP was about people doing stuff for themselves.

Source: Laraine Sommella and Maxine Wolfe, "This Is About People Dying; The Tactics of Early ACT UP and Lesbian Avengers in New York City," in *Queers in Space: Communities, Public Places and Sites of Resistance*, ed. Gordon Brent Ingram, Anne-Marie Bouthillette, and Yolanda Retter (Seattle: Bay Press, 1997), pp. 407–437.

*   *   *

The defining moment of 1987 for gay activism was the second National March on Washington for Lesbian and Gay Rights. Betty Berzon, a lesbian psychotherapist, author, and former president of the Gay Academic Union, remembered her feelings being a participant at the March:

DOCUMENT 121: National March on Washington for Lesbian and Gay Rights (1987)

Saturday afternoon, October 10, on a blocked-off street in front of the Internal Revenue Service Building, jammed into a crowd of several thousand people attending The Wedding [officiated by Metropolitan Community Church founder, Rev. Troy Perry], my lover of fourteen years and I got married. We didn't really need a ceremony to seal our commitment, but I...felt compelled to take part in this historic celebration of the relationships that are, after all, ground zero for our being gay.

Sunday morning, at sunrise, we stood silently at the site of the Names Project AIDS Memorial Quilt, watching the unfolding of the last of the three and a half tons of panels volunteers had worked all night to unload. When the slow reading of the names began, I was struck by the care each name was given, as though to make sure we knew that each belonged to an individual whose life was unique and deserving of our undivided attention. It was almost unbearably solemn and it went on for three hours.

In the afternoon the sadness of the quilt experience gave way to exhilaration as, under gray and overcast skies, the marchers stepped off in an explosion of energy, shouting, singing, and chanting the rallying cries of gay pride. From our vantage point on the Mall, watching the giant mass of humanity slowly moving over the horizon toward us was an extraordinary experience. They seemed to be spilling out of the sky and there was no end to that mass—which, in a sense, was true because beyond the body of marchers lay the entire country, the millions of gays and lesbians who were in spiritual unity with those who were physically present in Washington, D.C.

The National March on Washington for Lesbian and Gay Rights was a turning point for many of the participants, who left for home ready as never before to mobilize and organize—to make a difference in the shaping of public policy that would directly affect their lives. A new cycle of gay and lesbian advocacy was emerging, born of anger about AIDS and of the sense of historical relevance that activism bestows....

As a psychotherapist working in the gay and lesbian community for many years, I began to see the effects of these developments in the new ways my clients talked about being gay. I was hearing more pride of ownership in a community feeling its strength, speaking out, acting up, demanding attention to its needs. Clearly this transition, at any level, from a victim's mentality to an activist mindset was having a positive impact on the self-esteem of many gays. Other signs of gays feeling good about ourselves were seen in the emergence of black gays and lesbians organizing to build a leadership base, and more gay men and lesbians choosing to become parents. Prerogatives in gay life were increasing. The old myths about what you could or couldn't do because you were gay were being dispelled.

Source: Betty Berzon, "Acting Up," in Thompson, *Long Road to Freedom*, p. 308.

*   *   *

In the late 1980s and early 1990s, a generation of activists who had worked in a number of social movements, including the lesbian and feminist movements, moved into their senior years. To many this did not mean sedentary retirement. It meant another envelope that needed to be pushed. In 1987, the first old lesbians conference was held near Los Angeles. Some of these women went on to found a national organization called Old Lesbians Organizing for Change (OLOC), open to women over sixty. Their mission is to raise awareness about ageism and how most people buy into the notion that young is better. They also work to ensure that old lesbians will have support and community.

DOCUMENT 122: Old Lesbians Organizing for Change (1987)

OLOC is committed to:

Confronting ageism within our own and the larger community.
Exploring who we are and naming our oppression.
Analyzing the experience of ageism by sharing individual stories.
Developing and disseminating educational material.
Facilitating the formation of new groups and stimulating existing groups to confront ageism—making our presence a visible force in the women's movement and the lesbian community.

Why We Call Ourselves "Old":

Society calls us old behind our backs while calling us "older" to our faces. "Old" has become a term of insult and shame. To be "old" means to be ignored and scorned, to be made invisible and expendable. We refute the lie that it is shameful to be an "old" woman. We name ourselves "old lesbians" because we no longer will accommodate to language that implies in any way that "old" means inferior. We call ourselves OLD with pride. In doing so, we challenge the stereotypes directly. Thus, we empower and change ourselves, each other, and the world.

Ageism Is a Social Disease:

It is ageist:
to consider "young" a compliment, "old" a derogatory synonym for ugly, decrepit, out-of-date. ("You don't look your age.")
to speak/do for an old lesbian instead of letting her speak/do for herself, and to assume she needs help.

to view an old lesbian either as a burden or a role model, rather than as an equal with whom a reciprocal relationship is desirable.

to patronize a courageous old lesbian by trivializing her anger as "feistiness." (Would you call Superman "feisty"?)

to categorize an outspoken old lesbian as "complaining," "difficult," or "crotchety."

to assume automatically than an old lesbian is asexual.

to be unsupportive of an old lesbian looking for a partner, or disrespectful of an old lesbian's choice to be single.

not to confront ageist remarks because they are "not really meant that way."

Source: OLOC Web site [http://www.oloc.org/]

* * *

Randy Burns (Northern Paiute), Barbara Cameron (Lakota Sioux), and others cofounded the first gay and lesbian American Indian group (Gay American Indians [GAI]) in 1975. They also served as the first cochairs of GAI. Like many activist gay and lesbian people of color, Randy points out that gay American Indians "face double oppression— both racism and homophobia."

DOCUMENT 123: Randy Burns—Gay American Indians (1988)

Many Indian agencies now eager to receive AIDS funding have been antigay for years. Gay Indian parents must fight long court battles for the custody of their children. Members of our community, some who are pipe-bearers themselves, have been excluded from Sun Dances—even though, among some tribes, finding and cutting the center pole for the ceremony was a traditional gay role!...Gay American Indians was founded...to serve the needs and interests of the gay American Indian community. We came together to share a common identity, to give and receive emotional support, and to share our rich heritage as American Indians. We were the first gay Indian organization in the United States....GAI grew beyond our wildest dreams....GAI's programs include referral services, cultural and educational projects, and active involvement within local networks of Indian organizations and agencies....In 1984 we formed the Gay American Indian History project, to collect information on our history, and to make it available to the larger community....Today GAI is active in education and training programs related to the AIDS crisis....We are advocates for not only gay but American Indian concerns as well. We are turning double oppression into double opportunity—the chance to build bridges between communities, to create a place for gay Indians in both of the worlds we live in, to honor our past and secure our future.

Sources: Randy Burns, "Preface" in *Living the Spirit: A Gay American Indian Anthology*, ed. Will Roscoe (New York: St. Martin's Press, 1988), pp. 1–5. See also Dean Gengel, "Gay American Indians (G.A.I.)" in *Gay American History*, Jonathan Ned Katz, (New York: Crowell, 1976), pp. 332–334.

* * *

Journalist Judith Levine argued in 1988 that, even in the age of AIDS, it is necessary to keep pleasure at the center of the debate over sexuality. She sees gay rights as one part of the larger struggle for sexual liberation, and argues that people should be able to enjoy sex as long as they do it in ways that do not hurt others. She happily endorses monogamy for those couples who feel no need for sexual contact with others, but also feels that those who want to enjoy multiple-partner eroticism should be able to do so without condemnation. She criticizes the new sexual puritans for using AIDS to attack nonconventional sex.

DOCUMENT 124: AIDS Should Not Prevent Sexual Pleasure (1988)

We must militantly stand up for everybody whose sexuality falls outside "acceptable" bourgeois arrangements—even far outside them. But you can't do this without asking fundamental questions about sex. Questions like, is monogamy better? (My answer: not necessarily.) What's wrong with kids having sex? (Often, nothing.) Why is it worse to pay for sex than to pay for someone to listen to your intimate problems or care for your infant? (You tell me.)....

We need to keep pleasure as a vital part of the progressive vision at the same time as we confront AIDS....Teaching abstinence as "right" is not only puritanical and ineffective in limiting sexual activity, but it fuels prejudice....

Where can we look for prosex messages in the AIDS era? I found one in the most threatened quarter, the gay community, in the educational comic books distributed by the Gay Men's Health Crisis. These depicted...everyone having phone sex, masturbating, or role-playing, all with minimum risk and maximum heat. Explicitly, humorously sexual, indeed happily pornographic, these pamphlets were pragmatic: they met their constituency where it lived and did not try to preach living differently. But they implied more—that it's unnecessary to foment aversion to sex through moralizing or hyperbolizing. Death is aversion enough. It's driven many back into the closet and made celibates of countless more. Instead, the lascivious comic-book hunks are saying: affirm sex. While death is all around us, let us nurture pleasure—for pleasure is life. Even now, especially now.

Source: Judith Levine, "Thinking About Sex," *Tikkun* March-April 1988. [Reprinted in Lisa Orr, ed., *Sexual Values: Opposing Viewpoints* (San Diego: Greenhaven Press, 1989), pp. 26–31.]

*   *   *

Coming out to one's family, friends, and co-workers remains the single most effective strategy in reducing antigay prejudice. Research shows that heterosexuals who are aware of knowing at least one gay or lesbian friend, co-worker, or relative tend to have less antigay prejudice. Knowing this, National Gay Rights Advocates, a legal reform group, designed National Coming Out Day (NCOD) to encourage more gays and lesbians to "come out of the closet" to their friends, family, and co-workers. In later years the project was expanded to a week, and has been coordinated by the Human Rights Campaign on a national level. The popularity of NCOD, in promoting lesbian and gay visibility on college campuses, in workplaces, and in local areas, shows the impact that focused activist groups can make. The idea is that, no matter how closeted or open one might be, everyone can take a single step to be more visible. By encouraging massive numbers of lesbians, gay men, bisexuals, and transgendered persons to become more open, and to discuss gay and lesbian rights with their friends and family, National Coming Out Day has had a major impact. Los Angeles's *Lesbian News* commented on NCOD.

DOCUMENT 125: National Coming Out Day (1988)

This day will be celebrated by people from coast to coast....Last year's October 11th March on Washington energized the Gay community across the country, as it took our strength and spirit to the nation's capitol. This year the strength comes home, to the local grassroots organizations that are the backbone of the Gay movement. Coordinated by National Gay Rights Advocates (NGRA) and co-sponsored by The Experience Weekend, the event is a reminder to all Gay men and Lesbians that the time has come to go forward in the campaign for civil rights, the time has come for them to "take their next step."

To excite Gay and Lesbian organizations in local communities, the organizing body of NCOD has begun a large scale campaign of its own. The national media has been put on alert, three full time staff members have been hired by NGRA to work exclusively on the event and "Coming Out Kits" have been mailed to thousands of grassroots Gay organizations nationwide. The kits, which include dozens of different ideas for "coming out"…[such as] dances, dinners, seminars, letter writing campaigns and celebrations that are in the works. NCOD is making available a wide variety of support materials…about obtaining media support as well as an informational circular on how to start a Gay support group.…

Says Jean O'Leary, Executive Director of NGRA and co-chair of NCOD…"Last year's march clearly showed that, even in the face of the deadly AIDS epidemic, our community is vibrant and growing. We need, more than ever, an annual event to celebrate life, one that will help us renew our commitments to one another. Ours is a community that is coming out of the closet forever."

Source: "A Tribute to Coming Out," *Lesbian News* (Los Angeles) v. 14, n. 3 (October 1988), p. 1.

*   *   *

One of the leading voices in the federal government in opposition to gay and lesbian rights in the 1980s was Congressman William Dannemeyer, Republican representative from Orange County, California. In 1989 he published *Shadow in the Land*, alerting people to what he perceived as the dangers to society in the United States if it accepted lesbian and gay equality. He predicted vast epidemic death rates due to AIDS and other sexual diseases brought on by the gay rights movement, which would be so severe as to lead to the collapse of Western civilization as a whole. The only way to respond to this health threat, he said, would be to repeal all gay rights laws and reinstate sodomy laws in every state.

DOCUMENT 126: Congressman William Dannemeyer Opposes Gay Rights (1989)

America is surrendering to this growing army of [gay rights] revolutionaries without firing a shot, indeed, without more than a word or two of protest. The homosexual blitzkrieg has been better planned and executed than Hitler's.…When they can march down our main thoroughfares, with our official permission and the protection of the police, they have become not a klatch of sexual deviates but a "movement.…"

[Homosexuals'] demands endanger the very survival of the family as we know it, and the only way to make certain that such recommendations are not put into practice is to reinstitute laws against sodomy in all states. By so doing we would settle the question of rights and prerogatives now in dispute, saying emphatically that homosexuals per se have no rights other than those they enjoy by virtue of being citizens of the United States.

In passing such laws, we would also affirm a normative way of life for all Americans: that they are born and nurtured in traditional families where children have both mothers and fathers and hence learn to understand the marvelous union of man and woman that continually leads to the rebirth of life and love and hope on earth....

We must reinstate traditional prohibitions against homosexuality in order to establish a sense of order and decency in our society, to reconnect us with our normative past....The choice we make will determine whether or not we survive as a people....We have the capacity to make the wrong choice and plunge our people, and indeed the entire West, into a dark night of the soul that could last hundreds of years before the flame is again lit. It has happened before. It can happen again. It is in full knowledge of such a grim possibility that I have written this book.

Source: Congressman William Dannemeyer, *Shadow in the Land: Homosexuality in America* (San Francisco: Ignatius Press, 1989), pp. 121–122, 217–219, 221, 228.

* * *

Minority groups that have been the target of hate crimes are not always tolerant of others who are different from them. Like other minority groups, Jewish people have expressed a mixed reaction toward lesbians and gays. The Reform branch of Judaism welcomed gay and lesbian Jews into the Union of American Hebrew Congregations in 1973. The Conservative and Orthodox branches, however, have been much less tolerant.

Below is an account by a rabbi whose attitudes and beliefs were profoundly changed after she chose to serve as the spiritual leader of Beth Chayim Chadashim (BCC), the first known Jewish gay and lesbian congregation in the world. Founded in 1972 in Los Angeles, BCC organizers interviewed Janet Marder (a heterosexual) for the position of rabbi. Though she considered herself open-minded, Marder lacked knowledge about the lesbian and gay experience, and carried stereotypes about homosexuals. Others warned her that it would hurt her career to serve in a gay and lesbian congregation. The BCC interview committee told her that they preferred to have a gay or lesbian rabbi but did not want to discriminate against her as others discriminated against lesbians and gays. She was hired and served as the BCC rabbi for five years. Later she wrote about her experiences.

DOCUMENT 127: Jewish Rabbi Acceptance of Gay and Lesbian Rights (1989)

Today, after many trials and many more errors, I hardly recognize myself. My beliefs have changed slowly, but in profound ways that affect my entire outlook on life....My attitude toward homosexuality has moved from uncertain tolerance to full acceptance. I see it now as a sexual orientation offering the same opportunities for love, fulfillment, spiritual growth and ethical action as heterosexuality....[At first] I could find no published rabbinic statements declaring homosexuality an acceptable Jewish way of life. And so I had to decide how much did it matter to me that the voice of my tradition, without exception, ran counter to the evidence of my experience and the deepest promptings of my conscience?

In fact, the Jewish values and principles I regard as eternal, transcendent and divinely ordained do *not* condemn homosexuality. The Judaism I cherish and affirm teaches love of humanity, respect for the spark of divinity in every person, and the human right to live with dignity....There is no Jewish *legal* basis for this belief; my personal faith simply tells me that the duty to love my neighbor as myself is a compelling mitzvah [duty] while the duty to condemn and to kill homosexuals for committing "abominations" most certainly is not....

I know that prejudice against lesbians and gays is deeply rooted, but I also know from my own experience that it is possible to become educated and to change profoundly....There is simply no substitute for an open mind and direct contact with gay people....Lesbians and gay men are all around, and all it takes to bring them out is a friendly, sensitive and respectful manner.

Source: Janet Marder, "Getting to Know the Gay and Lesbian Shul: A Rabbi Moves from Tolerance to Acceptance," in *Twice Blessed: On Being Lesbian or Gay and Jewish*, ed. Christie Balka and Andy Rose (Boston: Beacon Press, 1989), pp. 209–217.

* * *

Queer Nation, a direct action group, was founded in New York City in 1990 by four gay men. The mission of the organization was to combat homophobia and hate crimes against lesbians and gays. The word "Queer" asserted difference and the word "Nation" suggested community and common goals. The group popularized the slogan: "We're here, we're queer, get used to it!" It held kiss-ins in restaurants, demonstrated at the 1992 Academy Awards, held protests against companies that discriminated against homosexuals, and outed closet celebrities. Below is part of the "Queer Nation Manifesto," published anonymously:

DOCUMENT 128: Queer Nation (1990)

WHY QUEER?

Queer!

Ah, do we really have to use that word? It's trouble. Every gay person has his or her own take on it. For some it means strange and eccentric and kind of mysterious. That's okay; we like that. But some gay girls and boys don't. They think they're more normal than strange. And for others "queer" conjures up those awful memories of adolescent suffering. Queer. It's forcibly bittersweet and quaint at best—weakening and painful at worst. Couldn't we just use "gay" instead? It's a much brighter word. And isn't it synonymous with "happy"? When will you militants grow up and get over the novelty of being different?

Why Queer...

Well, yes, "gay" is great. It has its place. But when a lot of lesbians and gay men wake up in the morning we feel angry and disgusted, not gay. So we've chosen to call ourselves queer. Using "queer" is a way of reminding us how we are perceived by the rest of the world. It's a way of telling ourselves we don't have to be witty and charming people who keep our lives discreet and marginalized in the straight world. We use queer as gay men loving lesbians and lesbians loving being queer. Queer, unlike *gay*, doesn't mean *male*.

And when spoken to other gays and lesbians it's a way of suggesting we close ranks, and forget (temporarily) our individual differences because we face a more insidious common enemy. Yeah, *queer* can be a rough word but it is also a sly and ironic weapon we can steal from the homophobe's hands and use against him.

Source: Anonymous. "Queer Nation Manifesto" at Web site: http://userwww. service.emory.edu/~lderose/docs/politics/qnation/qnation.html#Twelve

*   *   *

In the early 1990s Loraine Hutchins and Lani Ka'ahumanu helped to develop an activist philosophy for bisexuals with the publication of their book *Bi Any Other Name: Bisexual People Speak* [Boston: Alyson Publications, 1991]. One part of this trend has been to get those who identify as gay or lesbian to acknowledge that not everyone is either heterosexual or homosexual, but that many people have a mix of attractions to both males and females. Bisexuals' demand for inclusiveness, along with that of transgendered, transsexual, and intersex people, led to a transformation of the gay and lesbian movement into a movement for the rights of all sexual minorities. As Hutchins and Ka'ahumanu said in *The Advocate*, the real enemy of the queer movement is sexual intolerance. With this greater inclusiveness, the new queer viewpoint welcomes everyone to identify as being queer in some way, so that rigid categories of homo/hetero are broken down.

DOCUMENT 129: Bisexuals and Gay Rights (1991)

Bisexuals are here, we're queer, get used to it. Bisexuals are part of the gay movement. We always have been, and we always will be. In fact, many gay men and lesbians behave bisexually. Many bisexuals behave and/or identify as lesbian or gay. Some are also transgender or transsexual people. Some identify primarily with the straight community. We all share the experience of bisexuality.

The real question is: Why do some gays and lesbians have trouble admitting bisexuals are part of the movement? The truth is that bisexuality, or for that matter heterosexuality, is not the enemy. The enemy is sexual intolerance. The enemy is any cultural or political worldview that defines a certain group as "other," inferior, sick, or criminal. Those who invent an other are the real enemy.

The gay movement has been diminishing its own strength and breadth by acting exclusively. Whenever people refuse to add the word *bisexual* to titles of gay organizations (as happened a decade before when lesbians demanded that the word *lesbian* be included), whenever AIDS educators include bisexual in the title but not in the body of a brochure or workshop, whenever a truly bisexual hero or heroine is appropriated as supposedly really gay, whenever we ape straight expectations rather than standing tall for sexual diversity as a whole, we betray the larger goals of sexual and human liberation. This not only ostracizes a whole class of supporters and members but also perpetuates the illusion that we can appease the larger society and win concessions from it without radically transforming how it deals with sex....

Source: Loraine Hutchins and Lani Ka'ahumanu, "Do Bisexuals Have a Place in the Gay Movement?" *The Advocate* June 4, 1991, p. 94, quoted in Thompson, *Long Road to Freedom*, p. 387.

* * *

Many leaders in the Republican Party expressed antigay sentiments in the 1990s. A good example is Patrick Buchanan, who repeatedly attacked gay and lesbian rights in his speeches and newspaper columns. For example, in a 1991 column he condemned lesbian and gay Irish Americans for daring to march in the New York Saint Patrick's Day Parade. He defended discrimination and prejudice against homosexuals, reasoning that

DOCUMENT 130: Gays in the Republican Party (1991)

To discriminate is to choose. We all discriminate in our choice of associates and friends. And prejudice simply means prejudgment. Not all prejudgments are rooted in ignorance; most are rooted in the inherited wisdom of the race. A visceral recoil from homosexuality is the natural reaction of a healthy society wishing to protect itself.

[In 1977 he wrote] Homosexuality is not a civil right. Its rise almost always is accompanied, as in the Weimar Republic, with a decay of society and a collapse of its basic cinder block, the family.

Source: Quoted in "The Other Minority," *The New Republic* March 30, 1992: 7.

*   *   *

In response to attacks like those of Patrick Buchanan and other Republican leaders, Marvin Liebman, a prominent Republican fund-raiser, came out as gay and challenged the Republican Party officials to drop their heterosexist rhetoric and policies. He wrote in *The Advocate* in 1991:

Although many of us vote Republican, are active in the party, and are even elected Republican officials, other Republicans don't know it. I would guess that most openly gay and lesbian people fall into the liberal category, i.e., the Democratic Party. I would also guess that the vast number of closeted and uncounted gays and lesbians in our society are equally, if not more, Republican and conservative. But the few open and many hidden conservatives in this vast group remain in the political closet.

They may vote Republican, but they are fearful of taking any political action. This is a sad waste of human resources. It prevents the realization of legislation that would provide gay and lesbian Americans with the same rights and privileges as every other American. It is vital for the conservative members of our community to get involved in Republican politics in the same numbers as others do in Democratic politics.

To be gay, conservative, and Republican is not necessarily a contradiction. I'm proud to be all three. The Republican-conservative view, based as it is on the inherent rights of the individual over the state, should be the logical political home of gays and lesbians. It is up to us to help the overwhelming majority of decent Republicans reject the bigots and hypocrites who are attempting to control the party—just as the John Birch Society tried in the sixties. The Birchers failed, and the bigots will ultimately fail. The Republican Party will provide a base for gays as well as all others. The future of the party rests on the politics of inclusion; it is the duty of gays and lesbians to lead the way.

Source: Marvin Liebman, "Is There a Place for Gays in the Republican Party?" quoted in Thompson, *Long Road to Freedom*, p. 386.

* * *

As the Democratic Party moved to be more accepting of gay and lesbian rights as an integral part of its human rights emphasis, state and local parties adopted policy statements in support of gay rights. An example is this statement adopted at the Oregon Democratic Convention on March 1, 1992:

DOCUMENT 131: Democratic Party Progay Rights (1992)

As Democrats, we believe that our nation can only be as strong as our commitment to liberty, justice, and equality. The Democratic Party of Oregon is committed to individual liberty, dignity, and opportunity. Individual rights, including the right to privacy, must not be limited because of race, national origin, sex, sexual orientation, age, religion, disability, medical history, reproductive choice, marital or financial status, or political affiliation.

The Democratic Party of Oregon believes that among the "inalienable rights" referred to in the Declaration of Independence and the rights reserved to the people in the Ninth Amendment to the United States Constitution, our forefathers intended the right to be left alone, or, in contemporary language, the right to privacy. Nowhere is this more necessary to human dignity and self-determination than in the right to bodily integrity and the right to associate with and love whomever one will. Thus, we believe that all attempts...to discriminate on the basis of sexual orientation...are unacceptable, illegal, and unAmerican.

Source: Oregon Democratic Platform, March 1, 1992; quoted in *Voters' Pamphlet*, State of Oregon General Election, November 3, 1992, p. 122.

* * *

In 1985 Jeffrey Wasson met a man in a local park in Lexington, Kentucky. After talking for about twenty minutes, Wasson invited the man to come home with him. When the man suggested sexual activities, Wasson agreed. At this point, the man revealed himself as an undercover policeman, and arrested Wasson for soliciting to commit sodomy, a criminal act. Wasson's attorney defended him on the basis that Kentucky's sodomy law violated his right to privacy. In addition, by prosecuting people for sexual activity performed by members of the same sex while not criminalizing similar acts between males and females, Wasson's attorney said that this violated the guarantee in Kentucky's constitution of equal treatment under the law.

After Wasson won in the local and appellate courts, the state government appealed these decisions to the Kentucky Supreme Court. In 1992 the state Supreme Court upheld the lower courts. Since these decisions were based entirely on the Kentucky state constitution, they could not be appealed to federal courts. While *Bowers v. Hardwick* (1986) did not abolish sodomy laws, it did at least allow each state to repeal its own sodomy law. By this decision, Kentucky joined those states which declared that consensual sex acts practiced by adults in the privacy of their own home were not criminal, and thus the police could no longer arrest people for asking someone to come home with them for sex. This decision in Kentucky was also important as a precedent for other states because it challenged the reasoning of *Bowers v. Hardwick*, and declared that homosexuals were an identifiable class of persons who were deserving of equal protection under state laws. After this, only a minority of states continued to have sodomy laws.

DOCUMENT 132: *Kentucky v. Wasson* (1992)

Opinion of the Court by Justice Leibson.

I. RIGHT OF PRIVACY

Kentucky has a rich and compelling tradition of recognizing and protecting individual rights...upholding the right of privacy against the intrusive police power of the state....Immorality in private which does not operate to the detriment of others, is placed beyond the reach of state action by the guarantees of liberty in the Kentucky Constitution....We view the United States Supreme Court decision in *Bowers v. Hardwick* as a misdirected application of the theory of original intent. To illustrate: as a theory of majoritarian morality, miscegenation [interracial sex] was an offense with ancient roots. It is highly unlikely that protecting the rights of persons of different races to copulate was one of the considerations behind the Fourteenth Amendment. Nevertheless in *Loving v. Virginia* (1967), the United States Supreme Court recognized that a contemporary, enlightened interpretation of a liberty interest involved in the sexual act made its punishment constitutionally impermissible.

II. EQUAL PROTECTION

Certainly, the practice of deviate sexual intercourse violates traditional morality. But so does the same act between heterosexuals, which activity is de-

criminalized. Going one step further, *all* sexual activity between consenting adults outside of marriage violates our traditional morality. The issue here is not whether sexual activity traditionally viewed as immoral can be punished by society, but whether it can be punished solely on the basis of sexual preference....In the final analysis we can attribute no legislative purpose to this statute except to single out homosexuals for different treatment for indulging their sexual preference by engaging in the same activity heterosexuals are now at liberty to perform....Simply because the majority...finds one type of extramarital intercourse more offensive than another, does not provide a rational basis for criminalizing the sexual preferences of homosexuals.
Justice Lambert, dissenting.

This decision will be regarded as the imprimatur of Kentucky's highest court upon homosexual conduct. The moral opprobrium of the majority will be lost and the popular perception will be that if the Constitution protects such conduct, it must be okay....Those who oppose the portrayal of homosexuality as an acceptable alternative lifestyle will encounter the majority opinion as a powerful argument to the contrary.

Source: Commonwealth v. Wasson 1992 Ky. LEXIS 140 (Sept. 24, 1992).

* * *

Conservative antigay forces opposed gay rights laws on the local level, rallying around the slogan "No Special Rights" for homosexuals. They focused on Colorado, where an amendment to the state constitution was put before the voters. This Amendment 2 was a reaction to gay rights laws that had been passed by liberal City Councils in Denver, Boulder, and other urban areas. The text of this Amendment 2, which received a slight majority of the votes cast, states:

DOCUMENT 133: Colorado Amendment 2 (1992)

Neither the State of Colorado, through any of its branches or departments, nor any of its agencies, political subdivisions, municipalities or school districts, shall enact, adopt or enforce any statute, regulation, ordinance or policy whereby homosexual, lesbian or bisexual orientation, conduct, practices or relationships shall constitute or otherwise be the basis of, or entitle any person or class of persons to have or claim any minority status, quota preferences, protected status or claim of discrimination.

Source: Article 2, Section 30, of the Colorado State Constitution, as amended in 1992.

* * *

In Oregon in 1992, a conservative antigay group called the Oregon Citizens Alliance (OCA) placed an initiative as Measure 9 on the ballot to amend Oregon's state constitution. The OCA attempted to gain support for Measure 9 by lumping homosexuality with other sexual practices which were even more condemned than homosexuality. Passage of Measure 9 would mean that gay pride rallies could not be held on public property, homosexual teachers and police officers could be fired if they tried to defend the rights of gays and lesbians to nondiscrimination, books with positive gay themes could be pulled from the shelves of public libraries, and school counselors would be required to advise gay and lesbian students— or children whose parents are gay or lesbian—that homosexuality is "abnormal, wrong, unnatural, and perverse." After a wide array of leaders in the state, including Governor Barbara Roberts, came out against Measure 9, Oregon voters rejected the measure by 57 percent to 43 percent. However, it passed in many rural counties. Measure 9 is worded as follows:

DOCUMENT 134: Oregon Measure 9 (1992)

(1) This state shall not recognize any categorical provision such as "sexual orientation," "sexual preference," and similar phrases that includes homosexuality, pedophilia, sadism or masochism. Quotas, minority status, affirmative action, or any similar concepts, shall not apply to these forms of conduct, nor shall government promote these behaviors.

(2) State, regional, and local governments and their properties and monies shall not be used to promote, encourage, or facilitate homosexuality, pedophilia, sadism or masochism.

(3) State, regional and local governments and their departments, agencies and other entities, including specifically the State Department of Higher Education and the public schools, shall assist in setting a standard for Oregon's youth that recognizes homosexuality, pedophilia, sadism and masochism as abnormal, wrong, unnatural, and perverse and that these behaviors are to be discouraged and avoided.

The following arguments pro and con regarding Measure 9 were submitted by groups which paid a $300 fee to have them included in the *Voters' Pamphlet*:

ARGUMENT IN FAVOR

Carol A. Petrone and Phillip Ramsdell, Oregon Catholics for Life

Gay Rights activists have attempted to pass special rights laws through the Oregon legislature for years, but the voters have consistently thwarted their efforts. Now, the tactic seems to be to force special "gay rights" laws and policies through government entities such as city councils, commissions and educational facilities—thereby avoiding a vote of the people. Measure 9 will insure that special rights based on private behavior, including affirmative action and quotas for declared homosexuals, will not be forced on Oregonians. Homosexual activists have made their behavior central to their self-identification and they insist that society give it immunity from moral judgment. Further, they seek to propose legislation which forbids other citizens to disapprove of their lifestyle, which has the effect of compelling social acceptance. Portland's Future Focus program to promote "cultural diversity" includes phrases such as "embracing and celebrating," which could be used to force acceptance of homosexual lifestyles. In addition, the National Education Association's position paper, "Affording Equal Opportunity to Gay and Lesbian Students through Teaching and Counseling," tells teachers to censor books from school libraries that do not give positive treatment to the subject of homosexuality.

With these facts in mind, there is evidence that homosexual propaganda can sway some young people into homosexuality and, perhaps, permanent orientation in that direction. Because some persons enter adolescence with sexual orientation unresolved, the state should defend the rights of children not to be subject to such influences in school. This is not homophobia, but rather the assertion of parents' rights over those of civil rights activists. Homosexuals, as humans, have the same rights as all. However, homosexual orientation is an objective disorder and the acting out of its lifestyle threatens the rights of the family.

ARGUMENT AGAINST

Rev. Gary L. Davis, United Church of Christ

Measure No. 9 is founded in fear, hatred, and deceit. Measure No. 9 is disguised as an initiative banning a selection of "perverse behaviors." In truth, its aim is to legitimate discrimination against those born with a homosexual orientation. The backers of Measure 9 claim that the initiative is necessary because men and women who are homosexual seek to win "special rights" for themselves. This is the same argument once used against African-Americans, women, people with disabilities, and other non-dominant groups to deny them their basic civil rights. People of homosexual orientation do not seek special rights; they simply seek the same freedom others have to work and live where they want, without fear, and to maintain their lives in peace.

The truth about homosexuality refutes myths and stereotypes....Heterosexual and homosexual persons alike condemn crimes against children. Statistics confirm that the vast majority of child abusers are heterosexual, not homosexual. With people of homosexual orientation numbering at least one in ten in the population, they are among your friends, neighbors, co-workers, and family members.

The Bible has been misused by backers of Measure 9. Proponents of Measure 9 claim that homosexuality deserves condemnation because they interpret the Bible as condemning it. However, in similar ways, the Bible has been twisted in the past to wring interpretations condemning minorities and women to secondary status. In the Bible, God commands us to love, not hate. We cannot imagine Jesus condemning people on the basis of who God created them to be. Measure 9 targets for discrimination those guilty of nothing more than being born a certain way. Discrimination is wrong. Hatred is wrong. This initiative is wrong. We must stand up for one another. We must speak out against injustice.

Source: Voters' Pamphlet, State of Oregon General Election, November 3, 1992, pp. 93–127.

*   *   *

When Bill Clinton was running for president, he pledged to appoint qualified people to public office who reflected the reality of the diversity of America's population. Among the high-level appointees he sent for confirmation by the Senate was Roberta Achtenberg to be the assistant secretary for Fair Housing in the Department of Housing and Urban Development (HUD). Achtenberg was a former law school dean, had been elected to the San Francisco Board of Supervisors, and in all ways seemed qualified. But this was the first time a president had appointed a gay activist to a high federal position that required Senate confirmation, and Achtenberg had a high profile. She was founder of the Lesbian Rights Project, executive director of the National Center for Lesbian Rights, and her lover Mary Morgan was the nation's first openly lesbian judge. When asked if he would vote to confirm Achtenberg, Senator Jesse Helms opposed her appointment "because she's a damn lesbian. I'm not going to put a lesbian in a position like that. If you want to call me a bigot, fine." In response, Senator Claiborne Pell revealed that his daughter was lesbian, and he said he would not want to see her barred from holding a government job because of her orientation. Despite the opposition of conservative Republicans, the Senate voted to confirm Ms. Achtenberg on May 25, 1993, making it easier for presidents to appoint openly gay persons in the future. The Senate Record Vote Analysis summarized the positions that various senators expressed, pro and con, on Achtenberg's appointment.

DOCUMENT 135: Lesbian Appointed to Federal Government (1993)

Those favoring confirmation contended:

Argument 1: Roberta Achtenberg has a wealth of professional experience as a civil rights attorney and a locally elected official....She has a results-oriented, accommodating approach that will serve her well at HUD. Some of our colleagues do not share our view of her reasonableness. Several charges, all of which we find baseless, have been raised....The most oft-repeated charge is that she has mercilessly attacked the Boy Scouts of America for failing to admit homosexuals....Her vote was just one vote out of a unanimous, 34–0 vote in favor of denying funds. Local law prohibited funding for organizations that discriminate on the basis of sexual orientation, so her vote merely upheld local law. Roberta Achtenberg has assured us that she will not use this post to try to block Federal housing funds for organizations that discriminate on the basis of sexual orientation, because Federal law does not specify that such discrimination is illegal....

Her status as the first openly homosexual high-level Government appointee to appear before the Senate for confirmation is a milestone in America's civil rights history. We commend President Clinton for courageously standing up to the bigotry that still confronts this lifestyle in America. The only way we will ever dispel unwarranted prejudice against sexual orientation is by fighting it wherever it is found.

Argument 2: We find the lifestyle chosen by this nominee to be morally offensive....However, we must admit that she is qualified for this position. Though we certainly would not have nominated her, the President has the right to choose his own Administration officials so long as they are capable....

Those opposing confirmation contended:

Argument 1: Ordinarily, we defer to a President's selections...[but] when his choices very likely will lead to disastrous public policy consequences, we must exercise our constitutional duty of advice and consent to speak out....Her expertise is in advancing the legislative agenda of homosexual "rights" groups....She has actively supported the imposition of her views on others, against their deeply held religious and personal beliefs....We are very bothered by her willingness to abuse her authority as a public official to wage a campaign against the Boy Scouts of America. As a member of the San Francisco Board of Supervisors she introduced a resolution "urging the Boy Scouts to abolish its policy of barring lesbians, gays, and bisexuals from working with the group," and called for changes in State and Federal laws to repeal favorable treatment of the Boy Scouts. In February of 1992, as a member of the United Way board, she voted to suspend funding for the Scouts....

We fear she intends to do the same at HUD. If confirmed, she will have veto authority over billions in Federal housing aid. She has stated that she does not intend to withhold funding based on discrimination against homosexuals, but, in all candor, we do not trust her....

Argument 2: In choosing this nominee, President Clinton is endorsing a type of moral relativism which is rejected by the vast majority of Americans, and which has been repudiated by three decades of failure in social experimentation. Traditional family values such as monogamy, faith in God, civic duty, and individual accountability are not seen by many liberals as any more valuable than other, competing values, and they often are seen as less valuable. The resulting social disintegration has led to a five-hundred-fold increase in Government social service spending but the decline has not been stemmed. Teen pregnancy rates, abortion rates, the number of broken marriages, suicide rates, the amount of violent crime, and many other indicators of societal breakdown continue to climb. Still, the solution offered by many is more of the cause of the problem. The radical homosexual movement, as embodied by Roberta Achtenberg, holds as anathema the core values upon which America was built. A vote in her favor is a vote in favor of the proposition that we need to accelerate, not stem, societal collapse.

Source: Senate Record Vote Analysis, Achtenberg Nomination/Confirmation, 103d Congress, 1st Session, May 24, 1993, 4:29 P.M., page S–6356, Temporary Congressional Record, Vote No. 122.

*   *   *

Investigative journalist Randy Shilts interviewed hundreds of veterans and active duty military personnel for his book on lesbians and gay men in the United States armed forces. Shilts had to promise the strongest confidentiality to those on active duty since they could be immediately discharged if their homosexuality or bisexuality became known. They might not only lose their career, but also their educational or retirement benefits. The majority of military personnel discharged for homosexuality are women; and Shilts concluded that lesbianism was a convenient excuse for the military old guard to get rid of women. Shilts explained the old guard's hostility toward gay men as also being related to their reluctance to accept women in the military, since the presence of women and gay men was threatening to their concept of masculinity. The controversy, Shilts suggested, was a reflection of tensions over society's changing definitions of manhood.

Yet, despite persistent hostility toward openly gay and lesbian personnel, Shilts found that homosexuality is common in the military. In his confidential interviews with heterosexual generals and admirals, they told him—off the record—that they knew of many lesbians and gay men who were fine soldiers, but they did not want this to be publicized. In some areas where persistent shortages of personnel occur, such as the medical corps, officers admitted that if the government discharged all the lesbian and gay doctors, nurses, and medics, the armed forces' medical centers would be forced to close down. During times of war, when the need for troops is most acute, discharges for homosexuality decline sharply. This trend shows that gays and lesbians are kept in the service at precisely the time when skilled personnel are most needed, giving lie to the idea that lesbians and gay men are not competent to serve in a combat situation. Shilts concluded that the United States armed forces are far less concerned about homosexuals in the service, than with having people *think* there are no homosexuals in the service.

DOCUMENT 136: Lesbians and Gay Men in the Military (1993)

A vast gay subculture has emerged within the military, in every branch of the service, among both officers and enlisted. Today, gay soldiers jump with the 101st Airborne, [and] wear the Green Beret....Gay marines guard the president in the White House honor guard and protect U.S. embassies around the world. Gay military personnel are among the graduates of Annapolis, West Point, and the Air Force Academy in Colorado Springs. At least one gay man has served in the astronaut program. Recent gay general-staff officers have included one army four-star general, renowned in military circles, who served as head of one of the most crucial military missions of the 1980s. In the past decade, gay people have served as generals in every branch of the armed forces. The Marine Corps has also had at least one gay person at four-star rank since 1981, and at least one gay man has served on the Joint Chiefs of Staff....

[And yet, the armed forces] encourage lesbians and gay men to resign...under the vague rubric of "conduct unbecoming." Such quiet separations help conceal the numbers of lesbians and gay men the military turns out of the service, as many as two thousand a year during the past decade. In the past decade, the cost of investigations and the dollars spent replacing gay personnel easily amount to hundreds of millions. The human costs are incalculable. Careers are destroyed; lives are ruined.... [Discharges send a message that homosexuals] are undeserving of even the most basic civil rights. Such policies also create an ambience [of] discrimination, harassment, and even violence....The way women can prove themselves to be nonlesbians is to have sex with men. Thus antigay regulations have encouraged sexual harassment of women. Those who will not acquiesce to a [male] colleague's advances are routinely accused of being lesbian and are subject to discharge.

Source: Randy Shilts, *Conduct Unbecoming: Lesbians and Gays in the U.S. Military, Vietnam to the Persian Gulf* (New York: St. Martin's Press, 1993).

*   *   *

On January 29, 1993, President Clinton directed Secretary of Defense Les Aspin to review government policy on homosexuals in the military. On April 6, Aspin convened a Military Working Group, consisting of one general or admiral from each branch of the armed services, to prepare recommendations. This group issued its report on June 8, stating that the military should not ask recruits about their sexual orientation, which in their view should remain a personal and private matter. However, this report recommended that homosexuals should continue to be discharged from the armed forces if their same-sex feelings became known. This policy became known as the "don't ask, don't tell" policy.

The officers' report, while practically ignoring lesbianism, gave several reasons for opposing open homosexuality among males in the armed forces. Gay activists pointed out that similar reasons had been given by the military establishment in the 1940s to oppose President Harry Truman's executive order for the integration of black and white soldiers. In dealing with racism, the military does not exclude African Americans, but expects recruits with strong prejudices to change their attitudes. If recruits who were raised with racist values cannot work well in a diverse military, Pentagon policy suggests, they should not reenlist. Gay activists contrasted the military's effective antiracism educational programs to reduce racial prejudices, with its refusal to allow antihomophobia education among recruits. To understand this argument, substitute the term "nonwhite" in this statement every time "homosexual" is mentioned.

DOCUMENT 137: Military Working Group on Homosexuality (1993)

Military members bring their values with them when they enter the service. Whether based on moral, religious, cultural, or ethical considerations, those values and beliefs are often strongly held and not amenable to change. While we indoctrinate and train recruits, leadership and discipline cannot—and generally should not—attempt to counter the basic values which parents and society have taught. Indeed, efforts to do so will likely prove counterproductive.

Military operations are team operations—units win wars, not individuals. The rights and needs of the group are emphasized while individual rights and needs are often set aside.... The presence of open homosexuals in a unit would, in general, polarize and fragment the unit and destroy the bonding and singleness of purpose required for effective military operations. This phenomenon occurs whether or not homosexual acts are involved. By simply stating that he or she is a homosexual, the individual becomes isolated from the group and combat effectiveness suffers....

Introduction of individuals identified as homosexuals into the military would severely undermine good order and discipline. Moral and ethical beliefs of individuals would be brought into open conflict…[and] would be perceived by many servicemembers as the imposition of a political agenda by a small group—an agenda which is seen as having no military necessity.…Core values of the military profession would be seen by many to have changed fundamentally if homosexuals were allowed to serve. This would undermine institutional loyalty and the moral basis for service.…

Male homosexuals in the military could be expected to bring an increased incidence of sexually transmitted diseases and other diseases spread by close personal contact.…A significant number of servicemembers say they would not reenlist if open homosexuals were allowed to serve.…[Military education] should not include sensitivity training or attempt to change deeply held moral, ethical, religious values.

Source: Summary Report of the Military Working Group on Recommended Department of Defense Homosexual Policy, 8 June 1993. Quoted in Robert M. Baird and M. Katherine Baird, eds., *Homosexuality: Debating the Issues* (Amherst, NY: Prometheus Books, 1995), pp. 158–170.

*   *   *

When Senator Barry Goldwater of Arizona was the Republican nominee for president in 1964, he established his reputation as a leading conservative thinker. He chaired the Senate Armed Services Committee, and as an experienced air force pilot he was thoroughly familiar with the realities of military life. However, though a strong supporter of the Defense Department, he thought the Joint Chiefs of Staff were wrong to discharge trained military personnel simply because of their homosexual orientation. The ban on qualified gay and lesbian troops serving their country was, in the Republican senator's words, "just plain un-American." Goldwater wrote an editorial in the *Washington Post National Weekly* and it was widely quoted in the debate on gays in the military.

DOCUMENT 138: Barry Goldwater on Gays in the Military (1993)

After more than 50 years in the military and politics, I am still amazed to see how upset people can get over nothing. Lifting the ban on gays in the military isn't exactly nothing, but it's pretty damn close.…When the facts lead to one conclusion, I say it's time to act, not to hide. The country and the military know that eventually the ban will be lifted. The only remaining questions are how much muck we will all be dragged through, and how many brave Americans like Tom Paniccia and Col. Margarethe Cammermeyer will have their lives and careers destroyed in a senseless attempt to stall the inevitable....It's high time to pull the curtains on this charade of policy.

Source: Barry M. Goldwater, "The Gay Ban: Just Plain Un-American," *Washington Post National Weekly* July 21–27, 1993, p. 28.

* * *

In 1991, two lesbian couples and a gay male couple asked Daniel R. Foley, an attorney in Honolulu, to represent them in a lawsuit. One of the lesbian couples in the case, Ninia Baehr and Genora Dancel, explained that the denial of their right to marry left them without the legal and economic benefits provided to husbands and wives. The gay male couple had lived together in a committed relationship for fifteen years. Like other people who are in love, they wanted to be able to recognize their marriage formally. Yet when they applied for a marriage license, they were refused on the basis that state law specified a person can marry only someone of the other sex.

These couples appealed to several attorneys to challenge the state law that denied same-sex couples the right to marry, but none of them wanted to take a case that they seemed certain to lose. Foley was their last chance. He had previously focused on civil rights law relating to racial minorities and women, and he had served as legal director of the American Civil Liberties Union of Hawai'i, but he had never argued a gay rights case before a court. Nevertheless, Foley decided to take the case, and he took it all the way to the Hawai'i Supreme Court. In 1993 the Court decided that the Hawai'i state government must prove it has a "compelling interest" in refusing to allow same-sex couples the right to marry. After sending the case back to the State Circuit Court, Judge Kevin Chang ruled three years later that the state had failed to prove it had a compelling interest in preventing such marriages.

These court decisions made headlines across the nation, and same-sex marriage became a major issue in the struggle for gay and lesbian rights. It also highlighted the role of heterosexuals working for gay and lesbian rights. In this 1996 interview with Walter L. Williams, Foley explained his three-part motivation for his involvement in the case: his Buddhist religion, his civil liberties ideology, and having a gay relative.

DOCUMENT 139: Hawai'i Same-Sex Marriage Court Case (1993)

Did you consider taking a same-sex marriage case before this one?

I had never thought about marriage as anything other than between a man and a woman. But when these couples approached me, I could see that they had loving, committed relationships that reminded me of how my wife and I feel about each other. I knew it would be a case that would be practically impossible to win. But I'm a Buddhist, and in the Soka Gakkai Buddhist organization I belong to, a major teaching is that we must challenge and surmount those things that might seem to be impossible.

What does Buddhism say about gay rights?

Daisaku Ikeda, the president of the Soka Gakkai International (SGI) says that nothing is more important than respect for human dignity. The SGI's prime goal is to promote happiness among people. Ikeda repeatedly stresses the need to respect diversity, and the importance of human rights. The Charter of the SGI emphasizes the principle of not discriminating against any individual on any grounds. Diversity is a positive good, Buddhist teachings attest; it is the source of creative energy in life.

With this in mind, I began researching the issue of marriage law. I discovered there are hundreds of rights and benefits that accrue to people who are legally married, such as survivorship, property rights, employment benefits, health insurance, bereavement leave, inheritance rights, probate, public assistance, taxation, and other rights. Gay and lesbian couples can get none of those protections, simply because they cannot get legally married.

I'm really committed to the ideals of the Declaration of Independence. When it declares that the fundamental goal of government is to protect the right of all people to "life, liberty and the pursuit of happiness," what could be more basic than the right of someone to marry the person of their choice?

Still, what gave you a personal motivation to take on this case? You knew it would be an uphill battle, and that you would not make much money on it. You're a happily married heterosexual.

I thought of my deceased uncle. Our family realized he was gay, but we never talked about it with him. He was brilliant and talented, but he wasted a lot of his potential because he was forced to live in the closet. He never was able to overcome the intense prejudice against homosexuals, and he died without fulfilling his promise.

That certainly is a strong statement in favor of gay people coming out to their families.

Buddhism asks us to do everything we can to help others reach their highest potential. We did not do that in my family with my uncle, and I felt bad about that. After meditating about the issue, and talking with my wife, I decided to take the case as a memorial to my uncle. I knew that if I didn't take the case, no other lawyer in Hawai'i would either. I decided that, from that day forward, I would do everything I could to make sure that younger gays and lesbians don't have to endure the pain of tortured silence that so sapped my uncle's spirit. That's what, in fact, finally killed him.

Denial of the right of same-sex couples to marry is not in accord with my Buddhist ideals of equal rights for everyone. My gut feeling was that the gay position needed to be heard by the courts. I thought to myself, who am I to deny these couples the right to have the same benefits and joys of marriage that I have? Why should I be entitled to have all these benefits, while they are not?

What happened when you took the case to court?

I filed a complaint in the Circuit Court of the State of Hawai'i in 1991, but the judge threw out my complaint. The couples were discouraged, but I wasn't surprised at the negative ruling. After all, this was a new area of law where little precedent existed. I determined to never give up, no matter how discouraging the circumstances. So, I filed an appeal of the case *Baehr v. Lewin* to the Hawai'i Supreme Court. In 1992, the Supreme Court agreed to hear arguments. The State Attorney General argued from precedent, that no federal or State court had ever granted marriage rights to lesbian or gay couples. Furthermore, he said, heterosexual marriage was the basis for morality in society, and was needed to continue the human race. I realized this reasoning was based on Judeo-Christian morality, rather than on the Constitution. Despite the fact that humanity's problem today is *too many* people, the Attorney General was appealing to old ideas from a time when humans were not overpopulated like today. I hoped the justices would realize this outdated reasoning for what it was.

How did you argue your case?

I conceded right away that I would lose if I were in a federal court. But, I pointed out, the Constitution of the State of Hawai'i is more explicit that the United States Constitution in its protections for individual rights. It states that no person in Hawai'i can be denied "the equal protection of the laws" or be discriminated against on the basis of "race, religion, sex, or ancestry." I made the case that gay and lesbian Hawai'ians deserve the right to privacy in deciding their own private intimate decisions about who they wish to marry, and they should have the equal protection of the law in their marriage desires, just as other people do.

I also pointed out that the law which prohibits a person from marrying someone of the same sex, is a direct violation of the Hawai'i Constitution, which specifies that discrimination could not be made on the basis of sex. If the plaintiff Ms. Baehr could marry a man, but could not marry Ms. Dancel just because she was a woman, then this was a clear example of sex discrimination.

Didn't you also use the analogy of state laws in the South prohibiting persons of different races from marrying?

Yes. In Virginia in the 1960s, an African-American woman and a white man challenged that state's miscegenation law. The Virginia courts ruled against this interracial couple, claiming that God did not intend for the races to mix. It was precisely the same argument, based on religion, as is now being used, to say God does not intend for people of the same sex to marry. We don't have such a belief in Buddhism, in fact we don't even believe there is some all-powerful god laying down rules of "don't do this or that." So it wasn't hard for me to argue against that idea.

The U.S. Supreme Court overturned miscegenation laws in 1967, ruling that a state's laws must be based on the Constitution, with its guarantees of equal protection of the laws for everyone, rather than on Christian ideas of some people being "saved" and above others. The Supreme Court in that case ruled that the right to marry who one wishes is a fundamental right, guaranteed by the Constitution's equal protection clause. From this decision as precedent, I argued Hawai'i should fulfill its own constitution, and guarantee lesbian and gay couples the equal protection of the laws.

Were you surprised at the judges' decision in your case?

Not really. I had gotten the impression that they carefully considered my arguments. What I was surprised about was that the majority opinion held that the sexual orientation of my clients was irrelevant to the case. The real issue, they said, was over the issue of whether a person could be denied the right to marry another person, simply because that other person was of the same sex. Using the 1967 miscegenation decision as precedent, the Court suggested that a law prohibiting someone from marrying another person of the same sex was indeed sex discrimination.

The fundamental issue, they said, is equality. And a person's freedom to choose whom they wish to marry. They ruled that the only way the State can limit that right is to prove that it has a "compelling State interest" in doing so.

This decision is also an advance for the rights of women, isn't it?

Absolutely. The Court stated that discrimination on the basis of sex should receive the strictest scrutiny by the courts, meaning that in the future any case on sex discrimination will be accorded special attention. This decision grants far greater legal protections for women in Hawai'i, than previous cases had done. This case in behalf of gay and lesbian couples gained an additional major benefit in the area of women's rights. This case demonstrates that a victory for one group suffering discrimination is, in a larger sense, a victory for others as well.

What is the current status of the case?

The Hawai'i Supreme Court's decision returned the case to the lower court for a final decision, and given the firmness of the justices' words, it was unlikely the Attorney General could prove that the State had a compelling interest in prohibiting same-sex marriages. Now that the Circuit judge has decided in our favor, it is only a matter of time before the State Supreme Court will make its final ruling. The Lambda Legal Defense and Education Fund, and the Hawai'i Equal Marriage

Rights Project, have been very supportive. My clients are already making plans for their wedding ceremonies. Genora Dancel and her partner Ninia Baehr have asked me to be their "Best Man...." The Hawai'i lesbian and gay community went wild with joy. Honolulu newspapers endorsed the decision. The President of the Hawai'i Bar Association congratulated the justices for showing "moral courage."

This case has certainly put you in the spotlight. It's being hailed as the greatest legal victory for lesbians and gays ever.

Yes, all major national newspapers gave front page coverage to the decisions. I've been swamped with requests for interviews by journalists and television news shows on all the major networks. Law Review journals are publishing articles on the case. With Hawai'i's law as precedent, this decision will make it easier for same-sex couples in other States to argue similar cases....We really rocked the nation! No one in the legal community thought we could accomplish so much so soon.

How does this tie in with your Buddhist viewpoint?

This decision will help improve society because it will encourage more people to be happy in their life. It stands to reason that the more people you have who are happy, because they can marry who they want, the more of a contribution they will make to society. This is also a case promoting women's equality. Everybody concerned with women's rights and women's equality ought to be backing this effort....

In 1993 the American Civil Liberties Union presented you with its annual award for outstanding attorney.

Yes, that was nice. But there's little doubt in my mind that unless I was a Buddhist I could not have achieved this victory. My chanting gave me the strength to keep fighting against all odds and to never give up. The advocacy I did in this case is consistent with SGI Buddhist practice. Buddhism stands for diversity and the sacredness of each individual life. The Soka Gakkai stands for compassion and public service. These are not just ideas; they are embodied and applied in our daily practice.

Source: Unpublished interview of Daniel R. Foley by Walter L. Williams, Los Angeles, December 20, 1996. [See also Daniel Woog, *Friends and Family: The True Stories of Gay America's Straight Allies* (Los Angeles: Alyson, 1999).]

*   *   *

With hope that pressure on Congress would prompt it to pass some of the progay policies that Clinton proposed, activists called for another March on Washington for Gay and Lesbian Rights in 1993. This time, the march organizers agreed to include "bisexual" in the title of the march, but they still resisted including "transgender" as too controversial. Still, the third march on Washington was more representative of the diversity of the queer communities than either the 1979 or 1987 marches had been.

A major purpose of another national march was not only to pressure Congress, but also to inspire people across the country to tackle issues of equality in their own local areas. Perhaps the biggest impact of a march is on the marchers themselves. The psychological impact that comes from being part of a large crowd of like-minded people is significant for minorities who often feel outnumbered and isolated. The march helped inspire much progress on state and local levels. For example, later in 1993, after an effective lobbying campaign by hundreds of high school students, the Massachusetts State Legislature passed, and Republican Governor William Weld signed, a law to protect gay and lesbian public school students from discrimination. This was the first such law passed in the nation, to protect students from harassment, enable them to form support groups, and prevent discrimination.

One of the speakers at the April 25, 1993, March on Washington was Urvashi Vaid, then executive director of the National Gay and Lesbian Task Force (NGLTF). Vaid, who was born in India and came to the United States with her parents while still a young child, is an American immigrant success story. While attending college and law school she became a civil rights activist, and then worked as an attorney with Lambda Legal Defense and Education Fund. After joining NGLTF, she held several positions and became director of the organization's research arm, the NGLTF Policy Institute.

As a person of color, Vaid has unfailingly stressed the need for a strong progressive alliance between all the struggles for civil rights. In her speech she articulated the real danger of the right-wing Christian opponents of gay and lesbian rights.

DOCUMENT 140: March on Washington (1993)

With hearts full of love and the abiding faith in justice, we have come to Washington to speak to America. We have come to speak the truth of our lives and silence the liars. We have come to challenge the cowardly Congress to end its paralysis and exercise moral leadership. We have come to defend our honor and win our equality. But most of all we have come in peace and with courage to say, "America, this day marks the return from exile of the gay and lesbian people. We are banished no more. We wander the wilderness of despair no more. We are afraid no more. For on this day, with love in our hearts, we have come out, and we have come out across America to build a bridge of understanding, a bridge of progress, a bridge as solid as steel, a bridge to a land where no one suffers prejudice because of their sexual orientation, their race, their gender, their religion, or their human difference...."

The far right threatens the construction of that bridge....[But] to call our opponents "The Right," states a profound untruth. They are wrong—they are wrong morally, they are wrong spiritually, and they are wrong politically.

The Christian supremacists are wrong spiritually when they demonize us. They are wrong when they reduce the complexity and beauty of our spirit into a freak show. They are wrong spiritually, because, if we are the untouchables of America—if we are the untouchables—then we are, as Mahatma Ghandi said, children of god. And as god's children we know that the gods of our understanding, the gods of goodness and love and righteousness, march right here with us today.

The supremacists who lead the anti-gay crusade are wrong morally. They are wrong because justice is moral, and prejudice is evil; because truth is moral and the lie of the closet is the real sin; because the claim of morality is a subtle sort of subterfuge, a stratagem which hides the real aim which is much more secular....Christian supremacist leaders...don't care about morality, they care about power. They care about social control. And their goal, my friends, is the reconstruction of American Democracy into American Theocracy.

We who are gathered here today must prove the religious right wrong politically, and we can do it. That is our challenge. You know they have made us into the communists of the '90s. And they say they have declared cultural war against us. It's war all right. It's a war about values. On one side are the values that everyone here stands for...traditional American values of democracy and pluralism. On the other side are those who want to turn the Christian church into government....

We believe in democracy, in many voices co-existing in peace, and people of all faiths living together in harmony under a common civil framework known as the United States Constitution. Our opponents believe in monotheism. One way, theirs. One god, theirs. One law, the Old Testament. One nation supreme, the Christian Right one. Let's name it. Democracy battles theism....

To defeat the Right politically, my friends, is our challenge when we leave this March. How can we do it? We've got to march from Washington into action at home. I challenge you to join the National Gay and Lesbian Task Force to fight the Right. We have got to match the power of the Christian supremacists, member for member, vote for vote, dollar for dollar....Volunteer! Every local organization in this country needs you. Every clinic, every hotline, every youth program needs you, needs your time and your love.

And I also challenge our straight liberal allies, liberals and libertarians, independent and conservative, republican or radical. I challenge and invite you to open your eyes and embrace us without fear. The gay rights movement is not a party. It is not a lifestyle. It is not a hair style. It is not a fad or a fringe or a sickness. It is not about sin or salvation. The gay rights movement is an integral part of the American promise of freedom.

We, you and I, each of us, we are the descendents of a proud tradition of people asserting our dignity. It is fitting that the Holocaust Museum [in Washington, D.C.] was dedicated the same weekend as this March, for not only were gay people persecuted by the Nazi state, but gay people are indebted to the struggle of the Jewish people against bigotry and intolerance. It is fitting that the NAACP marches with us, that feminist leaders march with us, because we are indebted to those movements.

When all of us who believe in freedom and diversity see this gathering, we see beauty and power. When our enemies see this gathering, they see the millennium. Perhaps the Right is right about something. We call for the end of the world as we know it. We call for the end of racism and sexism and bigotry as we know it. For the end of violence and discrimination and homophobia as we know it. For the end of sexism as we know it. We stand for freedom as we have yet to know it, and we will not be denied.

Source: "Urvashi Vaid Speaks at the March on Washington" on the Internet at [www.cs.cmu.edu/afs/cs.cmu.edu/user/scotts/bulgarians/vaid-mow.html]

*   *   *

By the late twentieth century, subgroups within the gay and lesbian community were gaining attention. Deaf people, for example, must fight for their rights within an "ableist" world. What this means is that those who have certain abilities are often not sensitive to the needs and experiences of those who are not as able. A person who is both hearing-impaired and gay must negotiate multiple cultures as she or he moves between the deaf and the hearing worlds. In some cases this negotiation leads to activism for specific rights. For example, Charisse Heine founded the Lambda Society at the world-renowned Gallaudet University for the deaf. Tome Kane has traveled to many locations to lecture on deaf gay culture, established the Deaf Names Project to identify deaf people who died of AIDS, and chaired a national retreat for deaf people with AIDS.

In 1993, *Eyes of Desire*, a book about deaf gays and lesbians, was published. In this book, an anonymous young African American deaf gay man compared the civil rights of black, deaf, and gay people.

DOCUMENT 141: Deaf, Black, and Gay: Comparative Rights (1993)

The main concern of all my identities is my gayness….Because I see that I have my own rights as a black person already. Then again I have my own rights as a deaf person. As for my rights as a gay person, they are not quite established….

Unfortunately for the black community, homosexuality does not exist in their belief system, because religion plays such a big role in their lives. Many black gays fear that if their families ever found out, they'd be thrown out of the house....The black community should wake up and try to educate its people to accept homosexuality....

I'm thankful that I was born in the right year—if I were any older, I would've been beaten up by white people. Or I would've been sent to a deaf residential school due to my deafness. Or I would've been beaten to death because of my gayness....

Of course, I'll always struggle to prove that I can do it as a black person by being educated, as a deaf person by being successful, and as a gay person by preserving my rights. If I were living in a different time in another world, I wouldn't have all those privileges. I wouldn't be here and you wouldn't be able to interview me like this....

I'd like to tell every black deaf gay person: "You are not alone in this country. Be glad that you have friends around to give you support. If you don't have any friends, then go find a gay organization that interests you...[or] move somewhere else that can provide you with a list of gay resources. That way you can get all the support you need. It's also important not to lose your true identities. They make you a whole person."

Source: Raymond Luczak, ed., *Eyes of Desire: A Deaf Gay and Lesbian Reader* (Boston: Alyson Publications, 1993), pp. 39–42.

*   *   *

Gay activists realized they could not be successful in the struggle for equality as long as they were not portrayed accurately in the mass media. The National Lesbian and Gay Journalists Association began to impact the broadcast and print news media. The story of how that change occurred was presented by Richard Rouillard, editor of *The Advocate*:

DOCUMENT 142: Impact of Gays on the Media (1994)

"If it ain't on the six o'clock news, it ain't news," an editor at one of the Hearst newspapers once told me. In 1990, NBC, CBS, and ABC couldn't avoid us anymore. Week after week, we were six o'clock news. We had always made news, but the networks and mainstream newspapers had been able to ignore us with impunity. Twenty years of gonzo gay activism paid off handsomely....

Journalists flocked to the new controversies like moths to a flame, charring their own prejudices in the process. Straight journalists got gayed up, and began questioning their own attitudes toward gays. Once again,

American journalism at work demonstrated that prejudice revealed is prejudice reviled....

Another challenge to American media quietly emerged. Leroy Aarons, the gay executive editor of the *Oakland Tribune*, a highly respected California daily, conducted a survey of more than two hundred self-identified gay and lesbian journalists from mainstream publications across the country. The results—the majority of reporters maintained that their papers were doing a mediocre job covering gay issues—were presented to the all-powerful American Society of Newspaper Editors (ASNE) by Aarons. ASNE directors subsequently asked editors to prohibit antigay discrimination at their papers....When *Houston Post* columnist Juan Palomo attempted to come out in his column and was censored by his editors, Aarons was there, this time with a small but burgeoning coalition of reporters and editors, the core group of what has become the eight-hundred-strong National Lesbian and Gay Journalists Association. The *Post* caved in to the ensuing bad-mouthing they received. Palomo kept his job.

Operating on two fronts in 1990—inside the newsrooms and outside on the streets—the gay nation changed forever the anachronistic ways in which we had been portrayed by the American media: neurotic, tragic, and morally perverse. Reporters and editors came out in droves, not to advocate but to mediate. The gay and lesbian caucuses at the nation's largest dailies, *The New York Times* and the *Los Angeles Times*, began to convince their straight editors that newsworthy stories existed in the gay community, justifiably newsworthy by any paper's objective standards. They argued that the media could no longer ignore the facts of our existence. And they were heard.

Source: Richard Rouillard, "Year of the Queer," quoted in Thompson, *Long Road to Freedom*, pp. 357–358.

*   *   *

After the defeat of Measure 9 in Oregon in 1992, the antigay Oregon Citizens Alliance (OCA) sponsored Measure 13, still another state-level referendum to try to prevent gay rights. Their effort in 1994 was opposed by a coalition of groups, including Parents and Friends of Lesbians and Gays (PFLAG). Over the years, parents in PFLAG have not only helped personal acceptance in families on an individual level, but they have become active supporters of gay and lesbian rights.

The main focus of debate on Measure 13 was whether or not homosexuals could be classified as a minority group for protection under the law. The OCA said laws prohibiting discrimination constituted "special rights" for homosexuals, whereas opponents said antidiscrimination laws only provided protections for homosexuals to have the same rights as everyone else.

Scott Lively, representing the Oregon Citizens Alliance, wrote in the 1994 Oregon state *Voters' Pamphlet* that Measure 13

DOCUMENT 143: PFLAG Supports Gay and Lesbian Children (1994)

Stops minority status, affirmative action, quotas, and special rights based on homosexuality (section 1). Prohibits promotion of homosexuality to children by schools, teachers, or agencies (section 2). Preserves existing marriage laws as a union of one man and one woman—not two or more homosexuals (sub-section 2a)....The most important part of Measure 13 is the protection of our children in the public schools. For several years homosexual and pro-gay teachers and administrators have been pushing for approval of homosexuality in the school system. Many schools, such as South Eugene High, have held "Gay-Pride" celebrations and/or sponsored activist homosexual speakers. Age of the children has not been a deterrent. In Cottage Grove the Head Start program used the lesbian "children's" book, "Heather Has Two Mommies."...Existing school policies are obviously not enough to protect our children from this aggressive political agenda. We need a no-nonsense law that keeps this agenda away from our kids. Protect our children.

In response, Candace Steele, of Parents, Families and Friends of Lesbians and Gays, wrote in the *Voters' Pamphlet*:

My family is one of hundreds in Oregon which have beloved children and other cherished family members who happen to be gay or lesbian. In the shadows are thousands of other Oregonians who fear discrimination for themselves and their loved ones in the climate of intolerance and prejudice that this measure creates.

Our loved ones right now can be fired from the jobs they competently perform, or can be forced from their homes, simply because they are gay or are perceived to be gay. Today in Oregon this is perfectly legal. This ballot measure's intent and action is to make permanent this discrimination against our families. It specifically targets homosexuals as the only group to be barred forever from protection against intolerance and prejudice. This measure violates our nation's constitutional principles of equal protection.

Our loved ones do not ask for quotas nor affirmative action. These are specifically prohibited in the Oregon State Constitution. What they seek are exactly the same protections that all other citizens of Oregon and the United States possess. In the name of basic justice, prevent this senseless wrong! Vote no on 13!

Our gay and lesbian young people do not choose their orientation, nor are they recruited by others. Our gay teens are often taunted, physically attacked, and sometimes killed. They are told lies that they are worthless and evil. They survive in isolation and fear, dropping out of school, and running away from home. Some are driven to alcohol and drugs, or to suicide. This cruel, mean-spirited measure permanently denies them accurate knowledge about themselves. Other children will grow up in the ignorance that leads to bigotry. Will you destroy the hope of all our children to be productive and valued? *All* children, ours and yours, need and deserve love and respect. Please vote no on 13 to nurture all Oregon's children.

Source: Voters' Pamphlet, State of Oregon General Election November 8, 1994, pp. 77, 78, 85, 90.

*   *   *

In a public letter to Catholics in Oregon in 1994, Monsignor William B. Smith, a professor of moral theology at St. Joseph's Catholic Seminary in Yonkers, New York, argued in favor of Measure 13. He referred to homosexuality as "an intrinsic moral evil" and as "disordered," a term that was popularized by Pope John Paul II in 1986. Despite Rev. Smith's appeal, Oregon voters rejected Measure 13 by a margin of 52 percent to 48 percent.

DOCUMENT 144: Catholic Condemnation of Homosexuality (1994)

Homosexuality is a behavior to which no one has a moral right and therefore to legislate against it or to deny it privileged and protected status in civil law offends no human nor civil right and is not therefore a form of invidious discrimination. It is of course deplorable that homosexual persons have been or are the object of malice in speech or action. Nevertheless it is improper to accept homosexual behavior as normal in reaction to any crimes committed against homosexual persons or to claim that the homosexual condition is not disordered. It is also wrong to protect behavior to which no one has any conceiveable [sic] right, such as the behavior of homosexuality.

"Sexual orientation" as a condition or inclination does not constitute a quality comparable to race or ethnic background. It is not just inappropriate but positively erroneous and misleading to compare or equate homosexual orientation as the legal or social equivalent of race, color, religion, gender, age or national origin. None of these is ordered toward an intrinsic moral evil; whereas, homosexual orientation is so ordered.

Source: Msgr. William B. Smith, S.T.D., "To Oregon Catholics," *Voters' Pamphlet*, State of Oregon General Election November 8, 1994, p. 80.

*   *   *

By the 1990s, organizations which opposed gay and lesbian rights used personal testimony from individuals who had been actively homosexual, but who later rejected their participation in the gay community. Some of these individuals had become nonsexual or celibate, while others claimed to have become heterosexual. Their reasons for being disillusioned with a gay relationship varied, but personal unhappiness seemed to be the most common reason. Just as with people who had experienced an unhappy heterosexual relationship and switched to a same-sex relationship, what this phenomenon demonstrated was the ability of some people to have flexibility in their sexual object choice. A statement by Richard Weller, who belonged to an organization called Ex-Homosexuals for Truth, was used by the Oregon Citizens Alliance to support their antigay agenda in 1994.

DOCUMENT 145: Ex-Gays Condemn Gay Rights (1994)

My name is Richard Weller. When I was 17 I was recruited into the gay lifestyle by an older homosexual man. Like so many young people who get drawn into homosexuality I was lonely and naive. Eleven years and six homosexual relationships later I finally sought help. Now I am a normal heterosexual man, dedicated to helping young people avoid the mistakes I made.

For many years I told people I was just born gay to get acceptance. If we were born gay that took away any personal responsibility for our behavior and made people feel sorry for us. All along we knew it was a convenient lie, but it was our word against theirs. Today I am living proof that homosexuals can and do change. I was deep in the lifestyle, spending nine years in one relationship and even thought about getting "married."

Homosexuals put on a good public image, but MANY homosexual men try to recruit young boys and often succeed. All pedophile-rights groups in America are made up of homosexual men. The North American Man/Boy Love Association (NAMBLA) which has advertised in Oregon gay newspapers is just one of several. Most boys who get picked up by homosexuals are not part of the statistics. They are usually older, from 12–17, and they don't have good parental supervision. They usually don't report the sex because they are ashamed or believe they are old enough to decide for themselves.

The problem with "gay rights" is that it makes kids more willing to go along with homosexuality. When the government and teachers tell kids that homosexuality is just another normal lifestyle, they are easier for adult predators to seduce. I know what I'm talking about. I was one of those kids.

I am only one voice against all the pro-gay bias in the media, but mine is the voice of experience.

Source: Richard Weller, "The Voice They Want Silenced," *Voters' Pamphlet*, State of Oregon General Election November 8, 1994, p. 79.

* * *

Sexual minority youth experience all the challenges of adolescence and in addition must often deal with feelings of being different and of being rejected by family, church, and friends. In this essay, a bisexual eighteen-year-old in Wisconsin writes about how she dealt with acknowledging her bisexuality, coming out, and finding a supportive community.

DOCUMENT 146: Bisexual Young Woman Speaks Out (1994)

Most of the time, I call myself bisexual, but I dislike labels. They tend to box you in. My sexuality changes from day to day....I realized I wasn't straight about three years ago....I became very scared [and] avoided the issue for another year....But then I fell in love with one of my teachers—a married woman. This time I couldn't deny what I felt....It scared me to death. I was obsessed with keeping it a secret....I was suicidal many times during that period. I had very low self-esteem. I had problems with my parents, and was getting low grades in school....

[After I came out I attended a gay pride parade in Milwaukee, where I saw] thousands of gay people, all over the place. Loud and proud! It was incredible. Nothing made me feel better than being surrounded by all these people who were just like me....I have a wide network of friends who listen when I have problems with my parents or get sick of the straight world....Sometimes I wish I was straight. I wish I was "normal" like everyone else. But being gay and being involved in the gay community has made me a stronger person. I am not ashamed of what I am. I feel pride when I see one of "my people" in Congress; honor when I see them battling discrimination in the military; respect when my friends risk arrest to fight AIDS; and dignity when I speak to a high school group and tell them we are people, just like them.

I want to do something for the gay community, especially gay and lesbian youth. We carry the heaviest burden. We are already dealing with everything that all teenagers have to go through. Then, on top of that, we have to deal with society's taboos against our sexuality, rejection from family and friends, gay bashers and AIDS. I'm surprised any of us makes it.

Source: Jennifer Hanrahan, in *Two Teenagers in Twenty: Writings by Gay and Lesbian Youth*, ed. Ann Heron (Boston, Alyson Publications, 1994), pp. 172–176.

*   *   *

By the time her son Tyler was born in 1991, Sharon Bottoms was divorcing her husband. The court awarded custody of the infant to her. Though Tyler lived with and was cared for primarily by Sharon, he also spent a lot of time with Sharon's mother Kay Bottoms. A year later Sharon met a woman named April Wade, and they fell in love. After several months, they moved in together and decided to raise Tyler as their son. April continued to work at her job as manager of a gift shop, in order to support Sharon so she could stay at home as a full-time mother raising the infant boy.

Kay Bottoms was upset that Sharon had decided to keep Tyler full time. When Kay found out that Sharon and April were in a lesbian relationship, Kay was disgusted. She sued in court to gain custody of her grandson. Normally courts give a mother custody rights over a grandparent, but Kay claimed that Sharon was unsuitable as a mother because she had become a lesbian. No evidence was introduced to show that either Sharon or her partner April had mistreated or neglected Tyler, but that did not prevent the Virginia trial court from awarding custody of the boy to the grandmother. Because Sharon Bottoms was honest about admitting in court testimony that she engaged in oral sex with April, that statement put her in violation of the Virginia sodomy law. With this admission, the court ruled that she was a habitual criminal and a felon, and therefore not a fit mother for a child. Sharon was given limited visitation rights with her son, but only if April was not present.

DOCUMENT 147: Sharon Bottoms Child Custody Court Case (1994)

Sharon appealed this decision to the Virginia Court of Appeals, which ruled in 1994 that the lower court had erred. The Court of Appeals Decision is excerpted:

In this child custody appeal, we find the evidence insufficient to support the trial court's decision to remove custody of a three-year-old child from his natural parent....A child's best interest is presumed to be served by being in the custody of the child's natural parent, rather than a non-parent. A non-parent is granted custody over a parent only when the parent is unfit....The evidence showed that Sharon Bottoms is and has been a fit and nurturing parent who has adequately provided and cared for her son....Bottoms' open lesbian relationship has had no visible or discernible effect on her son. While the child has spent considerable time with his grandmother, Kay Bottoms, the evidence proved that he and his mother, Sharon Bottoms, have had a close, loving mother-child relationship....Unless a parent, by his or her conduct or condition, is unfit or is unable and unwilling to provide or care for a child, a court is not entitled to...take custody of a child from his or her parents....In this instance, the open lesbian relationship and illegality of the mother's sexual activity are the only significant factors that the court considered in finding Sharon Bottoms to be an unfit parent. The fact that a parent is homosexual does not per se render a parent unfit to have custody of his or her child.

Source: Sharon Bottoms v. Pamela Kay Bottoms, Court of Appeals Record No. 1930–93–2.

*   *   *

After the above decision, Kay Bottoms appealed to the Virginia Supreme Court. In 1995 the Supreme Court reversed the decision of the Appellate Court, declaring that Tyler's best interest was living with his grandmother. Sharon Bottoms continued to try to get her son back, but finally gave up in exhaustion. Tyler Bottoms continues to reside with his grandmother, as a result of this majority decision, written by Justice Compton:

Although the presumption favoring a parent over a non-parent is strong, it is rebutted when certain factors, such as parental unfitness, are established by clear and convincing evidence....Other important considerations include the nature of the home environment and moral climate in which the child is to be raised....Conduct inherent in lesbianism is punishable [under the Virginia sodomy law] as a Class 6 felony in the Commonwealth, Code 18.2–361; thus that conduct is another important consideration is determining custody....The record shows a mother who, although devoted to her son, refuses to subordinate her own desires and priorities to the child's welfare....Living daily under conditions stemming from active lesbianism practiced in the home may impose a burden upon a child by reason of the social condemnation attached to such an arrangement, which will inevitably afflict the child's relationships with his peers and with the community.

Source: Sharon Lynne Bottoms v. Pamela Kay Bottoms, Virginia Supreme Court, Record No. 941166.

*   *   *

After the 1993 Hawai'i Supreme Court decision in support of same-sex marriage, civil rights attorney Daniel Foley approached the Hawai'i chapter of the Japanese American Citizens League (JACL), and asked them to endorse same-sex marriage. Both the Hawai'i chapter and the national board of JACL approved a supportive resolution in early 1994. However, the Mormon-dominated JACL chapter in Utah objected and called for a vote at the League's National Convention, held in Salt Lake City in August 1994.

In response, several Asian American gays and lesbians in San Francisco and Los Angeles formed an ad hoc committee to lobby JACL members on behalf of the board's decision to support same-sex marriage. They asked J Craig Fong, a Chinese American civil rights attorney and director of the western office of Lambda Legal Defense and Education Fund, Inc., which was serving as co-counsel in the Hawai'i same-sex marriage case, to address the convention. According to Fong:

DOCUMENT 148: Japanese American Citizens League Supports Legalizing Same-Sex Marriage (1994)

The ad hoc committee, with keen knowledge and experience of both [Japanese American and gay] communities, performed spectacularly. They created brochures that explained the economic benefits of marriage, [and distributed] a question-and-answer handout that dispelled particular Asian myths about queers....Finally, the committee organized a cadre of about one dozen pan-Asian queers that went to Salt Lake City, set up an information booth, and lobbied JACL members.

I addressed the convention on Friday, August 5. I highlighted the civil rights connection between queer issues and those confronting Japanese-Americans....I pointed out mainstream America's long history of dehumanizing people of color by dictating who can and cannot be included in their families—that slaves were forbidden to marry, that slave families could be torn asunder, and that, as recently as 1967, interracial couples were illegal in sixteen states. The prohibition against same-sex marriage is, I said, another example of the government telling people what their families should look like. As I spoke, I could see eyebrows furrowing and heads nodding as, at least for some delegates, the connection was made. For them it was no longer about sex; it was about family. Now some of them understood that it was not a special right but a civil right.

Final debate of the issue on Saturday, August 6, was acrimonious. Although I felt my own presentation had gone well the afternoon before, I was not convinced that enough minds had been changed. Then U.S. Congressman Norm Mineta, a Japanese-American with a long respected history in JACL, rose and asked to address the convention. Mineta's remarks clearly framed the issue: JACL's credibility as a civil rights organization was at stake. [He said:]

I believe it would be disastrous if this Convention were to repudiate the action of our National Board in this matter. There are those who have argued that gay rights issues are not Japanese-American issues. I cannot think of any more dangerous precedent for this organization to set than to take a position on an issue of principle based solely on how it directly affects Americans of Japanese ancestry.

When we fought our decade-long battle for redress [for Japanese-Americans interned in relocation camps during World War II], we won. We could not have done so if we had stood alone in that fight. Where would we be today if the [African American] NAACP, or the [Latino] National Council of La Raza, or the National Gay and Lesbian Task Force had taken the position that redress was a Japanese-American issue—and had nothing to do with African Americans, Hispanic Americans, or gay and lesbian Americans? Those organizations, and their members, joined us because they understood and believed in our argument that a threat to the civil rights of one American is a threat to the rights of all Americans. They acted based on that principle—and not on a narrow evaluation of how redress affected their own communities. How can we as an organization turn around today and say that the civil rights of other Americans have nothing to do with us?

Mineta also scolded the delegates, reminding them that without the support of Massachusetts representative Barney Frank, redress for Japanese-American internees might not have happened. Frank, a gay congressman with only a tiny Japanese-American constituency, was instrumental in reporting the redress bill out of the House Administrative Law Subcommittee, where it had been stuck for many years.

The convention floor fell silent. I could physically feel the last opposition weaken and melt away. The vote was called, and the national convention voted overwhelmingly to continue its endorsement of same-sex marriage. The members of the ad hoc committee embraced one another and cried....

The fear that legions of conservative JACL members would bolt the organization did not materialize. Only a few members resigned. Further, JACL found new members, as the ad hoc committee swelled to become one of its newest chapters, the Asian Pacific Islander Lambda chapter. And the gay and lesbian community gained a new ally—an ally with over twenty-five thousand members nationally....

The ad hoc committee was simply a group of queer Asian Pacific Islanders who realized that there was a job to do, though none was an acknowledged, high-profile leader of the national queer community.... Queers and people of color alike must recognize that homophobia, racism, sexism, anti-Semitism, discrimination based on physical ability, anti-immigrant xenophobia, and other discriminatory isms all have the same roots. The same social dynamic created them all: the mainstream population's ability to isolate particular groups and characterize them as unequal, apart, and unworthy.

The radical right has also been successful in dividing us at a time when we should be standing together....Which group will next be in the radical right's gunsights? The social dynamic is the same. Only the targets change....

If we as a movement do not find the wherewithal to approach, work with, ally with, and maintain meaningful contact with other groups, we have little hope to create the environment needed to secure our liberties and our place at the political table....At stake is not only our freedom as queers, but the freedom of all people who can be singled out by a vicious, mean-spirited majority. If we cannot understand this and stand united against the tide, I despair of winning the liberty so cherished by us all.

Source: J Craig Fong, "Building Alliances: The Case of the Japanese American Citizens League Endorsement of Same-Sex Marriage," in *Overcoming Heterosexism and Homophobia: Strategies That Work,* ed. James T. Sears and Walter L. Williams (New York: Columbia University Press, 1997), pp. 375–379.

* * *

Lesbians of color are caught between an allegiance to themselves as women and allegiance to their cultural/ethnic/racial communities, which too often are sexist and homophobic. Like many other lesbian groups, lesbians of color groups also work on behalf of a variety of social causes. Lesbians of color continue to work with their brothers of color in cogender organizations, but in order to meet their specific needs they often form separate committees within the larger organization. In some cases, they have separated totally and/or formed their own lesbian-only groups. Below is a statement from the 10th Anniversary Celebration program of Lesbians Unidas, a Latina lesbian group active in Los Angeles between 1984 and the mid-1990s.

DOCUMENT 149: Lesbianas Unidas (1994)

As Latinas and as women we are hidden from history....Our herstory is scattered here and there in boxes, file cabinets and garages....In 1978 a group of Asian, African American, Latina and Native Americans gathered to form Lesbians of Color (LOC). It was the first time in L.A....that lesbians of color organized specifically for the purpose of politically and publicly demanding recognition....On another front, Gay Latinos was formed in 1981 by a small group of men who felt the need to create an organization that was culturally and politically relevant to who they were....Eventually a few Latina lesbians joined the group…the (Lesbian Task Force) was formed to encourage more Latina participation…the name of the [larger] organization was changed to include the word lesbian and became Gay and Lesbian Latinos Unidos…[in] 1984, the name of the [lesbian] task force was changed to Lesbianas Unidas.

Lesbianas Unidas (LU) was initially formed to serve as a support group and to address the specific needs of politicized, feminist Latina lesbians (many of whom were also lesbian separatists). Our original stated purpose included not only working for the elimination of negative stereotypes but also working to address racism, classism, homophobia and sexism which was then (and which remains now) present both in society as well as our own communities.…

It is important to note a few of our accomplishments…an annual retreat since 1984, [marching] in the 25th anniversary of the Chicano Moratorium, marches with César Chavez and Jesse Jackson against the Simpson-Mazolli bill [to prevent "illegal" immigration], Dia de La Mujer [Woman's Day celebration], Primer Encuentro de Lesbianas Feministas de Latinoamerica y el Caribe [First Gathering of Feminist Lesbians from Latin America and the Caribbean]…support groups…donations of money and labor [to]: Project 10 [a high school lesbian and gay support program], a hospital in Nicaragua, a lesbian group in Mexico [working] with earthquake victims…LU continues to provide the space and encouragement for Latina lesbians to develop their potential as leaders and organizers. Que viva[n] lesbianas Caribenas, que viva[n] lesbianas Chicanas, Que viva[n] lesbianas Latinas [long live Caribbean lesbians, long live Chicana lesbians, long live Latina lesbians].

Source: Lesbianas Unidas 10th Anniversary Program, 1994.

*   *   *

By the 1990s, the queer community had overcome its defensiveness against the attacks of fundamentalist religious leaders, and instead began attacking the contradictions of the religious right itself. A typical example was published by two lesbian and gay theologians in 1995.

DOCUMENT 150: Exposing the Religious Right (1995)

Portraying homosexuals as the aggressors has been an effective ploy in garnering support for the religious right's ideals and in creating an atmosphere of paranoia. But this caricature of homosexuals is as laughable as the ant who threatened to trample the elephant underfoot. The most threatening demand made by homosexuals is that they be permitted to openly exist without the fear of being assaulted, murdered, or fired from their jobs. The misrepresentation of homosexuals [is] the ubiquitous "them" lurking invisibly in our midst....If openly expressing who you are is not considered radical for straights, then how can it be viewed as combative behavior when applied to homosexuals?...

Some right wing politicians have had the bald-faced audacity to refer to homosexuals as a "special interest group," with the implication that they are a group who seek some sort of privilege which the rest of the country does not already enjoy. The unassailable civil liberties which the majority take for granted take on the status of "special interests" when extended to homosexuals. What makes them so special when applied to gay men and lesbians as opposed to anyone else? This is an obvious double standard. Are homosexuals to be blamed because they take issue with paying dues to a club which refuses to admit them?...

The time has finally come for the [heterosexual] patriarch (and his loyal spouse) to justify the privileges which they have enjoyed without restraint in terms which do not boil down to some "special interest" of their own....

In a country where a rape occurs every six minutes, the hypothetical threat to society posed by homosexuality is a red herring....Not one conservative Christian figurehead has made a national issue out of the rape epidemic....[Why is there no] fear and concern among Christians who purport to be concerned about society as a whole?

Source: Theresa Murray and Michael McClure, *Moral Panic: Exposing the Religious Right's Agenda on Sexuality* (New York: Cassell, 1995), pp. 28–29, 51.

* * *

Concerned about the lack of action on lesbian rights, in 1992 six activist women in New York City founded a group called the Lesbian Avengers. Their goal was to get lesbians involved in dramatic nonviolent actions that would focus media attention on lesbian and gay issues. Their first action was in support of a plan to educate students in New York public schools about diversity. What was called the Rainbow Curriculum included information on gays and lesbians. After heterosexist activists tried to prevent the curriculum from being used, the Lesbian Avengers planned an action at an elementary school in the suburb of Queens.

As with other examples given in this book, the founding of the Lesbian Avengers shows the power of every-day people—sometimes only one person or a few people—to take history into their own hands and make a difference in social change. In a media-driven society, sometimes only dramatic action can attract attention. The direct action tactics of the Avengers attracted both support and criticism. Some critics felt that their tactics provoke a conservative backlash. Maxine Wolfe, one of the original Avengers, was interviewed by Laraine Sommella in 1995 about the 1992 beginnings of the group.

DOCUMENT 151: The Lesbian Avengers (1995)

We decided that we would give out club cards at Gay Pride, which was coming up in June. We each chipped in thirty-three dollars to pay for the making of eight thousand club cards. Sarah [Schulman] and someone else wrote the original text of the club card, which said something like "Lesbians, dykes, gay women: Cold-blooded liars like George Bush in the White House—what did they ever do for us? Religion. The State. Who cares. We want revenge and we want it now. What have you got to lose?" And then we put down the phone number of the telephone in the upstairs part of my house and set up a tape machine. When you called the number, the tape said "You have reached the Lesbian Avengers. We're planning our first action for the first day of school in September against the community school boards that have refused to accept the Rainbow curriculum. If you want to be part of the planning, come to our first meeting."…We gave the cards out only to lesbians who were not in the March. We did not want women who were already committed to nine thousand other groups. We wanted to reach women who were new. Seventy lesbians showed up.…

We decided that the only way to do anything about this was to do something that nobody else would do. The women who came to the first meeting were all willing to do this. They were risk-takers. They had called a number they knew nothing about that they got from a card handed to them by someone they did not know. They knew that they were coming to a meeting about doing something on the first day of school about the Rainbow curriculum. Then word-of-mouth kicked in, and every week new women would show up. And what were their biggest issues? Their biggest issues were, "Aren't we using children, who are going to school on the first day, when it's already so chaotic and so upsetting to them already, and isn't this going to be terrible for kids?" And I said, "As someone who has two kids, this is what's going to happen. The first day of school is going to be great. The first day of school, these kids are going to get balloons and marching bands. They're going to think, 'Wow! This is fantastic!' And then the second day of school we're not going to be there and they're going to think, 'Oh my God. This is so boring. I can't believe it.'"…

The other issue was that we had come up with this idea to make balloons that said "Ask about lesbian lives." People were really upset about that—these new women who would come in later weeks to the planning meeting. And we would have to go through the same argument again and again. They said "How can you give those balloons to children? That's really manipulating them." And I would then say, "What if the balloons said 'Save the Whales'?" The trademark of what the Avengers wanted to do was to be in a place and confront the issue that is the "no-no." Gay people connected to kids. That's where everyone falls apart—especially in Queens sub-urbs....So we actually marched around the school and the kids were coming in for the first day of school and we handed out balloons and we had a marching band and sang songs like "We Are Family."...

That became our trademark—to do cutting edge stuff—out in places where people don't want us to be out....Lesbians have always been at the forefront of all movements for social change and most often in the leadership, especially in the women's movement, but they've been closeted. We wanted to be out and we wanted to do something for ourselves because no one ever does anything for lesbians. No one....

We [also] have a Lesbian Avengers civil-rights organizing project....This year we sent [representatives] to live and work in rural northern Idaho to do "out" organizing against Proposition One there—much to the chagrin of the mainstream lesbian and gay campaign there, who were once again going to do a campaign that did not mention lesbians and gay men, even though the right wing mentions us all the time....In New York City, we just did a series of coalition actions...with Las Buenas Amigas...and African American Women Organized for Societal Change....We [also] went to the Alice Austen House which is a National Historical Landmark [on Staten Island]. Alice Austin was a dyke photographer at the turn of the century...but the people who run the house refuse to admit that she was a lesbian and that she lived in it for 33 years with her lover....We went out there when they had "nautical day" dressed as turn-of-the-century life guards and carrying big life preservers that said "dyke preserver" on them...we do serious politics.

Source: Interview with Maxine Wolfe by Laraine Sommella. "This Is About People Dying: The Tactics of Early ACT UP and Lesbian Avengers in New York City," in *Queers in Space: Communities, Public Spaces, Sites of Resistance*, ed. Gordon Brent Ingram, Anne-Marie Bouthillette, and Yolanda Retter (Seattle: Bay Press, 1997), pp. 407–437.

* * *

Even in the 1990s, anyone who dresses in the clothes of the other gender takes their life in their hands. For transgender persons who pass as the other sex, being exposed publicly can subject them to violence and even murder. A case in point is a Female-To-Male (FTM) transgen-der person whose birth name was Teena Brandon, but who in 1993 moved from Lincoln, Nebraska, to the nearby small town of Humbolt and began living full time as a man under the name of Brandon Teena. Brandon easily passed as a man, and was befriended by two men, John

Lotter and Marvin Nissen. At one point the local police arrested Brandon for forging a check, and after seeing the "F" (for "Female") on Brandon's driver license did a physical inspection and publicly released this information to the local newspaper. After Lotter and Nissen read the newspaper story they confronted and forcibly stripped Brandon, then subjected Brandon to rape. When Brandon went to the police for protection, the police did not respond, and several days later Lotter and Nissen searched out their former friend and killed Brandon and two of Brandon's friends in a bloody murder. The local murder trial, in which Lotter was sentenced to death and Nissen to life imprisonment, was commented upon by Davina Anne Gabriel of FTM International.

DOCUMENT 152: Brandon Teena Murder Trial (1996)

The Brandon Teena murder shocked us all, even though it should have come as no real surprise to any of us. I think back on it today, and even now it fills me with rage....[It] is a good example of just what is wrong with the world we live in. Brandon Teena was someone who was trying to live his own life in the only way he knew how. He made a lot of mistakes, but none of them deserved a death sentence....

Richardson County sheriff Charles B. Laux...stat[ed] of Brandon that "you can call it 'it' as far as I'm concerned...." Local authorities have denied that their outing of Brandon in any way contributed to his killers' motives, and have declined to classify it as a hate crime. However, Lotter's sister has confirmed that both Lotter and Nissen were enraged after learning that Brandon was anatomically female, but had been living as a man and was even dating a local woman....

When one is willing to kill a "friend" who violates the gender binary system, it makes one realize how strong it is. Leslie Feinberg [stated]..."It's fair to ask if Brandon Teena would still be alive today if authorities and the local newspaper had not forcibly outed him after he had successfully passed as a male...." Riki Anne Wilchins of Transexual Menace says, "He died for the right to be a man—to be Brandon Teena."

Source: Davina Anne Gabriel, "Brandon Teena Murderer Sentenced," Internet Web site [http://songweaver.com/gender/teena-sentencing.html] posted on February 21, 1996. See also [http://www.ftm-intl.org/Hist/Bran/]

*   *   *

After a slight majority of voters in Colorado's 1992 election passed Amendment 2 of the state's constitution, to prevent gay rights laws from being enacted by local governments in the state, the American Civil Liberties Union (ACLU) and Lambda Legal Defense and Education Fund filed suit. They were successful in getting the Colorado Supreme Court to agree that the amendment was unconstitutional, but supporters of Amendment 2 appealed that decision to the United States Supreme Court. In 1996 the United States Supreme Court upheld the Colorado Supreme Court in *Romer v. Evans*. When the news arrived about this un-precedentedly supportive decision by the United States Supreme Court, Matt Coles, director of the ACLU's Lesbian and Gay Rights Project, re-called his presentation to ACLU's National Board of Directors.

DOCUMENT 153: *Romer v. Evans* (1996)

I don't think I will ever forget the Board meeting that day. I had barely begun speaking when it began to hit me, so strongly it seemed almost pal-pable: a wave of pure joy cascading across the room. These folks were not merely happy about a job well done; they were not just gratified that an im-portant idea had finally won acceptance on the Court. The women and men of the ACLU Board were thrilled because winning this case about equality for lesbians and gay men was something they cared about deeply, not just in their heads, but in their hearts. To the Board, this was not just a victory for lesbians and gay men; this was "our" victory....

Romer v. Evans is undoubtedly the greatest gay rights victory in court of all time. The Court overturned Amendment 2 and restored the power of states and cities to pass gay rights laws. Even more stunning, it swept aside the essentially political argument that gay rights laws were "special rights" by observing that there is nothing "special" about the right to participate in day to day life on an equal footing with everyone else. But maybe most im-portant of all, the Court issued an opinion that treated lesbians, gay men and bisexuals with respect. The legal and political damage done by *Bowers v. Hardwick* was over.

But of course, the fight for lesbian and gay rights is not. The Colorado case did not end the fight for gay rights; it simply ensured that we could keep fighting in the courts and in the legislatures. And keep fighting we will. Along with Lambda Legal Defense...[and] the National Center for Lesbian Rights, the ACLU is challenging systemic discrimination against lesbian and gay youth in schools...challenging bans on adoption by lesbians and gay men...striking down sodomy laws...and in passing an employment nondiscrimination law. And we'll keep at it....Until equality and dignity for our families is not an aspiration, but reality. Until it is all over, and the guar-antees enumerated in the Bill of Rights apply equally to all of us.

Source: Matt Coles, "Looking Back: Lesbian and Gay Rights, AIDS, and the ACLU," *Lesbian & Gay Rights, AIDS/HIV, 2000: An ACLU Report* (New York: American Civil Liberties Union, 2000), pp. 4, 8.

*   *   *

Prompted by the Hawai'i same-sex marriage court case, members of Congress who were opposed to same-sex marriages introduced a bill into the United States Congress that would allow any state to deny legal recognition to a marriage between two persons of the same sex even if it was recognized in another state. This Defense of Marriage Act, introduced into the House of Representatives on January 3, 1996 (as House Resolution 3396), voided the "full faith and credit" clause of the United States Constitution, which requires one state to recognize the laws passed in another state.

The Defense of Marriage Act also amended Chapter 1 or title 1, of the United States Code, to the end of section 7, the definition that, "the word 'marriage' means only a legal union between one man and one woman as husband and wife, and the word 'spouse' refers only to a person of the opposite sex who is a husband or a wife." Thus, even if a state legalized same-sex marriages, the United States government would not allow a United States citizen to gain legal residence for a noncitizen immigrant spouse unless that spouse is of the other sex. This act thus incorporates legal discrimination against same-sex couples into federal law.

In the House of Representatives, Democratic Congressman Henry Waxman from California saw the Defense of Marriage Act as a cynical attempt by Republicans to force President Clinton either to betray his gay and lesbian supporters, or to suffer a major controversy just as he was campaigning to be reelected to a second term.

DOCUMENT 154: Defense of Marriage Act (1996)

The proponents of H.R. 3396 would have us believe that this legislation is necessary to save the institution of marriage. The real purpose of H.R. 3396 is to create a wedge issue for Republicans in the upcoming elections. In a shameless attempt to divide the American public, the Republican party is espousing official bigotry. It is promoting discrimination against individuals who seek the same responsibilities and opportunities other Americans seek when they form a lifelong union with someone they love. It is scapegoating a segment of our society to fan the flames of intolerance and prejudice. And it is doing this to try to improve its standings in the polls.

Discrimination against people who are gay and committed to one another does nothing to defend marriage or to strengthen family values. It does, however, continue to deny them legal rights that married couples simply take for granted—inclusion in a spouse's health insurance plan, pension and tax benefits, the ability to participate in medical decisions, and the right to visit a dying spouse in the hospital.

Our nation's families deserve better from their leaders than this cynical effort to raise fears and create divisions for political gain. They need leaders who will recognize the true needs of families and who are willing to work for adequate healthcare, access to educational opportunities, a decent wage, and a livable environment. Let's work together on the real challenges we face as a nation. Let's not allow our Republican leaders to create scapegoats to distract the public's attention from the failure of this Congress to address issues the American public cares about. I urge my colleagues to stand up to bigotry and discrimination. I urge you to vote against this mean-spirited legislation.

Source: Congressman Henry Waxman (D–California), speech before the House of Representative in Committee of the Whole House, July 17, 1996. *Congressional Record*, E1299. [http://www.house.gov/waxman/issues/issues_gay_rights.htm]

* * *

Despite the efforts of liberal Democrats to kill the bill, the Defense of Marriage Act passed the House of Representatives and was introduced into the Senate. North Carolina's conservative Republican Senator Jesse Helms led the successful effort to pass the act, while he opposed another bill sponsored by Democratic Senator Edward Kennedy to prohibit employment discrimination on the basis of sexual orientation. Helms began his speech with the slogan:

"God created Adam and Eve—not Adam and Steve...." Homosexual and lesbian leaders...are demanding that homosexuality be considered as just another lifestyle—these are the people who seek to force their agenda upon the vast majority of Americans who reject the homosexual lifestyle. Indeed, Mr. President, the pending bill—the Defense of Marriage Act—will safeguard the sacred institutions of marriage and the family from those who seek to destroy them and who are willing to tear apart America's moral fabric in the process.

Isn't it disheartening, Mr. President, that Congress must clarify the traditional definition of marriage? But inch by inch, little by little, the homosexual lobby has chipped away at the moral stamina of some of America's courts and some legislators, in order to create the shaky ground that exists today that prompts this legislation....Homosexuals and lesbians boast that they are close to realizing their goal—legitimizing their behavior.

Mr. President, Bill Bennett has championed the cause of preserving America's culture; he contends that we are already reaping the consequences of the devaluation of marriage. And he warns that "it is exceedingly imprudent to conduct a radical, untested, and inherently flawed social experiment on an institution that is the keystone and the arch of civilization."

Bill Bennett is everlastingly right, and I believe the American people in the majority understand that the Defense of Marriage Act is vitally important. It will establish a simple, clear federal definition of marriage as the legal union of one man and one woman, and it will exempt sovereign states from being compelled by a half-baked interpretation of the U.S. Constitution to recognize same-sex marriages wrongfully legalized in another state.

If the Senate, tomorrow, makes the mistake of approving the Employment Nondiscrimination Act proposed by [Edward Kennedy] the senator from Massachusetts, it will pave the way for liberal judges to threaten the business policies of countless American employers, and, in the long run, put in question the legality of the Defense of Marriage Act. The homosexual lobby knows this and that is why there is such a clamor favoring adoption of the Kennedy bill.

Mr. President, at the heart of this debate is the moral and spiritual survival of this nation....We will decide whither goeth America. It is solely up to us.

Source: Senator Jesse Helms (R–N.C.), speech in the Senate, July 11, 1996, *Congressional Record*, pp. S10067–S10068.

*   *   *

When Michael Galluccio and Jon Holden first saw the boy that would become their son, he was three months old and sickly. His liver was enlarged, his lungs were filled with fluid, and he was almost certainly infected with HIV, because his mother was dying of AIDS. He did not have a name. Nonetheless, the two men took him in as a foster child, named him Adam, and nursed him back to health. Fortunately, Adam tested HIV-negative.

After the death of Adam's mother, Galluccio and Holden began the long process necessary to adopt Adam. The state of New Jersey did not have a problem with their sexual orientation, but they did prohibit both homosexual and unmarried heterosexual couples from adopting a child jointly. Galluccio would have to adopt Adam, and then Holden would have to go through the entire expensive and time-consuming process again, only to give him stepparent status. The ACLU filed suit to overturn the regulation preventing joint adoptions in New Jersey in 1997. In October of that year, Judge Sybil R. Moses awarded a joint adoption to Galluccio and Holden, saying that it was in Adam's best interest; this decision was limited only to Adam's adoption. Two months later, Judge Moses expanded her ruling by brokering an agreement with the ACLU and New Jersey's Division of Youth and Family Services; New Jersey became the first state to allow joint adoptions for unmarried couples.

While only one state—Florida—specifically prohibits adoption by homosexuals, only New Jersey specifically treats same-sex couples in the same manner as heterosexual couples. The success of the ACLU's argument had been lauded by gay rights activists, who view it as recognition of the legitimacy of gay parenting. Below is the Introduction to the original ACLU lawsuit.

DOCUMENT 155: Galluccio-Holden Adoption Lawsuit (1997)

1) Plaintiffs bring this civil rights class action for injunctive relief against the New Jersey Department of Human Services ("DHS"); the Division of Youth and Family Services ("DYFS"); William Waldman, Commissioner of DHS; and Michelle Ghul, Deputy Commissioner of DYFS, for violation of New Jersey's adoption statute and the New Jersey and United States Constitutions.

2) N.J.S.A. 9:3–43(a) provides that "[a]ny person may institute an action for adoption, except that a married person may do so only with the written consent of his spouse or jointly with his spouse in the same action." Notwithstanding this statutory language, the administrative regulations of DYFS state that "[I]n the case of an unmarried couple co-habitating, only one person can legally adopt a child." Manual IIM, Sec. 21, Subsec. 31, DYFS Adoption Services (hereinafter referred to as "DYFS's regulation"). Plaintiffs JON HOLDEN, MICHAEL GALLUCCIO, and LAMBDA FAMILIES bring this class action, on behalf of lesbian and gay couples who live together in the State of New Jersey and would like to jointly adopt, challenging the legality of the DYFS regulation.

3) Plaintiffs JON HOLDEN and MICHAEL GALLUCCIO are two men in a long-term, committed relationship who share a home in Maywood, New Jersey and who seek to jointly adopt children together as a family. Plaintiffs HOLDEN and GALLUCCIO applied to DYFS for permission to adopt a child and were approved together as an adoptive family. However, the State of New Jersey will not consent to their joint adoption because they are not married.

4) Under DYFS's regulation a qualified married couple can jointly adopt a child, but a qualified unmarried couple like Plaintiffs HOLDEN and GALLUCCIO must go through a cumbersome and costly two-step process: first, one member of the couple must petition for adoption with the consent of the State, and then the other parent must file a petition for a "second parent adoption" with the courts. This regulation is not authorized by New Jersey's adoption statute, but instead conflicts with the statute because it does not serve the best interests of children. It is therefore ultra vires and invalid.

5) In addition, by allowing a qualified married couple to jointly adopt, requiring a qualified unmarried couple to adopt through a cumbersome and costly two-step process, the DYFS regulation creates a classification that treats unmarried couples differently from married couples. Because there is no rational basis for this differential treatment, the DYFS regulation violates the Equal Protection guarantees of the United States and New Jersey Constitutions. Plaintiffs HOLDEN, GALLUCCIO

and LAMBDA FAMILIES therefore file this class action for injunctive relief and ask this Court to declare the DYFS regulation invalid and enjoin its enforcement.

*   *   *

   An important area of progress for gay and lesbian rights has occurred due to changes in public attitudes, partly as a result of the changing image of homosexuality presented in the mass media. Before the 1970s the dominant images presented of gays and lesbians were sad, pathetic characters who were usually murdered or committed suicide. In 1973 ABC-TV became the first United States television network to air a made-for-TV movie, *That Certain Summer*, which presented gay men as full characters who were presented in a nonstereotypical way. Since the 1970s many movies and television dramas, comedies, and talk shows have dealt with homosexuality as an issue in contemporary culture. These changes have not come about by accident, but because of hard work by gay and lesbian activists operating behind the scenes to influence media executives. The existence of strong gay and lesbian communities in the media capitals of Los Angeles and New York have had a dramatic impact, by organizing letter-writing campaigns, street protests, and one-to-one conversations. A history of this impact is presented by sociology professor Peter Nardi, who was president of the Los Angeles chapter of the Gay and Lesbian Alliance Against Defamation.

DOCUMENT 156: Gay and Lesbian Alliance Against Defamation (1997)

   Attitudes are shaped by the media, and if the media persist in presenting images favorable to the status quo, then is it any wonder that a variety of groups with least access to the control of the media and least visibility in the media should be activists and advocates of reform?...Individuals can have a big effect on the media through letters and calls, [but] it often helps to have the clout and legitimacy of larger organizations and media. Several strategies that have been very successful in combating homophobia and heterosexism include the development of media watchdog organizations and the creation of media by and for lesbian and gay people.

   In 1973 the Gay Activists Alliance (GAA) in New York was one of the first organizations to take on the media when it confronted executives at ABC-TV about unfavorable treatment of homosexuality. A group of GAA members later split to form the National Gay Task Force (NGTF), which then formed a Gay Media Task Force (GMTF) in Los Angeles, under the direction of Newt Deiter. The Association of Gay and Lesbian Artists (AGLA) also started in the early 1980s as a support group of gay media people to lobby the industry, consult on projects, and present awards for positive depictions of gays and lesbians.

Although GMTF and AGLA no longer exist, their efforts led to the formation of the Gay and Lesbian Alliance Against Defamation (GLAAD), begun in New York in 1985, then in 1988 in Los Angeles. Today GLAAD is the largest and most influential national organization, with chapters around the country devoted to monitoring the media's portrayals of gays and lesbians, responding with organized letter-writing actions and protest marches, and consulting with [media] executives and creative staff.

In addition to organizations structured to resist and change stereotypical images, another form of response has been the creation of lesbian and gay media. From cable TV public access shows to computer E-mail, the Internet, newspapers, and slick magazines, gays have developed an impressive communications network.

With the beginning of the modern homophile movement in the early 1950s in Los Angeles, *ONE* became the first widely circulated homosexual magazine…[which] helped create an incipient sense of community. The tradition carries on with…many [national and] local lesbian and gay newspapers.

With the growing power of openly gay and lesbian filmmakers, television and newspaper reporters, and writers, a most effective form of resistance to the hegemonic force of the dominant media is occurring, namely to speak for oneself. However, there is no lesbian or gay equivalent to the Christian cable networks or the numerous syndicated conservative religious radio and television shows that mobilize thousands of followers to write or call politicians instantly. For gays and lesbians, access remains limited, especially in the powerful electronic national media.

Source: Peter Nardi, "Changing Gay and Lesbian Images in the Media," in *Overcoming Heterosexism and Homophobia: Strategies That Work*, ed. James T. Sears and Walter L. Williams (New York: Columbia University Press, 1997), pp. 430, 440–441.

* * *

Part of the progress of the gay and lesbian rights movement is due to the many lesbian and gay publishers that have emerged within the last four decades. With books, journals, magazines, and newspapers, those persons who feel isolated by their sexual minority status can read of others like themselves. With the Internet explosion of the late 1990s, even more exposure for lesbian and gay writing has occurred. Electronic publications have had an enormous impact on spreading the message of gay and lesbian rights around the world. One of these Internet sources is the *International Gay & Lesbian Review*. Books that deal with lesbian, gay, bisexual, and transgendered rights are reviewed, including memoirs of activists, reports by gay rights organizations, queer theory books that apply themselves to political issues, debates over same-sex marriage, and books on overcoming heterosexism.

For example, in 1997 Julie Anderson wrote a review of a book titled *Coming Home to America: A Roadmap to Gay & Lesbian Empowerment* (New York: St. Martin's Press, 1996) by Torie Osborn. A longtime activist, Osborn was executive director of the National Gay and Lesbian Task Force. She brought her own personal activist experience, as well as research, into the writing of this book. Osborn's main conclusions are that

DOCUMENT 157: Internet Publication for Gay and Lesbian Rights (1997)

Coming out, building local gay and lesbian community centers, supporting our leaders as opposed to attacking them, and getting involved politically and/or in social service organizations that take care of gays and lesbians should be important priorities during the next phase of the gay and lesbian movement. She also suggests that it will be important to share with the rest of America gays' and lesbians' diverse spirituality, creativity, inclusive approach to problem-solving, skills in building unity out of diversity, community ethic of caring, and the ability to rejoice in the face of pain and horror.

Coming Home to America opens with an historical look at the gay and lesbian movement in the United States. Osborn suggests that many of the recent gay and lesbian civil rights losses (i.e., the 1993 military issue) were due to the radical right's financial power and ability to influence policy makers with inaccurate and demeaning information about gays and lesbians. The right's campaigns continue to portray gays and lesbians as sick, sinful, and desperate, sexually obsessed child molesters. Osborn also attributes these losses to lack of strategy and vision, bitter infighting between key gay and lesbian groups and individuals, along with negative public perceptions about gays and lesbians. A 1993 *Newsweek* poll found that only 43 percent of Americans reported even knowing someone gay. She cites another recent poll that found that about 60 percent of Americans still consider homosexuality to be immoral. Negative perceptions, fear, and ignorance set the stage for her call for all gays and lesbians to come out to everyone....

Osborn's vision of [the] next important phase of the movement involves bringing gay and lesbian culture, community, and movement out of the big cities and into the smaller towns, suburbs, and rural areas of America. She suggests that there should be gay and lesbian community centers in every town. In her opinion, these are places where ideas, leadership, activism, values, and vision emerge. She also believes that community centers send a message that "We take care of our own."

Osborn warns that while the movement progresses, gays and lesbians must deal with...infighting [which] hurts the ability of organizations to operate efficiently and effectively. She suggests with strong leadership and ethics, the gay and lesbian community will be able to effectively fight the real enemies—the right-wing Christian political extremists.

Source: Julie Anderson review of *Coming Home to America: A Roadmap to Gay & Lesbian Empowerment*, by Torie Osborn, in *International Gay & Lesbian Review* (1997) [www.usc.edu/gayreview *or* www.usc.edu/isd/archives/iglr]

*   *   *

Some babies are born with a mix of female and male genitals or "ambiguous genitals." Others, classified as female are born with only one X chromosome. Well-meaning parents and medical staff immediately try to assign a specific gender to the child if need be by operating on her or him. A pattern of secrecy and shame goes along with this process. It is only in the past few years that people who have suffered as intersexual children have come out of the closet and demanded recognition, a voice, and a choice. Groups like the Intersex Society of North America are leading the challenge against traditional methods and attitudes. Intersex liberation activists often ally with other "sexual outlaws" such as gays and lesbians. Like gays and lesbians they argue that to live one's life without socially imposed stigma or shame is a basic human right.

DOCUMENT 158: Intersex Society of North America (1997)

In modern Western culture, the events of an intersexual's birth are hidden in shame and half-truths. Parents most often will not reveal their ordeal to anyone, including the child as s/he comes of age. The child is left physically damaged and in an emotional limbo without access to information about what has happened to them. The burden of pain and shame is so great that virtually all intersexuals stay deep in the closet throughout their adult lives....Intersexual children's bodies combine male and female characteristics, and the decision to register the child's birth as a girl or as a boy is made...largely on the basis of the prognosis for genital plastic surgery....Surgeons find it easier to assign the child as a girl, construct an opening, and remove enlarged clitoral tissue, than to assign the child as a boy and try to enlarge and reshape the small penis....[Physicians] are careful to avoid words like "hermaphrodism" or "intersexuality," and speak only of "improperly formed gonads"....

Secrecy and taboo disrupt emotional development and stress the whole family....Many intersexual children are subject to repeated surgeries....As a growing number of adult intersexuals have come forth to speak about their experiences, it is apparent that surgery had generally been more harmful than helpful....A few are now beginning to organize to oppose this silence....Parents and medical staff must be reeducated about sexuality. Intersexual children need early access to a peer support group where they can find role models and discuss medical and lifestyle options.

Source: Bo Laurent, "Intersexuality—A Plea for Honesty and Emotional Support" at Web site [http://www.ahpweb,org/pub/perspective/intersex.html]

*   *   *

Author Leslie Feinberg is a leading voice for transgender liberation. A masculine/androgynous female-born person who identifies as a bisexual transgenderist, Feinberg began working as a social activist in the labor movement. Seeing the direct relationship between the strength of union leaders at the bargaining table and the size of the picket line outside, Feinberg gained an awareness about the need to attract as many different people and groups into a large queer alliance in order to challenge sexual and gender oppression. Feinberg points out that androgynous, transgender, transsexual, and intersexed people have been at the forefront of the efforts for lesbian and gay liberation, and their issues should not be sacrificed on the altar of "respectability" favored by gender-conformist lesbians and gay men.

Transgender people have specific problems in their daily lives due to official forms, like state drivers' licenses and passports, that require listing oneself as "male" or "female." Trans activists have lobbied to eliminate gender references on such forms, in the same way that "race" is no longer listed. In public places, toilets that are labeled "men's" or "women's" restrooms can be oppressive for an androgynous or intersex person. Some activists suggest adding an unlabeled private single-person toilet which could be used by anyone. Although trans people face unique issues, they share a common oppression of job discrimination, harassment, and violence with gays, lesbians, and bisexuals. It is on the level of common interests that Feinberg directs a call for unity among lesbian, gay, bisexual, and trans people.

DOCUMENT 159: Transgender Liberation (1998)

We fought to defend our sexual freedom, and to fight the discrimination and violence we face because of our sexuality. And those oppressions are inextricably linked with trans liberation. In a society in which heterosexuality and male/female dress and behavior are decreed and enforced by law, gay, lesbian, bisexual, and trans people are all gender transgressors. There are no boundaries between the territories in which we live; our populations over- lap. We cannot separate the demands for lesbian, gay, bisexual, and trans liberation. We have our own pasts, and yet our histories have commingled. Wherever oppression has reared its ugly head, we have been thrown to- gether into jail cells and concentration camps by cops, prosecutors, judges, and military brass who view us as guilty of the same crime: "queerness."...

We will all benefit from seeing the interconnectedness....Whenever a new fight against oppression emerges, some people have conflicting feel- ings. They know that a struggle against any form of bigotry and discrimi- nation is ultimately good for everyone. But they feel anxious about how those changes will affect their own lives....No one's sex reassignment or fluidity of gender threatens your right to self-identity and self-expression. On the contrary, our struggle bolsters your right to your identity. My right to be me is tied with a thousand threads to your right to be you. We're not trying to barricade the road you travel; we're trying to open up more av- enues to self-definition, and identity and love....

An injury to one is an injury to all! When we allow ourselves to be split along lines of oppression, we always lose. But when we put forward a col- lective list of demands together, and fight to defend each other from at- tacks, we frequently win.

Source: Leslie Feinberg, *Trans Liberation: Beyond Pink or Blue* (Boston: Beacon Press, 1998), pp. 98–102.

* * *

The Southern Baptist Convention, the Christian denomination that most strongly defended slavery in the nineteenth century, and offered the most resistance to the African American civil rights movement in the 1950s and 1960s, shifted their resistance to gay and lesbian equality in the late twentieth century. It was only in the 1990s that the Southern Baptist Convention issued an apology to African Americans for their earlier proslavery and prosegregationist statements, but this change did not lessen their certainty in condemning queer activism. At their 1998 annual convention, the Southern Baptists passed several resolutions condemning same-sex love.

DOCUMENT 160: Southern Baptist Convention Condemns Homosexuality (1998)

One resolution singled out *Corpus Christi*, a play by noted play- wright Terrence McNally that focused on the loving relationship between Jesus and his disciple John. The resolution condemned this off-Broadway play as an example of

indecent, blasphemous photographs or performances that ridicule, attack or debase the Christian religion....A despicable show...is entitled "Corpus Christi," in which our sinless Lord and Savior, the Lord Jesus Christ, is depicted as a sexually perverted person engaging in acts against nature with his disciples.

* * *

A different resolution, opposing legal recognition of same-sex marriages, defined marriage as:

the uniting of one man and one woman in covenant commitment for a lifetime. It is God's unique gift to reveal the union between Christ and His church....A husband is to love his wife as Christ loved the church. He has the God-given responsibility to provide for, to protect and to lead his family. A wife is to submit herself graciously to the servant leadership of her husband.

* * *

Another Southern Baptist resolution objected to a 1998 executive order signed by President Bill Clinton that forbade employment discrimination on the basis of sexual orientation, in the civilian departments of the executive branch of the federal government. Clinton's executive order exempted the military, the largest number of federal employees, but even his limited action raised the ire of the Southern Baptists. Note the irony, given their previous resistance to racial justice, that the Baptist resolution complimented "the moral movement to stop discrimination against race."

WHEREAS, homosexuality is immoral, contrary to the Bible (Leviticus 18:22, 1 Corinthians 6:9–10) and contrary to traditional Judeo-Christian moral standards, and the open affirmation of homosexuality represents a sign of God's surrendering a society to its perversion (Romans 1:18–32); and

WHEREAS, on May 28, 1998, President William Jefferson Clinton signed an amendment to an executive order which "prohibit(s) discrimination based on sexual orientation...; and

WHEREAS, homosexual politics is masquerading as "civil rights," in order to exploit the moral high ground of the civil rights movement even though homosexual conduct and other learned sexual deviance have nothing in common with the moral movement to stop discrimination against race and gender; and

WHEREAS, what God has established in His eternal law to be morally wrong, man should never assert in temporal laws as a legal right.

Therefore, be it RESOLVED, that we, the messengers to the Southern Baptist Convention...call upon Congress to nullify the president's action through legislation unless the president first rescinds his order; and

Be it finally RESOLVED, that we oppose all efforts to provide government endorsements, sanction, recognition, acceptance or civil rights advantage on the basis of homosexuality.

Source: SBC Bulletin, Report of Committee on Resolutions, Southern Baptist Convention, June 9–11, 1998. Also reprinted on the Internet, "Dr. Dobson on Homosexuality" (July 1998 letter) at [www.uhuh.com/laws/homosex.htm]

*   *   *

An active conservative Christian organization in the 1990s, Focus on the Family, led by James Dobson, often complained about homosexuality as a major sin. Like Republican leader Pat Buchanan, who in 1992 called for a "cultural war" against godless liberals, Dobson refers to a "great civil war of values." Raising the specter of a gay and lesbian takeover of the government, Dobson said he would "fight...the battle" if his supporters would send more money. In a fund-raising letter to his followers in July 1998, Dodson admitted that recent contributions had been "anemic," and hoped that his antihomosexual letter would increase the collection.

DOCUMENT 161: Focus on the Family (1998)

Dear Friends:

In June I devoted this monthly letter to the subject of homosexuality and the striking cultural gains made in recent years by gay and lesbian activists. Shortly after [that]...President Bill Clinton issued an executive order on May 28, 1998, establishing what amounts to an affirmative action program for homosexuals....All of the civil rights policies that have applied historically to minorities will now be enforced on behalf of homosexuals. The potential for costly legal battles and the intimidation of government officials is difficult to overstate....

Thus, another milestone in the homosexual agenda quietly became federal administrative law, with few people noticing or even appearing to care. Immediately after the signing, Clinton announced his intention of promoting the Employment Non-Discrimination Act (ENDA), a bill that...will extend the spirit of the president's executive order to the entire nation....

Be assured, as conservative Christians continue to lose ground in the great civil war of values, that the [liberal] cultural elites will continue their campaign to marginalize and paralyze us….Is this treatment going to weaken my determination to defend righteousness in the culture? Not for a minute….I will remain in the battle as long as I have reason to believe that our friends and supporters are behind us. But I can't fight it alone. If you identify with the pro-family and pro-moral positions I have taken, I would appreciate hearing from you….

As the moral free fall gathers momentum…[we] are called "intolerant" and "judgmental" for believing in traditional morality, as though the greatest human virtue is to recognize no differences between right and wrong and to accept them both on equal terms. That is the popular culture's definition of tolerance.

A writer once stated, "Tolerance is the virtue of people who do not believe in anything." When we become so accommodating of evil that we neither recognize nor oppose it, our moral collapse is imminent….

We especially need your encouragement at this time. The contributions to Focus have been rather anemic.

Source: James Dobson, "Dr. Dobson on Homosexuality" (July 1998), on the Internet at [www.uhuh.com/laws/homosex.htm]. See also [www.family.org/docstudy/newsletters/a0002203.html].

* * *

Many conservatives were alarmed by the 1993 decision of the Hawai'i Supreme Court that said a state law which prohibited people from marrying another person of the same sex was a violation of the Hawai'i State Constitution's prohibition of discrimination on the basis of sex. This successful court suit, argued by civil rights attorney Daniel R. Foley, seemed to be the final word on the subject. However, in 1998 antigay activists moved to amend the state's Constitution, declaring that marriage is limited as a special right only between one man and one woman. On May 30, 2000, Daniel Foley gave an interview to Walter L. Williams about recent events in Hawai'i.

DOCUMENT 162: Hawai'i Voters Reject Same-Sex Marriage (1998)

Please explain what has happened in the Hawai'i case since the pro-same-sex marriage Court decisions.

In 1994 the Hawai'i state legislature had passed a face-saving statute to limit marriage to a man and a woman. This statute would not have outweighed the Supreme

Court decision in favor of same-sex marriage because it would still be seen as a violation of the equal protection clause of the state constitution. However, it did provide legislators with an excuse for irate voters that they had in fact voted to restrict marriage to heterosexuals, even though they knew the act would have no impact against a Supreme Court ruling to the contrary. It was just a cover.

Those who were most opposed to same-sex marriage felt that nothing could be certain to stop it except a constitutional amendment to the Hawai'i state constitution. In 1997 the Mormon, Catholic, and Evangelical Protestant churches, abandoning any pretense of separation of church and state, proposed legislation to amend the state constitution to limit marriage solely to a man and a woman. We had been successful in opposing such a constitutional amendment up until that time, but they marshaled resources like never before. Due to their pressure, in 1997 the state legislature passed a proposed constitutional amendment that would give the legislature the power to limit marriage to opposite-sex couples. However, to balance this conservative limitation the legislature also passed a companion Reciprocal Beneficiary Act to extend the majority of rights and benefits of marriage to non-traditional couples. This Act gave benefits not just to same-sex couples, but also included other types of two people who could not marry. For example, a parent and a child over age eighteen could register under this Act, so that the child could remain on the parent's health insurance plan after reaching adulthood.

What are the tangible benefits provided by the Reciprocal Beneficiary Act?

Non-traditional couples at least can now receive many benefits that they had been denied before. For example, before this only man-woman married couples could acquire and register land tenancy in the entirety. The Reciprocal Beneficiary Act provides that same-sex couples who buy real estate together can own it as one, and do not have to pay taxes when one member of the couple dies. The surviving same-sex partner now gets the same tax break that a heterosexually married spouse receives.

With the Reciprocal Beneficiary Act, one person in a couple cannot be sued for a debt made individually by their partner, just as a married couple have this benefit. For the first time non-traditional couples can have peace of mind in probate proceedings, where the surviving partner can inherit just as married people do. If one partner dies without a will, the other partner can inherit their property without another relative being able to challenge it in court. And the partner in a registered couple has hospital visitation rights, and can participate in decision-making if the other partner is medically incapacitated.

There are many legal benefits that are provided by marriage, and same-sex couples can now qualify for many of them. In this respect, the Act is an improvement. However, it is still not as good as marriage because there is no legal protection for couples once they go beyond Hawai'i state boundaries. Furthermore, beneficiary status is still second class citizenship for non-traditional couples, because there are other benefits of legal marriage that are not provided to same-sex couples.

There are two important categories of exceptions: first, in rights provided in family court cases (for example, child support and custody, alimony and divorce proceedings), and second, where state law interfaces with federal law (for example, in federal tax issues, social security, and immigration and naturalization). This federal exception was thought to be necessary because Congress had passed the Defense of Marriage Act in 1996, which stated that for federal purposes, marriage shall be defined only to be between a man and a woman. This reactionary Act had been pushed through Congress by conservatives who were appalled by what we were doing in Hawai'i.

It was a case of two steps forward, and one step back. Despite the disappointment about removing same-sex couples from being able to legally marry, it is still important to remember that this Reciprocal Beneficiary Act provided for the most sweeping rights package for non-traditional couples, including same-sex couples, in the history of the United States up to that time.

Tell us what happened in the vote to amend the state constitution.

Even though the legislature passed this package in 1997, the constitutional amendment to limit marriage to opposite-sex couples could not be voted upon until the next election in November 1998. I hoped that there was still a chance for us to get the state Supreme Court to rule in favor of same-sex marriage before that time....

To our great disappointment the Supreme Court delayed its ruling until after the results of the constitutional amendment vote would be known. The Supreme Court justices had been subject to a lot of criticism over their original decision in favor of same-sex marriage, and basically they lacked the courage to follow through as they should have done. We did not anticipate this retreat by the Supreme Court, in which the justices lost their will.

How did this constitutional amendment manage to pass?

In 1998 the Utah-based Mormon Church stepped in to do everything they could to pass the constitutional amendment. The Mormons spent more money in the fight against same-sex marriage in Hawai'i than all the other churches combined. They did the same thing in fighting against recognition of same-sex marriage in California later. With all of the money at their disposal, they vastly outspent the pro-gay side in television and radio ads. They very effectively used scare tactics to convince many of the undecided voters that same-sex marriage would be a threat. For example, they claimed that legalization of same-sex marriages would lead to churches losing their right to perform any marriages if they refused to hold weddings for same-sex couples. The Hawai'i courts explicitly ruled that this would not happen, and that no clergyman is legally required to perform any wedding they do not want to. But the Mormons still made that claim, even though they knew it was not accurate. The religious coalition overwhelmed the pro-gay side, and voters approved the constitutional amendment in November 1998.

I remember that the pro-gay side did not push the basic issue of the rightness of same-sex marriage much in the campaign. Why not?

Some of the gay people in Hawai'i wanted to take on the issue of church interference in the political process, but polls indicated that if we did this we would lose the election. Polls of voters suggested that our side would be more likely to win by sticking to a message of "don't change the Hawai'i Constitution" and seeing the amendment as a threat to civil liberties in general. As a result, not much was said in the campaign defending the right of people to marry someone of the same sex. Unfortunately, despite this cautious approach the campaign was not effective in getting enough people to vote against the amendment.

Then maybe would it have been more effective to take a long-range view, and make the argument for equality anyway?

Looking at it from the short run, polls suggested this was the best strategy to try to win the election, and I don't want to criticize those brave activists who decided to follow this strategy. But now, having seen that the short-term strategy did not work, it is clear that we should have used the money raised to get out the basic message that gay and lesbian couples deserve equal rights to have legal marriage with the person they love, and that discrimination is wrong. This is the long-range strategy that, even if it might not have been immediately effective in the 1998 election, would have probably more effectively changed public opinion in the long run. It is the dilemma of short-term versus long-term thinking. But now that we learned this lesson the hard way in Hawai'i, activists in other states should learn from our mistake and look at such battles as merely one step in the long-term effort to change public opinion. If we are going to have to spend all this money on television ads, we might as well use the money effectively to have the most long-term impact.

How did the Hawai'i Supreme Court react to this vote?

After the constitutional amendment had been passed by the voters, the Supreme Court ruled that this vote enacted and legalized the 1994 statute passed by the legislature that limited marriage to opposite-sex couples. As a fall-back position we made a second argument that even if marriage is limited to a man and a woman, all the rights and benefits of marriage should still be extended to same-sex couples. On December 9, 1999 the Supreme Court dismissed our complaint without addressing this issue. I was very disappointed, of course, but I am still not giving up. I am filing new court actions to get them to answer this question. The basis of my challenge is that the Supreme Court has never reversed its original 1993 conclusion in *Baehr v.*

Lewin that not providing these benefits constitutes discrimination on the basis of sex. Therefore, even though we cannot call it marriage, same-sex couples deserve the same rights that opposite-sex couples get when they legally marry.

What do you think is going to happen in Hawai'i in the future?

As a compromise, we think that within the next year or so Hawai'i will pass legislation that will essentially be similar to the civil union legislation passed in 2000 by the Vermont state legislature. That legislation gives all the same rights to same-sex couples that married heterosexual couples now have, even though it is not called marriage. There is a chance, depending on the outcome of the 2000 elections, that the United States government will create a federal civil union category. Democratic nominee Al Gore has already come out in support of such a category, but Republican nominee George W. Bush opposes it. So we will have to see what happens. But the point is that none of this would be happening now if we had not pushed the issue in Hawai'i in the early 1990s.

The success of civil unions in Vermont is a direct result of what we did, and the Vermont Supreme Court cited the Hawai'i Supreme Court decision in their own 1999 ruling supporting the equal rights of same-sex couples. The Vermont Supreme Court recommended their state legislature to use the 1995 report of the Hawai'i Commission on Sexual Orientation and the Law as a model for Vermont. Now, in turn, what has happened in Vermont—as well as in several other nations around the world—is having an impact in Hawai'i. When we consider that same-sex marriage was never even considered until Denmark moved toward legal recognition in 1989, this is a very quick international movement. The synergy of what happens in one part of the world has an impact in another area.

What our Hawai'i court case did was to make the issue of equal rights for same-sex couples respectable in American politics. It moved along the effort to enact domestic partnerships, or what are now being called civil unions, as a compromise. For example, when it looked like Hawaii might enact fullfledged marriage for same-sex couples, conservative columnist William Safire wrote a column in the *New York Times* supporting domestic partnerships as a moderate solution. That would never have happened if we did not push for total equality in marriage. Many voters in Hawai'i who opposed granting marriage to lesbian and gay couples in 1998 have now come to accept that justice requires giving equal rights to everyone in some form.

What are public opinion polls in Hawai'i showing about changes in attitude toward same-sex marriage?

Polls have been pretty consistent from 1991 to 1998, that Hawai'i voters remained about two to one against legalizing same-sex marriage. But that does not mean those figures would remain the same if the Supreme Court had ruled firmly in favor of same-sex marriage at the beginning. To compare it to the question of interracial marriage, a Gallup Poll in 1968, a year after the United States Supreme Court ruled firmly in favor of a black-white couple in *Loving v. Virginia*, showed seventy percent of Americans opposed interracial marriage. But because the Court ruled firmly, and state miscegenation laws were declared unconstitutional, gradually the issue of interracial marriage became a non-issue. After interracial marriage was legalized, people saw that the sky did not fall. They saw that much of what conservative reactionaries said about the destruction of civilization did not turn out to be true. People gradually got used to the idea that someone should have the right to marry another person of a different race if they wanted. This idea has now been incorporated into the list of rights that any American can expect to have in our legacy of freedom. Interracial marriage is now a non-issue in American politics, even though it was a major controversy only a few decades ago.

It is the experience of interracial marriage being part of the way things are, that convinced most people that it is OK. There is a synergy between legal decisions and public opinion that follows this experience. That is how social change occurs, and I predict that a similar pattern will occur with gay and lesbian equality. One day people will look back on the controversy of same-sex marriage, and wonder what all the fuss was about.

Therefore, even though the term "marriage" still remains a sticking point for many people, the new idea of civil unions is becoming more acceptable. This is a transition stage, because it still is not totally equal. It is separate and unequal, just like decisions trying to provide for some rights of black people in the segregated South before the United States Supreme Court ruled firmly in 1956 that separate is inherently unequal. That time will come in the area of gay and lesbian rights. We did not get equality in Hawai'i as quickly as I thought it would happen, but we will get there. What we are going through now is a major step in the larger effort for equality.

Source: Unpublished interview of Daniel R. Foley by Walter L. Williams, Honolulu, May 30, 2000. See also Daniel Woog, *Friends and Family: The True Stories of Gay America's Straight Allies* (Los Angeles: Alyson, 1999).

*   *   *

Matthew Shepard was a gay twenty-two-year-old student at the University of Wyoming who was beaten to death by two young men who (according to one of the men's girlfriends) wanted "to teach him a lesson" for allegedly coming on to him. In contrast to numerous other murders of gays and lesbians, when this case came to the attention of the national media in October 1998 it generated newspaper and magazine headlines. A few weeks before that, an African American man named James Byrd was tortured and killed by white racists in Texas. The Byrd and Shepard cases sparked a renewal of the effort to pass hate crime laws on both the state and national levels. On March 23, 1999, Matthew's mother Judy Shepard spoke at a press conference organized by the Human Rights Campaign and the Leadership Conference on Civil Rights.

DOCUMENT 163: Mrs. Shepard Speaks in Support of Hate Crimes Laws (1998)

Before Matthew died, my husband and I had given little thought to the issue of hate crimes legislation. We, of course, deplored reports of violence that would from time to time come to us through the media, but we focused very little on what our government could do about it....While it is true [that] perpetrating violence on another individual is against the law regardless of the motivation, violence motivated by hate has deep ramifications and is often times meant to intimidate entire groups of people. Hate crimes laws first send a message that these crimes will not be tolerated in our society, a message that sadly needs to be heard by some people....

There is ample evidence that hate crimes laws are needed. My heart stands with Daryl Varrette who is with us today. The savagery of what occurred to his uncle, James Byrd is beyond human comprehension....There is no guarantee that these laws will stop hate crimes from happening. But they can reduce them. They can help change the climate in this country, where some people feel as though it is OK to target specific groups of people and get away with it. If just one is stopped, if just one potential perpetrator gets the message of this legislation and there is one less victim, then it will be worthwhile.

Source: "Mrs. Shepard Speaks in Support of Hate Crimes Legislation," April 1, 1999, [http://www.wiredstrategies.com/Shepardx.html]

* * *

While decrying hate crimes, James B. Jacobs, professor of law at New York University, feels that existing criminal laws are adequate to address hate crimes. He is opposed to adding more criminal laws, and argues that enforcing existing laws makes more sense. The same argument was used to oppose civil rights laws in the 1960s, when the United States government began to prosecute racists for "violating the civil rights" of African American murder victims, when those persons had not been convicted of murder by local courts.

DOCUMENT 164: Hate Crimes Laws Won't Stop Hate (1998)

I don't know what "the answer" is to stopping horrific crimes like the murder of Matthew Shepard, the gay University of Wyoming student, or whether there is an answer....President Clinton and gay activists say that the tragedy demonstrates a need for more state and Federal "hate crime" laws. Such calls are well-meaning but misguided....As with the men who chained James Byrd to a pickup truck and dragged him to his death in Jasper, Texas, last summer, the suspects in Wyoming were quickly arrested and charged by the local police. Why must the Federal Government also come to the rescue? It is hard to see the current outcry as anything more than another chance for politicians to go out on a limb and declare themselves against hate and prejudice.

The Federal bill would put the F.B.I. in a very difficult situation. It could not possibly respond to even a fraction of the offenses labeled as bias or hate crimes. Victims and advocacy groups would clamor for F.B.I. intervention, if only to make a symbol of a particular crime. How could the bureau refuse to intervene if it meant alienating important constituencies and politicians who control its budget? Moreover, there is no evidence that local law-enforcement agencies are not doing a competent job or that the F.B.I. has an advantage over them.

A Federal hate-crime law would also put another nail in the coffin of our constitutional protection against double jeopardy. After all, every Federal crime would also be a state crime, like assault, robbery or murder. Thus the defendants could be tried twice if special interests judged the first trial to have ended in an unjust acquittal.

Source: James B. Jacobs, "New Laws Won't Stop Hate," *New York Times* October 14, 1998, section A, page 23.

*　*　*

Acknowledging to others and/or yourself that you are lesbian, gay, bisexual, or transgender (LGBT) is known as "coming out." The term comes from "coming out of the closet," which is a place to hide (one's identity or inclinations). Coming out is for many LGBT people both a major step in their lives and in many cases a liberating one. Each person must decide for her- or himself *if, when,* and to *whom* they will come out to. Below are several commonly asked questions about the coming-out process.

DOCUMENT 165: Coming Out (1998)

WHAT IS *COMING OUT?*

Coming out is about being open and honest with the world about who you are. This is a personal process. You are in control. You can come out to whomever you please, whenever you please. *Coming out* does not need to be done in skywriting or by taking out a full page advert in the newspaper.

You can start with a close friend, move on to your circle of friends, your parents or family…entirely at your own pace.

WHY SHOULD I *COME OUT?*

Health: The best reason to come out is for your own mental health. If you are not open about yourself, it means that you are ashamed of who you are. It's like believing subconsciously that you are "a bad person." This is simply not true—and if you persist in believing it you will damage yourself.

Happiness: Expressing love is fundamental to human happiness. You don't have to deny yourself the most basic of human drives. If you're gay the only full and satisfying (and natural) way to do this is with someone of the same sex. The sooner you confront your sexuality the sooner the road to happiness and fulfilment will be clear.

Respect: People who are true to themselves win respect from other people and are most sought out for friendship. Nobody likes a "yes-person." People with independent minds and self-confidence win friends and influence people a lot easier than those who just try to conform.

True Friendship: You may be afraid that if you admit to people that you're gay, they'll hate you. Some will of course, but most won't. You'll see who your real friends are and stop wasting time on those who aren't worth the effort.

Don't waste time: Gay counselor Terry Sanderson says: "The saddest aspect has been the cry from elderly gay people that they have "wasted" their lives. However materially successful they have been…they have denied themselves the comfort and satisfaction of human love.…"

Politics: The more people who are out and proud to be out, the more visible homosexuality becomes and the more society will learn to accept it. It sends a message to other gay people that it is safe to come out and that they are not alone.…

PERSONAL STATEMENTS

"One of the first people I came out to was my best friend—whom I'd known since high-school. He said: 'Well, don't think that anyone actually cares.' I thought those were the kindest words that anyone could say. It's true, nobody who cares about you really cares whether you're gay or straight, short or tall, black, white, green or blue.…Once you realise that the world isn't actually watching you, waiting for you to mess up or something, it's very liberating."—Fred, age 25.

Source: Rhodes University [South Africa] Society for Gay, Lesbian and Bi Students Web site [http://www.ru.ac.za/societies/step/comeout.htm]

* * *

Through E-mails that disperse messages quickly around the world, the Internet has become even more of an inexpensive, increasingly accessible, and important tool in the struggle for lesbian, gay, bisexual, and transgender rights. Below is an article discussing the recent importance of E-mail activism. Through the Internet, injustice is sometimes averted, awareness is increased, and social change is promoted.

DOCUMENT 166: Cyberactivism (1999)

GLAAD [Gay and Lesbian Alliance Against Defamation] was among the pioneers of online gay activism nearly three years ago when it started GLAADLines, a weekly E-mail bulletin that provides news and breaking stories about gay men and lesbians. The bulletin usually includes information on where readers can E-mail or call to express their views on the particular stories featured....The alerts routinely spark thousands of responses and are credited with encouraging ABC to allow Ellen De-Generes's sitcom alter ego to come out in 1997.

Indeed, the charm of cyberspace is its ease, the fact that a simple E-mail can be forwarded to thousands of people at almost no cost. [United States navel officer Timothy] McVeigh proved how effective this tactic can be....The sailor was on the brink of discharge in the fall of 1997 after Navy investigators discovered that an America Online screen profile containing the word gay belonged to McVeigh....AOL's divulgence of McVeigh's identity to the Navy certainly broke the company's rule against revealing personal information about users. McVeigh pointed this out in an E-mail he sent to every AOL member whose profile also contained the word gay.

The E-mail prompted an outpouring of mail to the White House, the Pentagon, and Congress, and that support encouraged McVeigh to sue the Department of Defense, which resulted in a federal judge's preventing his discharge....

And the speed at which such issues are bubbling up to the mainstream continues to increase. In January it took just two days of E-mail buzz from activists offended by Merriam-Webster's online thesaurus listing gay slurs as synonyms for homosexual to bring the story to the attention of established media outlets. A cybersecond later, *The New York Times*, the Associated Press, and *The Wall Street Journal* ran items on the flap, and an apologetic Merriam-Webster and AOL, which had licensed the service, both shut down the thesaurus.

While McVeigh sought the support of the masses through the Internet, it was the masses who sought the support of the Internet when Matthew Shepard died. As news of the brutal October slaying spread, the world's gay and gay-friendly Netizens went online to express their anger over the atrocity and to push for more hate-crimes legislation....

[T]he Internet has helped gay groups around the country combine and expand their activism efforts. In January, in a gay Internet version of the Exxon-Mobil merger, GLAAD fused with Digital Queers, the groundbreaking group that has worked to bring gay organizations online since 1992 and was one of the first to predict the potential of gay online activism....

The Internet has also let gay activists reach abroad to cultures and communities even more remote than small-town America, to places where cyberspace is the only form of a free press. Rex Wockner, who operates an E-mail list that alerts journalists and advocates to gay news, ticks off several instances in the past year when the medium provided the message to the world. The most prominent example is that of the president of Zimbabwe, Robert Mugabe, whose virulently antigay statements and policies Wockner documented online. "Basically, Mugabe can't go anywhere in the first world without there being a protest by gays outside of whatever building he's in, and that's because of the Internet," Wockner says....

[John] Aravosis [a specialist in progressive Internet advocacy] says the cyberactivism successes of the past year, which astonished even those who engineered them, still need to be picked apart and analyzed. "We all have our shining moments, but none of us have figured out a consistent way to tap into the Internet," he says. "We're all still trying to figure out how to make this effective in the long term."

Source: Steve Friess, "Forget street demonstrations—the Internet is the newest avenue for organizing and protesting" [http://www.advocate.com/html/stories/0299/0299_cyberactivism.html]

* * *

In the 1990s, the battle over same-sex marriage expanded to other states besides Hawai'i. Three couples in Vermont—Stan Baker and Peter Harrigan, Holly Puterbaugh and Lois Farnham, Nina Beck and Stacy Jolles—filed a suit in Vermont state court, seeking to obtain marriage licenses which they had been denied by county clerks. The couples' suit did not claim they were being discriminated against by Vermont's marriage laws on the basis of their sexual orientation. Rather, Baker and the others argued that the state of Vermont offered to married couples benefits that were denied to unmarried couples, thereby violating Vermont's constitutional guarantee of equal treatment to all.

The State Attorney General of Vermont, however, argued that defining marriage as between one man and one woman sanctioned the link between procreation and child rearing—in essence, the state was using

weddings to link making babies with raising babies. Opponents, including the plaintiffs, dismissed this as ridiculous, pointing out not only
that some heterosexual couples do not have children—either because
they cannot or because they choose not to—and that many same-sex
couples were raising children. Holly Puterbaugh and Lois Farnham, for
example, had a four-year-old daughter at the time the suit was filed.

The Vermont Supreme Court decided that the state legislature had a
choice: either they should amend the marriage statutes to allow same-
sex unions or, alternatively, to pass equitable domestic partnership legislation. Vermont's legislature responded by passing a civil union law
which decrees that unmarried partners, including those in same-sex relationships, may enjoy all of the same state-level benefits that married
partners do. The significance of the Vermont legislation is that it was not
a political compromise, as the domestic partnership law was in
Hawai'i; rather, a judicial body had decreed that gay men and lesbians
were entitled to equal treatment, regardless of political concerns.

The decision of the Vermont Supreme Court was written by Chief Justice Jeffrey L. Amestoy.

DOCUMENT 167: *Stan Baker v. State of Vermont* (1999)

May the State of Vermont exclude same-sex couples from the benefits
and protections that its laws provide to opposite-sex married couples? That
is the fundamental question we address in this appeal, a question that the
Court well knows arouses deeply-felt religious, moral, and political beliefs.
Our constitutional responsibility to consider the legal merits of issues
properly before us provides no exception for the controversial case. The
issue before the Court, moreover, does not turn on the religious or moral
debate over intimate same-sex relationships, but rather on the statutory
and constitutional basis for the exclusion of same-sex couples from the secular benefits and protections offered married couples.

We conclude that under the Common Benefits Clause of the Vermont
Constitution, which, in pertinent part, reads, "That government is, or
ought to be, instituted for the common benefit, protection, and security of
the people, nation, or community, and not for the particular emolument or
advantage of any single person, family, or set of persons, who are a part
only of that community...."

Vermont Constitution chapter 1, article 7, plaintiffs may not be deprived
of the statutory benefits and protections afforded persons of the opposite
sex who choose to marry. We hold that the State is constitutionally required
to extend to same-sex couples the common benefits and protections that
flow from marriage under Vermont law. Whether this ultimately takes the

form of inclusion within the marriage laws themselves or a parallel "domestic partnership" system or some equivalent statutory alternative, rests with the Legislature. Whatever system is chosen, however, must conform with the constitutional imperative to afford all Vermonters the common benefit, protection, and security of the law.

Plaintiffs are three same-sex couples who have lived together in committed relationships for periods ranging from four to twenty-five years. Two of the couples have raised children together. Each couple applied for a marriage license from their respective town clerk, and each was refused a license as ineligible under the applicable state marriage laws. Plaintiffs thereupon filed this lawsuit....

In denying them access to a civil marriage license, the law effectively excludes them from a broad array of legal benefits and protections incident to the marital relation, including access to a spouse's medical, life, and disability insurance, hospital visitation and other medical decisionmaking privileges, spousal support, intestate succession, homestead protections, and many other statutory protections....Vermont law affirmatively guarantees the right to adopt and raise children regardless of the sex of the parents, and challenge the logic of a legislative scheme that recognizes the rights of same-sex partners as parents, yet denies them—and their children—the same security as spouses....

The words of the Common Benefits Clause are revealing....Chief among these is the principle of inclusion...[which] underscores the framers' resentment of political preference of any kind. The affirmative right to the common benefits and protections of government and the corollary proscription of favortism in the distribution of public emoluments and advantages reflect the framers' overarching objective not only that everyone enjoy equality before the law or have an equal voice in government but also that everyone have an equal share in the fruits of the common enterprise....

The reality today is that increasing numbers of same-sex couples are employing increasingly efficient assisted-reproductive techniques to conceive and raise children....The Vermont Legislature has not only recognized this reality, but has acted affirmatively to remove legal barriers so that same-sex couples may legally adopt and rear the children conceived through such efforts....

Therefore, to the extent that the state's purpose in licensing civil marriage was, and is, to legitimize children and provide for their security, the statutes plainly exclude many same-sex couples who are no different from opposite-sex couples with respect to these objectives. If anything, the exclusion of same-sex couples from the legal protections incident to marriage exposes their children to the precise risks that the state argues the marriage laws are designed to secure against. In short, the marital exclusion treats persons who are similarly situated for purposes of the law, differently....

The past provides many instances where the law refused to see a human being when it should have. See *Dred Scott* (concluding that African slaves and their descendents had "no rights which the white man was bound to respect")....The extension of the Common Benefits Clause to acknowledge plaintiffs as Vermonters who seek nothing more, nor less, that legal protection and security for their avowed commitment to an intimate and lasting human relationship is simply, when all is said and done, a recognition of our common humanity....

> Justice J. Johnson dissented with the majority decision to turn over the matter to the Vermont legislature. Instead, she wanted the Court to legalize marriage for couples of the same sex.

Plaintiffs come before this Court claiming that the state has unconstitutionally deprived them of the benefits of marriage based solely upon a discriminatory classification that violates their civil rights....The majority agrees that the Common Benefits Clause of the Vermont Constitution entitles plaintiffs to obtain the same benefits and protections as those bestowed upon married opposite-sex couples, yet it declines to give them any relief other than an exhortation to the Legislature to deal with the problem. I concur with the majority's holding, but I respectfully dissent from its novel and truncated remedy, which in my view abdicates this Court's constitutional duty to redress violations of constitutional rights. I would grant the requested relief and enjoin defendants from denying plaintiffs a marriage license....

Denying same-sex couples a marriage license is viewed by many as indicating that same-sex relationships are not entitled to the same status as opposite-sex relationships....Singling out a particular group for special treatment may have a stigmatizing effect more significant than any economic consequences....With respect to regulation of morals, the police power should properly be exercised to protect each individual's right to be free from interference in defining and pursuing his own morality but not to enforce a majority morality on persons whose conduct does not harm others....Allowing plaintiffs to obtain a license would further the overall goals of marriage, as defined by the majority—to provide stability to individuals, their families, and the broader community by clarifying and protecting the rights of married persons....

Courts [must] act independently and decisively to protect civil rights guaranteed by our Constitution....[Concerning] discrimination based on sex or sexual orientation rather than race, I would not prioritize among types of civil rights violations; our duty to remedy them is the same....Groups that have historically been the target of discrimination cannot be expected to wait patiently for the protection of their human dignity and equal rights while governments move toward reform one step at a time....

The majority declares that plaintiffs have been unconstitutionally deprived of the benefits of marriage, but does not hold that the marriage laws are unconstitutional, does not hold that plaintiffs are entitled to the license that triggers those benefits....The protections conferred on Vermonters by the Common Benefits Clause cannot be restricted by the outmoded conception that marriage requires one man and one woman....

This case is undoubtedly one of the most controversial ever to come before this Court. Newspaper, radio and television media have disclosed widespread public interest in its outcome, as well as the full spectrum of opinion as to what that outcome should be....The Vermont Constitution does not permit the courts to decline to adjudicate a matter because its subject is controversial, or because the outcome may be deeply offensive to the strongly held beliefs of many of our citizens....However much history, sociology, religious belief, personal experience or other considerations may inform our individual or collective deliberations, we must decide this case, and all cases, on the basis of our understanding of the law, and the law alone.

Source: Stan Baker et al. v. State of Vermont. No. 98–032, Supreme Court of Vermont 744 A.2d 864 (December 20, 1999 filed).

* * *

Ever since *Bowers v. Hardwick* (1986), when the United States Supreme Court refused to declare sodomy laws unconstitutional, the American Civil Liberties Union and Lambda Legal Defense focused on overturning sodomy laws on the state level. By the end of the twentieth century, after years of time-consuming and expensive litigation, this legal approach was accomplishing significant results. In contrast to 1960, when every state in the United States had a sodomy statute, by the beginning of the twenty-first century only thirteen states still enforced such a law. Challenges to those laws, in both the state and federal court levels, were continuing. The struggle to overturn antigay laws became one of the success stories for the gay and lesbian rights movement, demonstrating the importance of legal strategies in accomplishing change.

DOCUMENT 168: Overturning State Sodomy Laws (1999)

Legal challenges to state sodomy laws met with astonishing success in 1999. The tone was set before the year began, in November 1998, when the Georgia Supreme Court ruled that Georgia's sodomy statute violates the right to privacy under that state's constitution. This case was a sweet victory after repeated unsuccessful attempts to bring down the Georgia law, which became the "crown jewel" of sodomy laws after the U.S. Supreme Court's infamous 1986 decision in *Bowers v. Hardwick* upholding the statute.

The [ACLU] Lesbian and Gay Rights Project rang in the new year with a January 1999 consent decree invalidating two Maryland statutes which created felonies for anybody engaging in anal sex and for gays and lesbians engaging in oral sex....After the Baltimore County Circuit Court ruled in favor of the ACLU challenge...Maryland agreed to enter into a global consent decree eliminating both laws.

The action continued in February 1999, when a trial judge issued a promising decision rejecting a motion by Puerto Rico's Department of Justice to dismiss an ACLU challenge to Puerto Rico's sodomy statute. That same month, a Louisiana appellate court reversed a man's conviction for engaging in sodomy with a woman, holding that Louisiana's sodomy statute violated the state constitution's right to privacy. Two Louisiana trial courts quickly followed suit, striking down the statute in a civil challenge brought on behalf of lesbians and gay men....And in April 1999, the conservative Arkansas Supreme Court rejected state efforts to dismiss a challenge to Arkansas' sodomy statute filed by Lambda [Legal Defense]....

Why the sudden surge forward? There are probably several explanations. First, we have spent the 1990s building a solid foundation for sodomy challenges with hard-won decisions striking down sodomy statutes in Kentucky (1993), Tennessee (1996), and Montana (1997). We may be starting to reap the benefits of this growing body of case law in our favor. Second, some of the recently successful sodomy challenges (Georgia, Louisiana) have been brought on behalf of heterosexuals who have become entangled in sodomy statutes. Courts in conservative states may find it easier to strike down sodomy statutes in cases that don't raise the gay rights flag. And finally, the success of our sodomy challenges may be improving as a result of increasing social acceptance of gay men and lesbians. Indeed, even the decisions striking down sodomy statutes in cases involving heterosexuals may evidence this, since those courts have made no efforts to distinguish between gay and straight people but instead have assumed that the same constitutional protections apply to all. Whatever the explanation, it's safe to say we're on a roll.

Source: "A Banner Year for Attacking Sodomy Statutes," *Lesbian & Gay Rights, AIDS/HIV, 2000: An ACLU Report* (New York: American Civil Liberties Union, 2000), pp. 22–23.

* * *

James Dale served as assistant scoutmaster for a Boy Scout troop in New Jersey while attending Rutgers University, but he was dismissed from this position when scout leaders found out that he was copresident of the University's Lesbian/Gay Alliance. Dale sued the Boy Scouts of America (BSA), claiming that his dismissal violated New Jersey's Law Against Discrimination which prohibits discrimination on the basis of sexual orientation. The BSA asserted that its right to freedom of association allowed them to exclude homosexuals. Below are excerpts of the unanimous ruling of the New Jersey Supreme Court, as well as the concurring opinion of Justice Handler.

DOCUMENT 169: *Dale v. Boy Scouts of America* (1999)

Justice C. J. Poritz, writing for a unanimous Court.

The issue in this appeal is whether New Jersey's Law Against Discrimination (LAD), prohibits Boy Scouts of America (BSA) from expelling a member solely because he is an avowed homosexual....

James Dale became a member of BSA in 1978 at the age of eight. He remained a youth member of BSA until his eighteenth birthday in 1988. Dale was an exemplary scout. During his long membership, he earned many badges and honors, including the award of an Eagle Scout Badge, an honor achieved by only the top three percent of all scouts. On March 21, 1989...BSA accepted and approved his application for the position of Assistant Scoutmaster of Troop 73, where he served for approximately sixteen months.

In July 1990...Dale's photo appeared in the *Star-Ledger* [local newspaper] with a caption identifying him as co-president of the Rutgers University Lesbian/Gay Alliance. Later that month, Dale received a letter from BSA Monmouth Council Executive James W. Kay, revoking Dale's BSA membership [and indicating] that the standards for leadership established by the BSA specifically forbade membership to homosexuals....In July 1992, Dale filed suit against BSA....

We find that...Dale's expulsion constituted discrimination based solely on his status as an openly gay man. The United States Supreme Court has not hesitated to uphold the enforcement of a state's antidiscrimination statute against an expressive association claim based on assumptions in respect of status that are not a part of the group members' shared expressive purpose....

When contrasted with its all-inclusive policy, Boy Scouts' litigation stance on homosexuality appears antithetical to the organization's goals and philosophy. The exclusion of members solely on the basis of their sexual orientation is inconsistent with Boy Scouts' commitment to a diverse and representative membership. Moreover, this exclusionary practice contradicts Boy Scouts' overarching objective to reach all eligible youth. We are satisfied that Boy Scouts' expulsion of Dale is based on little more than prejudice and not on a unified Boy Scout position; in other words, Dale's expulsion is not justified by the need to preserve the organization's expressive rights.

The invocation of stereotypes to justify discrimination is all too familiar. Indeed, the story of discrimination is the story of stereotypes that limit the potential of men, women, and children who belong to excluded groups. By way of example, we observe that certain claimed propensities of character were once invoked to advocate the subjugation of women....The human price of this bigotry has been enormous. At a most fundamental level, adherence to the principle of equality demands that our legal system protect the victims of invidious discrimination. New Jersey has long been a leader in this effort....Thus, even if Dale's membership works some slight infringement on Boy Scouts' members right of expressive association, we find that the infringement is justified because it serves New Jersey's compelling interest in eliminating discrimination based on sexual orientation....

Justice J. Handler, concurring opinion.

Dale's statement of his [gay] identity does not express a view about homosexuality...any more than a Scout admitting he is Catholic amounts to a teaching that Catholicism is the only proper religion. As the Court recognizes, Dale has never used his leadership position or membership to promote homosexuality, or any message inconsistent with Boy Scouts' policies....Dale appears to have heeded and lived by Boy Scouts' dictate that individual conscience should guide a Scout's moral decisionmaking.

...One particular stereotype that we renounce today is that homosexuals are inherently immoral. That myth is repudiated by decades of social science data....[Stereotypes] reveal nothing about that individual's moral character, or any other aspect of his or her personality....Plaintiff's exemplary journey through the BSA ranks is testament enough that these stereotypical notions about homosexuals must be rejected....

Another particularly pernicious stereotype about homosexuals is implicit in Boy Scouts' arguments: the sinister and unspoken fear that gay scout leaders will somehow cause physical or emotional injury to scouts. The myth that a homosexual male is more likely than a heterosexual male to molest children has been demolished....[Research studies show] that the adult heterosexual male constitutes a greater sexual risk to underage children than does the adult homosexual male....In light of this evidence, the belief that a gay scoutmaster poses a risk to young boys because of his sexual orientation is patently false, and...must be rejected as an unfounded stereotype....

The 1979 repudiation of New Jersey's sodomy statutes is further evidence of the evolution in social thinking about homosexuality. Sodomy laws and their implicit moral assumptions about homosexuals very much parallel miscegenation statutes, which were grounded in similar stereotypical notions concerning the morality of African Americans.…The indefensibility of basing contemporary moral views regarding race on those laws is obvious. The same is true of placing current reliance on the archaic moral views underlying sodomy laws, which are totally inconsistent with present day conceptions of homosexuality.

It is not tenable to conclude that because at one time "traditional moral values" were based on unsupportable stereotypes about homosexuals, those values have survived and endured unchanged in contemporary times. It is similarly untenable to conclude…that Boy Scouts—a federally chartered and nationally recognized organization with significant ties to governmental institutions and public entities that fully adhere to contemporary laws rejecting anachronistic stereotypes about homosexuality—remains entrenched in the social mores that existed at the time of its inception.…Such stereotypes, baseless assumptions, and unsupported generalizations reflecting a discredited view of homosexuality as criminal, immoral and improper are discordant with current law and public polity.

Source: *James Dale v. Boy Scouts of America* 160 N.J. 562 (Decided August 4, 1999).

*   *   *

After James Dale won his case in the New Jersey Supreme Court, the Boy Scouts appealed that decision to the United States Supreme Court. The Supreme Court was split. In a close five-to-four decision, in which gay and lesbian rights in the United States hinged upon the vote of one person, Chief Justice Rehnquist was joined by Justices O'Connor, Scalia, Kennedy, and Thomas, to rule that the Boy Scouts have a legal right to discriminate against gay scouts. Quoted first here are excerpts from Rehnquist's majority decision, which repeatedly refers to James Dale as "an avowed homosexual," and shows that some jurists have trouble dealing with a gay person as a full human being rather than as a label. This majority opinion is followed by excerpts from an impassioned dissent.

DOCUMENT 170: *Boy Scouts of America v. Dale* (2000)

The Boy Scouts is a private, not-for-profit organization engaged in instilling its system of values in young people. The Boy Scouts asserts that homosexual conduct is inconsistent with the values it seeks to instill. Respondent is James Dale...an avowed homosexual and gay rights activist....

Implicit in the right to engage in activities protected by the First Amendment is a corresponding right to associate with others....Freedom of association...plainly presupposes a freedom not to associate....It is not the role of the courts to reject a group's expressed values....The Boy Scouts [court brief] asserts that it "teaches that homosexual conduct is not morally straight"....We accept the Boy Scouts' assertion. We need not inquire further to determine the nature of the Boy Scouts' expression with respect to homosexuality....

Dale's presence in the Boy Scouts would, at the very least, force the organization to send a message, both to the youth members and the world, that the Boy Scouts accepts homosexual conduct as a legitimate form of behavior....The presence of an avowed homosexual and gay rights activist in an assistant scoutmaster's uniform sends a distinctly different message from the presence of a heterosexual assistant scoutmaster....

A state requirement that the Boy Scouts retain Dale as an assistant scoutmaster would significantly burden the organization's right to oppose or disfavor homosexual conduct. The state interests embodied in New Jersey's public accommodations law do not justify such a severe intrusion on the Boy Scouts' rights to freedom of expressive association....It appears that homosexuality has gained greater societal acceptance. But this is scarcely an argument for denying First Amendment protection to those who refuse to accept these views. The First Amendment protects expression, be it of the popular variety or not....[The government of New Jersey cannot] compel the organization to accept members where such acceptance would derogate from the organization's expressive message.

> Justice Stevens wrote a dissent to Rehnquist's opinion, and was
> joined by Justices Souter, Ginsburg, and Breyer. If only one other justice
> had joined them, this would have been the majority opinion.

It is plain as the light of day that neither...[the *Boy Scout Handbook*, or any instructions given to scouts] says the slightest thing about homosexuality....Scouts are advised to seek guidance on sexual matters from their religious leaders (and Scoutmasters are told to refer Scouts to them); BSA surely is aware that some religions do not teach that homosexuality is wrong. [Moreover, the *Boy Scout Handbook* states that it is] a Scout's duty to be "obedient" and "obey the laws," even if "he thinks the laws are unfair...." BSA's public posture—to the world and to the Scouts themselves...[is] one of tolerance, welcoming all classes of boys and young men....

The right to associate does not mean that in every setting in which individuals exercise some discrimination in choosing associates, their selective process of inclusion and exclusion is protected by the Constitution....For example, we have routinely and easily rejected assertions of this right by expressive organizations with [racially] discriminatory membership policies, such as private schools, law firms, and labor organizations. In fact, until today, we have never once found a claimed right to associate in the selection of members to prevail in the face of a State's antidiscrimination law. To the contrary, we have squarely held that a State's antidiscrimination law does not violate a group's right to associate simply because the law conflicts with that group's exclusionary membership policy.

In *Roberts v. United States Jaycees* (1984), we addressed just such a conflict. The Jaycees was...described as a "young men's organization," in which regular membership was restricted to males between the ages of 18 and 35. But Minnesota's Human Rights Act, which applied to the Jaycees, made it unlawful to "deny any person the full and equal enjoyment of...a place of public accommodation because of...sex." The Jaycees, however, claimed that applying the law to it violated its right to associate—in particular its right to maintain its selective membership policy. We rejected that claim. Cautioning that the right to associate is not "absolute," we held that "infringements on that right may be justified by regulations, adopted to serve compelling state interests, unrelated to the suppression of ideas...." We found the State's purpose of eliminating discrimination is a compelling state interest....

We took a similar approach in *Board of Directors of Rotary Int'l v. Rotary Club of Duarte* (1987). Rotary International, a nonprofit corporation, was founded as "an organization of business and professional men...." Though California's Civil Rights Act, which applied to Rotary International, prohibited discrimination on the basis of sex, the organization claimed a right to associate, including the right to select its members. As in *Jaycees*, we rejected the claim....If California's law worked a "slight infringement on Rotary members' right of expressive association, that infringement is justified because it serves the State's compelling interest in eliminating discrimination against women...."

The relevant question is whether the mere inclusion of the person at issue would "impose any serious burden," "affect in any significant way," or be "a substantial restraint upon" the organization's "shared goals...." The evidence before this Court makes it exceptionally clear that BSA has, at most, simply adopted an exclusionary membership policy and has no shared goal of disapproving of homosexuality....New Jersey's law "requires no change in [BSA's] creed...[and] does not require [BSA] to abandon or alter any of its activities...."

The majority [United States Supreme Court opinion] insists that we must "give deference to an association's assertions regarding the nature of its expression" and "we must also give deference to an association's view of what would impair its expression...." Once the organization "asserts" that it engages in particular expression, "we cannot doubt" the truth of that assertion. This is an astounding view of the law. I am unaware of any previous instance in which our analysis of the scope of a constitutional right was determined by looking at what a litigant asserts in his or her brief and inquiring no further. It is even more astonishing in the First Amendment area....

[The right of association] is not a freedom to discriminate at will, nor is it a right to maintain an exclusionary membership policy simply out of fear....If this Court were to defer to whatever position an organization is prepared to assert in its briefs, there would be no way to mark the proper boundary between genuine exercises of the right to associate, on the one hand, and sham claims that are simply attempts to insulate nonexpressive private discrimination, on the other hand. Shielding a litigant's claim from judicial scrutiny would, in turn, render civil rights legislation a nullity, and turn this important constitutional right into a farce.

BSA has not contended, nor does the record support, that Dale had ever advocated a view on homosexuality to his troop [of Boy Scouts]....Surely many members of BSA engage in expressive activities outside of their troop, and surely BSA does not want all of that expression to be carried on inside the troop. For example, a Scoutmaster may be a member of a religious group that encourages its followers to convert others to its faith....BSA does not discourage or forbid outside expressive activity, but relies on compliance with its policies and trusts Scouts and Scoutmasters alike not to bring unwanted views into the organization....There is no basis for BSA to presume that a homosexual will be unable to comply with BSA's policy not to discuss sexual matters any more than it would presume that politically or religiously active members could not resist the urge to proselytize or politicize during troop meetings....BSA does not expel heterosexual members who take that view [that homosexuality is not immoral] *outside* of their participation in Scouting, as long as they do not advocate that position to the Scouts. And if there is no reason to presume that such a heterosexual will openly violate BSA's desire to express no view on the subject, what reason—other than blatant stereotyping—could justify a contrary presumption for homosexuals?...

The majority, though, does not rest its conclusion on the claim that Dale will use his position as a bully pulpit. Rather, it contends that Dale's mere presence among the Boy Scouts will itself force the group to convey a message about homosexuality....[This means] the right of free speech effectively becomes a limitless right to exclude....That cannot be, and never has been, the law.

The only apparent explanation for the majority's holding, then, is that homosexuals are simply so different from the rest of society that their presence alone—unlike any other individual's—should be singled out for special First Amendment treatment. Under the majority's reasoning, an openly gay male is irreversibly affixed with the label "homosexual." That label, even though unseen, communicates a message that permits his exclusion wherever he goes. His openness is the sole and sufficient justification for his ostracism. Though unintended, reliance on such a justification is tantamount to a constitutionally prescribed symbol of inferiority....

It is equally farfetched to assert that Dale's open declaration of his homosexuality, reported in a local newspaper, will effectively force BSA to send a message to anyone simply because it allows Dale to be an Assistant Scoutmaster. For an Olympic gold medal winner or a Wimbledon tennis champion, being "openly gay"...certainly does not follow that they necessarily send a message on behalf of the [Olympics or Wimbledon] organizations that sponsor the activities in which they excel. The fact that such persons participate in these organizations is not usually construed to convey a message on behalf of those organizations any more than does the inclusion of women, African Americans, religious minorities, or any other discrete group. Surely the organizations are not forced by antidiscrimination laws to take any position on the legitimacy of any individual's private beliefs or private conduct.

The State of New Jersey has decided that people who are open and frank about their sexual orientation are entitled to equal access to employment as school teachers, police officers, librarians, athletic coaches, and a host of other jobs filled by citizens who serve as role models for children and adults alike. Dozens of Scout units throughout the State are sponsored by public agencies, such as schools and fire departments, that employ such role models....

Unfavorable opinions about homosexuals have ancient roots....For too much of our history there was the same inertia in distinguishing between black and white. Over the years, however, interaction with real people, rather than mere adherence to traditional ways of thinking about members of unfamiliar classes, have modified those opinions....That such prejudices are still prevalent and that they have caused serious and tangible harm to countless members of the class New Jersey seeks to protect are established matters of fact that neither the Boy Scouts nor the Court disputes. That harm can only be aggravated by the creation of a constitutional shield for a policy that is itself the product of a habitual way of thinking about strangers. As Justice Brandeis so wisely advised, "we must be ever on our guard, lest we erect our prejudices into legal principles."

Source: Boy Scouts of America v. James Dale 530 U.S. 1 (n. 99–699, decided June 28, 2000).

*   *   *

In the 1990s the American Civil Liberties Union began filing court cases on behalf of transgendered and transsexual people. Employees are often fired from their jobs when a male begins to dress in women's clothes, or a female begins to dress in men's clothes. Other court cases involve child custody, housing, benefits access, and marriage recognition. The ACLU Lesbian and Gay Rights Project has taken on these cases, explaining why they do so in their 2000 annual report:

DOCUMENT 171: Transgender Rights and the ACLU (2000)

Transgender issues are important to our work on two levels: both as part of the larger struggle for civil liberties, and as an element of the struggle for lesbian, gay and bisexual civil rights. The ACLU's mission is to preserve individual civil liberties. That includes protecting our rights to make choices about our bodies and about how we define ourselves, without interference or discrimination on account of those choices. Fighting prejudice against transgendered individuals fits closely within that commitment.

But transgender issues also challenge one of society's most closely held (though fluid) notions: what it is to be male, and what it is to be female. The hate and disgust that transgendered people can provoke is a fear of people who do not fit stereotypes of appropriate sex roles. And that is the same fear that often fuels discrimination against lesbian and gay people. The butch woman and the effeminate man do not conform; they stir fears that our ideas of what a woman or a man is "supposed" to be may not be fixed and reliable. And indeed, they are not. Making society comfortable with that idea is at the heart of all our work in the LGBT community.

Source: "Why Do We Work on Transgender Issues?" *Lesbian & Gay Rights, AIDS/HIV, 2000: An ACLU Report* (New York: American Civil Liberties Union, 2000), p. 23.

* * *

By the end of the 1990s Laura Schlessinger had become the nation's most popular radio talk show host. She hoped to expand that into a television counseling show titled "Dr. Laura," even though her education is not in the field of psychotherapy. A convert to Orthodox Judaism, she readily applies biblical references to contemporary issues and speaks often of "God's law." One subject that she has commented on extensively is homosexual behavior, quoting the condemnation in the Bible's book of Leviticus. She also called lesbians and gay men "a biological error."

DOCUMENT 172: Laura Schlessinger Radio Show (2000)

Given the opportunity by *Time* magazine to clarify her statement, she replied in an interview:

Homosexual behavior deviates from the norm of heterosexuality and is forbidden by Scriptures....My concern is always the well-being of children. And since your average child human being is heterosexual, it seems to me self-evident that the best environment is with the polarity of a mother and a father joined in love, who raise that child with the image of what his future life will be....

We have vaginas and penises. We were biologically meant to give birth to more people. Not being able to relate normally to a member of the opposite sex is some kind of error. I do not see that as insulting at all. It is a statement of biological fact.

Source: Jeanne McDowell, "Preacher, Teacher, Nag: Dr. Laura Speaks Her Mind," *Time* July 3, 2000, pp. 59–60.

*   *   *

In reply, an anonymous person wrote this satirical letter which was distributed widely on the Internet in 2000.

Dear Dr. Laura,

Thank you for doing so much to educate people regarding God's law. I have learned a great deal from you, and I try to share that knowledge with as many people as I can. When someone tries to defend the homosexual lifestyle, for example, I simply remind him that Leviticus 18:22 clearly states it to be an abomination. End of debate. I do need some advice from you, however, regarding some of the specific laws and how to best follow them.

When I burn a bull on the altar as a sacrifice, I know it creates a pleasing odor for the Lord (Lev. 1:9). The problem is my neighbors. They claim the odor is not pleasing to them. How should I deal with this?

I would like to sell my daughter into slavery, as it suggests in Exodus 21:7. In this day and age, what do you think would be a fair price for her?

I know that I am allowed no contact with a woman while she is in her period of menstrual uncleanliness (Lev. 15:19–24). The problem is, how do I tell? I have tried asking, but most women take offense.

Lev. 25:44 states that I may buy slaves from the nations that are around us. A friend of mine claims that this applies to Mexicans but not to Canadians. Can you clarify?

I have a neighbor who insists on working on the Sabbath. Exodus 35:2 clearly states he should be put to death. Am I morally obligated to kill him myself?

Also, a friend of mine feels that even though eating shellfish is an abomination (Lev. 10:10), it is a lesser abomination than homosexuality. I don't agree. Can you settle this?

Lev. 20:20 states that I may not approach the altar of God if I have a defect in my sight. I have to admit that I wear glasses. Does my vision have to be 20/20, or is there some wiggle room here?

I know you have studied these things extensively, so I am confident you can help. Thank you again for reminding us that God's word is eternal and unchanging.

*   *   *

While Vermont was considering legalizing same-sex marriage, Republican State Senator Pete Knight tried to convince the California state legislature to pass a law prohibiting same-sex marriages performed in another state. The California legislature refused to do this. Knight's family was fractured as a result of his efforts, with his own son writing an editorial in the *Los Angeles Times* decrying his father's close-minded bigotry. Despite this opposition, Pete Knight placed a referendum on the ballot that would limit legal marriage as a heterosexual privilege. Proposition 22, known as the Knight Initiative, said that marriage in California is legal only when it is between a man and a woman. This Proposition provided that if another state legalized same-sex marriages, a gay or lesbian couple could not have their marriage recognized if they moved to California.

Despite the progress of the previous five decades, passage of Proposition 22 showed that equality for sexual minorities was far from a reality. The battle for gay and lesbian rights would be ongoing into the new century.

The Knight Initiative passed in California partly as a result of huge monetary contributions and strong support from Utah's Mormon Church. Although homosexuality had not been a major issue for the Mormons until the 1960s, in recent decades the church had become stridently opposed to gay and lesbian rights. Mormons who came out as lesbian or gay were ordered to be forever celibate, or else they were excommunicated from the church. For many who grew up in the close-knit Mormon community, leaving the church or being excommunicated was emotionally devastating.

At the height of the debate over the Knight Initiative, Stuart Matis, a thirty-two-year-old devout gay Mormon in Santa Clara, California, became distraught over the numerous "Yes On Prop 22" signs that blanketed his Mormon neighborhood. Matis had finally decided that he could not continue to live, with the conflict between the reality of his overpowering attractions for males and the antigay teachings of his church. He drove to the local Mormon Church and shot himself in the head. After his death *Newsweek* magazine did an investigative article interviewing Matis's family and friends. Reporter Mark Miller learned from Matis's friends that from age seven,

DOCUMENT 173: Suicide of a Gay Mormon (2000)

Matis began harboring a terrifying secret: he realized he was attracted to boys. For the next 20 years he kept the secret from everyone he knew, and prayed fervently for God to make him heterosexual. He tried to make up for what he considered his shortcoming by being perfect in other areas of his life. He studied hard in school and attended every church function he could. Though he deeply loved his family, he showed little outward affection, fearing he would blurt out his secret in an avalanche of emotion. "He would punish himself if he had a [homosexual] thought," says his childhood friend....He would sit in his room and read Scripture. He set goals for himself not to think about boys for a certain length of time....

As he got older, it became more difficult to keep his feelings hidden. He enrolled at Brigham Young University in Utah, spending hours in the library looking for a technique for becoming straight....Finally, early last year, his agony spilled into the open. Depressed and desperate, he [came out to his family]. To Matis's surprise, his family accepted his homosexuality. They spent many evenings talking and crying into the night. He was able to tell them how much he loved them. Unburdening himself to his family was a relief; yet it did little to lift his depression. He struggled to figure out how to live as a gay man without disobeying the teachings of the church...."Straight members have absolutely no idea what it is like to grow up gay in this church," he wrote. "It is a life of constant torment, self-hatred and internalized homophobia." Matis...was able to reject Mormon teachings on homosexuality intellectually...but emotionally he couldn't....[He was] praying for an answer [from God] that never came.

Source: Mark Miller, "To be Gay—And Mormon," *Newsweek* May 8, 2000, pp. 38–39.

*   *   *

By the beginning of the twenty-first century, despite substantial progress in the European Union and in other nations, the United States Congress had still not passed a law prohibiting discrimination on the basis of sexual orientation. Activist groups like the Human Rights Campaign and the National Gay and Lesbian Task Force responded by pushing for more restricted bills. The Employment Nondiscrimination Act, which covered only employment issues, was supported by President Clinton and a majority of Democratic congress members. But most Republican members of Congress opposed this bill and prevented it from being passed. Even adding the words "sexual orientation" to a national law against hate crime violence generated intense opposition in Congress.

Faced with this lack of action by the federal government, the American Civil Liberties Union decided to focus on hate crimes on the local level. They were successful in several court suits concerning hate crimes, particularly against local public school districts which had taken no action to protect gay, lesbian, bisexual, and transgendered students from violence and harassment. Motivated by fear of substantial court fines, if nothing else, school administrators in many areas of the nation took measures to enforce policies that protect students from hate crimes.

DOCUMENT 174: Antigay Hate Crimes in High Schools (2000)

We heard a lot in the press this year about hate crimes. The brutal murder of Matthew Shepard was the most notorious anti-gay crime, but there were many others. Billy Joe Gaither was tortured and burned in his small rural hometown in Alabama for being gay. Gary Matson and Winfield Scott were killed in their bed in Happy Valley, California because they were gay. And these are only the crimes that were widely reported: unknown numbers more have been assaulted, beaten, left to die in anti-gay attacks around the nation.

Many politicians and members of the lesbian and gay community responded by calling for new laws which would impose tougher sentences for crimes motivated by hate, so-called "hate crime" laws.

Hate crime laws are not a bad idea. Their critics to the contrary, being beaten in a random attack and being beaten because you are black or Asian or Jewish or gay is not the same thing to the victim. Victims of hate crimes are more depressed, lose more of their sense of safety, and have a harder time adjusting back to a normal life.

Perhaps more important, one of the major reasons why we have hate crimes is the widespread belief that society does not value some lives much, if at all. Perpetrators often think that the society in which they live really does not think there is much wrong with assaulting minorities, including gay people. A hate crime law is one way to begin reversing that perception....

But if hate crimes laws are a decent start on dealing with the problem of hate violence, they are no more than a start. The message that society does not value the lives of lesbians and gay men much will not get undone until society says in a meaningful way that discrimination based on sexual orientation is wrong, and that lesbians, gay men, bisexuals and transgendered people are entitled to the same basic respect every citizen gets. We need comprehensive anti-discrimination laws....

There may be no more important place to begin getting that message of respect out than in our schools....One of the purposes of school is to teach society's values. Simply leaving respect for gay people out of the curriculum would send the wrong message in itself. But in all too many schools, the problem is not just omission: schools are not a safe place for lesbian, gay, bisexual and transgendered students.

A study of Massachusetts high school students just published in the journal *Pediatrics* reported that more than 25% of gay teens had recently missed school because of fear for their safety. When compared to heterosexual students, they are four times as likely to be threatened with a weapon at school, four times as likely to be assaulted to the point that medical attention is needed. And school authorities themselves are part of the problem: another study showed that 53% of high school students report hearing homophobic slurs such as "faggot" from their teachers.

If schools are the most important place to teach values based on equality and respect for all, most schools, at least until very recently, want nothing so much as to avoid dealing with the problems of lesbian and gay students entirely. The avoidance option is disappearing. Several high profile [legal] cases have ruled that schools have a responsibility to make their environments safe for all students, gay and straight alike. If they do not, the administrators may be liable for damages. The Supreme Court ruled this past year that schools can be liable if they let sexual harassment flourish unnoticed, even when the harassment comes from other students.

School-by-school litigation is not the answer. It takes far too long, and it is much too expensive. But a few cases can make school districts realize that failure to do something about abuse of lesbians, gay men, bisexuals and transgendered students can lead to protracted litigation with expensive outcomes. The next step is to help them take action. At the start of the school year in 1999, the [ACLU Lesbian and Gay Rights] Project and GLSEN (the Gay, Lesbian, Straight Education Network) published a piece collecting the most often asked questions about school non-discrimination and harassment policies, and providing clear answers. Together we mailed it to every school district in America....

The process of getting America's schools to teach respect will not be finished overnight. But it's worth being persistent, because in the long run, it is likely to be the most effective answer to hate.

Source: Jennifer Middleton and Matt Coles, "Is High School the Answer to Hate Crimes?" *Lesbian & Gay Rights, AIDS/HIV, 2000: An ACLU Report* (New York: American Civil Liberties Union, 2000), pp. 18–19.

*   *   *

On April 30, 2000, several hundreds of thousands of people came to the nation's capital for the fourth national March on Washington. Rather than name it "for gay and lesbian rights" the march organizers titled it a March for Equality. The need for absolute and total equality was the theme of the speeches given at the rally. C-SPAN television channel broadcast to a national audience these speeches, including one by Lorri L. Jean. A longtime activist, Ms. Jean was executive director of the Los Angeles Gay and Lesbian Center, and later led the National Gay and Lesbian Task Force. She represented the feelings of many activists with her frustration at the slowness of social change. However, the very fact that she could call for absolute equality in all aspects of life for lesbian, gay, bisexual and transgendered persons is a measure of how far the movement has come.

DOCUMENT 175: Millennium March on Washington (2000)

Today we have heard from some of the most venerable pioneers in our movement, and some of the most vivacious young people. Some say that these youth are our future. I say that they are our here and now, and to-gether, we must work to create a future that is worthy of all of us.

That's why we're here today—we're fighting for our future. And that's important. It's good to stand up for what is right. And sometimes we even have fun doing it. But I am *not* having fun today. I am not having fun be-cause I'm mad. I marched here for our rights in 1979; I had just come out and I was afraid. I marched again in 1987, without fear and full of pride. I marched again in 1993, filled with excitement about the promise of a new President. But now it's the year 2000, and I'm not afraid and I'm not excited. I'm tired. I'm tired of marching. And I'm MAD! I'm mad because we should not have to be here.

We have seen the dawning of a new millennium and in a country that is supposed to be the freest on earth, we are still having to march. We are still having to fight for the most basic freedoms that every single one of our straight brothers and sisters take for granted. That's wrong, and I'm mad as hell about it!

I am mad that we live in a society where it is still permissible to discrimi-nate against millions of people simply because of our sexual orientation. In some states, it is legal to take away our homes. In others, it is legal to break up our families and take away our children. In 39 states, it is still legal to fire us from our jobs for no reason other than who we love. And still, in the final years of the Clinton Administration, we have no federal laws to guarantee these most basic of protections. ALL OF THESE THINGS ARE WRONG.

All we want is the freedom to love. The freedom to love whomever we choose, without fear, without bigotry, without discrimination. That's it. LOVE. Why is there such a big fuss about love?

If you ask Pat Robertson or Jesse Helms, they don't talk about love. Their hearts are so full of hatred that they're *afraid* of love. Instead, they say we have "a gay agenda." Well, let's admit it. We DO have a gay agenda, and it's the very one upon which this nation was founded: liberty, equality. That's all. We simply want to be treated fairly and equally in all aspects of our society; to have the same rights and responsibilities as every other American.

But not everyone believes in freedom and fairness and equality. That's why we HAVE to march. In fact, some have the gall to look us right in the eyes and say that they *believe* that we should be second class citizens, without equal rights, like the right to marry. And these aren't just our enemies, sometimes these are politicians who claim to be our friends.

Well, to these enemies and so-called friends, I say this: there is no such thing as *partial* freedom or virtual equality. If we are not entirely free, then we are not really free at all. If we do not have the *same* rights, we do not have equal rights. And we're not going to go away until we do. We are not going away, not now, not *ever*.

So, as we enter the new millennium, it is time for a new vision, a new message. A message that is worthy of those who started this battle decades ago, and of the youngest among us who have picked up their torch.

From this point forward, let us adopt a policy of ZERO TOLERANCE. Zero tolerance of discrimination, zero tolerance of bigotry and ignorance, zero tolerance for elected officials who refuse to support our full and complete participation in this society—especially those politicians who take our money! It is *not* OK to tell us that, on one hand, we are welcome to join "the big tent," but on the other hand, we don't deserve the same rights as our tent mates. I say it again, if we are not *completely* free, then we are not really free at all.

This is the agenda that our movement leadership should be promoting, boldly and without compromise. We must stop settling for crumbs. We must stop being apologists for allies who refuse to promote our FULL equality. We must never, *never* be willing to compromise our own freedom, or give others permission to do so. Because if WE fail to stand firm for true justice, others will think they don't have to either. If we won't stand up for total justice for ourselves, how can we expect anyone else to do so?

Some might say that it's not the right time to demand full equality. I say that if we had listened to those who said that it wasn't the right time, or that it couldn't be done, we'd never be where we are today. Freedom can *never* come too soon. It *can* be done! It *must* be done! It *will* be done! This is not a radical message, it is the only acceptable message. We must never lose sight of the fact that what we want and what we demand and what we deserve and what we WILL have is full equality—full equality and nothing less.

Let this be our rallying cry for the new millennium—full equality and nothing less. This is our *birth right*. We are *entitled* to it. And ours is a noble cause because we are engaged in a fight for the very promise of America. Let us not forget that this is a patriotic battle of the highest order, a battle to secure the principle that forms the bedrock of our society, and upon which our nation was founded: life, liberty and the pursuit of happiness.

We must follow the vision of Dr. Martin Luther King, Jr. when he said: "No! No! We are not satisfied until justice rolls down like water and righteousness like a mighty stream."

FULL EQUALITY & NOTHING LESS!

Let this message ring through the land to friend and foe alike. We deserve to participate in the promise of America, and we will not be denied. Whether it takes 20 years or 200 years, we will never give up. And rest assured, we WILL win, because right is on *our* side. History will judge harshly those foes who opposed our freedom, just as it will those friends who lacked the courage and the character to do what is right.

So, when you return home to towns and cities all over this nation, do not forget our message for the new millennium: ZERO TOLERANCE!

FULL EQUALITY, NOTHING LESS!

We demand it, we deserve it and we WILL have it!

Source: "Remarks of Lorri L. Jean, Millennium March on Washington.

*   *   *

Conclusion

The struggle for gay and lesbian rights demonstrates the power of small numbers of individuals to change the course of history. When Henry Gerber organized the first group of American homosexuals for protection of individual rights in 1924, when Edythe Eyde took the initiative to type a lesbian newsletter in 1947, when Mattachine Society member Dale Jennings challenged police entrapment in 1952, when a few original thinkers in Los Angeles founded *ONE* magazine in 1952 as a publication to present the homosexual viewpoint, when the editors sued the United States government for the right to send *ONE* in the mail, and when Jose Sarria ran for public office as an openly gay person in 1961, they each did something that had never been done before.

By taking the initiative, by organizing to do pioneering work on behalf of a minority despised by many, these selfless pioneers laid the basis for millions of people to be able to live their lives openly and with less oppression. In the early years of the movement, newsletters had to be mimeographed secretly in basement offices, closeted homosexuals had to be convinced to take action, letters to the editor had to be written, phone banks had to be staffed, protest marches had to be organized, demonstrations had to be sparked, politicians and media officials and clergy and bureaucrats had to be lobbied, lawsuits had to be filed in court, and—most important—people had to come out of the closet to their relatives, friends and co-workers.

A small number of radical activists had to do what they did, to question the very basics of social values, so large numbers of people could live their lives in all the ways that heterosexuals take for granted. To be left alone without harassment by police or interfering neighbors, to legally marry, to be able to adopt or retain custody of one's children, to serve in the armed forces, to have a house with a white picket fence in the suburbs—these are far from being revolutionary stances. And yet, ironically, a revolution was necessary so sexual minorities could enjoy these aspects of everyday life. All of this is not much different from the role of activists who led the American Revolution in 1776, and who enshrined the principles of individual freedom and liberty into the Bill of Rights in 1791.

The original patriots of 1776 knew, from bitter experience, how government could infringe upon the many details of their intimate daily lives. Under the British colonial system they did not feel free to speak and write their opinions, assemble with their peers, choose their own religious values without coercion by others, feel secure in the privacy of their own homes, and in other ways pleasantly and fully live their own lives as they saw fit. The history of all the struggles for freedom in the United States, from 1775 to the present, has focused on the details of intimate behavior. The nineteenth and twentieth centuries witnessed a gradually expanded idea of freedom, from the abolition of slavery and women's legal subordination, to the right of privacy, and protection from discrimination on the basis of race, sex, and religious nonconformity. The right for people to be left alone, to live their lives as they themselves choose, is a basic tenet in the political ideology of the United States of America.

The fact that it has required such bitter struggles to accomplish these mundane rights—from a civil war over slavery that resulted in the deaths of over 600,000 Americans, to a protest movement lasting seventy years before women could vote—is testament to the powerful forces that exist against equality within the population of the United States. Over the years many Americans have not been committed to the idea of liberty for all. The fact that certain groups have had to struggle for many years to gain equal rights shows that liberty cannot be taken for granted.

One reason the Founders of the republic attached such importance to things like the separation of church and state was because they had seen firsthand, in the colonial era, the disastrous results that occurred when Christian religious zealots had control over the body politic. They rejected the notion that one church—any church—could outlaw or persecute those who did not participate in that church. Though the vast majority of Americans were Protestant Christians, the Founders required tolerance for Catholics, Jews, atheists, and other religious nonconformists. It is supremely ironic that the Catholic Church and the Mormons, two minority religious groups that have experienced much intolerance and prejudice in the past, overcame the prejudice against their own groups only to emerge at the forefront of the effort to deny a similar tolerance to homosexuals. They seem not to have learned an important lesson of American history, that if we expect others to respect our own right to be unique and different, we need to respect the rights of others who are different from us. The flame of liberty is flickering; for it to exist for one, it has to be guaranteed for all.

The main contribution of the struggle for gay and lesbian rights to political ideology is the notion that the right to love is of central importance to human liberty. The history of other social struggles in the United States indicates that justice is not something that happens immediately. It requires many years of challenge, reaction, disagreement, and conflict. The historical record also shows, however, that ultimately the struggles for individual rights result in an expansion of the idea of freedom. Just as with the other freedoms of intimate behavior that are stated in the Bill of Rights, this right to love is part of a larger trend toward respect for individual freedom. These accomplishments—in support of life, liberty, and the pursuit of personal happiness—are the most important gifts the United States of America has given to the modern world.

Given the reality that decades of struggle are necessary to secure the blessings of liberty, the movement for gay and lesbian rights has made amazing progress during its half century of existence in the United States. In 1950, homosexuality was universally condemned by all segments of American society. Churches unanimously considered it a sin, psychiatrists considered it a mental illness, the law considered it a crime, and society considered it a shameful practice. Many homosexuals internalized this hatred, and hid their inclinations from their families and co-workers. Because so many people were leading hidden lives, it was common for a young person to grow up thinking that he or she was the only person in the world to have same-sex attractions. If a person's same-sex feeling did become known, it was treated as a scandal or, at best, as a dirty little secret. People were fired from their jobs, lost their homes, ostracized by their families, beaten up, imprisoned, mutilated by brain surgery, or killed. Under such pressures, many were literally driven insane, suffered depression, alcoholism, drug abuse, or committed suicide.

Fifty years later, few young people in the United States could think they were the only persons in the world with same-sex feelings. Openly gay teachers, business owners, doctors, entertainers, government officials, neighbors, relatives, and friends were a part of the mosaic of society in the United States. Knowing a person involved in a same-sex relationship became a commonplace experience for many Americans. Despite the thousands of people lost to AIDS in the 1980s, the gay and lesbian community continued to grow. Bisexual, transgendered, and intersex persons, or people who simply refused to attach a label to their gender and sexuality, were inspired by the gay and lesbian rights movement to come out of their own closets. Visibility emerged in many aspects of life, from the mass media to the local neighborhood association. The more the opposition tried to crush the movement for personal liberation, the more stubborn and diverse its growth became. While discrimination was far from eliminated, those who engaged in discrimination were put on the defensive. Battles that once took place in the major cities were beginning to take place in small towns. Lesbians, gay men, bisexuals, and transgendered people gained respect for standing up for their right to be treated as equal members of society. Liberation became a positive, even a celebratory, aspect of life in the United States at the dawn of the twenty-first century.

Though the debate over sexual liberation is continuing in the twenty-first century, the story of the struggle for gay and lesbian rights will be seen as an important part of the great movement for human rights that engulfed the United States in the last half of the twentieth century. The activists represented in this book are an integral part of that history.

Glossary

Some of these definitions are social concepts. No single definition can encompass all the variations within socially defined groups of people. Below are general definitions to help clarify specific words, sometimes quoting from Steve Hogan and Lee Hudson, *Completely Queer: The Gay and Lesbian Encyclopedia* (New York: Henry Holt, 1998). Readers are encouraged to look to definitions supplied by the groups themselves.

Bill of Rights. The first ten amendments to the United States Constitution, which were added to provide guarantees of civil liberties and individual rights to the people. Many state constitutions also have their own specified Bill of Rights. The U.S. Bill of Rights was strengthened in 1868 by the addition of the Fourteenth Amendment which prohibited state governments from violating the equal protection of the laws.

Bisexual. A person who is sexually attracted to both males and females. Bisexual activists describe themselves as "people who are attracted to individuals rather than to persons of a particular gender or biological sex" [*Completely Queer*, p. 88].

Civil rights. Rights to legal and social equality that everyone is supposed to possess regardless of race, creed, age, national origin, sex, gender, sexual orientation, and disability.

Coming out. A shortened phrase to describe a person who "comes out of the closet" by letting oneself and/or others know of one's homosexual inclinations.

Equal protection of the law. A guarantee in the Fourteenth Amendment of the United States Constitution that no person or class of persons shall be denied the same protection of the laws enjoyed by other persons.

FTM. Female to male transsexual person.

Gay. A term used to refer to both male and female homosexuals. Also used within the homosexual community to refer to male homosexuals only, which use is usually combined with the term "lesbian" for female homosexuals.

Heterosexual. A person of any sex who is sexually attracted primarily or solely to persons of another sex.

Heterosexism. The belief that heterosexuality is superior to other types of sexuality.

Homophile. Members of the first activist phase of the gay and lesbian movement for civil and human rights, mainly used in the 1950s and 1960s.

Homophobia. Prejudice, discrimination, harassment, or acts of violence directed against sexual minorities, including lesbians, gay men, bisexuals, transgendered/transsexual/intersex persons, or persons of indeterminant gender.

Homosexual. A person of any sex who is sexually attracted primarily or solely to other persons of the same sex. Homosexual identities do not need proof of sexual behavior in order to qualify as such, anymore than heterosexual identities do.

Intersexual. "Individuals born with anatomy or physiology which differs from cultural ideals of male and female" [http://www.isna.org/about/index.html].

Invert. Term used in the early twentieth century to refer to homosexuals, especially gender nonconforming persons.

Lesbian. A woman whose primary affectional and sexual attraction is to women. Lesbianism was named after the island of Lesbos, the home of the ancient Greek female poet Sappho.

LGBT. Acronym for lesbian, gay, bisexual and transgender people.

MTF. Male to female transsexual person.

Queer. Though originally an insult word meaning "abnormal," in the 1980s some activists began to use it as a badge of transgression. Queer describes persons whose "sexual desires or gender identity do not conform to socioculturally constructed norms…[and also suggesting] anti-assimilationism defiance, and pride in non-conformity." It is sometimes used as an umbrella term for all lesbian, gay, bisexual, transgender, transsexual, intersexual and sexually undefined people [*Completely Queer*, pp. 463–464].

Sapphist. Early twentieth-century term for lesbians, named after the ancient Greek poet Sappho who lived on the island of Lesbos.

Transgender. "Increasingly used to describe persons who assert a gender identity different from their biological sex, but who choose not to undergo sex reassignment surgery." [*Completely Queer*, p. 545].

Transsexual. "Persons whose gender identity differs from what is culturally associated with their biological sex at birth…[or] persons who have had an operation to change their congenital sex." [*Completely Queer*, p. 544].

List of Gay, Lesbian, Bisexual, and Transgender Organizations

The Advocate
   http://www.advocate.com/
AIDS Memorial Quilt
   http://www.aidsquilt.org/
BCC (First LGBT Jewish Congregation)
   http://www.bcc-la.org/
Bisexual Resource Center
   http://www.biresource.org/
Children of Lesbians and Gays Everywhere (COLAGE)
   http://www.colage.org/
Committee on Lesbian and Gay History
   http://www.usc.edu./isd/archives/clgh
Deaf Queer resources
   http://www.deafqueer.org/
Dignity (LGBT Catholics)
   http://www.dignityusa.org/
Evangelicals Concerned with Reconciliation (ECWR)
   http://www.ecwr.org/
Freedom to Marry Coalition
   http://www.freedomtomarry.org/
Gay Asian Pacific Support Network
   http://www.gapsn.org/
Gay and Lesbian Alliance Against Defamation (GLAAD)
   http://www.glaad.org/
Gay and Lesbian Arabic Society
   http://www.glas.org/

Gay and Lesbian Organizations and Publications (extensive list from
Alvin Fritz)
   http://faculty.washington.edu/alvin/gayorg.htm
Gay, Lesbian, Straight Education Network
   http://www.glsen.org/templates/index.html
Human Rights Campaign
   http://www.hrc.org/
International Gay and Lesbian Human Rights Commission
   http://www.iglhrc.org/site/iglhrc/
International Gay and Lesbian Review
   http://www.usc.edu./gay review
Intersex Society of America
   http://www.isna.org/
Lambda Literary Foundation
   http://www.lambdalit.org/index_2.html
Lambda 10 Project (fraternities/sororities)
   http://www.lambda10.org/
Lesbian and Gay Aging Issues Network
   http://www.asaging.org/networks/lgain/index.html
Lesbian History Project
   http://isd.usc.edu/~retter/main.html
Lesbian News
   http://www.lesbiannews.com/
Michigan Womyn's Festival
   http://www.michfest.com/
National Gay and Lesbian Task Force
   http://www.ngltf.org/index.cfm
National Latina/o Lesbian and Gay Organization (LLEGO)
   http://www.llego.org/
ONE Institute and Archives (Los Angeles)
   http://www.oneinstitute.org/
Oscar Wilde Gay and Lesbian Bookshop (New York)
   http://www.oscarwildebooks.com/
OutProud! The National Coalition for Gay, Lesbian, Bisexual and Transgender Youth
   http://www.outproud.org/
Parents and Friends of Lesbians and Gays (PFLAG)
   http://www.pflag.org/
Planet Out Radio
   http://www.planetout.com/pno/gloradio/splash.html
Stop Violence.com: Hate crimes, Bias Crimes and Homophobia
   http://www.stopviolence.com/hate/lbgt.htm

United Lesbians of African Descent (ULOAH)
    http://members.aol.com/uloah/home.html
Universal Fellowship of Metropolitan Community Churches
    http://www.ufmcc.com/index2.htm
Washington Blade
    http://www.washblade.com/
Women and Children First Bookstore (Chicago)
    http://www.womenandchildrenfirst.com/NASApp/store/IndexJsp

Selected Bibliography

Adleman, Jeanne et al. *Lambda Gray*. North Hollywood, CA: Newcastle Publishing, 1993.

Baird, Robert M. and M. Katherine Baird, eds. *Homosexuality: Debating the Issues*. Amherst, NY: Prometheus Books, 1995.

Baird, Robert M. and Stuart E. Rosenbaum. *Same-Sex Marriage: The Moral and Legal Debate*. Amherst, NY: Prometheus Books, 1997.

Balka, Christie and Andy Rose. *Twice Blessed: On Being Lesbian, Gay and Jewish*. Boston: Beacon Press, 1989.

Beam, Joseph. *In the Life: A Black Gay Anthology*. Boston: Alyson, 1986.

Beemyn, Brett. *Creating a Place for Ourselves. Lesbian, Gay and Bisexual Community Histories*. New York: Routledge, 1997.

Berube, Allan. *Coming Out Under Fire: The History of Gay Men and Women in World War Two*. New York: The Free Press, 1990.

Berzon, Betty. *Setting Them Straight: You Can Do Something about Bigotry and Homophobia in Your Life*. New York: Plume, 1996.

Blasius, Mark and Shane Phelan, eds. *We Are Everywhere: A Historical Sourcebook of Gay and Lesbian Politics*. New York: Routledge, 1997.

Bull, Chris, ed. *Witness to Revolution: The Advocate Reports on Gay and Lesbian Politics, 1967–1999*. Los Angeles: Alyson Books, 1999.

Chauncey, George. *Gay New York: Gender, Urban Culture and the Making of the Gay Male World, 1890–1940*. New York: Basic Books, 1994.

Clarke, Cheryl. *"The Failure to Transform: Homophobia in the Black Community."* In *Homegirls: A Black Feminist Anthology*. Barbara Smith, ed. New York: Kitchen Table Press, 1983, pp. 197–208.

Clendinen, Dudley. *Out for Good: The Struggle to Build a Gay Rights Movement in America*. New York: Simon and Schuster, 1999.

Combahee River Collective. "A Black Feminist Statement." In *This Bridge Called My Back: Writings by Radical Women of Color*. Chere Moraga and Gloria Anzalda, eds. New York: Kitchen Table Press, 1983, pp. 210–218.

Cowan, Thomas. *Gay Men and Women Who Enriched the World*. New Canaan, CT: Mulvey Books, 1998.

Currah, Paisley and Shannon Minter. *Transgender Equality: A Handbook for Activists and Policymakers*. Introduction by Jamison Green. San Francisco: National Center for Lesbian Rights and The Policy Institute of the National Gay and Lesbian Task Force, 2000.

D'Emilio, John. *Sexual Politics, Sexual Communities: The Making of a Homosexual Minority in the United States, 1940–1970*. Chicago: University of Chicago Press, 1983.

Drucker, Jane. *Families of Value: Gay and Lesbian Parents and Their Children Speak Out*. New York: Insight Books, 1998.

Duberman, Martin. *Midlife Queer*. New York: Dutton, 1993.

———. *Stonewall*. New York: Dutton, 1993.

Due, Linnea. *Joining the Tribe: Growing Up Gay and Lesbian in the 90s*. New York: Anchor Books, 1995.

Eng, D. and Alice Hom, eds. *Q&A: Queer in Asian America*. Philadelphia: Temple University Press, 1998.

Faderman, Lillian. *Odd Girls and Twilight Lovers: A History of Lesbian Life in Twentieth-Century America*. New York: Columbia University Press, 1991.

Feinberg, Leslie. *Trans Liberation: Beyond Pink or Blue*. Boston: Beacon Press, 1998.

Fone, Byrne R.S. *The Columbia Anthology of Gay Literature: Readings from Western Antiquity to the Present Day*. New York: Columbia University Press, 1998.

Geis, Sally and Donald Messer, eds. *Caught in the Crossfire: Helping Christians Debate Homosexuality*. Nashville, TN: Abingdon Press, 1995.

Gershick, Zsa Zsa. *Gay Old Girls*. Los Angeles: Alyson Books, 1998.

Haggerty, George, ed. *Gay Histories and Cultures: An Encyclopedia*. New York: Garland Press, 2000.

Herek, Gregory M. and Kevin T. Berrill, eds. *Hate Crimes: Confronting Violence Against Lesbians and Gay Men*. Newbury Park, CA: Sage Publications, 1992.

Heron, Ann, ed. *Two Teenagers in Twenty: Writings by Gay and Lesbian Youth*. Boston: Alyson Publications, 1994.

Hoagland, S. and Julia Penelope, eds. *Lesbian Culture: An Anthology*. Freedom, CA: The Crossing Press, 1993.

Hogan, Steve and Lee Hudson. *Completely Queer: The Gay and Lesbian Encyclopedia*. New York: Henry Holt, 1998.

Howard, Kim and Annie Stevens, eds. *Out and About Campus: Personal Accounts by Lesbian, Gay, Bisexual and Transgender College Students*. Los Angeles: Alyson Books, 2000.

Hutchins, Loraine and Lani Ka'ahumanu, eds. *Bi Any Other Name: Bisexual People Speak Out*. Boston: Alyson Publications, 1991.

Ingram, Gordon Brent, Anne-Marie Bouthillette, and Yolanda Retter, eds. *Queers in Space: Communities, Public Places, Sites of Resistance*. Seattle: Bay Press, 1997.

Katz, Jonathan Ned. *Gay American History: Lesbians and Gay Men in the U.S.A.* New York: Thomas Crowell, 1976.

———. *Gay/Lesbian Almanac: A New Documentary*. New York: Harper & Row, 1983.

Kennedy, Elizabeth and Madeline Davis. *Boots of Leather, Slippers of Gold: The History of a Lesbian Community*. New York: Routledge, 1993.

Kepner, Jim. *Becoming a People: A 4,000 Year Chronology of Gay and Lesbian History*. Los Angeles: International Gay and Lesbian Archives, 1995.

Legg, W. Dorr, David Cameron, and Walter Williams. *Homophile Studies in Theory and Practice*. San Francisco: ONE Institute Press and GLB, 1994.

Luczak, Raymond, ed. *Eyes of Desire: A Deaf Gay and Lesbian Reader*. Boston: Alyson Publications, 1993.

Marcus, Eric. *Is It a Choice? Answers to 300 of the Most Frequently Asked Questions About Gays and Lesbians*. New York:HarperCollins, 1993.

———. *Making History: The Struggle for Gay and Lesbian Equal Rights, 1945–1990*. New York: HarperCollins, 1992.

Miller, Neil. *Out of the Past: Gay and Lesbian History from 1869 to the Present*. New York: Vintage Books, 1995.

Murphy, Lawrence. *Perverts by Official Order: The Campaign against Homosexuals by the United States Navy*. New York: Harrington Park Press, 1988.

Nava, Michael and Robert Dawidoff. *Created Equal: Why Gay Rights Matter to America*. New York: St. Martin's Press, 1994.

Nestle, Joan, ed. *The Persistent Desire: A Femme/Butch Reader*. Boston: Alyson Publications, 1992.

Nestle, Joan. *A Restricted Country*. Ithaca, NY: Firebrand Books, 1987.

Orr, Lisa, ed. *Sexual Values: Opposing Viewpoints*. San Diego, CA: Greenhaven Press, 1989.

Penelope, Julia, ed. *Out of the Class Closet: Lesbians Speak*. Freedom, CA: The Crossing Press, 1994.

———and Susan Wolfe, eds. *Lesbian Culture: An Anthology*. Freedom, CA: The Crossing Press, 1993.

Preves, Sharon E. *Intersex and Identity: The Contested Self*. New Brunswick, NJ: Rutgers University Press, 2003.

Ramos, Juanita, ed. *Compañeras: Latina Lesbians*. New York: Latina Lesbian History Project, 1987.

Ratti, Rakesh, ed. *Lotus of Another Color: An Unfolding of the South Asian Gay and Lesbian Experience*. Los Angeles: Alyson Publications, 1993.

Retter, Yolanda. "On the Side of Angels: Lesbian Activism in Los Angeles, 1970–1990." PhD Dissertation, University of New Mexico, 1999.

Richardson, Diane and Steven Seidman, eds. *Handbook of Gay and Lesbian Studies*. Thousand Oaks, CA: Sage Publications, 2002.

Roberts, Jo Ann and Dallas Denny. "Selected Readings on Transvestism, Transexualism and Related Subjects: Annotated Bibliography." [http://www.tgfmall.com/info/Biblio.html].

Roscoe, Will, ed. *Living the Spirit: A Gay American Indian Anthology*. New York: St. Martin's Press, 1988.

Russo, Vito. *The Celluloid Closet: Homosexuality in the Movies*. New York: Harper, 1981.

Rutledge, Leigh W. *The Gay Decades: From Stonewall to the Present: The People and Events That Shaped Gay Lives*. New York: Plume, 1992.

Sanlo, Ronni, ed. *Working with Lesbian, Gay, Bisexual and Transgender College Students: A Handbook for Faculty and Administrators*. Westport, CT: Greenwood Press, 1998.

Schlager, Neil, ed. *St. James Press Gay and Lesbian Almanac*. Detroit: St. James Press, 1998.

Sears, James T. and Walter L. Williams, eds. *Overcoming Heterosexism and Homophobia: Strategies That Work*. New York: Columbia University Press, 1997.

Shilts, Randy. *And the Band Played On: Politics, People and the AIDS Epidemic*. New York: St. Martin's Press, 1987.

Siker, Jeffrey, ed. *Homosexuality in the Church: Both Sides of the Debate*. Louisville, KY: Westminster Knox Press, 1994.

Stein, Marc. *City of Sisterly and Brotherly Loves: Lesbian and Gay Philadelphia, 1945–1972*. Chicago: University of Chicago Press, 2000.

Stewart, Chuck. *Sexually Stigmatized Communities: Reducing Heterosexism and Homophobia, An Awareness Training Manual*. Thousand Oaks, CA: Sage, 1999.

Stewart, Stephen. *Gay Hollywood Film & Video Guide: 75 Years of Gay and Lesbian Images in the Movies*. Laguna Hills, CA: Companion Publications, 1994.

Storr, Meri, ed. *Bisexuality: A Critical Reader*. London: Routledge, 1999.

Streitmatter, Rodger. *Unspeakable: The Rise of the Gay and Lesbian Press in America*. Boston: Faber and Faber, 1995.

Summers, Claude, ed. *The Gay and Lesbian Literary Heritage: A Reader's Companion to the Writers and their Works, from Antiquity to the Present*. New York: Henry Holt, 1995.

Swidler, Arlene. *Homosexuality and World Religions*. Valley Forge, PA: Trinity Press International, 1993.

Thompson, Mark, ed. *Long Road to Freedom: The Advocate History of the Gay and Lesbian Movement*. New York: St. Martin's Press, 1994.

Trujilio, Carla, ed. *Chicana Lesbians: The Girls Our Mothers Warned Us About*. Berkeley: Third Woman Press, 1991.

Tucker, Naomi, ed., with Liz Highleyman and Rebecca Kaplan. *Bisexual Politics: Theories, Queries and Visions*. New York: Harrington Park Press, 1995.

Vacha, Keith. *Quiet Fire: Memoirs of Older Gay Men*. Trumansburg, NY: The Crossing Press, 1985.

Wat, Eric. *The Making of a Gay Asian Community: An Oral History of Pre-AIDS* Los Angeles. Lanham, MD: Rowman and Littlefield, 2002.

Williams, Walter L. *The Spirit and the Flesh: Sexual Diversity in American Indian Culture*. Boston: Beacon Press, 1992.

Witt, Lynn, Sherry Thomas, and Eric Marcus, eds. *Out in All Directions: A Treasury of Gay and Lesbian America*. New York: Warner Books, 1995.

Zimmerman, Bonnie, ed. *Lesbian Histories and Cultures*. New York: Garland Press, 2000.

Index

Aarons, Leroy, 225
Abdill, Michelle, xlii
Abortion, xxix, 48, 141, 142, 180, 212
Abzug, Bella, xxxix
Achtenberg, Roberta, 210–12
ACLU. *See* American Civil Liberties Union
Act for the Suppression of Trade in, and Circulation of, Obscene Literature and Articles of Immoral Use, 48
Activism, 285–86; and Democratic Party, 188; and Foster, 105; and Gay Activists Alliance, 119–20; and Gittings, 107; and Homophile Action League, 115; and homophile movement, 71; and job discrimination, 191; and Lesbianas Unidas, 235; and lesbians, 123–24; and New York City, 117, 118, 120; and Oregon Measure 9, 209; and Perry, 114; personal change, 167; and Rivera, 117–18; and Sarria, 95–96; and transgender persons, 249. *See also* Militancy
ACT UP, xli, 188, 192–93
Adultery, 27
Advocate, The, xxxviii, 111, 112, 113, 291
Advocate Experience, The, 138
Affirmative action, 208, 226
African Americans, xl, 141, 223–24; and civil rights movement, 69, 70;

and *Dred Scott* decision, 266; and early United States, 36; feminist, 166–67; and Gay Liberation Front, 119; and Gittings, 107; and homophobia, 181–82; and Japanese American Citizens League, 233; and Kameny, 102; and March on Washington, 152; and marriage, xxx; and military, 214; and Milk, 149; and morality, 271; and New Netherland, 24–25; and Southern Baptist Convention, 250; and Third World Lesbian/Gay Conference, 153
African Ancestral Lesbians United for Societal Change, xl
Ageism, 195–96
AIDS/HIV, xl; and ACT UP, xli, 192–93; and American Indians, 196; and bisexuals, 203; and Christianity, 183–85, 187, 188; and Dannemeyer, 199; emergence of, 142, 160–61; and government, 188; and Holden and Galluccio, 243; and Hudson, 174; and lesbians, 142, 183, 184, 192; and Maupin, 174; and pleasure, 197–98; and religion, 183–85, 187; and service organizations, 174–75. *See also* Sexually transmitted disease
AIDS Quilt, 174, 194, 291
Aldredge, J. C., 57

Alice B. Toklas Memorial Democratic
    Club, 127, 140
American Civil Liberties Union
    (ACLU), 69; accomplishments of,
    139; and adoption, 243, 244; and
    civil liberties, 276; and Colorado
    Amendment 2, 239–40; and de-
    criminalization, xxxviii; and Foley,
    216, 220; and gay and lesbian
    rights, 97–98; and hate crimes,
    279–80; and Immigration and Nat-
    uralization Service, 110; and Ka-
    meny, 102; and marriage, 220; and
    Mattachine Society National Con-
    vention, 92; and National Gay and
    Lesbian Task Force, 130; and
    sodomy laws, 267, 268; and trans-
    gendered people, 275, 276; and
    transsexuals, 275
American Conservative Union, 159
American Foundation for AIDS Re-
    search, 174
American Indians: and AIDS/HIV,
    196; beliefs of, xl, 1–9, 21; and early
    United States, 36, 37; and Gage,
    100–101; and Gay American Indi-
    ans, 196–97; and Spain, 31–32
American Jewish Congress, xl
American Psychiatric Association,
    The, xxxix, 132–34, 139, 151
American Revolution, 36–38, 43,
    286
American Society of Newspaper Edi-
    tors, 225
American Sociology Association,
    xxxviii
Amestoy, Jeffrey L., 264–67
Amster, Joseph, 113
Anderson, Julie, 247–48
Androgyny, 2, 3, 8, 249
Animals, xxiii, xxvi, 26
Animism, 1, 2
Anita Bryant Ministries, 156
Anthony, Susan B., 125
Anza, Juan Bautista de, 32
Aravosi, John, 263
Asian Americans, 136–37, 153, 154,
    155, 232–34
Aspin, Les, 213

Assembly, 68, 75, 81
Association, freedom of, 272–73, 274
Association of Gay and Lesbian
    Artists (AGLA), 246
Atkinson, Ti-Grace, 126

Bachelors, 40–43
Baehr, Ninia, 216, 218, 220
Baehr v. Lewin, 218
Baines, Jim, 171
Baker, Stan, 263
Baker v. Nelson, 98
Baldwin, James, 182
Bars: and Fleischman, 78; and Mafia,
    77; owners of, 104–5; and police, 68,
    73, 77, 78–79, 94–95, 97, 104, 111;
    and politics, 104; problems with,
    104; and San Francisco, 94–95. See
    also Stonewall Inn
Bathhouses, 161
Bauman, Robert, 159–60
Beatniks, 83
Beck, Nina, 263
Behavior Modification Conference,
    121
Benefits, 254–55, 256, 264, 265, 267. See
    also Marriage
Bennett, William, 242–43
Ben-Shalom, Miriam, xl
Bergler, Edmund: Homosexuality:
    Disease or Way of Life?, 151
Bernsen, Sam, 110
Berrill, Kevin, 169
Berzon, Betty, 193–94
Bestiality, 26, 27
Beth Chayim Chadashim (BCC),
    xxxix, 200
Bible, 184; and AIDS/HIV, 185; and
    American Revolution, 36; attitudes
    in, 9–20; and Bill of Rights, 39; and
    Blackstone's Commentaries, 31; and
    Boyd, 156; and Bryant, 157; and
    Declaration of Independence, 38;
    and Falwell, 162; and fundamen-
    talism, 141; and John Paul II, 163;
    and Milk, 149; and Oregon Mea-
    sure 9, 210; and Puritans, 26, 27, 28;
    and Schlesinger, 276–78; and
    Southern Baptist Convention, 251;

and Vaid, 221; and women's rights, 42, 43

Bill of Rights. *See* Constitution of the United States

Biology, 3, 59, 248, 276, 277

Bird, Merton, 75

Birth control, xxix, 47, 69, 180, 187

Bisexual Forum, The, xl

Bisexuality, xxvi, 220, 229, 249

Bisexual Resource Center, 291

Bisexuals, 202, 203, 289

Black and White Men Together, 169

Black Cat bar, 95, 96, 111

Black Gay Leadership Forum, xli

Blackmun, Harry, 176–77, 178

Black Power Movement, 116, 119

Blackstone, Sir William, 30–31; *Commentaries,* 31

Blick, Roy E., 65

Block, Martin, 75

Bloomstein, Charles, 100

Blues, 169

Blunt, Frank, 48

Board of Directors of Rotary Int'l v. Rotary Club of Duarte, 273

Body, right to control, xxii

Bonny, Anne, 29, 30

Book of Exodus, 11–12

Book of Genesis, 10–11

Book of Leviticus, 9, 12–14, 16, 277–78

Book of Ruth, 14–15

Book of Samuel, 15–16

Boozer, Mel, xl, 158–59

Bottini, Ivy, 122

Bottoms, Kay, 230, 231

Bottoms, Sharon, 230–31

Bottoms, Tyler, 230, 231

Boutillier v. The Immigration and Naturalization Service, 97, 110

Bowers, Michael, 176

Bowers v. Hardwick, xli, 31, 176–77, 188, 206, 240, 267, 268

Boyd, Malcolm, 155; *Take Off the Masks,* 155

Boy Scouts of America, xlii, 211, 268–75

Boy Scouts of America v. Dale, 271–75

Brandon, Teena, 238–39

Bratman, Cheryl, xxxix, 134

Briggs, John, 144, 147, 149, 150

Briggs Initiative, The, xl

Brigham Young University, 145, 279

Brinkin v. Southern Pacific, 98

Brown, Howard, 130; *Familiar Faces, Hidden Lives,* 128–29

Brown, Rita Mae, 122, 135–36; *Rubyfruit Jungle,* 135

Brownmiller, Susan, 124

Bryant, Anita, 143–44, 147, 149, 150, 156–57

Buchanan, James, 41

Buchanan, Patrick, 203–4, 252

Buddhism, 216, 217, 218, 219, 220

Burger, Warren, 31

Burns, Randy, xl, 196–97

Burroughs, William, 83; *Naked Lunch,* 84

Bush, George H. W., xli, 188

Bush, George W., 257

Bush, Larry, 169

Bushel, Hyman, 55–56

Business, xxvii, 91, 192

Byrd, James, 258, 259, 260

California, colonial, 32

California Proposition 22, 278

Call, Harold, 91, 92

Cameron, Barbara, xl, 196

Cammermeyer, Margarethe, 215

Capitalism, xxvii

Carnes, Jim, 169–71

Carter, Jimmy, xl, 140

Castro, Fidel, 103

Cauldwell, D. C., xxxvii

Chang, Kevin, 216

Chapman, Bert, xxxix

Children of Lesbians and Gays Everywhere (COLAGE), 291

Children/youth: and adoption, xxix, 243–44; and American Indians, 4, 5, 7; and bisexuality, 229; and Bryant, 143; custody of, xxxix, 134–35, 176, 230–31; and early United States, 37–38; and Falwell, 162; and Hawai'i Reciprocal Beneficiary Act, 255; and homophobia, xxxii; and intersexed hermaphrodites, 248–49; and Lesbian Avengers, 236, 237–38; and

Children/youth (*continued*)
   molestation, 149, 150, 209, 247, 270;
   and Oregon Measure 9, 209; and
   Oregon Measure 13, 226–27; and
   Project 10, xli; recruitment of, xxix;
   and rejection, 131–32; and
   Schlesinger, 277; and Vermont marriage law, 263–64; and *Voeller v.
   Voeller*, 98; and Weller, 228–29
China, xxv
Christianity: and AIDS/HIV, 183–85,
   187, 188; and American Indians, 1,
   7, 32; and Bible, 9–20; and Blackstone's *Commentaries*, 31; and
   Bryant, 143; conservative, 183; conservative evangelical, 179; and
   English colonies, 33; and Falwell,
   162; and Foley, 218; fundamentalist, 140, 141–42, 143, 155–58, 170,
   179, 187, 188, 221; and Maupin,
   174; and media, 246; and Perry,
   112–14; and persecution, 67; and
   Playboy ethic, xxvii; and Religious
   Right, 235–36; and San Francisco
   activists, 105; and sexism, 157–58;
   and sodomy, 21; and United States,
   36; and Vaid, 221; and Whitman,
   44–45; and witchcraft, xxviii; and
   women, 21, 43, 70. *See also* Metropolitan Community Church; Religion; *specific sects*
Church of Jesus Christ of Latter-Day
   Saints, 145–46, 232, 254, 255–56,
   278, 279
Civil rights, 289; activism around, 69;
   and American Civil Liberties
   Union, 276; and Boyd, 155; and
   du Mas, 151; and Foley, 216; and
   Hawai'i State Constitution, 256;
   and Japanese Americans Citizens
   League, 232, 233; and Kameny, 102;
   and Kepner, 80; and law, 259; and
   love, 283; and National Gay and
   Lesbian Task Force, 130; and National Gay Task Force, 129; and
   sodomy law, 176; and Southern
   Baptist Convention, 250, 251
Civil Rights Act, 99, 140

Civil rights movement: and Boozer,
   159; and Gay Liberation Front, 119;
   and Gittings, 107; as inspiration,
   69–70; and Kameny, 102; and
   Rivera, 117; and Rustin, 98
Civil union, xlii, 257. *See also* Domestic
   partnership; Marriage; Union, ceremony of
Clarke, Cheryl: "Failure to Transform:
   Homophobia and the Black Community," 181–82
Class, xxvii, 44
Clinton, Bill, 133, 188–90, 191; and
   Achtenberg, 210, 211; and Defense
   of Marriage Act, 241; and Dobson,
   252; and Employment Nondis-
   crimination Act, 279; and hate
   crimes, 259; and military, xli,
   213–15; and Southern Baptist Con-
   vention, 251
Clothing, 5, 7. *See also* Transvestites
Coles, Matt, 97, 240
Colorado Amendment 2, 190, 207,
   239–40
Combahee River Collective, 166
Coming out, xli, 107, 116, 150, 153,
   260–61, 289
Committee of Lesbian and Gay His-
   tory, 291
Communism, 63
Communist Party, 72
Community, 68, 69, 140, 229
Comstock, Anthony, 48–49
Congo, Manuel, 25
Congress: and hate crimes, 279; and
   job discrimination, xlii, 65–66; and
   Kameny, xxxix; and March on
   Washington for Gay and Lesbian
   Rights (1993), 220, 221; and mili-
   tary, 190; and police reform, 169;
   and sexual orientation, 279; and
   Southern Baptist Convention, 252
Congress to Unite Women, 122, 124
Conservatism: and Achtenberg, 210;
   and Bauman, 159; and Colorado
   Amendment 2, 207; and fundamen-
   talist Christians, 142; and Japanese
   Americans Citizens League, 234;

and Liebman, 204; and military, 215; and Oregon Citizens Alliance, 208; and Osborn, 247; and personal change activism, 167; and Religious Right, 235–36; social, 141; and unnaturalness, 152; and Vaid, 221. *See also* Republican Party
Constitution of the United States, 39–40, 67; Bill of Rights of, 39–40, 67, 80, 81, 93, 240, 286, 287, 289; and Boozer, 158; and *Bowers v. Hardwick,* 177, 178; and Defense of Marriage Act, 190, 241; due process clause of, 177, 178; Fifth Amendment to, 177; First Amendment to, 272; Fourteenth Amendment to, 45–46, 177; full faith and credit clause of, 241; and Gerber, 51–54; and Homophile Action League, 115; and "A Homosexual Bill of Rights," 93; and Kepner, 80, 81; and marriage, 218; Nineteenth Amendment to, 70; Ninth Amendment to, 205; and religion, 254, 286; and *Romer v. Evans,* 240; and slavery, 45; and sodomy laws, 182; Thirteenth Amendment to, 45
Corbin, Joan, 88
Cordova, Jeanne, 134–35
Cornish, Richard, 23
Costanza, Midge, xl, 140
Council on Religion and the Homophile, 77
Council on Religion and the Homosexual, 105–6
Counterculture, 70, 83, 116
Courts, 108, 109, 130–31. *See also* Law; Supreme Court
Creedle, James, 169
Creoli, Jan, 25
Crittenden, S. H., Jr., 84–86
Crittenden Report, The, xxxviii, 84–86
Cuba, 103
Cyberactivism, 262–63

Dade County Commission, 143
Dale, James, 268–75
Dale v. Boy Scouts of America, 269–71

Daley, Jo, 147
Dancel, Genora, 216, 218, 220
Danforth, Samuel, 26–28
Dannemeyer, William: *Shadow in the Land,* 199–200
Darrow, Clarence, 51
Daughters of Bilitis (DOB), xxxviii; and Council on Religion and the Homosexual, 105; and Fleischman, 77; founding of, 68, 79–80; and gay bars, 104; and Gittings, 108; and Homophile Action League, 115; and National Organization for Women, 122; and ONE, Inc., 93
Davis, Gary L., 209–10
Davis, Madeline, xxxix, 127
Deaf Names Project, 223
Deaf people, 223–24
Deaf Queer Resources, 291
Declaration of Independence, 38–39, 52, 67, 150, 205, 217
Defense of Marriage Act (DOMA), xlii, 190, 241–43, 255
Deiter, Newt, 246
Delaney v. Florida, 97
Democracy, 39, 46–47
Democratic National Presidential Convention, xli, xxxix, 84, 127, 158–59
Democratic Party, 96, 105, 147, 158–59, 188, 189, 204, 205, 279
Desire, xxx, xxxi, 2
Diana, 64
Digital Queers, 263
Dignity, 179, 180, 291
Discrimination, xxix, xxxix, 219. *See also* Job discrimination
Diversity, xxiii, 17, 221
Dobson, James, 252
Domestic partnership, 257, 264, 265. *See also* Civil union; Marriage
Domination, xxxi, xxxii, 9, 43, 136, 141, 156
Donovan, Duncan, xli
Drag queens, 95, 117
Dred Scott decision, 266
Duberman, Martin, 129
Du Mas, Frank, 151

East Coast Homophile Organization, xxxviii

Economy, xxvii, 36–38, 91, 191

Education: and AIDS/HIV, 161; and American Civil Liberties Union, 98; and Briggs, xl, 144, 147; and discrimination, 221; and hate crimes, 280–81; and Homophile Action League, 115; and "A Homosexual Bill of Rights," 94; and Kepner, 80; and Lesbian Avengers, 236, 237; and Maupin, 173; and military, 214; and ONE, Inc., 76, 80; and Oregon Citizens Alliance, 208; and Oregon Measure 9, 209; and Oregon Measure 13, 226; and Project 10, xli; and religion, 141; and Sarria, 104; and segregation, xxix. *See also* Teachers

Effeminacy, xxxii, 32, 41, 49. *See also* Gender role

Egypt, ancient, xxvii

Eichberg, Rob, 138

Eisenhower, Dwight D., xxxvii, 42, 59

Ellis, Havelock, 57

Ellis, Roxanne, xlii

Emerson, Ralph Waldo, 44

Employment. *See* Job discrimination

Employment Nondiscrimination Act (ENDA), 242, 243, 252, 279

England, 22, 35–36, 39, 44

English Common Law, 30–31

Enslin v. Walford, 97

Episcopal Church, 49–50, 155, 179

Europe/Europeans, 1, 2

Evangelicals Concerned with Reconciliation (ECWR), 291

Executive Order 10450, xxxvii

Ex-Homosexuals for Truth, 228

Experience Weekend, The, 198

Eyde, Edythe, 60–64, 285

Fages, Pedro, 32–33

Falwell, Jerry, 142, 162

Family: and Achtenberg, 212; and American Indians, 4, 7; and Buchanan, 204; and Dannemeyer, 199, 200; and early United States, 36–37; and "A Homosexual Bill of Rights," 93; and Japanese Americans Citizens League, 232; and law, xxx; and marriage, xxvi; and Moore, 59–60; and Parents and Friends of Lesbians and Gays, 225; rejection by, 131–32; and stability, 145; and Weller, 228; and women, 41–42, 64

Farnham, Lois, 263, 264

F.B.I., 65, 159, 260

Feinberg, Leslie, 249–50

Feinstein, Diane, 148

Fellowship of Reconciliation, 98

Feminism, xxxii, 116, 124–25, 126, 135–36, 166–67. *See also* Women's movement

Field, Gertrude, 48

First National Coming Out Day, xli

Fiscal rights, 93

Fleishman, Flo, 77–79

Florida, 77, 244

Florida Orange Juice Commission, 156, 157

Focus on the Family, 252

Foley, Daniel R., 216–21, 231–32

Fong, J Craig, 232–34

Font, Pedro, 32

Fornication, 27

Foster, Jim, xxxix, 105, 127, 147

Frank, Barney, 233

Freedom, 39; and American Revolution, 36; of association, 272–73, 274; and Constitution of the United States, 39–40, 67; and Declaration of Independence, 67; of expression, 39–40; and love, 283, 286–87; of press, 88, 89; of speech, 89; and Whitman, 46–47; and women, 43–44. *See also* Constitution of the United States

Freedom to Marry Coalition, 291

Freud, Sigmund, xxx, xxxi, 55–56, 58

Friedan, Betty, 122, 125

Friede, Donald S., 53

Friendship and Freedom, xxxvii, 52–53

Fritz, Alvin, 291–92

From, Sam, 87

Gage, Elmer, 100–101

Gaither, Billy Joe, 280

Gallaudet University, 223
Galluccio, Michael, 243, 244
Gandavo, Pedro de Magalhaes, 6
Garland, Judy, 117
Gay, as term, 202, 289
Gay, Lesbian, Straight Education Net-
    work, 281, 292
Gay Academic Union, 129
Gay Activists Alliance, 119–20, 129,
    245
Gay American Indians (GAI), xl,
    196–97
Gay and Lesbian Alliance Against
    Defamation (GLAAD), xli, 188, 246,
    291
Gay and Lesbian Arabic Society, 291
Gay and Lesbian Librarians of Los
    Angeles, 181
Gay and Lesbian Organizations and
    Publications, 291–92
Gay and Lesbian Pride parades, 71
Gay and Lesbian Student Unions, 71
Gay Asian Pacific Support Network,
    291
Gay Asians, 136–37
Gay Community Services Center,
    xxxix
Gay Liberation Front, xxxviii, 71,
    118–19, 120
Gay Liberation Front Los Angeles,
    120, 121
Gaylord v. Tacoma, 98
"Gay Manifesto, A," 71, 116
Gay Media Task Force (GMTF),
    245–47
Gay Men's Health Crisis (GMHC),
    161, 192–93
Gay Pride festivals, 191, 208
Gay Pride marches, xxxix, 114, 120,
    140, 193
Gay Women's Service Center, xxxix
Gender, xxxi–xxxii, 1, 2, 9
Gender role, xxxii, xxxiii, 5, 6, 7, 8–9,
    22, 38
Genitals, ambiguous, 3, 248
Georgia, xxxvii, 57–58, 176–77, 267–68
Gerber, Henry, 51–54, 285
Germany, xxix, 51–52
Gernreich, Rudy, xxxvii

Ginsberg, Allen, 83, 84, 117
Gittings, Barbara, 71, 107–9, 129, 132
Gold, Ron, 132
Goldman, Emma, 51
Goldwater, Barry, 215
Gomorrah, 10–11
Goodstein, David, 138
Gore, Al, 257
Government: and AIDS/HIV, 188;
    and American Civil Liberties
    Union, 97; and Clinton, 189; and
    Constitution of the United States,
    39–40; and Declaration of Indepen-
    dence, 38–39; and equal rights,
    45–46; and hate crimes, 259–60; and
    job discrimination, 65–66; and Ka-
    meny, 101, 103; and Kepner, 81; and
    Oregon Measure 9, 208, 209; and re-
    ligion, 188; state, 45–46
Greeks, ancient, xxv, xxvi
Green, Bob, 156, 157

Hall, Radclyffe: The Well of Loneliness,
    xxxvii, 54–56, 64
Hammon, Mary, 25–26
Handler, J., 270–71
Hardwick, Michael, 176–77
Hargis, Billy James, 184
Harper's magazine, 119
Harrigan, Peter, 263
Hatch, Thomas, 23
Hate crimes, 201, 258–60, 279–81
Hate Crimes Act, xli
Haughland, David, 88
Hawai'i, xxvii, 216–21, 253–58, 264
Hawai'i Bar Association, 220
Hawai'i Equal Marriage Rights Pro-
    ject, 219–20
Hawai'i Reciprocal Beneficiary Act,
    254–55
Hawai'i State Constitution, 218,
    253–54, 255
Hay, Harry, xxxvii, 72, 76, 91, 114
Hays code, xxxvii
Heard, Gerald, 87
Heine, Charisse, 223
Helms, Jesse, 242–43, 282
Hennings, Thomas, 80
Herek, Gregory, xxxii, xxxiii

Hermaphrodites, 3, 32, 248–49
Heterosexism, xxxi–xxxii, 70, 290
Hill, William W., 3
Hirschfeld, Magnus, 51, 56
Hitchcock, Lorena, 58
HIV. *See* AIDS/HIV
Hoey Committee, 85
Holden, Jon, 243, 244
Homophile, 290
Homophile Action League, 114–15
Homophile movement, 68–69, 71, 73, 108, 129, 139, 140, 246
Homophiles, 102, 118
Homophobia, xxxii–xxxiv, xl, 95, 201–2, 290
Homosexual Action League, 71
Homosexual behavior, xxii–xxiii
"Homosexual Bill of Rights, A," 69, 92–94
Homosexuality, 290; authorities on, 102; as disorder, 132–33, 134, 139, 209; and electroshock treatment, 145, 146; as perversion, 73; and self-image, 138, 139, 173; as sickness, 73, 104, 107, 108, 120–21; and unnaturalness, xxi, 152
Hooker, Evelyn, 86–88
Howard, Charlie, 169–71
Hudson, Rock, 174
Hughes, Langston, 181, 182
Human Rights Campaign, xl, 99, 174–75, 279, 292
Hutchins, Loraine, 202–3
Hutchins, Robert, 80

Idaho Proposition One, 238
Identity, 67, 68, 69, 140
If Café, 61–63
Ikeda, Daisaku, 217
Illinois, xxxviii
Immigration, 97, 110, 153, 189
Immigration and Nationality Act, 110
Immigration and Naturalization Service (INS), 97, 110, 189
International Gay and Lesbian Archives, 76
International Gay and Lesbian Human Rights Commission, 292

International Gay and Lesbian Review, 246–47, 292
Internet, 246–47, 262–63
Intersexed persons, 3, 192, 248–49, 290
Intersex Society of America, 248–49, 292
Interweave, 170
Intolerance, xxx
Invert, 48, 290
Isherwood, Christopher, 87
Islam, 21

Jackson, Jesse, 188
Jacobs, James, 259–60
Japan, xxv, xxvi
Japanese Americans Citizens League, 232–34
Jean, Lori L., 282–84
Jefferson, Thomas, 36, 38
Jennings, Dale, xxxvii, 74–75, 140, 285
Jesus, 11, 16–19, 20, 251
Jews/Judaism, 70, 140, 141, 174, 179, 200–201, 218, 223, 276
Jim Kepner Library, The, 76
Job discrimination, xlii, xxix; and activism, 191; and American Civil Liberties Union, 97, 98; and Briggs Initiative, xl; and Congress, 65–66; and Dade County Commission, 143; and Gerber, 54; and Helms, 242, 243; and "A Homosexual Bill of Rights," 93; and Kameny, 101; and Kennedy, 242, 243; and Kepner, 81; and Maupin, 173; and Oregon Citizens Alliance, 208; and Oregon Measure 13, 226; and transvestites, 275–76; and University of California, Berkeley, 165–66
John Paul II, 162–63, 180
Johnson, J., 266–67
Johnston, Jill: "Lesbian Nation," 125, 126
Jolles, Stacy, 263
Jorgensen, Christine, xxxvii
Julber, Eric, 88
Justice, Inc., 164

Ka'ahumanu, Lani, 202–3

Kameny, Frank, 71; activism of, 101–3; and American Psychiatric Association, 132, 133, 134; and Gittings, 107, 108–9; and Mattachine Society of Washington, 103–4; and National Gay Task Force, 129; and politics, xxxix

Kantrowitz, Arnie, 175–76

Kato, Nancy Reiko, 167–68

Kay, James W., 269

Kennedy, Edward M., 242, 243

Kennedy, Flo, 124

Kennedy, John F., 42

Kent, Samuel, 44–50

Kentucky, 205–7, 268

Kepner, Jim, 76–77, 80, 83–84, 92, 111

Kight, Morris, 119, 121

Kilhefner, Don, 121

King, Coretta Scott, 99

King, Martin Luther, Jr., xxxviii, 98, 99, 113, 155, 284

King, Rufus, 41

Kinsey, Alfred, 80–81, 87

Kinsey Report, xxxvii, 80–81

Knight, Pete, 278

Knight Initiative, 278

Knights of the Clock, 75

Koch, Edward, xxxix, 169

Kramer, Larry, 160–61, 188, 193

Ladder, The, xxxviii, 79, 107–8, 112

Lahusen, Kay Tobin, 107

Lambda Legal Defense and Education Fund, 131, 219–20, 221, 232, 240, 267, 268

Lambda Literary Foundation, 292

Lambda 10 Project, 292

Latino/Latina, xxxix, xl, 153, 233, 234–35

Laux, Charles B., 239

Law: accomplishments in, 139; activism around, 69; antidiscrimination, 163–64, 172; and Bible, 36; and Briggs, 144; and Bryant, 143–44; and civil rights, 259; and Colorado Amendment 2, 190; and Comstock, 48–49; and decriminalization, xxxviii, 71, 140; and Defense of Marriage Act, xlii, 190; due process of, 39; and English colonies, 33, 34; English Common, 30–31; equal protection of, 289; and family, xxx; and Gay Liberation Front, 119; for gay rights, 71; and Gerber, 53–54; and Gittings, 108; and government job discrimination, 66; and Hall, 54–55; and hate crimes, 258–60; and Illinois, xxxviii; and immigration, 110, 153; and Jean, 282–83; and Jefferson, 36; and Kameny, 102; and Kepner, 81; and Magnuson, 171–72; and marriage, xxviii, xxix, xxx, 216–21; and Mattachine Society National Convention, 92; and Moore, 59–60; and National Gay and Lesbian Task Force, 130–31; and New York City, 175–76; and North American Man-Boy Love Association, 83; and sexual orientation, xxxix; and sodomy, xxxvii, 48, 57–58, 176–77; and unnaturalness, xxii; and Virginia colony, 22–23; and Wisconsin, 163–64

LCE News, 104

League for Civil Education, 104

Lee, Sylvia. See Rivera, Rey

Legg, W. Dorr, 75, 80, 88, 89, 92–93, 111

Lesbian and Gay Aging Issues Network, 292

Lesbian and Gay Rights Project, 97

Lesbianas Unidas, 234–35

Lesbian Avengers, 236–38

Lesbian History Project, 292

Lesbian News, 292

Lesbian Rights Project, 210

Lesbians, 290; and activism, 123–24; and AIDS/HIV, 142, 183, 184, 192; and child custody, 134–35; and co-gender groups, xxxix; and Congress to Unite Women, 122; and Daughters of Bilitis, xxxviii, 79–80; and Eyde, 60–64; and feminism, xxxii, 124–25, 135–36; and Fleishman, 77; and Hall, 55; Latina, xl, 234–35; and military, 212, 214; and National Organization for Women, 122, 124–25; old, 195–96; and piracy, 30; and

Lesbians *(continued)*
    politics, 123, 124, 126; and race, 128;
    and separatism, xxxix, 123, 168;
    and sexism, xxxix; and sodomy
    law, 57–58; as term, xxv; and *Vice
    Versa,* 61–64; violence against,
    164–65; and Women's Army Corps,
    58–59; and women's movement,
    122–24
Lesbians of Color, xli, 234
Lesbians of Color Conference, 167–68
Lesbian Tide, The, xxxix
Levine, Judith, 197
Liberationists, 129, 142
Liberty. *See* Freedom
Liebman, Marvin, 204
Liette, Pierre, 5
Lincoln, Abraham, 41
Lincoln, Mary Todd, 41
Lind, Earl, 48
Lively, Scott, 226
LLEGO. *See* National Latina/o Les-
    bian Gay Bisexual and Transgender
    organization
Lorde, Audre, 153
Los Angeles, xxxvii, xxxix; activism
    in, 111; and gay/lesbian popula-
    tion, 126; and New York City, 120;
    and poets, 83; and politics, 68
Los Angeles Gay and Lesbian Center,
    xxxix
Los Angeles Lesbian Center, xxxix
Los Angeles Lesbians of Color, 168
Lotter, John, 238–39
Louisiana, 268
Love, 46–47, 45, 282–83, 286–87
Loving v. Virginia, 206, 258
Loy, Tana, 154
Lutherans, 179
Lyon, Phyllis, 107, 147

Mabry, Shawn, 171
Madison, James, 36
Mafia, 77
Magnuson, Roger, 171–72
Manford, Jeanne, 132
Manford, Marty, 132
Mangaoang, Gil, 137

March for Equality, 281
March on Washington, xxxviii, 98–99,
    152
March on Washington (2000), 281
March on Washington for Gay and
    Lesbian Rights, 188
March on Washington for Gay and
    Lesbian Rights (1979), xl, 83, 152–54
March on Washington for Gay and
    Lesbian Rights (1987), xli, 193–94,
    198–99
March on Washington for Gay and
    Lesbian Rights (1993), 220–21
Marder, Janet, 200–201
Marmor, Judd, 132, 133–34
Marquette, Jacques, 5
Marriage: and Achtenberg, 212; and
    American Indians, 1, 2, 3, 6; and
    benefits, xli; and Bible, 9, 17;
    Boston, 42; and Bryant, 156–58; and
    California Proposition 22, 278; and
    Comstock, 48–49; and Defense of
    Marriage Act, xlii, 190, 241–43; and
    early United States, 37–38; and
    Foley, 216–21; and Hawai'i, 216–21,
    253–58; interracial, xxx, 218, 219,
    258; and Japanese Americans Citi-
    zens League, 232, 233; and Ken-
    tucky sodomy law, 207; and
    Knight, 278; and law, xxix, xxx; and
    Lincoln, 41; and McNeill, 179; and
    Meininger, 53; and morality, 218;
    and Philadelphia bachelors, 40; and
    religion, 218–19; and sex, xxviii,
    141, 183, 187, 207, 219; sex outside,
    69; and Southern Baptist Conven-
    tion, 251; and Vermont, 263–67; and
    women, 43, 64; and Women's Army
    Corps, 58–59; and world culture,
    xxv–xxvi. *See also* Benefits; Civil
    union
Martin, Del, 92, 106, 107, 128
Masochism, 208
Massachusetts, 221, 281
Massachusetts Bay Colony, 24, 26
Masturbation, 24, 26, 27, 48
Matis, Stuart, 278–79
Matlovich, Leonard, xl

Matson, Gary, 280
Mattachine Review, The, 112
Mattachine Society, 285; and Council
    on Religion and the Homosexual,
    105; and Gay Activists Alliance,
    119–20; and gay bars, 104; and Git-
    tings, 107; and Hay, 114
Mattachine Society National Conven-
    tion, 92
Mattachine Society of Los Angeles,
    xxxvii; development of, 91–92;
    founding of, 68, 72–75; and Hooker,
    86, 87; and Kepner, 76–77, 92
Mattachine Society of New York, 70,
    117
Mattachine Society of Washington
    (MSW), 102, 103–4
Maupin, Armistead, 172–74
McCarthy, Joseph, 59, 64
McConnell v. University of Minnesota,
    98
McGovern, George, 127
McNally, Terrence: *Corpus Christi,*
    250–51
McNeill, John J.: *The Church and the
    Homosexual,* 179
McVeigh, Timothy, 262
Means, Russell, 8
Media: challenges to, 224–25, 245–46;
    changes in, 245; and Gay Activists
    Alliance, 119; and Gay and Lesbian
    Alliance Against Defamation, 188;
    and Gerber, 53–54; and Gittings,
    109; increased exposure in, 191; and
    Kameny, 109; and Lesbian
    Avengers, 236; and Mattachine Soci-
    ety, 92; and National Coming Out
    Day, 199; and National Gay Task
    Force, 130; support in, 192; use of, 69
Meininger, Al, 53
Men, xxxii, 2, 4, 5, 6, 9, 136, 141
Metropolitan Community Church
    (MCC), xxxviii, 77, 79, 113–14
Miami, 143
Michaels, Dick, 112
Michigan Womyn's Festival, 292
Militancy, xli, 102, 104, 188. *See also*
    Activism; Protest/demonstration

Military, xxix, 212–16; and American
    Civil Liberties Union, 97–98; and
    Clinton, xli, 190; and Crittenden
    Report, xxxviii; and cyberactivism,
    262; discharge from, xl; and Kent,
    49–50; and Kepner, 81; and mobi-
    lization, 68; regulations of, xxxvii;
    and World War II, 58–59
Military Working Group, 213–15
Milk, Harvey, xl, 69, 140, 146–50
Millennium March on Washington,
    282–84
Miller, Mark, 278–79
Millett, Kate: *Sexual Politics,* 124
Mineta, Norma, 232–33
Minority status, 226
Miscegenation. *See* Marriage
*Mississippi Gay Alliance v. Mississippi
    State University,* 98
Mixner, David, 138
Monette, Paul, 82–83
Montana, 268
Moore, Thomas, 59–60
Morality, xxi–xxxiv; and Achtenberg,
    211; and African Americans, 271;
    and Bible, 11–12; and Christianity,
    21; and *Dale v. Boy Scouts of America,*
    270; and government job discrimi-
    nation, 65–66; and Jews, 201; and
    Kent, 50–51; and Kentucky sodomy
    law, 206, 207; and marriage, 218;
    and military, 214–15; and Paul the
    Apostle, 19; and sex, 69; and sexual
    pleasure, xxviii; and Southern Bap-
    tist Convention, 251; and stereo-
    types, 271; and United States, 36;
    and Vaid, 221; and Vermont mar-
    riage, 264, 266; and vicarious sex,
    xxvii; and Whitman, 46–47
Moral Majority, The, 142
Morgan, Mary, 210
Mormons, 145–46, 232, 254, 255–56,
    278, 279
Morris, Anna, 48
Moscone, George, xl, 147, 148
Moses, 11
Moses, Sybil R., 243, 244
Mugabe, Robert, 263

Municipal Elections Committee of Los Angeles (MECLA), xl, 138, 140
Muslim Moors, 21

Nadleeh, 3–4
Names Project, The, 174, 194
National Association for the Advancement of Colored People (NAACP), 129, 130
National Center for Lesbian Rights, 210
National Coming Out Day, 188, 198–99
National Education Association, 209
National Gay and Lesbian Black Leadership Forum, xli
National Gay and Lesbian Task Force, xxxix, xl, 130, 221, 222, 279, 292
National Gay and Lesbian Task Force v. Oklahoma, 98
National Gay Rights Advocates, 198
National Gay Task Force, xxxix, 128–30, 132, 140, 169, 245
National Institute of Mental Health, 88
National Latina/o Lesbian and Gay Organization, 292
National Latina/o Lesbian Gay Bisexual and Transgender organization, xli
National Lesbian and Gay Journalists Association, 224
National Lesbians of Color Conference, xli
National Organization for Women, 122, 124–25, 139
National Women's Rights Convention (1852), 43–44
Native Americans. See American Indians
Nature, xxiii, xxvi
Navy, xxxviii, 47–49, 84–86, 262. See also Military
Nazism, xxix
Ness, Daniel, 171
New England, 42; colonial, 24, 26
New Guinea, xxv, xxvi
New Haven colony, 26

New Jersey, 243, 244, 271, 272
New Netherland, 24–25
New Right coalition, 162
New York City, xxxix; and activism, 117, 118, 119, 120; and gay/lesbian population, 126; and Gay Liberation Front, 119; and gay rights law, 175–76; and Stonewall Inn riots, xxxviii
New York Parents of Gays, 132
New York Society for the Suppression of Vice, 48
New York University, 119
Nissen, Marvin, 239
Nixon Administration, 88
Noble, Elaine, xl
Norman, Sarah, 25–26
North American Man-Boy Love Association, 83, 228
Novak, Michael, 144–45

Obscenity/indecency, xxxvii, 48, 55, 88, 89
Ogden, Roy, 170, 171
Old Lesbians Organizing for Change (OLOC), xli, 195–96
O'Leary, Jean, 199
Oleson, Otto, 88
ONE, Inc., xxxvii, xxxviii; and assimilationists, 93; and Daughters of Bilitis, 93; formation of, 68, 75–76; and Gittings, 107; and Hooker, 86, 87; and media, 246
ONE, Inc. v. Oleson, 88
ONE Institute, 69, 80–82, 92–93, 111
ONE Institute and Archives, 292
ONE Magazine, xxxvii, xxxviii, 52, 75, 84, 88–90, 111, 112, 285
Oregon, 205
Oregon Catholics for Life, 208–9
Oregon Citizens Alliance, 208, 225, 226, 228
Oregon Measure 9, 208–10, 225
Oregon Measure 13, 225–26
Osborn, Torie: Coming Home to America, 247–48
Oscar Wilde Gay and Lesbian Bookshop, 292

OutProud! The National Coalition for Gay, Lesbian, Bisexual and Transgender Youth, 292

Page, Carroll, 50
Palomo, Juan, 225
Palou, Francisco, 33
Paniccia, Tom, 215
Parents and Friends of Lesbians and Gays (PFLAG), xl, 131–32, 225, 292
Paul the Apostle, 10, 19, 20, 21, 43, 163
Pedophilia, 208, 228
Penetration, xxxi
People of color, xl, 153, 181–82, 232
People v. Onofre, 98
Perdue, Betty, 76
Perry, James, 50
Perry, Troy, xxxviii, 71, 112–14, 194
Personal Rights in Defense and Education (PRIDE), 111, 112
Perversion, xxix, xxxvii, 65–66, 73, 209
Petrone, Carol A., 208–9
Peurifoy, John, 64
Phelps, Nell "Johnnie," 59
Philadelphia, 40
Piracy, 28–30
Plaine, William, 24
Planet Out Radio, 292
Playboy ethic, xxvii
Plymouth Colony, 25–26
Police: and Brandon, 239; changes in, 139–40, 148; and du Mas, 151; and Fleischman, 78–79; and gay bars, 68, 73, 77, 78–79, 94–95, 97, 111; and government job discrimination, 65–66; and Kepner, 81; and Oregon Citizens Alliance, 208; and Perry, 114; reform of, 168–69; resistance to, 69; and Rivera, 117; and San Francisco New Year ball, xxxviii; and Society for Individual Rights, 105; and Stonewall Inn, xxxviii; and White trial, 148
Politics: accomplishments in, 140; and ACT UP, 193; and Clinton, 188–89; and Council on Religion and the Homosexual, 105–6; and Foster,

127, 147; and gay bars, 104; and Gay Liberation Front, 119; and Gerber, 54; and Gittings, 108; and Homophile Action League, 115; and Kameny, xxxix; and lesbians, 123, 124, 126; and Los Angeles, 68; and marriage, xxvii; and Mattachine Society, 72, 74; and Milk, 147; and Municipal Elections Committee of Los Angeles, 138; participation in, 68; and personal change activism, 167; and personal issues, 138, 154; retreat from, 167, 168; and Rivera, 117; and Rustin, 98; and Sarria, xxxviii, 95–96; and Sarris, 165; and Smith, 167; and Southern Baptist Convention, 251; and Whitman, 47; and women, 43
Population, xxix
Poritz, J., 269–70
Post Office, xxxviii, xxxix, 54, 89
Powell, Lewis, 176–77
Privacy, 286; and bachelors, 41; and Bowers v. Hardwick, xli, 176, 179; and Buchanan, 41; and Constitution of the United States, 40; and Kentucky sodomy law, 205, 206; and Kepner, 81; and marriage, 218; and military, 214; and Oregon Measure 9, 209; and sex, 41–42; and sodomy laws, 268; and urban population, 68
Project 10, xli
Protect America's Children, 156
Protest/demonstration, 70, 71, 102, 103–4, 119. See also Activism; Militancy
Psychology/psychiatry, xxx–xxxi, 59–60, 90; authority of, 102; and Eyde, 63; and Freud, 56–57; and Gay Liberation Front Los Angeles, 121; and Gittings, 108; and government job discrimination, 66; and Hooker, 86–88; and Kameny, 102, 103; and Mormons, 146
Public Health Service, 88
Publishing, 246–47
Puerto Rico, 268

Puritans, 26–28
Puterbaugh, Holly, 263, 264

Quakers, 179
Queer, 290
Queer Nation, xli, 201–2
Quotas, 208, 226

Race/racism, 167, 286; and associa-
    tion, 273; and homophobia, 182;
    and Japanese American Citizens
    League, 232, 233; and lesbians, 128;
    and marriage, xxx, 218, 219; and
    Martin, 128; and military, 214; and
    people of color, 181–82; and Vaid,
    223
Radicalesbians, 123
Rainbow Coalition, 188
Rainbow Curriculum, 236, 237
Ramsdell, Phillip, 208–9
Rand, Bill, 112
Randolph, A. Philip, 98, 99
Read, Mary, 29–30
Reagan, Ronald, 142, 162, 167, 174,
    187
Reform Jewish Congregations, 179
Rehnquist, William, 271–72
Religion, xxv, 1–33, 224; and
    AIDS/HIV, 183–85, 187; and Boyd,
    155–56; and Boy Scouts of America,
    272; and Bryant, 156–58; and Con-
    stitution of the United States,
    39–40, 254, 286; and education, 141;
    and Fleischman, 78; freedom of,
    286; and fundamentalism, 140–43;
    and government, 188; and "A Ho-
    mosexual Bill of Rights," 94; and
    Howard, 169–71; and John Paul II,
    162–63; and Kameny, 103; and mar-
    riage, 218–19; and Maupin, 174;
    and Milk, 149, 150; and Moore,
    59–60; and persecution, 67; and re-
    production, xxvi; and San Fran-
    cisco activists, 105; and Sarris, 164,
    165; and unnaturalness, xxii; and
    Vermont marriage, 264; and Whit-
    man, 46–47; and women's rights
    movement, 70. See also Christianity;
    Jews/Judaism

Religious Right, 235–36
Reno, Janet, 189
Repression, xxx
Reproduction, xxvi–xxx, 152, 218; and
    early United States, 34–35; and Fal-
    well, 162; and Kepner, 82; and
    Novak, 144–45; and Schlesinger,
    277; and sex, 141; and Vermont
    marriage, 263–64, 265
Republican Party, 96, 142, 159–60, 187,
    190, 203, 204–5, 210, 241, 242, 279
Reyes, Antonio, 75
Riesman, David, 81–82
Rist, Darrell Yates, 182
Rivera, Rey, 117–18
Roberts, Barbara, 208
Robertson, Pat, 282
Roberts v. United States Jaycees, 273
Roman Catholic Church, 1, 33, 179–80,
    187, 227, 254. See also Christianity;
    Religion
Romer v. Evans, 190, 240
Roosevelt, Eleanor, 58
Roosevelt, Franklin D., 42, 58
Rose, Ernestine, 43
Roth v. U.S., 89
Rouillard, Richard, 224–25
Rowland, Chuck, xxxvii
Rustin, Bayard, xxxviii, 71, 98–100

Sadism, 208
Safire, William, 257
Salsa Soul Sisters, xl
Sanderson, Terry, 261
San Francisco, xxxix; Castro area of,
    146, 147; and Foster, 105; and
    gay/lesbian population, 126–27;
    and New York City, 120; and poets,
    83
San Francisco Board of Supervisors,
    xxxviii, 69, 147, 148, 210, 211
San Francisco Commission on the Sta-
    tus of Women, 147
San Francisco Democratic Party, 105
San Francisco Human Rights Com-
    mission, 147
San Francisco Police, xxxviii
Sapphist, 290
Sappho, 79

Sarria, Jose, xxxviii, 69, 95–96, 104
Sarris, Kathleen, 164
Save Our Children, 143, 147
Schlegel v. U.S., 97
Schlesinger, Laura, 276–78
Scientific Humanitarian Committee, 51
Scott, Tom, 138
Scott, Winfield, 280
Scott v. Macy, 97
Seattle Lesbian Resource Center, xxxix
Separatism, xxxix, 123, 168
Sepulveda, Juan Gines de, 22
Sex: and AIDS/HIV, 160–61; and American Indians, 1–2, 6; anal, 26; with animals, 26, 27; and Bible, 9, 10, 11, 12–13, 14; and Boy Scouts of America, 272; and discrimination, 286; and Freud, 56–57; and Gage, 101; and Kentucky sodomy law, 207; and love, xxvii; and marriage, xxviii, 69, 141, 183, 187, 207, 219; and McNeill, 179; and morality, 69; multiple–partner, 197; and *ONE Magazine*, 88; and Paul the Apostle, 19, 20; and Philadelphia bachelors, 40–41; and pleasure, xxvii, 2, 69, 141, 197–98; and preference, xxiv; and privacy, 41–42; reasons for, xxvi–xxvii; and reproduction, xxvi–xxvii, 36–37, 82, 141, 144–45, 152, 162, 218; and stress, xxvii; and Whitman, 44–45
Sexism, xxxix, 116, 223
Sexually transmitted disease, 69, 184, 185, 199, 215. *See also* AIDS/HIV
Sexual revolution, 69, 83, 116
Shepard, Judy, 258–59
Shepard, Matthew, xlii, 258–59, 262–63, 280
Shibley, George, 74
Shilts, Randy, 212–13
Slater, Don, 75, 111
Slavery, 36, 45–46, 266, 286
Smith, Barbara: *Home Girls*, 166–67
Socarides, Charles, 133
Society, xxxii; ancient, xxiii, xxv, 42; and early United States, 37; and government job discrimination,

65–66; and "A Homosexual Bill of Rights," 93, 94; and Moore, 59–60
Society for Human Rights, xxxvii, 50–53
Society for Individual Rights (SIR), xxxviii, 70, 105, 114–15, 127
Society for the Suppression of Vice, 53
Sodom, 9, 10–11, 26–28, 31
Sodomy, xxxvii; and American Indians, 1, 5–6, 32; and Christianity, 21; and Comstock, 48–49; and Constitution of the United States, 39; and New Haven colony, 26; and New Netherland, 24–25; and Plymouth Colony, 25–26; and Spain, 21–22; and Virginia colony, 22–23
Sodomy law, 176–77, 188, 205–7; and American Civil Liberties Union, 98; and Bottoms, 230–31; and Comstock, 48–49; and Dannemeyer, 199, 200; and New Jersey, 271; repeal of, 140; and Supreme Court, 267–68; and Thompson, 57–58
Soka Gakkai International, 217
Sommella, Laraine, 237
Southern Baptist Convention, 250–52
Southern Poverty Law Center, 169
Spain/Spaniards, 1, 21–22, 32–33
Speed, Joshua, 41
Spirituality, 1–2, 4, 7, 8, 9, 44, 47
Stan Baker v. State of Vermont, 264–67
Stanley v. George, 178
Starr, Adele, 132
Starr, Larry, 132
Steinem, Gloria, 124
Stephenson, Bob, 114
Stephenson, Peggy, 114
Stereotypes, 108, 200, 246, 270, 271, 276
Stevens, John Paul, 272–75
Stigma, xxiv, xxv, xxix, 2, 4, 6
Stonewall Inn, xxxviii; anniversary of, xxxix, 152, 154; commemoration of, 120; and Milk, 149; and riots, 117–18; and Rivera, 117; significance of, 70–71, 111, 114
Stop Violence.com, 292
Strait, Guy, 104
Student Homophile League, xxxviii

Students for a Democratic Society, 115
Supreme Court, 269; and Blackstone's
    Commentaries, 31; *Board of Directors
    of Rotary Int'l v. Rotary Club of
    Duarte,* 273; *Boutillier v. The Immi-
    gration and Naturalization Service,*
    110; *Bowers v. Hardwick,* xli, 31,
    176–77, 188, 240, 267, 268; and Boy
    Scouts of America, xlii; *Boy Scouts of
    America v. Dale,* 271–75; and Col-
    orado Amendment 2, 240; and edu-
    cation, 281; and Kameny, 101;
    Loving v. Virginia, 206; *Roberts v.
    United States Jaycees,* 273; *Romer v.
    Evans,* 190, 240; *Roth v. U.S.,* 89; and
    Sarria, 96; and sexual harassment,
    281; and sodomy laws, 31, 176–77,
    182, 188; *Stanley v. George,* 178

Tavern Guild, 104–5
Taylor, Elizabeth, 174
Teachers, xl, 208, 226. *See also* Education
Teaching Tolerance project, 169
Teena, Brandon, xli, 238–39
Tennessee, 268
That Certain Summer, 245
Third World Lesbian/Gay Confer-
    ence, 153
Thompson, Ella, 57–58
Thompson, Mark, 138
Thompson, Merritt, 80
Thoreau, Henry David, 42
Thurmond, Strom, 99
Time magazine, xxxix, 71
Transgender people, 5, 7, 32, 46, 53, 131,
    220, 238–39, 249–50, 275, 276, 290
Transsexual people, xxxvii, 249,
    275–76, 290
Transvestites, 3, 4, 5, 30, 32–33, 46,
    275–76. *See also* Clothing
Truman, Harry S., 64, 190, 214
Tsang, Daniel, 153
Two-Spirit person, 2, 3, 5, 6, 7, 8–9,
    100–101

Union, ceremony of, 179. *See also* Civil
    union
Union of American Hebrew Congre-
    gations, 200

Uniqueness, xxiii–xxiv, 3
Unitarian Church, 91, 170, 171, 179
United Church of Christ, 179, 209–10
United Lesbians of African Descent,
    292
United States Conference of Mayors,
    xli
Universal Fellowship of Metropolitan
    Community Churches, 293
University of California, Berkeley,
    165–66
Urban population, 37, 67, 68
Uribe, Virginia, xli

Vaca, Alvar Nunez Cabeza de, 22
Vaid, Urvashi, 221–23
Variation, xxiv, xxvi
Vermont, xlii, 257, 263–67
Vermont Constitution Common Bene-
    fits Clause, 264, 265, 266, 267
Vice Versa, xxxvii, 61–64
Vietnam War, 70, 117, 141, 155
Violence, xli, xlii, 182–83, 239,
    258–59
Violence Project, xl, 169
Virginia, 218–19, 230–31
Virginia colony, 22–23
Voeller, Bruce, 129, 132–34
Voeller v. Voeller, 98
Vote, 104, 105
Voting Rights Act, 99

Wade, April, 230
Wallace, Henry, 72
Wall Street, 192, 193
Washington, D.C., 120
Washington, George, 36
Washington Blade, 293
Wasson, Jeffrey, 205
Wat, Eric, 136–37
Watkins, Perry, xl
Waxman, Henry, 241–42
Wealth, xxxii, xxxiii
Weld, William, 221
Weller, Richard, 228–29
West Coast Lesbian Conference, 128
West Hollywood, City of, xli
Whan, Del, 121
Wherry, Kenneth, 65

White, Dan, xl, 148
White Night Riot, 148
Whitman, Walt, 44–45; "Calamus,"
    44–45; *Democratic Vistas*, 46–47
Wicker, Randy, 71
Wilkins, Roy, 99–100
Williams, Cecil, 105
Williams, Walter L., 3, 6, 8, 216
Wilson, Woodrow, 50
Winston, Sam, 112
Winthrop, John, 24
Wisconsin, xl
Wisconsin Antidiscrimination Law,
    163–64
Witchcraft, xxviii
Wittman, Carl, 115–16
Wockner, Rex, 263
Wolf, Irma "Corky," 75
Wolfe, Maxine, 192–93, 236–38
Women: and American Indians, 2, 4, 5,
    6, 7, 9; and American Revolution, 43;
    and Bible, 9; and Christianity, 21;
    and discrimination, 219; and early
    United States, 36–38; and family, 64;
    and finances, 43; and heterosexism,
    xxxi–xxxii; and homophobia, xxxiii;
    and independence, 43, 64; and les-
bians, xxxix; and marriage, 64; and
    military, 212; and New Haven
    colony, 26; and Novak, 144–45; and
    ONE, Inc., 93; and piracy, 29–30; and
    Plymouth Colony, 25–26; and poli-
    tics, 43; rights of, 43–44; and
    sodomy, xxxvii; as spinsters, 42;
    subordination of, xxxi, 9, 70, 136,
    141, 156, 157, 270, 286; violence
    against, 149, 150, 164–65; and witch-
    craft, xxviii; and Wittman, 116;
    woman identified, 123
Women and Children First Bookstore,
    293
Women's Army Corps, 58–59
Women's movement, 122–24, 141. *See
    also* Feminism
Women's rights, 59, 68
Women's rights movement, 70
Woo, Merle, 165–66
World War II, 58–59, 68
Worldwide Church of God, 185

Yolles, Stanley, 88
Young Americans for Freedom, 159

Zap, 119

About the Editors

WALTER L. WILLIAMS is Professor of Anthropology, History, and Gender Studies at the University of Southern California. He is the author of *The Spirit and the Flesh: Sexual Diversity in American Indian Culture,* which won the 1986 Gay Book of the Year Award from the American Library Association. He is also coeditor of *Homophile Studies in Theory and Practice* (1994) and *Overcoming Heterosexism and Homophobia: Strategies That Work* (1997). He is founding editor of the International Gay and Lesbian Review.

YOLANDA RETTER is a lesbian history and visibility activist. She is the coeditor of *Queers in Space: Communities, Public Places, Sites of Resistance* (1997), which won a Lambda Award. She manages the Lesbian History Web site and the Lesbian Legacy Collection of ONE Institute and Archives in Los Angeles.